THE UNIVERSITY OF ILLINOIS

# THE UNIVERSITY

# ENGINE
# OF ILLINOIS
# INNOVATION

Edited by Frederick E. Hoxie

**UNIVERSITY OF
ILLINOIS PRESS**
Urbana, Chicago, and Springfield

Library of Congress Control Number: 2016957907
ISBN 978-0-252-04082-5 (hardcover)
ISBN 978-0-252-09932-8 (e-book)

# CONTENTS

PART TWO. WORLD-CHANGING INVENTIONS

Created and Nurtured on the University of Illinois Campus, Then Spread to the World

PART THREE. PLACES OF INNOVATION
Where Ideas and People Meet to
Produce Innovation

# Changing the World from a Very Small Place

Frederick E. Hoxie

More than two thousand years ago, Archimedes explained that the power of the simple lever was limited only by human imagination. "Give me a place to stand," he declared, "and I shall move the earth." The Greek mathematician's audacity was fueled by his love of technology as well as the intoxication of a new idea. Archimedes's declaration remains inspirational today because it reminds us that fresh insights, innovative ideas, and startling discoveries have the potential to "move the earth."

For 150 years the community of scholars and students at the University of Illinois in Urbana-Champaign has generated and nurtured ideas that have changed the world. These ideas have arisen from across the disciplines and in a variety of settings—from laboratories and librar-ies to classrooms to the outdoor spaces of the midwestern prairie—but all have been nurtured by the remarkable community of thinkers and actors gathered here. In this sense, the university has been an engine of innovation.

Viewed from a departing airplane, the university campus quickly shrinks and soon disappears into an ocean of towns and farms. It is a very small place. But size is deceiving, for the innovations produced here have changed lives, opened countless doors, and improved communities across the globe. Unlike Archimedes, we at the University of Illinois are not looking for a place to stand. We have discovered it beneath our feet. This book tells the story of this place, of some of the world-changing innovations that have emerged here, and of the community that has nurtured and sustained them for fifteen decades.

# A University for Learning and Labor

Frederick E. Hoxie

The University of Illinois was not born with an educator's vision but with a political deal sealed by a roll call vote in the Old Illinois State Capitol on February 20, 1867. The Morrill Act, passed by Congress in 1862, had promised a federal subsidy (in the form of a "grant" of public land in the West) to every state in the Union that pledged to create a university to educate its citizens in "agriculture and the mechanic arts." The 480,000 acres promised to Illinois triggered a competition across the state to determine both the shape and the location of the new school.

The debate over the exact nature of the state's land-grant university lasted more than four years. At first, older, well-established sectarian institutions like Knox and Wheaton Colleges offered to open agricultural pro-grams that they argued would qualify them to receive the land-grant subsidy. Representatives from Chicago proposed splitting the new school's agricultural and mechanical missions and creating a polytechnic institute in their growing metropolis. Over time, however, the most powerful voices came from the state's farm community, led by the State Agricultural and Horticultural Societies, who parried the other interests by pushing for a single, new institution to be located in a rural location. Despite the state's meager history of support for public education—it had passed its first statute calling for universal public schools (limited to whites) barely a decade earlier—the prairies were suddenly awash in supporters of higher learning. But the question that seemed to attract the most attention was not the educational mission of the new school; they wanted to know which town would win the new campus.

As the contest over the location of the university reached its climax in the winter of 1867, proponents of four candidates—Jacksonville, Bloomington, Lincoln, and Urbana-Champaign—lobbied furiously for the prize. (Previous maneuvering by farm backers had sidelined Chicago and the denominational schools.) When the governor signed the enabling legislation on February 28, the outraged citizens of Bloomington, Lincoln, and Jacksonville charged that bribery and political horse trading had won the day for Champaign County. All four towns had sent lobbyists to Springfield, but it was clear that Representative Clark Robinson Griggs, a railroad promoter and former mayor of Urbana, had stolen a march on the competition. Political deals sealed over the previous six months, together with generous receptions and dinners dispensed from rooms at Springfield's swanky Leland Hotel, had brought uncommitted legislators to Griggs's side. He and his associates had offered the state nine hundred acres of land on the prairie midway between the Urbana court house and the Champaign train station, together with $100,000 in cash (to be raised by issuing bonds) and an empty five-story brick building that town boosters had previously tried to peddle as a seminary. While the other towns had more assets (Bloomington offered $400,000, and the city fathers of Jacksonville promised to turn over the entire campus of Illinois College to the state), Griggs had the votes. Not only was he an accomplished late-night host, he had also pledged his support for new roads in Chicago, a new state house in Springfield, and a new prison in southern Illinois. And Governor Richard Oglesby was in his corner as well. As the House took up Griggs's motion on February 20, Oglesby and the state's attorney general sat conspic-

> "All four towns had sent lobbyists to Springfield but it was clear that Representative Clark Robinson Griggs, a railroad promoter and former mayor of Urbana, had stolen a march on the competition."

uously close to Urbana's champion, ready to congratulate him as the roll call was completed.

Because of its contested and politically charged birth, it was not exactly clear in 1867 what the citizens of the state expected from the "Illinois Industrial University" that would soon occupy a muddy stretch of treeless prairie in Urbana-Champaign. The school had a seal and a slogan—"Learning and Labor"—but no one really knew what that would mean once its doors opened and students arrived. Representative Griggs and his supporters expected the institution to trigger the flow of federal dollars into the local economy and hoped that other public funds would soon follow. State legislators anticipated a place where farmers and mechanics could receive practical training, and their emphasis on everyday skills seemed to impress the authors of the university's charter. This founding document assured the public that "classical and scientific studies" would not be excluded from the curriculum, but it stipulated that lessons would produce practical skills had hardy midwestern values. The charter stipulated that "no student shall at any time be allowed to remain in or about the university in idleness or without full mental or industrial occupation" and declared that, in contrast to the practice of most colleges and universities of the time, "no degrees shall be conferred nor diplomas awarded." The charter further noted that "all certificates of scholarship" as well as all "names and terms on labels, samples, specimens, books charts and property" would be in the English language.[1] (In other words, there would be no pretentious documents printed in Latin or Greek.)

Casting our imaginations back to these founding moments, it is difficult to detect a distinctive institutional identity for the new school other than opportunism, a commitment to practicality, and a determination not to create another elite institution modeled on universities in the East. And based on those vague founding ideas, it would be impossible to predict the future that lay ahead for the new university. Even the most prescient observer could not have imagined the process by which an abandoned seminary building set amid nine hundred acres of empty prairie would grow into the imposing campus of today. By what magic did the modest concerns expressed in the university's original charter blossom into the clusters of classroom buildings, auditoriums, and laboratories that now crowd around Green Street, Wright Street, and Goodwin Avenue and ring the central quadrangle? What triggered the creation of one of the largest university libraries in the world, an enormous performing arts complex, or the acres of experimental farms and research stations that stretch to the southern horizon? Philanthropic generosity is certainly an important part of the story, as is the fierce loyalty of alumni and the largesse of the state legislature. All of these provide partial answers, but they also raise a more fundamental question: What sparked this lavish attention in the first place?

The essays in this book arise from the striking observation that almost from the moment that students, faculty, and campus leaders first gathered in Urbana-Champaign, a mysterious combination of idealistic students, committed teachers, and a location set apart from both the distractions of city life and the immediate pressures of state politics created an environment that fostered opportunities for new ideas to germinate. Most of these ideas and the actions they inspired were unplanned, but the volatile mix of new knowledge, creativity, and an undeveloped space allowed them to find supporters and take root.

The most significant unplanned events in the first years of the university were triggered in large part by the appointment of the school's first president (called "regent" until 1892). The trustees' decision to hire John Milton Gregory was made with only a vague sense of his educational philosophy; they were drawn initially to the fact that he, like many of them, was a Baptist. Several trustees were suspicious of Gregory's background as a Michigan school superintendent, but they had little comprehension of his specific educational methods or priorities. He did not even meet with the board until a month after his appointment. But Gregory went quickly to work in the year prior to the arrival of students, laying out a vision for the empty prairie that awaited him in Urbana-Champaign. In the process he established several enduring elements of an institutional identity. For example, despite the promise of Urbana boosters that the new school would operate solely on its federal endowment, Gregory moved quickly to request an annual appropriation from the state legislature. His requests were repeated regularly during his tenure, and the initial flow of state funds for new buildings and programs tied the institution to the fortunes of the state in ways few had expected.

Gregory also revealed a single-minded commitment to the application of academic knowledge to the problems of the world. He insisted that rather than simply teaching farming and factory skills, the new institution should explore the basic principles that governed and shaped those activities. And those explorations, he argued, necessitated the careful study of languages, literature, and history. He demanded a great deal more "learning" than the advocates of an education for "labor" alone had imagined. As Winton Solberg wrote in his history of the university's founding, Gregory sought "a golden mean, avoiding the old sterile learning at one extreme and the new utilitarianism at the other."[2]

Other changes occurred on the new campus. Despite resistance from some trustees and the pressures created by shifting economic fortunes, the university admitted fifteen women as undergraduate students in 1870 (after a narrow 5–4 vote by the trustee executive committee). As their numbers grew, women not only altered the tone of campus social life, they also pressed for the inclusion of their concerns in the curriculum. Spurred by the arrival of women, the university soon offered the first courses in domestic science (and later art and music). Regent Gregory was fascinated by the extent to which European universities, especially those in Germany, involved themselves in agricultural and technical research. His regular tours of European universities not only encouraged him to hire European faculty members, they also produced the idea that professors should not only teach but should also use

> "State legislators anticipated a place where farmers and mechanics could receive practical training, and their emphasis on everyday skills seemed to impress the authors of the university's charter."

libraries and laboratories for basic research in their disciplines. Within a decade, a library, chemistry and botany laboratories, and greenhouses devoted to plant research became features of the campus landscape.

Gregory, of course, played a prominent role in shaping the identity of the university, but he was not alone. As the school established its course of study and organized its faculty into departments, other strong personalities arrived. Austrian Edward Snyder was among the first faculty members Gregory appointed. A veteran of the Austrian army, Snyder had joined the Union cause when he came to America in 1862 and used his military training to help win the war. He served as commander of the university's military cadets when the school opened. He also taught French, German, and Italian, but the bachelor Snyder was best remembered at the time as someone who could be counted on to make small private loans to students facing financial difficulties. Don Carlos Taft, an eccentric former Congregational minister who had studied with geologist Edward Hitchcock at Amherst College, arrived to teach geology (and raise a family that included his famous artist son, Lorado). The study of botany soon became the province of Thomas J. Burrill, a remarkable local high-school teacher whom Gregory hired after the young man returned from an expedition to the Rocky Mountains with specimens that formed the basis for the university herbarium. Frederick Prentice, educated in England and Scotland, began teaching courses in veterinary medicine using a papier mâché horse ordered from Paris. On a more exalted level, Gregory raised private funds to create a campus art gallery and fill it with plaster casts of classic European statues and lithographic and photographic images of famous paintings and Italian landscapes.

Gregory's ambition, together with the bustle of new courses and academic programs, caused worry among the trustees who were committed primarily to the idea of the university as a place for practical instruction. Their leaders included Matthias Dunlap of Champaign and Samuel Edwards, one of the founders of the Illinois State Horticultural Society. During the university's first academic year these two managed to persuade the state legislature to pass a resolution demanding the administration offer courses solely for the benefit of farmers and mechanics,

and they engineered a trustee vote reducing Gregory's authority over the university curriculum. Gregory's enemies were aided by Jonathan Turner, a longtime champion of Illinois agriculture and widely celebrated as one of the original instigators of the land-grant idea. Turner charged that Gregory did not understand the purpose of the Morrill Act. Gregory's critics proposed replacing the regent with Turner himself.

The university faculty, who enjoyed support from the *Chicago Tribune* and educational reformers from Illinois and across the Midwest, fought back. Gregory's critics succeeded, however, securing in 1873 new legislation that reduced the size of the board of trustees and eliminated the regent as a member of that group. The new arrangement made it clear that the regent would serve at the pleasure of the board. State lawmakers also stipulated that, in the future, all students should study "such branches of learning as are adapted to promote the liberal and practical education of the industrial classes."[3] Gregory viewed the latter order as an infringement on students' academic freedom, but he soldiered on, guiding the university through political opposition and controversy until 1880.

The ongoing debate over the university's mission and the struggles between, on the one hand, an emerging community of educators and students and, on the other, a politically appointed board of trustees created a dynamic tension that would shape the institution's future. Ambitious professors and administrators, excited at the prospect of creating something new—a public university—would continue to explore new subjects, open new lines of study, and test the limits of their assigned roles. At the same time, boards of trustees charged with setting priorities and managing resources in a state with no previous commitment to higher education struggled to fulfill their responsibility to the wary citizens of Illinois. Both camps agreed that the university was obligated to serve the public—that it would not become an isolated refuge for scholars—but the extent of the infrastructure needed to accomplish that goal, as well as the exact nature of the lessons to be learned, remained in dispute. How broad should the curriculum be? How theoretical should learning be? How influential should faculty experts be in the development of new programs? And given the ongoing struggles over state subsidies, where should the school's priorities lie?

In the late nineteenth century all the land-grant colleges created by the Morrill Act were asking these broad institutional questions, but at Illinois they carried special meaning because of the school's location and recent history. The university was being created on a vacant prairie. Political support for the enterprise was both divided and thin. There was no comparable institution in the state to serve as a model. Also troubling was the fact that the faculty and staff in Urbana-Champaign appeared to be a collection of outsiders—a regent from Michigan and professors who were either untested locals or newcomers from Europe and the East Coast. It is remarkable, therefore, to recognize that during the first decades of the university's existence a solution appeared to calm these tensions. While trustees and regents were busy squaring off over curriculum plans and budgets, busy members of the campus community began producing a new commodity that everyone could celebrate: innovation.

It might have started with the Morrow Plots, the brainchild of Manly Miles, appointed professor of agriculture in 1875. Despite the skepticism of local farmers, Miles and his successors soon demonstrated that rigorous trials and timely interventions could boost crop yields to levels few had previously imagined. In a similar vein, Thomas Burrill, the resident professor of horticulture, developed both a broad theory of plant disease and a solution to the devastating fire blight that had afflicted orchards across the state. Architect Nathan Ricker proved to developers eager to rebuild Chicago's fire-ravaged downtown that professionally trained, University of Illinois architects could reliably manage the construction of steel-framed skyscrapers, producing buildings that would be both innovative and safe. Illinois graduate Arthur Palmer

"By the turn of the twentieth century, it was clear that the University of Illinois would be an engine of innovation, a place where faculty, students, and campus leaders would stimulate and nurture new ideas that could change the world."

demonstrated the effectiveness of modern chemistry in protecting the public's safe water supply. And so on.

These innovations were not created by geniuses working alone. Neither were they the simple, "practical" lessons the university's critics had been calling for. They were something else: powerful ideas, creative inventions, and new practices that promised to alter dramatically and improve forever the society beyond the boundaries of the campus. Over time, of course, these innovations would take many forms (including theoretical breakthroughs that would earn Illinois faculty members the highest academic accolades), but the ever-increasing stream of new ideas and inventions that flowed outward from the college at Urbana-Champaign during its first decades of existence won the institution its first bands of loyal followers while clarifying and solidifying its identity and its mission. By the turn of the twentieth century, it was clear that the University of Illinois would be an engine of innovation, a place where faculty, students, and campus leaders would stimulate and nurture new ideas that could change the world. Innovation would be the institution's central focus and its greatest product.

This book will provide an overview of the history of innovation at Illinois. It takes its inspiration from the thirty-one historical markers that now dot the campus, reminding visitors of the community's most important innovators and inventions.[4] But these markers are merely a beginning. They offer only a peek into the tradition of innovation at Illinois because they say nothing about the creative energy and rich environment that inspired and sustained the achievements they celebrate. They also say little about the impact of these innovations on the world at large. Discovering the true extent of the innovations created on the prairie along Green Street requires a wider lens and deeper reflection. It also requires the service of expert guides who can explain the sources of campus achievements and trace their reverberations beyond Urbana-Champaign. Knowledgeable guides can also make clear the achievements that have, as yet, remained unmarked by monuments. These "missing markers" can reveal additional stories of innovation and expand our understanding of the university's complex history as an engine of change.

*Engine of Innovation* includes twenty-two essays written especially for this volume by experts on the topics described. While the majority of these experts are either members of the university's History Department or among its recently trained doctorates, the authors also include a prominent musician/composer, an agronomist, a historian of mathematics, an engineer, and a writing teacher. The volume includes an additional twenty-four short descriptions of individual topics that will help convey the range of innovation that has taken place on the campus. All of these essays—or sketches—were written by University of Illinois undergraduates, most of them majors in history. Finally, at the end of the volume an illustrated series of snapshots will help orient readers to the context for the stories being told in the individual contributions. The forty-six literary markers included here, like the markers on campus, do not constitute a comprehensive history of innovation at Illinois. They reveal, however, the scale of this story and its range across the disciplines and across the campus.

Each essay and sketch investigates the sources and meaning of a single innovative discovery or idea and describes its effect on the society beyond our campus. In some cases these discoveries were unique to Illinois, while in others, innovations at Illinois joined with and provided crucial strength to national and international movements for change that had many sources. In every case, however, those changes were inspired by ideas that arose and were nurtured here.

The people and events commemorated in these essays represent the history of innovation at Illinois from three perspectives.

First, they focus on singular individuals who introduced challenging ideas to the campus community and fueled enormous change both here and in the world at large. These range from widely celebrated campus heroes like John Bardeen, winner of two Nobel prizes, to lesser known (and "unmarked") figures such as Alta Gwinn Saunders, a pioneering professor of business, and Clarence Shelley, a central figure in the racial integration of the campus.

A second group explores "inventions" (both physical and intellectual) by describing the people who produced them and by tracing their impact across the globe. Again, this section includes inventions celebrated by campus markers (supersweet corn, professional architecture) as well as those that are not. The latter include the idea of affordable higher education (a principal feature of the Morrill Act) and experimental music.

A final set of essays describes major campus "arenas of innovation"—places designed to produce and sustain innovation and new ideas. These include grand temples of research and innovation such as the Beckman Institute and the Krannert Center for the Performing Arts, as well as more modest gathering places—the Farmers' Institutes and Ebertfest. This section also features a fascinating essay on the university's century-long connection to China, reminding us that "places" of innovation have also included locations far from campus where people and ideas nurtured here have had a lasting influence.

While obviously falling far short of conveying the entire history of innovation at Illinois, the essays here should give readers a good sense of how widely varied and dispersed the products of this "engine" have been. They also provide insight into the process of innovation itself—demonstrating, for example, that great innovations, while often attributed to a single individual, are generally the product of deep engagement by many people, often stretching across generations. In addition, they also show us that an innovation in one arena—computer science, for instance—can stimulate echoing inventions in other fields, such as music. And finally, because so many innovations are produced through the interaction of one researcher with students or colleagues, the essays help us see that interaction and debate are essential elements of the innovation process. Innovation is unpredictable and can be unsettling—even threatening to those committed to old ways. In retrospect, all successful innovations look appealing; at the time of their creation, however, there were no guarantees. Illinois farmers were quite dubious at first of Professor Morrow's experimental plots. We should not be surprised if modern critics and skeptics express similar concerns.

Today the University of Illinois remains an engine of innovation. This tradition continues to define one of the institution's core missions, thereby uniting the campus and drawing together faculty, students, alumni, and all who share the ambition to change the world. Despite the passage of 150 years, the commitment to innovation remains a stirring reflection of the institution's original aspiration to be a place of "Learning and Labor."

## Notes

1. For an excellent summary of the events surrounding the university's founding see Winton U. Solberg, *The University of Illinois, 1867–1894: An Intellectual and Cultural History* (Urbana: University of Illinois Press, 1968), 75–83.

2. Ibid., 92.

3. Quoted in Solberg, 116.

4. The university website offers a listing of these markers, as well as a "virtual tour" of their locations on campus. See http://publicaffairs.illinois.edu/markerstour.

# PART ONE

# SINGULAR PEOPLE

Remarkable Individuals
Who Triggered Innovation at the
University of Illinois and Beyond

# Isabel Bevier

## Bringing Science into the Home

Elisa Miller

When Isabel Bevier recorded her first impressions of the University of Illinois campus in the spring of 1900, she captured a distinctive feature of the Illinois landscape. "I thought I had never seen so flat and so muddy a place," she wrote. "No trees, no hills, no boundaries of any kind." But rather than be repelled by the stark scene before her, Bevier observed that the expansiveness of the midwestern prairie mirrored the openness and ambition of the campus community. "This lack of boundaries," she added, "the open-mindedness of the authorities and their willingness to try experiments . . . opened up a whole new world to me."[1] When she became a member of the faculty that fall, Bevier discovered how prescient her words had been. She joined a group of faculty and administrators engaged in academic reforms and experiments that were having an influence in higher education across the United States. As the first chair of the school's new Household Science Department, Bevier constructed a program that placed it at the forefront of the burgeoning home economics movement. In her twenty-one years at Illinois, Bevier earned an international reputation as a scholar and academic leader who helped define a new field grounded in rigorous standards of excellence and science.

Despite, or perhaps because of, her academic and professional accomplishments and national prominence, Bevier faced criticism and suspicion about her new department at the University of Illinois and in the local community. Some of this criticism came from male colleagues who doubted the academic credibility of home economics and viewed its courses and students as weakening the

Isabel Bevier on campus

Isabel Bevier's role as an academic pioneer was made possible by important changes in American higher education in the second half of the nineteenth century. The Morrill Act of 1862, which had triggered the founding of the Illinois Industrial University (renamed the University of Illinois in 1885), dramatically expanded access to higher education to men and women from rural and working class backgrounds. The University of Illinois was part of that trend. Women attended classes from the year of its founding and became eligible for degrees three years later. Despite the presence of women, however, most administrators at the new public institution believed that men and women should be educated differently and separately, in line with the mid-nineteenth-century gender ideology of "separate spheres." They argued that men should be trained for public careers in business, farming, and politics, while women should focus their attention on the home and private pursuits. Followers of the separate-spheres ideology held that women's place was in the home, where their natural tendencies for nurturing would protect their family's health, happiness, morality, and religion. These advocates agreed that women should be educated with men, but that the focus of their training should be on developing skilled mothers and homemakers.

Soon after their founding, the new land-grant universities created new gender-specific curriculums for their women students in domestic education. At the University of Illinois, founding president John Milton Gregory set out to create a curriculum that was "especially adapted to the wants of women."[2] Heavily influenced by Catharine Beecher, an advocate for women's education and author of bestselling domesticity manuals, Gregory argued that the university should offer a "domestic education" that prepared female students for their future duties as wives, mothers, and homemakers.[3] He successfully lobbied the Illinois legislature for funds to create a school of domestic education for women at the university and in 1874 hired Professor Louisa C. Allen to implement the program as a unit within the College of Agriculture. The domestic economy program at Illinois in the 1870s was one of the first academic programs of its kind in the country, but its progress was disrupted in 1879 when Professor Allen married President Gregory and they both left the university. Greg-

standards and reputation of the university. More damaging attacks, however, came from farmwomen in the community who viewed Bevier's commitment to scientific principles in the department as a betrayal to the practical needs of rural housewives. These tensions were grounded in larger discourse about the role of women in education and American society at the beginning of the twentieth century. In order to develop the new program, Bevier had to negotiate these complicated academic and social obstacles. In addition, they reveal the kind of resistance and backlash that academic innovation can engender.

ory's successor, Selim H. Peabody, opposed the domestic science program and gender-specific education in general and encouraged the board to discontinue the program.

Domestic education for women at the university was abandoned in the 1880s, but over the next decade, a growing group of alumnae began a campaign to revive the effort Allen and Gregory had initiated. The women argued that the institution had a public duty to offer equal educational opportunities to Illinois women. These new advocates of a women's curriculum were progressive activists who, with counterparts across the nation, pressed American institutions to allow their sisters and daughters to participate fully in education, social reform, and politics. These "new women" viewed domestic science as an integral entry point for women seeking to accomplish political, social, and educational reforms. The alumnae argued to the board of trustees in a petition that it was time to make the university "a *Co-educating* as well as a *Co-educational* institution" and demanded a Domestic Science department and more women faculty members.[4]

At the same time, a complementary lobby for domestic science was emerging among Illinois farming families. The Illinois Farmers' Institutes and its counterpart for women, the Illinois Association of Domestic Science, were at the forefront of this effort. The organizations promoted farm work and rural life, and they became vocal at a time when the population of the nation's cities was surging. Afraid that political leaders were paying too much attention to urban issues, these new groups lobbied for formal and informal education to preserve rural life and instill its values and practices in children and young adults. In particular, they hoped to convince young women that their futures would be better spent on farms than in cities. In Illinois these rural advocates identified domestic education as a critical factor that would enable rural women to live up to their household duties and thereby ensure the future of rural America.

The university's first women trustees quickly became important allies in the new campaign for domestic science. Among these influential advocates was Mary Turner Carriel, daughter of Jonathan Baldwin Turner, the Illinois educator who was widely credited for inspiring the land-grant education movement. Carriel and her colleagues argued that re-establishing the domestic science program was an issue of equity for women and promised to produce graduates who could make a vital contribution to social reform in the state and country. During the 1890s, President Andrew Draper resisted these entreaties, but dramatic continued lobbying, together with increases in the number of women students at the university, ultimately changed his mind. (Between 1894 and 1900 the size of the student body increased from eight hundred to twenty-five hundred, but the percentage of women on campus rose even more dramatically, from 18 percent to 28 percent.)[5]

Once it became evident that a domestic science department would likely pass, President Draper initiated a national search for a director. His inquiries led him to Isabel Bevier, then teaching at Lake Erie College in Painesville, Ohio. A veteran of ten years teaching chemistry and natural science at women's colleges in Ohio and Pennsylvania, Bevier was a committed laboratory researcher who had studied with pioneering nutritionist W. O. Atwater and Dr. Ellen Richards, a chemist who had been the first female student at MIT and was a founder of the home economics movement. Following her arrival on campus, Bevier found ready allies in President Draper and Eugene Davenport, dean of the College of Agriculture. Both men encouraged her ambition to create a program grounded in scientific principles, and they welcomed her proposal to call the new unit the Department of Household Science. Bevier and Davenport also agreed that one quarter of the courses required in the new major would focus exclusively on domestic topics; the remainder of the curriculum would expose students to traditional science and liberal arts classes.[6] Bevier also insisted that the department should house "laboratories, apparatus, . . . specimens of various kinds of building material, and exhibits demonstrating chemical composition and products obtained in the manufacture of certain foods."[7]

Under Bevier's leadership, the household science program expanded rapidly, from twenty students in 1900 to

"These 'new women' viewed domestic science as an integral entry point for women seeking to accomplish political, social, and educational reforms."

Isabel Bevier's colleagues celebrate her birthday

more than 150 four years later. Significantly, these new students shared Bevier's vision of household science as an avenue for social reform and a stepping stone to careers outside the home. An investigation of the twenty-eight graduates of the program by 1907, for example, found twenty-one women working outside the home or teaching at schools and universities.[8] Household science students also embraced the rhetoric and ideology of women's importance to the home and nation. A student from the class of 1907 explained, "There is no place more fateful for good or evil in the life of the individual or nation than the home," adding that "household science should be offered in every state university."[9] Anna Riehl, from the class of 1904, echoed this sentiment, explaining that household science offered a woman "the privilege to throw her influence upon the side of the movement which will be of such great benefit to society."[10]

Bevier added graduate training to the program in 1904 with a new master's degree in household science and later hired Dr. Nellie E. Goldthwaite to train and supervise graduate students in the program. As she took up her post, Goldthwaite, whose previous appointments had been at Mt. Holyoke College and the Rockefeller Institute of Medical Research, became the first person hired

by a department of home economics for an exclusively research role. Bevier and Goldthwaite's students soon took up leading posts across the country. Ruth Wardall (bachelor's degree 1903, master's 1907), for example, became the director of household science at both the University of Ohio and the Agriculture College of South Dakota before succeeding Bevier at Illinois in 1921. Edna H. Day, a graduate fellow in 1905, earned her PhD at the University of Chicago in 1906 and served as head of the Department of Household Science at the University of Missouri.[11]

Despite her national prominence and acclaim, Isabel Bevier attracted an array of local critics, a reflection of the resistance and backlash that academic innovation frequently engenders. Traditionalists on the faculty viewed home economics as an inappropriate topic for higher education. These opponents—overwhelmingly male—argued that classes in cooking and sewing belonged in high schools and trade schools, not in rigorous universities. (They also suggested that coeducation itself weakened the reputations of universities.) Bevier believed that her most committed, and condescending, critics resided among the male faculty in the liberal arts. Bevier recalled an incident in which the dean of the College of Literature and Arts asked her, "How much credit are you asking for bread baking?" to which she responded, "Not much, because we're not baking much bread." In contrast, Bevier believed that her scientific peers on campus recognized her program as upholding principles of scientific rigor and excellence. She recalled that when science colleagues were introduced to the program, "they would make some statement that left no doubt that they understood my language." Students, too, usually responded to such condescending comments by following Bevier's lead in emphasizing the program's scientific basis as well as its potential for promoting social reform. One student argued that her classes prompted her to seek out "board of health reports from various places" and to learn, for example, that "the average mortality increases with the density of population; which usually means [that] crowded tenements, with air made impure through lack of ventilation and uncleanliness, are conditions under which these micro-organisms thrive."[12] Those who enrolled in the courses in Bevier's program came to understand and embrace the new field of household science.

For the most part, Bevier was able to maneuver successfully around the misgivings that many on campus had about household science. President Andrew Draper, a friend and strong supporter, remarked, "I was somewhat skeptical as to whether such a department could be established in a University so as to make it really worth the time and cost. [But] with very many obstacles in her way, Miss Bevier steadily pushed her work to success."[13] In 1905, though, Draper stepped down from the presidency and was replaced by Edmund J. James, a Harvard-trained political scientist who Bevier feared would be hostile to women's education. Early in his administration, James confronted Bevier, charging that her department was "not made up of college students." The new president accused the Household Science Department of skirting university admission standards and lowering the quality of education at the university. Bevier later recalled, "To have this said to me after I had really battled for ten years to have chemistry as a requirement for admission to our work and thereby, I had offended some of those in high places, was too much to stand."[14] Despite this early conflict, Bevier and James developed a good working relationship based on mutual respect.

During these years, however, Bevier faced opposition from other, often more vocal, factions. For all the criticism directed at the Household Science Department for not being academic enough for a first-rate university, Illinois farmwomen and the powerful farming organizations attacked the domestic science program for being too rigorous in its application of academic and scientific standards to homemaking. This faction's opposition almost cost Bevier her job.

Despite the fact that farmwomen had been instrumental in the campaign to establish the Domestic Science Department, Bevier's relationship with local farmwomen and their organizations had been contentious. She and the farmwomen's groups held conflicting visions of the field. Bevier had struggled to create a department based on rigorous scientific and academic standards, but local women now felt that she had gone too far. It had become difficult for young rural women to meet the department's entrance requirements. Moreover, they believed that Bevier's program contained too much science and not enough practical homemaking. As department head, Bevier was caught in an academic no-woman's-land, unable to please either her academic or her domestic critics.

"New students shared Bevier's vision of household science as an avenue for social reform and a stepping stone to careers outside the home."

The major focus of contention between Bevier and the farming leaders was the department's curriculum. The Illinois Association of Domestic Science repeatedly asked for the inclusion of more practical courses in household duties, such as dressmaking, that they believed were more important for future homemakers than science and liberal arts. Bevier responded that such a shift would jeopardize "the good name of home economics in the mind of educators."[15] Bevier considered practical skills as inappropriate emphasis for the department and the University of Illinois, a priority, however secondary, that would undermine her effort to insure the credibility of Illinois as a research university. She tried also to highlight the positive national attention the Illinois program was receiving.

Bevier told the farmwomen, "The President of Ohio State University made the statement recently that all roads in domestic science, leading to progress and efficiency, seemed to center out of the University of Illinois."[16]

Bevier tried to win converts to scientific homemaking by giving speeches at association meetings and farmers' institute conferences. She utilized the farming lexicon and examples to appeal to rural residents. At one conference, she observed that farmers had learned "the benefit of science" and had started "sending [their] boys to agricultural colleges to learn the principles of physics, chemistry and bacteriology. . . . Is there any good reason," she asked "why the girl should not apply her knowledge of chemistry to bread and of bacteriology to the processes of fermentation?"[17]

But despite her best efforts, Bevier found working with the farming community challenging. She complained that many of the farmwomen were "suspicious of these newfangled notions about food. Chemistry and bacteriology were high-sounding terms, and science they did not know; but they could cook!"[18] Bevier's scientific curriculum seemed more suited for developing future educators and scientists than homemakers. The majority of her household science students went on to careers outside the home—often as home economists, dietitians, and social workers—and so her curriculum appeared threatening to the traditional homemaker role.

The farming associations continued to criticize Bevier. In the fall of 1909, she began a sabbatical during which she examined and participated in research programs throughout the country, including at Yale and Columbia's Teachers College. During her absence from the University of Illinois, the dean of agriculture conducted an investigation of Bevier and the Department of Household Science.[19] Although Davenport was a strong supporter and close friend of Bevier's, alienating the local farm leaders and organizations was both politically and financially risky. Davenport decided that there was no alternative but to ask for Bevier's resignation. He took the step reluctantly, though, as he still considered her "the leading woman in household science."[20]

As university administrators struggled to resolve Bevier's status, they turned to leaders in the field for advice.

The response was overwhelming. A. C. True, the director of the Office of Experiment Stations of the United States Department of Agriculture, for example, provided the university with a glowing recommendation for Bevier: "I doubt if there is a more influential woman on this subject in the American colleges today."[21] Buoyed by this support, the university leadership decided to defer acting on Davenport's recommendation, Bevier returned to campus in 1910, and the department weathered the crisis. The program's enrollment and status continued to increase in subsequent years, and Bevier continued to play a prominent role in the domestic science field. In 1911 the American Home Economics Association chose her as its new president. Bevier was invited to speak at universities across the country, and she was in demand to serve on professional committees and review panels. She added to her profile with a series of influential publications, including *Food and Nutrition, Laboratory Manual* (1906), *The Home Economics Movement* (co-authored with Susannah Usher) (1906), *The House: Its Plan, Decoration and Care* (1907), and *Home Economics in Education* (1924).

Bevier further solidified her position on campus and nationally during World War I. Across the country, home economics played an important and high-profile role through women's war work in areas such as food conservation, nursing, and preparation of war supplies. As the field demonstrated its usefulness and patriotism during wartime, it helped to legitimize domestic science. Bevier was named chair of the Home Economics Advisory Committee in Herbert Hoover's Food Administration, and she organized a variety of service projects on campus: a hospital training class, a center on food conservation and the use of food substitutes, Red Cross projects in knitting and making surgical dressings, and a home nursing course. In addition, several staff members of the department served overseas as nurses and dietitians. By one account, the Home Economics Department reached "315,703 Illinois people through lectures, conferences, and demonstrations, and sent out 734 newspaper articles, 10,794 letters, and 127,557 bulletins and circulars" about the role of home economics to the war effort.[22] During the war years, student enrollment in household science at the university increased dramatically as home-front volunteerism by

Bevier inspecting the food laboratory

women during World War I highlighted growing career opportunities for women trained in home economics.

In 1921, at age sixty-one, Bevier decided to retire from the university, having served as director for twenty-one years. After Bevier's retirement, her successors maintained the scientific principles and national profile that she established for the department. The two women who succeeded Bevier as director of the program—Ruth Wardell (1921–1936) and Lita Bane (1936–1948)—had been trained and mentored by Bevier as students and workers at the University of Illinois. The program remained committed to preparing women students for professional careers after graduation. In her later years, Bevier supervised the implementation of home economic programs at both the University of California, Los Angeles, and the University of Arizona following the principles she had established at Illinois.

Isabel Bevier was an educational pioneer at the University of Illinois and a national leader in the field of household science, renamed home economics in the early twentieth century. Her commitment to a curriculum rooted in science and research, to graduate training, and to her own high-profile research and publishing established the University of Illinois as a center of innovation in women's education and helped women students and faculty gain acceptance in both the university and in the world of work. Bevier was instrumental in establishing home economics as an academic field and in defining a place for women in higher education and the professions, and in the broad effort to bring about social progress and equality for women in the United States.

## Notes

1. Quoted in Lita Bane, *The Story of Isabel Bevier* (Peoria, Ill.: Bennett, 1955), 29.

2. *Sixth Annual Report of the Board of Trustees of the Illinois Industrial University*, 50.

3. Winton U. Solberg, *The University of Illinois, 1867–1894* (Urbana: University of Illinois Press, 1968), 161; *Sixth Annual Report*, 15.

4. Meeting of September 8, 1891, *Sixteenth Report of the Board of Trustees of the University of Illinois*, 150.

5. Allen Nevins, *Illinois* (New York: Oxford University Press, 1917), 163.

6. Isabel Bevier, "Recollections and Impressions of the Beginnings of the Department of Home Economics at the University of Illinois," *Journal of Home Economics* 32 (May 1940): 291–92.

7. *Catalog of the University of Illinois, 1900–1901* (Urbana: University of Illinois, 1901), 149–50.

8. "Alumni Notes," *Illinois Agriculturist* 12 (February 1908): 164–66, UIA.

9. E. G., "Household Science in State Universities," *Illinois Agriculturist* 10 (September 1905): 5–6, UIA.

10. Anna Riehl, "Why Young Women Should Study Household Science," *Illinois Agriculturist* 8 (June 1904): 253–54, UIA.

11. Isabel Bevier, "Household Science at the University of Illinois," *Illinois Agriculturist* 12 (February 1908): 129, UIA; Susan Barr, "The Household Science Alumnae," *Illinois Agriculturist* 8 (April 1904): 163–64, UIA; "College and Alumni Notes," *Illinois Agriculturist* 15 (April 1911): 39–41, UIA.

12. Bevier, "Recollections and Impressions," 294; Lillian Blair, "How the Work Outlined in the Household Science Course Impresses the New Student and How Her Impression Changes," *Illinois Agriculturist* 7 (May 1903): 127–28, UIA.

13. Andrew S. Draper to L. H. Bailey, March 26, 1906, RS 8/11/20, box 1, Isabel Bevier Papers, 1879–1955, UIA.

14. Isabel Bevier, *The History of the Department of Home Economics at the University of Illinois, 1900–1921* (Urbana: University of Illinois, 1935), 32.

15. Isabel Bevier to Mrs. I. S. Raymond, February 25, 1907, RS 8/1/51, box 2, Agriculture, Dean's Office, Historical Material, 1904–1975, UIA.

16. Isabel Bevier to Mrs. Laura B. Evans, September 7, 1908, RS 8/1/51, box 2, Agriculture, Dean's Office, Historical Material, 1904–1975, UIA.

17. Isabel Bevier, "Household Science in a State University," *Illinois Association of Domestic Science, Yearbook 1901* (Bloomington, Ill.: Lloyd and Miller, 1901), 26.

18. Bevier, "Recollections and Impressions," 295.

19. Eugene Davenport, October 28, 1909, RS 8/11/20, box 1, Isabel Bevier Papers, 1879–1955, UIA.

20. Eugene Davenport to Isabel Bevier, November 22, 1909, RS 8/11/20, box 1, Isabel Bevier Papers, 1879–1955, UIA.

21. A. C. True to Edmund James, September 26, 1910, RS 8/1/51, box 2, Agriculture, Dean's Office, Historical Material, 1904–1975, UIA.

22. Richard Gordon Moores, *Fields of Rich Toil: The Development of the University of Illinois, College of Agriculture* (Urbana: University of Illinois Press, 1970), 198.

## Sources

The University of Illinois Archives in Urbana-Champaign house Isabel Bevier's personal papers and the records of the Department of Household Science.

For more background on the history of women's education and land-grant universities, see Laurence Veysey, *The Emergence of the American University* (Chicago: University of Chicago Press, 1965) and Barbara Solomon, *In the Company of Educated Women: A History of Women and Higher Education in America* (New Haven, Conn.: Yale University Press, 1985).

On the national home economics movement, see Sarah Stage and Virginia B. Vincenti, eds., *Rethinking Home Economics: Women and the History of a Profession* (Ithaca, N.Y.: Cornell University Press, 1997); Sarah A. Leavitt, *From Catharine Beecher to Martha Stewart: A Cultural History of Domestic Advice* (Chapel Hill: University of North Carolina Press, 2002); and Megan J. Elias, *Stir It Up: Home Economics in American Culture* (Philadelphia: University of Pennsylvania Press, 2008).

On nineteenth-century ideas about separate spheres and domesticity, see Barbara Welter, "The Cult of True Womanhood: 1820–1860," *American Quarterly* 18 (Summer 1966): 151–74; Kathryn Kish Sklar, *Catharine Beecher: A Study in American Domesticity* (New York: Norton, 1976); Nancy F. Cott, *The Bonds of Womanhood: "Woman's Sphere" in New England, 1780–1835* (New Haven, Conn.: Yale University Press, 1977); and Linda K. Kerber, "Separate Spheres, Female Worlds, Woman's Place: The Rhetoric of Woman's Place," *Journal of American History* 75 (June 1988): 9–39.

For information about "New Women" at the turn of the century, see Rosalind Rosenberg, *Beyond Separate Spheres: Intellectual Roots of Modern Feminism* (New Haven, Conn.: Yale University Press, 1982); Nancy F. Cott, *The Grounding of American Feminism* (New Haven, Conn.: Yale University Press, 1987); Ellen Fitzpatrick, *Endless Crusade: Women Social Scientists and Progressive Reform* (New York: Oxford University Press, 1990); Lynn Gordon, *Gender and Higher Education in the Progressive Era* (New Haven, Conn.: Yale University Press, 1990); and Sarah Deutsch, *Women and the City: Gender, Space, and Power in Boston, 1870–1940* (New York: Oxford University Press, 2000).

Sources on the rural-life movement include William L. Bowers, *The Country Life Movement in America: 1900–1920* (Port Washington, N.Y.: Kennikat, 1974); Lynne Curry, *Modern Mothers in the Heartland: Gender, Health, and Progress in Illinois, 1900–1930* (Columbus: Ohio State University Press, 1999; and Marilyn Irvin Holt, *Linoleum, Better Babies, and the Modern Farm Woman* (Lincoln: University of Nebraska Press, 2006).

# Arthur Palmer

## The Chemistry of Safe Water

*Kelsey Reinker*

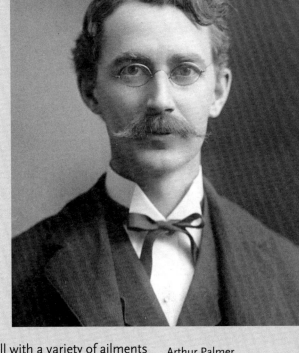

Arthur Palmer

Arthur Palmer (1861–1904) was born in London, England, but grew up in Elgin, Illinois. Palmer attended the University of Illinois and graduated with a Bachelor of Science degree in 1883. Palmer then headed east, first to Harvard, where he earned a doctorate in 1886, and later to Germany, where he conducted research in Berlin and Göttingen on arsine, an inorganic compound of arsenic. The chemist returned to Urbana-Champaign in 1889 and took up the post of assistant professor of chemistry.

During 1893, a typhoid epidemic struck several communities in Illinois. Most scientists believed typhoid and many other diseases originated in contaminated drinking water. In response, Palmer, who had become head of the Department of Chemistry at the university, proposed creating a survey to monitor the chemical content and quality of the state's water. The following year, the state legislature acted on the idea, and the Illinois board of trustees approved the university campus as the base for the survey's work. Palmer planned to use his chemistry laboratory to determine the sanitary conditions of wells, streams, and lakes, and to establish standards for drinking water across the state. The Illinois State Water Survey officially began its work in the fall of 1895.

In the first fifteen months of the survey's existence, Palmer and his team analyzed more than seventeen hundred samples of water from around the state. Unfortunately, all of these samples and related records were destroyed when a fire swept through the chemistry lab in late August 1896. Undaunted, Palmer salvaged what he could and pressed on. During next seven years, he accumulated 3,715 additional samples from nearly five hundred towns. His survey even extended to the Illinois River, where he tested the conditions of the water, including the tributaries from other states that fed into the river. Palmer's research was cut short on February 3, 1904, when he died suddenly at age forty-three. According to the Urbana *Courier*, Palmer's passing was a "shock" to the local community. He had been ill with a variety of ailments for several weeks, and their impact was ultimately compounded by the effects of the scientist's strenuous routine and relentless work habits. Nevertheless, Palmer's creation, the Illinois State Water Survey, continues to this day on the University of Illinois campus as part of the Prairie Research Institute, monitoring the state's rivers, lakes, and streams, and insuring that clean drinking water standards are upheld across the state and that water resources are managed wisely for economic development and a sustainable environment. The survey has grown to include areas of research in climate and atmospheric science, hydrology and hydraulics, and hazard assessment and management, and it is also home to the Illinois State Climatologist's office.

## Sources

The University Archives contains a number of documents related to Arthur Palmer's life and career. Most prominent is a pamphlet published on the occasion of a memorial service held for him in 1904. The University Archives also holds records related to the history of the Illinois State Water Survey. The notice of Palmer's death was carried in the Urbana *Daily Courier*, February 5, 1904.

# Austin Harding

## Inventor of the School Band

*Tim Brown*

A. A. Harding conducting the university band

In 1905, during his senior year in the engineering program at the University of Illinois, Albert Austin Harding (1880–1958) was suddenly and unexpectedly named the director of the school's military band. Despite the surprising nature of his appointment, Harding, an amateur musician from Georgetown in Vermillion County, Illinois, plunged headfirst into his new assignment. His principal goal was to expand the band's repertoire and extend its reach across campus. He happily conducted the military band for two years, but in 1907 he fulfilled a larger ambition when he landed the job of director of bands for the entire university. In that role—which he held for forty-three years—Harding created something new at Illinois: a symphonic band. From his new post, he became an ambassador for sophisticated band performance and a tireless advocate of music education. By the time of his retirement, he was universally recognized for his musicianship as well as for his impact on American popular culture.

Harding was an innovative band director. He moved band performances to the auditoriums in Huff Hall and developed the techniques that would enable a marching band to perform entertaining routines before massive audiences at football games and other events (his band performed at the nation's first homecoming, held at Illinois in 1910). Harding also crisscrossed the state with his band, promoting the Illinois music program and urging local educators to incorporate band performance into the school curriculum. Harding was also an innovative arranger of music. He shifted the band away from a sound dominated by brass instruments to a more balanced presentation that would feature a variety of woodwind and percussion instruments. Early in his career Harding had the good fortune to befriend John Philip Sousa, famed director of the United States Marine Corps band. Sousa became one of Harding's biggest supporters. He helped publicize Harding's program and declared the Illinois ensemble "the world's greatest college band."

Harding's combination of musicianship and advocacy earned him support from around the state and beyond. His band tours expanded interest in musical performance and popularized school bands. Harding encouraged his supporters to become part of a new network of performers and educators. He developed the first band clinics in America. The first clinic was held on the Illinois campus in January 1930. At his clinics, Harding emphasized the importance of sight reading so that performers could constantly expand their repertoire. He also argued that the key to a good band was a sophisticated leader who would work constantly to improve his or her musical knowledge. He encouraged bands to adopt a broad instrumentation and to perform a wide range of works to both educate and stimulate their audiences. The success of the clinics was evident from the start. In 1930, forty band directors drove through sleet and across icy roads to attend Harding's first session; they are still coming.

## Sources

The Sousa Archives and the Center for American Music, part of the University Archives, contains extensive holdings on Harding and his career.

# Victor E. Shelford
## Environmental Pioneer

George O. Batzli and Jeffrey D. Brawn

I am old and have had many troubles,
but most of them never happened.
—Sign in Victor Shelford's office

The early years of Victor Shelford's life (1877–1968) were not very promising. He was raised on a farm in upstate New York in a family with little extra money. As a result, he took a teaching job in a country school (1894) and did not complete high school until he was nearly twenty-two.[1] Throughout his life Shelford blamed the inadequate training in rhetoric and composition that he received during these years for his limited ability in public speaking and for the time it took to express himself in writing. These deprivations are surprising for a man who would become variously known as "the father of animal ecology in North America," "the father of physiological ecology of animals," and "the father of the Nature Conservancy." What explains these achievements? How could someone with such a limited background become an inno-vative scientist and a pioneer in the field of conservation? The answers to these questions lie in the combination of Shelford's remarkable personality, his training, his teaching and research career at the University of Illinois, and the development of his ideas through decades of activism.

Shelford's training as a biologist began when he entered the University of West Virginia as a premedical student in 1899. He took courses in zoology and botany and worked in several laboratories to support himself, but the greatest influence on his development as an undergraduate seems to have been his uncle, Assistant State Entomologist William Rumsey. Shelford lived with Rumsey, prepared lantern slides (glass slides for projection of images) for his lectures, and helped to curate the university insect collection. More important, however, were the walks

Victor Shelford

in the woods that he took with his uncle. During those explorations of the West Virginia countryside he began to seriously observe nature and to ask questions about the relationships of plants and animals to their natural habitats. After two years on the Morgantown campus, Shelford decided to pursue a career in biology and to transfer to a university that emphasized basic research. He so impressed his mentors with his industry, reliability, and excellent work that he received scholarship offers from Syracuse, Harvard, and the University of Chicago. Chicago—barely a decade old—made the most lucrative offer and landed the eager scholar.

While completing his undergraduate degree (1903) and doctorate (1907) in zoology at Chicago, Shelford's grades were not always stellar, but once again he impressed his mentors with his determination, enthusiasm, and hard work. In the early twentieth century, zoology was largely a laboratory and descriptive science. Morphology (the study of form) and physiology (the study of function) dominated the field. Ecology was just emerging as a self-conscious discipline with a focus on the natural history of individual species (autecology). Shelford's first research, which he began as an undergraduate and completed for his doctorate, was on the coloration, life history, and larval biology of a group of predaceous beetles (tiger beetles). Plant biologists were already recognizing relationships of groups of species (plant communities) to their environment, and Frederick Clements, building on the work of Eugenius Warming in Denmark, had begun his influential studies on the development of plant communities from simple to complex entities (a process called plant succession).[2] Early in his doctoral studies, Shelford sat in on a course in ecology by Henry Cowles (a follower of Warming), who had recently published his seminal work on the succession of plant communities in relation to changes in their physical environment. Cowles conducted his research in the nearby sand dunes on the south shore of Lake Michigan. He discovered that as one moves away from the lakeshore, one finds older dunes with greater stature and diversity of plants and with less frequent exposure to physical extremes.[3] Shelford was inspired by Cowles's approach, and he quickly came to see the necessity of field observations. As a result of continued association with Cowles, Shelford expanded his animal studies to include the spatial distribution of tiger beetles and other invertebrates in relation to plant communities amid the shifting physical conditions on the dunes.

When he finished his doctorate, Shelford so impressed his mentors with the thoroughness of his work and his superior performance on his final exam (summa cum laude) that Chicago offered him a position as "Associate in Zoology" to teach field natural history courses (the characteristics and relationships of organisms in their natural habitats). Now he began two contrasting approaches to ecology that, over the years, made Shelford's reputation.

Victor Shelford (far left) with graduate students from the University of Chicago

On the one hand, he developed laboratory studies of reactions of fish and invertebrates to physical conditions of the environment, particularly temperature, humidity, salt concentrations, oxygen concentrations, and pollutants. He used these results to help explain the distribution of organisms in nature. Today, such studies are more relevant than ever as we try to predict the responses of organisms to climate change. On the other hand, Shelford also championed community ecology, emphasizing the significance of relationships among multiple species in the same natural habitat. He came to see the study of these relationships as the proper focus for the emerging discipline of ecology.[4]

In 1913, after five years of teaching at Chicago and conducting field research at local sites, Shelford published *Animal Communities in Temperate America* (subtitled—*as illustrated in the Chicago region*), a compendium of the habitats and animal communities found near Chicago.[5] This work, a testimony to Shelford's industry, was completed at the same time as he developed laboratory equipment for testing the responses of fish and invertebrates to variable physical conditions, published a series of papers on succession in fish communities in response to changes in pond characteristics, published a monograph on physiological animal geography, and taught five courses per year!

In the preface of his book Shelford made it clear that *Animal Communities* emerged because "the need for some logical and philosophical background for the organization of natural history instruction into something more unified than haphazard discussions of such animals as were encountered in chance localities" was keenly felt. After introducing the nature of animals and describing their responses to environmental factors, Shelford marched through the various animal communities associated with aquatic and terrestrial habitats, providing maps, charts, photographs, and tables to illustrate the invertebrate and vertebrate members, successional sequences, and food webs (who eats whom) for each community. Finally, he discussed the factors that link species into particular communities and reviewed his "Law of Toleration," which states that limits to the distribution of organisms are set by one or more physical conditions (light, temperature, moisture, nutrients, oxygen, and the like) that are either below minimum or above maximum values beyond which the species can no longer survive and reproduce. Scientists teach this fundamental principle of physiological ecology in introductory ecology courses to this day.

"Shelford's book . . . was the first substantial volume on animal ecology ever published."

Shelford's book rapidly received national attention from biologists. It was the first substantial volume on animal ecology ever published, and it represented an enormous amount of field experience and analytical labor. One early admirer was Stephen A. Forbes, a professor at the University of Illinois and another founder of the field of ecology in North America. Forbes was well known for his early publications on the interaction of organisms in aquatic systems, for assessments of fish and bird populations, and for ecological studies of agricultural pests.[6] Forbes and Shelford knew each other from their joint work on the Ecological Survey Committee of the Illinois Academy of Sciences.

In spite of all Shelford's activity and innovation, his department head, who was a traditional zoologist trained in morphology and physiology, did not receive his work very enthusiastically. Shelford, now age thirty-six, began to look for another job. Apparently, in part to get a change of scene and in part to examine new animal communities, he arranged to spend the summer of 1914 at the Puget Sound Biological Station at Friday Harbor, Washington. Forbes, seventy years old but still the head of the Ento-

mology Department and the State Laboratory of Natural History (now the Illinois Natural History Survey, or INHS), encouraged Henry Ward, the head of the Zoology Department at Illinois, to hire Shelford. Although communication between Illinois and Puget Sound was slow, negotiations gradually progressed. As a final piece of the employment package, Shelford was offered the opportunity to help design and, later, move his laboratory into the space in a new vivarium (a building to house living organisms) and greenhouse (now the Victor E. Shelford Vivarium on Healey Street between Wright and Sixth Streets). To justify his salary, Shelford actually occupied two positions, as assistant professor of zoology and as biologist in the INHS (in charge of research laboratories), where he worked closely with Forbes. He immediately began designing more sophisticated equipment for examining responses of animals to physical factors in the laboratory and in the field.

At Friday Harbor, Shelford started a long-term study of the benthic (bottom-dwelling) animal communities and became particularly interested in the changes in light penetration as depth of water increased. He had read papers on marine bottom communities in Europe and was excited by the chance to develop his own ideas about their structure. After a trip to the Rocky Mountains and California in 1910–11 to observe tiger beetles in natural habitats apart from those of the Midwest, he began his ambitious, lifelong quest to visit all the major habitat types and biomes in North America. In addition to his spending every other summer at Friday Harbor for the next fifteen years, he began a series of field trips around North America that continued for more than three decades. Many trips during weekends, over academic breaks, and during summer included students from the University of Illinois and became legendary because of their scope and organization. Visiting remote places with a group of students required special logistics for travel, meals, camping equipment, and campsites. His students and colleagues praised Shelford as the master planner of these excursions.

Shortly after Shelford arrived at Illinois he was contacted by a friend, Robert Wolcott of the University of Nebraska, about the possibility of forming an ecological society. After discussing the matter with Henry Cowles, Shelford responded positively and soon found himself on the organizing committee. The Ecological Society of America (ESA) was formed in 1915 at a meeting of the American Association for the Advancement of Science (AAAS) with Victor Shelford and Stephen Forbes as charter members and with Shelford serving as the group's first president. Because he and other ecologists became concerned about human impact on the natural environment, he suggested that a committee of ESA be formed to locate natural areas that were unique or rare and, therefore, should be preserved. The ESA appointed Shelford chair of the Committee on Preservation of Natural Conditions (CPNC) in 1917. By 1921 the committee had fifty members and had identified six hundred areas preserved or worth preserving, most of them already owned by the federal government.

Working with other early advocates of nature on the national scene, such as Gifford Pinchot (National Forest Service) and Steven Mather (National Park Service), Shelford attended national meetings and organized ecologists to provide a scientific rationale for preserving natural areas. In 1926 this work culminated in the *Naturalist's Guide to the Americas* (North America, Central America, and northern South America), assembled and edited by Shelford, but with many contributing authors.[7]

Throughout those years of activism on the national stage, Shelford continued the research projects he had begun at Chicago, and he continued to teach. *Laboratory and Field Ecology*, published in 1929, was the culmination of his work on techniques and equipment designed for reliable measurement of animal responses to their physical environment. The book was an essential tool for students and colleagues. It contained diagrams, tables, and graphs showing the structure and explaining the use of the equipment for such things as the production of physical gradients and the simulation of climatic conditions.[8] Shelford also fulfilled his obligations to the INHS by completing two major studies of crop pests, the coddling moth and the chinch bug, and he continued to be in charge of studies in marine ecology at the Puget Sound Biological Station (PSBS).

In the 1930s Shelford resigned from his positions with the INHS and PSBS, reduced his work on responses of animals to the physical environment, and focused more keenly on animal communities. His travels then took him even farther afield—to the arctic tundra at Churchill, Manitoba, and to Mexico and Central America. He also continued his work on preservation of important natural environments. Because the ESA had active members who worked for government agencies and, therefore, could not serve as lobbyists, Shelford's public advocacy committee, the CPNC, was split in two. The CPNC continued to oppose government programs, such as predator control by the Bureau of Biological Survey, and the Committee for the Study of Plant and Animal Communities (CSPAC) became a fact-finding body to which federal employees could contribute. Not surprisingly, Shelford became chair of both committees. He simultaneously served on the Wildlife Committee and the Grassland Committee of the National Research Council (NRC) and was a trustee of the National Parks Association (a private organization that supported the designation of, monitored the use of, and lobbied the administration of the national parks). By the late 1930s Shelford had a local ally in his efforts for the preservation of nature, S. Charles Kendeigh, a former graduate student who had returned to Illinois as a faculty member in the Department of Zoology. Kendeigh, whose studies focused on birds, was destined to become an eminent ecologist in his own right. Shelford turned over the chairmanship of the CSPAC to Kendeigh so he could concentrate on the completion of a book co-authored with fellow ecologist Frederick Clements.

Shelford and Clements had begun their collaboration in 1923 when they agreed to review the ecological literature with the aim of characterizing animal and plant communities as single entities (the biome concept, first developed by Clements), but their sometimes contentious relationship did not bear fruit until the 1930s, when Clements repeatedly visited Shelford at Illinois to iron out their disagreements. Their jointly authored book, *Bio-ecology*, did not appear until 1939. After a brief history of ecology, their text considered community functions (the characteristics of plants and animals and their interrelationships), reactions (the ways in which organisms change their habitat), coactions (the ways plants and animals influence each other), the nature of animal population fluctuations and movements, succession and the development of mature (climax) communities, and, finally, application of these processes to North American grasslands and to aquatic biomes.[9] Throughout the writing of *Bio-ecology*, Shelford was traveling extensively during weekends, holidays, and summers to experience biomes first hand so he could complete his magnum opus, a book that described all the biomes of North America.

In the late 1930s Shelford became increasingly disenchanted with the leadership of the ESA. By 1937 he had been leading the committees on natural areas for twenty years with very little support from the society, a fact he resented. His discontent reached a breaking point that year when the executive committee of ESA rejected his proposal that thirty-five cents from each member's dues be directed to support his committees. He also feared that many ecologists missed the essential point that the unique contribution of ecological research was to elucidate the structure and function of natural communities, not just their species composition. The key for him was to examine the interaction of species with one another and with their natural habitats. He resolved the apparent contradiction of this emphasis on communities with his physiological approach to ecology by pointing out that the responses of animals to the physical conditions of their environments could explain their distribution, abundance, and life history (the schedule of reproduction, development, and survival) in the context of their natural habitats. He believed that for every biome there were only a few species that could be studied in detail, which made it essential to select for special scrutiny those with the greatest impact on the community. In 1937 Shelford summarized his reservations about the state of the ESA in a letter to the organization's president that severely criticized the limited program of

> "The key for him was to examine the interaction of species with one another and with their natural habitats."

the society, which now consisted of holding annual meetings and publishing the journal *Ecology* with little or no support for preservation activities.[10] His manifesto placed him at odds with the society's leaders.

Because of his extensive travels and activities in support of preservation, Shelford knew that natural areas were disappearing. Indeed, the outbreak of World War II made preservation efforts more difficult because people's concerns were elsewhere. As the chair of the Grassland Committee of the NRC and a trustee of the Grassland Foundation (a private organization formed at his suggestion), he nearly completed a plan to preserve one million acres of grassland in northwestern Nebraska and southwestern South Dakota, but the project fell by the wayside as the war started. Probably out of frustration, Shelford published a short article in the leading U.S. scientific journal *Science*, titled "Twenty-Five-Year Effort at Saving Nature for Scientific Purposes," that recounted the efforts of his committees and the lack of support from ESA.[11] He then sent the article and a questionnaire to 453 members of ESA without notifying the organization's officers. The respondents largely confirmed Shelford's belief that preservation was as important as ESA's other activities, and their support inspired Shelford to continue on his solitary course.

In 1944 Shelford published two open letters in the *Bulletin of the Ecological Society of America*.[12] In the first, addressed to members, he reviewed support for preservation work by the membership, the lack of support for this work by the society itself, and the need for a constitutional amendment to make clear the importance of activism in the future. The second, addressed to members and officers, pointed out that only 5 percent or fewer of members attended annual meetings where constitutional amendments were made (and, although he did not say it, where officers were elected), that the attendees of annual meetings varied widely, and that they sometimes approved policies that conflicted with earlier votes. Shelford argued that in the future the society should distribute ballots by mail to insure greater representation and that it should employ a paid secretary-treasurer to modernize the organization's business practices.

Charles Kendeigh, as chair of the CSPAC, proposed an amendment to the bylaws that established permanent committees for the study and preservation of natural areas, provided 10 percent of members' dues to support the committees, and empowered the committees to accept donations, hold property, and transact business. In September 1944 the executive committee responded by proposing to abolish the preservation committee (CPNC) altogether. Shelford railed against this proposal and condemned it as a plot by a cabal of senior officials of the NRC's Division of Biology and Agriculture (also officers of ESA) who wanted control of conservation activities from their offices in Washington, D.C.[13] In the end, a mail ballot conducted in 1945 produced a redefinition of the CPNC's duties that empowered it to provide information and advice to the public, but not to take direct action to influence legislation. Shortly thereafter Shelford began to organize the Ecologists' Union (EU) to carry on the work of the CPNC formerly done under the auspices of ESA.

By early 1946 the EU had eighty-three members, including four past presidents of ESA. Shelford, now age sixty-five and forced to retire at the University of Illinois, wanted to concentrate on completing his life's work (*The Ecology of North America*, a review of all the major biomes, which did not appear until 1963[14]), so Kendeigh took up the chairmanship of the new organization until a meeting of EU could be held in December. A board of governors that included Shelford was elected by the membership, now 168 strong, and lobbying of the federal government began in earnest. The EU grew rapidly and began to include members who were not professional ecologists. George Fell, a botanist who had taken courses from Shelford and Kendeigh at Illinois, took on an important leadership role and pushed for expansion of the organization so it could acquire land, as was done by the newly formed Nature Conservancy in Great Britain. In 1950 the EU changed its name to The Nature Conservancy, with Shelford and Kendeigh on the board. That organization rapidly expanded with funds from individual members and charitable foundations. It now has one million members and has protected 120 million of acres of natural areas in thirty-five countries.[15]

Throughout his career Victor Shelford demonstrated a remarkable set of personal qualities. He was highly organized, industrious, dedicated, tenacious, and fearless. Professionally, he pursued his passion for ecological study wherever his curiosity took him—from the laboratory to the field to the political arena. According to students and friends of Shelford, he was not a polished lecturer but instead was generally calm, highly organized, and enthusiastic in the field. He insisted on punctuality and discipline from his students but would go out of his way to help them. He chafed under bureaucratic regulations and restrictions, however, and occasionally lost his temper. He held strong views and directed them to everyone—students, colleagues, university presidents, and federal cabinet officers. His students, colleagues, and collaborators described his personality as dominant, even aggressive, but leavened with a sense of humor and desire to serve his students, his profession, and society at large.[16]

Shelford's basic drive to understand the structure and function of natural communities of organisms and his incredible industry combined to produce his extraordinary influence on the development of animal ecology in North America. His insistence on conducting research in the field led to his early recognition of the need for preservation of natural areas, and his tenacious and assertive personality propelled him to become one of the most important champions of conservation in North America in the first half of the twentieth century. His refusal to accept defeat ultimately resulted in the formation of The Nature Conservancy.

## Notes

1. Details of Shelford's life, career, and personality are well documented in Robert A. Croker's *Pioneer Ecologist: the Life and Work of Victor Ernest Shelford* (Washington, D.C.: Smithsonian Institution Press, 1991).

2. Donald Worster, *Nature's Economy: A History of Ecological Ideas* (New York: Cambridge University Press, 1977).

3. Henry Chandler Cowles, "The Ecological Relations of the Vegetation on the Sand Dunes of Lake Michigan," *Botanical Gazette* 27 (1899): 95–117, 167–202, 281–308, 361–91.

4. Victor Shelford, *Introduction to Laboratory and Field Ecology* (Baltimore, Md.: Williams and Wilkins, 1929).

5. Victor E. Shelford, "Animal Communities in Temperate America as Illustrated in the Chicago Region: A Study in Animal Ecology," *Geographic Society of Chicago Bulletin* 5 (1913).

6. Robert A. Croker, *Stephen Forbes and the Rise of American Ecology* (Washington, D.C.: Smithsonian Institution Press, 2001).

7. Victor E. Shelford, ed., *Naturalist's Guide to the Americas* (Baltimore, Md.: Williams and Wilkins, 1926).

8. Victor E. Shelford, *Laboratory and Field Ecology: The Responses of Animals as Indicators of Correct Working Methods* (Baltimore, Md.: Williams and Wilkins, 1929).

9. Frederick E. Clements and Victor E. Shelford, *Bio-Ecology* (New York: Wiley, 1939).

10. Letter from Victor Shelford to Robert Croker, President of the Ecological Society of America, October 15, 1937, University of Illinois Archives—Victor E. Shelford, box 1.

11. Victor E. Shelford, "Twenty-Five-Year Effort at Saving Nature for Scientific Purposes," *Science* 98 (1943): 280–81.

12. Victor E. Shelford, two open letters in *Bulletin of the Ecological Society of America* 25 (1944): 12–15.

13. Letters from Victor Shelford to members of the Ecological Society of America, June 6, 1945, and to W. S. Cooper, June 12, 1945; University of Illinois Archives—Victor E. Shelford, box 1.

14. Victor E. Shelford, *The Ecology of North America* (Urbana: University of Illinois Press, 1963).

15. See http://www.nature.org/about-us/index.htm?intc=nature.tnav.about.

16. Anonymous, "Victor E. Shelford: An Appreciation," *Bulletin of the Ecological Society of America* 36 (1955): 116–18. S. Charles Kendeigh, "Victor Ernest Shelford: Eminent Ecologist 1968," *Bulletin of the Ecological Society of America* 49 (1968): 97–100.

## Sources

Shelford's career can be studied through his 1991 biography, as well as his published works and additional materials in the University Archives.

# Katharine Sharp

## Shattering the Glass Ceiling of Library Leadership

*Nicholas Hopkins*

The University of Illinois system of more than two dozen libraries, along with its tradition of public service and its close ties to the highly rated Graduate School of Library and Information Science, has long been a source of pride on campus. But, perhaps because this resource has been so remarkable for such a long time, those responsible for organizing and maintaining its collection of thirteen million volumes and countless electronic and archival resources are routinely overlooked. Nevertheless, this major source of campus innovation has a history—and a heroine: Katharine L. Sharp (1865–1917), founder of the university's library school.

Sharp's extensive training and passion for improving library systems gave the library program at Illinois a foundation that stimulated high achievement and supported the massive expansion of the university's library holdings. Sharp grew up in Elgin, Illinois, and attended Northwestern University, where she graduated in 1885. Following her graduation, Sharp returned home to teach but she was soon drawn to the new professional field of librarianship. In 1888 she moved to Oak Park, Illinois, to become assistant librarian at the new Scoville Institute, a forerunner of the city's public library. Two years later, she enrolled in the New York State Library School, a new institution headed by library pioneer Melvil Dewey, inventor of the Dewey Decimal System of book classification. (Dewey had founded the nation's first professional library school at Columbia University but had moved the school to Albany when he relocated there in 1889.)

Katharine Sharp's enthusiasm and capacity for detailed work quickly impressed Dewey. As Sharp completed her studies, Dewey, then serving as president of the American Library Association (ALA), asked her to organize the association's exhibit for the 1893 Chicago World's Fair. Sharp's project at the exhibition, for which she catalogued, classified, and listed five thousand books chosen by the ALA, won her wide praise. Her work in Chicago also drew her closer to Dewey and his growing national network of (male) librarians.

Library science students and faculty, 1893

As the fair concluded, a new "institute of technology" in Chicago, the Armour Institute, approached Melvil Dewey about who the "best man" would be to direct its program in library science. "The best man," Dewey replied, "is a woman." Sharp remained at Armour (now Illinois Institute of Technology) for five years. She enjoyed serving as the leader of an important institute program, but she longed to develop a library program at a major university. It did not take her long, then, to consider University of Illinois President Andrew Draper's invitation to become university librarian and head of the Illinois State Library School. In the process Sharp became the first woman to hold such a post and, as a consequence, one of the most prominent librarians in the nation.

By the turn of the twentieth century, Sharp was supervising a faculty of six and a group of forty-seven library students. Together, they organized the library's forty thousand volumes and created a reference system to support the collection. At the same time—as she had in Albany and Chicago—she continued to be an active and vocal member of the growing library profession. By 1907 the Illinois library school had become a rival of Dewey's program in Albany. Unfortunately, Sharp's dedication to library science came at a price. Sickness beset Sharp throughout much of her career, brought about by her relentless schedule. When she was stricken with typhoid fever in 1897, her mentor Dewey had cautioned Sharp, saying, "You have magnificent possibilities of usefulness, but they are all contingent on your taking rest and husbanding your strength."

In 1907 Sharp decided to retire from the university. She was only forty-two, but she wrote in her resignation letter that she believed that "the pressure of administrative duties was preventing [her] from doing what [she] wished to do for the school. "It was," she added, "crushing the human element out of my life." Sharp's care for students and commitment to detail gave the library program its early success and stability. From the bedrock of her efforts, the library school would soon evolve into a graduate program and would play a leading role in the many innovations that ensued: distance education, digitization, and mentorship programs for undergraduate and graduate researchers. Through her prominent role in library administration, Sharp helped create the modern science of information management. Unfortunately, while she was the first woman to lead a major school within the university, her unprecedented rise was not soon duplicated. While many women later rose to prominence in the library field, it would be decades before other women would equal Sharp's rapid rise and nearly a century before Nancy Cantor would become the campus's first woman chancellor in 2001.

## Sources

Katharine Sharp's papers are housed in the University Archives. For an overview of her career, see Donald Krummel, "Katharine L. Sharp and the Creation of the University Library," in Lillian Hoddeson, *No Boundaries: University of Illinois Vignettes* (Urbana: University of Illinois Press, 2004).

Billingsley, Mary P., of the Kansas City, Missouri, Library. Letter to Frances Simpson, Assistant Director of the Library School, October 15, 1915. Katharine L. Sharp Memorial Correspondence, record series 18/1/22, box 1, folder "General correspondence about Sharp Memorial A–Z 1914–22."

Dewey, Melvil. Letter to Katharine Sharp, March 26, 1895. Katharine L. Sharp Papers, record series 18/1/20, box 1, folder "Correspondence—D."

Grotzinger, Laurel. "Remarkable Beginnings: The First Half Century of the Graduate School of Library and Information Science." In *Ideals and Standards: The History of the University of Illinois Graduate School of Library and Information Science*, edited by Walter C. Allen and Robert F. Delzell, 1–22. Urbana: Board of Trustees of the University of Illinois, 1992.

Hoddeson, Lillian. *No Boundaries: University of Illinois Vignettes*. Urbana: University of Illinois Press, 2004.

Robinski, George S., Jesse Hauk Shera, and Bohdan S. Wynar, eds. *Dictionary of American Library Biography*. Denver, Colo.: Libraries Unlimited, 1978.

Sharp, Katharine L. "Catechism for Librarians." Katharine L. Sharp Papers, record series 18/1/20, box 2, folder "Catechism for Librarians."

Katharine L. Sharp. Resignation letter (copy), donated by a former student, dated April 29, 1907. Katharine L. Sharp Papers, record series 18/1/22, box 5, folder "Resignation—copy of letter."

"Thirteenth-Million Volume Acquired." University of Illinois Archives website, September 7, 2013, http://www.library .illinois.edu/news/thirteenth_millionth_volume.html.

# Ven Te Chow
## Hydrologist, Educator, and Rainmaker

Marcelo H. Garcia

On July 30, 1981, Professor of Engineering Ven Te Chow, internationally respected for his research and leadership in water resources, hydrology, and hydraulic engineering, died suddenly and unexpectedly in Champaign, Illinois, bringing to an early end an unparalleled career that encompassed study of the hydrologic cycle, established the field of hydrology as a science, built the world-renowned Hydrosystems Laboratory at the University of Illinois, and led to the founding of the forum, the International Water Resources Association. For anyone concerned about water resources and the distribution of this precious resource to the people of the globe, Ven Te Chow's journey through the river of life offers both inspiration and an opportunity to learn the dimensions of a career marked by continuous achievement and innovation.

## The Making of a Hydrologist

Ven Te Chow was born August 14, 1919, in Hangzhou, China. Upon graduating from Fuh Tan High School in Shanghai in 1936, he entered National Chiao Tung University, receiving a bachelor of science degree in civil engineering, with honors, in 1940. After graduation he worked for several years as a teacher in his former high school, as an instructor at the Great China School in Shanghai, and as an assistant professor at several universities. Despite coming of age during a tumultuous time in China's history, Chow was both determined to make a difference and eager to share his knowledge through publications. His technical writings covered a wide range of topics. His first book, *Theory of Structures* (published in Chinese in

1943), written when he was twenty-seven years old, was quite wide ranging, but he also wrote on more esoteric subjects, particularly in essays published in popular magazines under such titles as "Bamboo and Its Engineering Uses" and "Savage Tribes in Formosa."[1] Toward the end of World War II, the Bureau of Public Works assigned Chow to the island of Formosa (known today as Taiwan), where he worked as a civil engineer on the reconstruction and maintenance of highways and bridges. Upon his return to mainland China in October 1946, Chow worked for nearly a year as an assistant professor of civil engineering at his alma mater in Shanghai before leaving for graduate school in the United States. National Chiao Tung University, where Chow completed his undergraduate work, is now Shanghai Jiao Tong University (SJTU). The school was established in 1896 by an imperial edict issued by Emperor Guangxu. It is one of the oldest and most prestigious and selective universities in China and a training ground for the nation's first generation of professionally trained engineers. Interestingly, when translated to English the motto of SJTU reads, "*When you drink water, never shall you forget its source; love your motherland and add credit to your Alma Mater.*" Ven Te Chow lived up to this alma mater's motto quite literally, devoting his life to water science and engineering and water resources policy.

In August 1947, while the civil war between Chiang Kai-shek's republican forces and the communists under Mao Zedong engulfed China, Ven Te Chow departed for the United States and began his graduate studies at Pennsylvania State College (renamed Pennsylvania State University in 1953). At Penn State, Chow majored in structural engineering, earning his master's degree in civil engineering in just one year. To support himself during his studies, he worked at the university's engineering experiment station as a graduate research assistant on hydraulic engineering research and applications. Being in a hydraulic laboratory renewed Chow's interest in finding solutions to the water problems he had first observed while stationed

> "Being in a hydraulic laboratory renewed Chow's interest in finding solutions to the water problems he had first observed while stationed in Taiwan."

in Taiwan. This experience must have influenced Chow's decision to leave Penn State and pursue a doctorate in civil engineering at the University of Illinois. Another factor that most likely pointed Chow toward the Midwest was the encouragement he received from Professor Frederic T. Mavis, a native of Macomb, Illinois, who received all of his civil engineering degrees from the University of Illinois and had recently served as department head at Penn State. Illinois College of Engineering annually awards the Frederic T. and Edith F. Mavis Memorial Fellowship to support graduate studies. Whatever might have been the motivation for Chow's move from the mountains of Pennsylvania to the prairie fields of central Illinois, the University of Illinois was about to welcome the future leader in the field of water resources and, by all accounts, a potential "rainmaker" who would make the modest Boneyard Creek, running east to west across the engineering quadrangle, famous through his books and publications.

Immediately upon his arrival on campus in the fall of 1948, Ven Te Chow, as an assistant to Professor James J. Doland in the Civil Engineering Department, started to work on the design of storm-water drainage for the Congress Expressway (later renamed Eisenhower Expressway) in Chicago. Professor Doland was well known in the field of hydraulic engineering, and the opportunity to work with him was attractive to Chow. Doland had co-authored with Professor Harold Babbitt the classic textbook *Water Supply Engineering* (first edition published in 1926), which had caught Chow's attention while at Penn State. As it turned out, Professor Doland's health was declining, and Chow began to take on an increasing share of his mentor's teaching load. By the time he had earned his doctorate in May 1950, Dr. Chow was teaching all of Doland's classes in addition to his own assignments as an assistant professor in the Civil Engineering Department. The title of his doctoral dissertation was "Probability Studies of Hydrologic Events and Their Applications to Hydraulic Design," reflecting a balance between hydrology (the science of water and its movements) and hydraulics (the science and technology concerned with the conveyance of water). Chow sustained this dual interest throughout his professional life.

As part of his dissertation, Chow had developed a methodology for frequency analysis of hydrologic data that could be applied to drainage problems in Chicago. Stemming from his work on the Congress/Eisenhower Expressway and his doctoral research, Chow's "frequency factor approach" for hydrologic design was further extended through unfunded studies that were published in University of Illinois Engineering Experiment Station Bulletin No. 414 in 1953. The frequency factor approach quickly became the dominant technique applied to hydraulic design throughout the world. Chow's work further elevated the field of engineering hydrology by developing techniques that could be used to analyze the propagation of flood waves as well as the dimensions of a spillway or a levee that could be constructed to prevent flooding. His approach was pioneering in the use of exceedance probabilities to estimate the frequency of extreme hydrologic events. In the process he devised a clever method for incorporating hydrologic estimates into the design of hydraulic structures. Long before other scientists considered such factors, Chow was factoring in the uncertainty associated with climate change and variability into hydrologic and hydraulic design.

Professor Chow had an amazing capacity for work. Even though he maintained a double teaching load in his early years at Illinois, he also found the time to begin writing his own books while simultaneously helping Professor Doland complete the publication of *Hydro Power Engineering: A Textbook for Civil Engineers* (New York: Ronald, 1954). Reading the book's preface must have been disheartening for Assistant Professor Chow, who, even though he did most of the work needed to complete the textbook, was not named a co-author. This did not seem to slow him down, however, for he continued to devote himself to his own writing as well. Five years after the publication of Doland's book, Chow published what would become his first bestseller: *Open-Channel Hydraulics* (McGraw-Hill, 1959). Chow's new book replaced Boris Bakhmeteff's *Hydraulics of Open Channels* (McGraw-Hill, 1932), which had

Ven Te Chow in his artificial rainmaking laboratory

been considered the definitive text on open-channel flows up to that time. This was no small accomplishment for the forty-year-old Ven Te Chow, given that Boris A. Bakhmeteff (1881–1951) had been a distinguished professor at Columbia University and a former Russian ambassador to the United States. With its clear descriptions and explanations of fundamental principles, Chow's book quickly gained a wide audience and has withstood the test of time. Despite the fact that computational technologies have evolved, the fundamentals have not changed, and for this reason Chow's book remains an indispensable reference that has been translated into several languages and is used around the world both as a textbook and a reference guide for practicing engineers. Despite the presence of some very minor mistakes in the text, there has never been a second edition of Ven Te Chow's classic.

In the preface of another highly popular book, *Open-Channel Flow* (1966), hydraulician Frank Henderson wrote, "No one can write on the subject matter of this book without becoming indebted to Ven Te Chow's recent authoritative treatise on the subject." *Open-Channel Hydraulics* has enjoyed a strong and sustained presence in the hydraulics profession and among several generations of students the world over who have learned the principles of hydraulics from its pages in both undergraduate and graduate courses. Indeed, when I took a course in open-channel hydraulics as an undergraduate in Santa Fe, Argentina, I used the Spanish version of Chow's book. Likewise, when teaching open-channel hydraulics at the University of Illinois, I maintain Chow's book as an important reference. It's one of those books that each time one reads it, something new comes up. It's simply timeless, and the work that went into writing it must have been monumental. Chow dedicated the book, "To Humanity and Human Welfare."

> "The frequency factor approach quickly became the dominant technique applied to hydraulic design throughout the world."

## Chow's *Handbook of Applied Hydrology* (1964)

Chow's relentless pursuit of academic excellence continued with his work on the preparation of a landmark tome published by McGraw-Hill in 1964 as the *Handbook of Applied Hydrology: A Compendium of Water-Resources Technology*. In the 1960s, before the publication of his handbook, Chow directed a number of graduate students who were working on adjacent aspects of hydrology. Among them were Krishnan P. Singh, V. C. Kulandaiswamy, Mordechai Haim Diskin, and Ramanand Prasad, who were working on several aspects of deterministic hydrology, while Sundaresa Ramaseshan was working on stochastic aspects of hydrology. In the handbook, Chow describes his General Hydrologic System Model based on the thesis of his doctoral student Kulandaiswamy (PhD 1964, the year that the handbook was published). This was the latest knowledge in the field at the time of the handbook publication, which had not gone through the peer review process. As one might expect, there were many vigorous discussions among the participants of this team and with Professors Ven Te Chow and Murray B. McPherson, all of whom had made substantial contributions to the handbook. Prior to the publication of Chow's *Handbook*, Stanford University professor Ray K. Linsley's *Applied Hydrology* (McGraw-Hill, 1949) had been the common text. After Chow's handbook appeared, however—a work prepared by a team of forty-five specialists, with the Illinois professor serving as editor-in-chief and author of several chapters—hydrology could no longer be taught as it had been in the past. Of Chow's forty-five contributors, twenty-three were government officials, seventeen came from academia, and five were from the world of consulting. The handbook was a comprehensive compendium on modern hydrology as it stood in the mid-1960s. It also contained results from the research produced by many of Chow's students. Chow's handbook benefited as well from contributions from many of the leaders in their respective fields at the time, including Arthur N. Strahler (Columbia) on drainage basins and channel networks; Hans A. Einstein (Berkeley) on river sedimentation; Murray B. McPherson (Illinois) on hydrology of urban areas; Chow on frequency analysis and runoff; Maury L. Albertson and Daryl B. Simons (Colorado State) on sediment transport; Gilbert F. White (Chicago) on floodplain analysis; David K. Todd (Berkeley) on groundwater; David R. Dawdy and Nicholas C. Matalas (USGS) on time series analysis; and Vujica M. Yevdjevich (Colorado State) on statistical analysis of hydrologic data.

## Chow's Boneyard Creek Hydrographs and Floods

Many international visitors who have studied from Chow's *Handbook of Applied Hydrology* are surprised when they come to the University of Illinois campus expecting finally to watch the "mighty" stream (dubbed Boneyard Creek) immortalized in Chow's *Handbook*. What they discover instead is a tiny waterway that is not much larger than a typical drainage ditch commonly found in central Illinois. Nevertheless, many generations of students have learned from the hydrologic observations Chow and his students made in Boneyard Creek. In fact, on a plaque located by the creek's bridge near the back of Engineering Hall in Urbana, one can read the history of the flow discharge gauging station operated and maintained by the U.S. Geological Survey (USGS) on the campus since the 1940s. The plaque highlights Ven Te Chow's major role in ensuring that the gauging station continued to operate, even at times when its existence was threatened due to shortages of federal funds.

Chow's vision to continue monitoring flows in Boneyard Creek became evident many years after his passing. Starting in the 1980s, as the twin cities Urbana and Champaign continued to experience growth, urban flooding became a major issue along Boneyard Creek, affecting especially the "campus town" neighborhood—indeed, it was not uncommon occasionally to see students having fun in canoes at the intersection of Green and Wright Streets. As the situation worsened, the university chancellor and the mayors of both Urbana and Champaign agreed to collaborate to identify a solution to the flooding problem. The data collected at the USGS gauging station on the Boneyard were very useful for the development of flood-control measures and new infrastructure to eliminate the bothersome overflow. Such data were also used to conduct a flow-conveyance analysis for detecting bottlenecks and to calibrate scale hydraulic models of Boneyard Creek as it flows under Wright Street and Lincoln Avenue. Both were built at Ven Te Chow's Hydrosystems Laboratory of the Civil and Environmental Engineering Department. Once again, Professor Chow's earlier efforts to promote hydrologic data collection paid dividends by reducing local flooding. One would imagine that this might have been Chow's way to pay it forward to the Urbana-Champaign community that welcomed him when he started his career at Illinois.

## Watershed Experimentation System (WES)

Long before the university built the Hydrosystems Laboratory under Chow's leadership, the hydrologist used an old laboratory located directly behind the Physics Department (now Loomis Lab) to construct hydraulic systems for his students. Following the success of those efforts, Chow decided to simulate nature's efforts in his own laboratory, the Watershed Experimentation System (WES). With a grant from the National Science Foundation, plus the interest and assistance of colleagues like the late Professor Ben Chie Yen and students like Terrence Harbaugh, who went on to become a professor at the University of Missouri at Rolla, Dr. Chow developed a computer-controlled rainfall simulator that could produce what *Public Works Magazine* called "Rainstorms Made to Order." Professor Chow's rainfall simulator could produce storms of any intensity and duration as well as change the spatial and temporal distribution patterns, thus making it possible to measure quite accurately, and for the first time, the runoff hydrograph resulting from rainfall over all types of model terrains having a wide range of infiltration capacities. On this system, Chow's doctoral student Arie Ben-Zvi, who went on to become chief hydrologist with Israel's Hydrological Service, ran 588 experiments of steady uniform rains with different intensities and durations. The Illinois rainmaker even attracted the attention of *LIFE* magazine,[2] which ran a picture of Professor Chow with one of his students, both wearing raincoats, under intense rain and doing measurements of runoff in a scale model of California's San Fernando Valley.

## Watershed Hydrology at Illinois

By the time Ven Te Chow joined the University of Illinois faculty in 1950, the university had already enjoyed a national reputation as a center of research on hydraulics and watershed hydrology. Professor Arthur N. Talbot developed the renowned "Talbot formula" in 1887, which described an empirical relation that could be used to estimate the cross-sectional area needed to convey the floods resulting from intense rainfall on a watershed. In the ensuing sixty years, studies on watershed hydrology continued at a relatively local scope, most prominently through the work of George W. Pickels, who focused on Illinois floods during the 1920s and 1930s. In 1936, Professor Hardy Cross, a structural engineer, published his method to compute flow and head losses in pipe networks. The so-called Hardy Cross method has found its way around the world several times and has brought recognition to the University of Illinois. After his early work on the Eisenhower Expressway with his mentor Professor Doland, Ven Te Chow joined this tradition by starting what would become a thirty-year, multiphase research project on watershed hydrology at Illinois. This effort, supported by the U.S. Bureau of Public Roads, the Illinois Department of Highways, and the unfunded completion of the frequency factor approach, began with a report of practical value for agricultural basins, titled "Hydrologic Determination of Waterway Areas for the Design of Drainage Structures in Small Drainage Basins," issued by the Engineering Experiment Station in 1962. This publication reflected Chow's belief in the need to produce research results that improved the quality of life of people by preventing floods through sound drainage engineering. Despite his rising academic prominence, Chow never lost sight of the need to use science for the common good.

Chow's research on watershed hydrology engaged four separate areas: lumped system approaches to the rainfall-runoff relationship, experimental investigations of runoff from rainfall (as at Boneyard Creek), hydraulics-based theoretical modeling of runoff due to rainfall, and the analysis of spatial and temporal distributions of rainfall for watershed runoff. Some of this work is summarized in chapter 14 ("Runoff") in the *Handbook of Applied Hydrology*, a chapter Professor Chow himself wrote using hydrologic data collected for Boneyard Creek to make a formal presentation of Unit Hydrograph Theory, originally proposed by Leroy K. Sherman in the early 1930s. The theory seeks a relationship between rainfall and runoff distribution for individual storms over a watershed. Initial investigations, which started in 1950 right after Chow completed his own doctoral dissertation, led to several dissertations supervised by Chow on the nonlinear nature of unit hydrographs. Later, the validity of the Unit Hydrograph Theory in view of nonlinearity was investigated on hydrodynamic-based theoretical studies and laboratory experiments, which showed that unit hydrographs are in general nonlinear in nature and that the practice of superposition based on the linearity assumption should be used with caution. During the height of Professor Chow's academic career, from 1960 to 1981, he solely or jointly supervised twenty-nine doctoral dissertations on watershed hydrology, stochastic hydrology, and water resources systems—a remarkable record of productivity.

## Ven Te Chow's Hydrosystems Laboratory (VTCHL)

Toward the end of the 1960s it had become clear that Ven Te Chow's leadership in hydrologic sciences was fully established, was having a positive effect on the scientific community, and was receiving regular support from major funding agencies. Chow and his associates organized the First International Seminar for Hydrology Professors, held on July 13–25, 1969, on the Urbana-Champaign campus. Chow gave the plenary lecture communicating the latest advances in the field. Most remarkable was the announcement at the meeting that a new laboratory for hydrology and hydraulics had been under construction for a couple of years and would be inaugurated later in the year. With backing from Nathan M. Newmark, professor and head of the Civil Engineering Department, Professor Chow secured a major grant from the National Science Foundation, and with matching funds from the State of Illinois, the Hydrosystems Laboratory was built on the Urbana-Champaign campus. This was an incredible achievement, given that no experimental hydraulic laboratory had been built anywhere in the United States since the construction of the St. Anthony Falls Hydraulic Laboratory at the University of Minnesota in 1938 under the leadership of Professor Lorenz G. Straub (incidentally, an Illinois PhD).

The experimental bay in the Hydrosystems Laboratory covered an area of 170 feet by 64 feet and was to be serviced by an overhead crane. Several tilting flumes as well as weighing tanks for calibration of sensors and a cavitation tunnel, built in Germany, were the main experimental facilities available in the new lab when it first opened. Reflecting a general lack of industrial experience in building experimental facilities with such characteristics, the bidding process was set up so that whoever won the contract to construct the new building for the new Hydrosystems Laboratory also had to build the flumes and ancillary equipment, such as the large constant-head water tank, a pump room, and a sump to hold 400,000 gallons of water. The WES remained in the old Hydraulics and Hydrology Lab by Boneyard Creek. At the time of commissioning of the new laboratory in the fall of 1969, the Hydraulic Engineering Section of the Civil Engineering Department changed its name to Hydrosystems Engineering. The Hydrosystems group consisted of Professor Chow (hydraulic engineering), Associate Professors Cheng-lung Chen and Edward R. Holley (civil engineering), and Assistant Professors W. Hall C. Maxwell, Dale D. Meredith, J. Richard Weggel, Harry G. Wenzel, and Ben Chie Yen (civil engineering). It is fair to say that by 1970, Ven Te Chow and his associates had created one of the preeminent water resources engineering groups in the nation, and even worldwide. Chow's leadership was a crucial element in this success.

## A Consultant in High Demand

From Ven Te Chow's earliest days on the faculty at the University of Illinois, academics and government officials had sought him out for advice on hydrologic problems. As his fame spread, Chow had the increasing problem of budgeting his time between students and what was becoming a worldwide demand for his expertise. He was active on a number of U.S. national committees and boards, and he counseled the Department of State on water management in developing countries. The World Health Organization used his advice on the Danube River Projects in central Europe, and he provided guidance on several other international projects. He was a consultant to the United Nations, advising the U.N. Secretariat on world water problems, and a National Academy of Sciences advisory member to the U.S. Geological Survey on the use of spacecraft and remote sensing in water resources. He was also a member of the U.S. National Committee for the International Hydrological Decade and a consulting advisor to the Texas Water Development Board and both the Honolulu and Puerto Rico Departments of Public Works. He assisted in the establishment of a Centre of Applied Hydrology at the Universidade Federal do Rio Grande do Sul, Porto Alegre, Brazil, and helped in the planning of the National Institute of Hydrology in Lima, Peru.

The hydrosystems laboratory water tower. Photo courtesy of the University of Illinois Archives / UIHistories and Kalev Leetaru.

During the last sixteen years of his life, Chow was a consultant and lecturer to twenty-three foreign governments as well as many private organizations. Countries where he consulted included Argentina, Austria, Brazil, Canada, the People's Republic of China, Colombia, Costa Rica, the Dominican Republic, France, Ghana, Hungary, India, Israel, Japan, Korea, Mexico, the Netherlands, Peru, Puerto Rico, Turkey, the United Kingdom, and Yugoslavia. In the United States, he advised formally more than fifty foundations, development boards, engineering companies, and commissions. Somehow, he was able to maintain this busy schedule and still allow adequate time for class lectures and consultation with his graduate students. During this period he also authored more than two hundred technical publications, of which thirty were books, reports, and monographs. In 1963 he started the serial publication *Advances in Hydroscience* (Academic Press), which became a continuing compilation of the latest available information emerging from the study of water, until his passing.

At the time of his untimely death, Chow was working on an applied hydrology textbook; fortunately, he left enough notes for his book to be completed a few years later, appearing in 1988 as *Applied Hydrology* by Ven Te Chow, David R. Maidment, and Larry W. Mays. Both co-authors were very familiar with Chow's work and ideas: Professor Maidment (University of Texas at Austin) was a doctoral student under Dr. Chow, and Professor Mays (Arizona State University) was a graduate student in the Hydrosystems Group at Illinois, and Dr. Chow was a member of his doctoral committee. Both of these experts were later recognized with the Distinguished Alumni Award by the Civil and Environmental Engineering Department at the University of Illinois.

Throughout his career, Ven Te Chow himself garnered many prestigious awards and recognitions. He received honorary doctorates from universities in India, Korea, France, and Canada, and from the Louis Pasteur University in Strasbourg, France, where he also received the Louis Pasteur Medal. He was elected to membership in the National Academy of Engineering, a Fellow of the American Academy of Arts and Sciences, and Academician of the Academia Sinica and of the China Academy. Among his long list of awards was the Silver Jubilee Commemorative Medal of the International Commission on Irrigation and Drainage. Medals and awards galore came from such groups as the University of Illinois, the American Society of Civil Engineering, the Western Electric Fund, Fulbright-Hays, and the National Science Foundation, to mention a few. He was also president of the American Geophysical Union (AGU) Hydrology Section. The State of Texas named Chow an Honorary Citizen, and the American Society of Civil Engineering (ASCE) established the Ven Te Chow Award to recognize lifetime achievement in the field of hydrologic engineering, considered the most prestigious award given in Hydrology

and Water Resources by the ASCE Environmental and Water Resources Engineering Institute (EWRI).

## International Water Resources Association

It is difficult, if not impossible, to cover adequately all of Ven Te Chow's projects and achievements. However, his role in helping with the founding of the International Water Resources Association (IWRA) is one that has to be mentioned, since it brings to the forefront his organizational ability and the fulfillment of his humanistic vision of an inclusive world in which all those with an interest in the conservation and distribution of water could cooperate for the good of the planet. Founded in 1971 by fellow hydrologists Sandor Csallany, Gabor M. Karadi, and Herbert C. Preul, the IWRA turned to Chow almost from the start. The group elected him its first president in 1972, and he played a central role in the association's first signature event: First World Water Congress, held in Chicago the following year. The main theme of the gathering was "Importance and Problems of Water in the Human Environment in Modern Times." The meeting attracted participants from more than sixty-two countries who, on arrival, were confronted by principles that President Chow himself articulated and declared: the need to develop a significant new international and interdisciplinary approach regarding water resources to solve, through a cooperative and coordinated approach, many common problems that exist among nations and water users.

The Chicago conference amplified Chow's international commitments and underscored the hydrological community's commitment to international cooperation. The IWRA had been established in response to the strong support of many people who felt, as he did, the need for a continuing international forum to promote interdisciplinary communication between professionals with diverse backgrounds, one that would encompass the entire range of water resources problems. Serving as the group's president from 1972 to 1979, Chow devoted tremendous effort to make sure that the spirit of his vision for a truly international association fostering cooperation remained central to the organization's activities. As it

Ven Te Chow and Prime Minister Indira Gandhi of India.
Photo courtesy of *Water International* and Hall Maxwell.

turned out, the workload he assumed took a terrible toll on his health. Chow added to his already backbreaking commitments by becoming the founding editor of the IWRA's *Water International* journal and was deeply involved in the group's second World Water Congress in 1975 in New Delhi. Under the theme "Water for Human Needs," more than twelve hundred participants from forty-five countries gathered as Indian Prime Minister Indira Gandhi opened the congress alongside the organization's leader, Ven Te Chow.

Chow's impact on his association is felt to this day. After stepping down as president of IWRA in 1979, Dr. Chow insisted that the next president of IWRA should be a non-engineer (to invite a less academic and more multi-

disciplinary governance of the association). This resulted in the election of Guillermo J. Cano, a famous Argentinean lawyer in the water field, as the new president of IWRA. Chow became more absorbed in his teaching and consulting work. He also turned to possible collaborations with colleagues in his native China. The first time he was able to visit his motherland was in 1974 after the Nixon administration normalized diplomatic relations between the two countries. He had been away for nearly a generation. Extensive international travel soon took its toll, however. In 1980 Chow was hospitalized after a strenuous round of visits to projects around the world. After recovering, he resumed a busy travel schedule in both Latin America and Asia. In late July 1981 Chow was making a farewell speech to a group of foreign students at the Illini Union. He had complained about some distress earlier in the day but managed to finish his remarks before suffering a massive heart attack that ended his life. It was perhaps appropriate that his last earthly act was one shared with students. He died on July 30, 1981, at age sixty-one, leaving behind his wife Lora and their two children, Margot and Marana.

Lora Chow observed after her husband's death that "his books were still open on his desk—it was like a movie, just stopped." Ven Te Chow had lived up to this alma mater's motto as well as to the Chinese proverb: "When you drink water, honor the source."

## Notes

1. *Popular Science, The China Science Corp.* 10, no. 11 (June 1944): 524–27; *Popular Science* 13, no. 4 (April 1947): 245–50; *Popular Science* 13, no. 5 (May 1947): 331–34.

2. See vol. 66, no. 22 (June 6, 1969): 77.

## Sources

Ven Te Chow's major publications are still widely available. These include *Handbook of Applied Hydrology* (1964); *Open-Channel Hydraulics* (1959, 2009); and *Applied Hydrology* (with David R. Maidment and Larry W. Mays) (1988). His work is also featured in W. H. C. Maxwell and L. R. Beard, eds., *Frontiers in Hydrology* (Littleton, Colo.: Water Resources Pub., 1984). A profile of Ven Te Chow appeared in *Memorial Tributes: The National Academy of Engineering*, vol. 2 (1984), 47. The University Archives holds materials on his career at Illinois.

# Stuart Pratt Sherman

## Literary Criticism Comes to the University

*Kelsey Reinker*

Stuart Pratt Sherman

Stuart Pratt Sherman (1881–1926) grew up in Iowa, Arizona, and California, but he headed east for college and graduate school. After earning an undergraduate degree at Williams College, he went on to Harvard University, where he studied medieval and early modern literature. Sherman received his doctorate in 1906, but he was an irreverent student. He criticized the Harvard faculty in witty articles published in the national magazine *The Nation* (where he became a regular contributor) and called for a more engaging style of criticism in literary studies.

In 1908, after a year teaching at Northwestern University, Sherman joined the University of Illinois faculty; within six years, he had become chair of the English Department—at age thirty-three. The young professor quickly demonstrated that a university-based scholar could be both a nationally recognized literary critic and a forceful presence in academia. He pursued both callings simultaneously and with gusto. Sherman served as associate editor of *The Cambridge History of American Literature* (1917), yet during World War I he won wide praise for his patriotic writing (*American and Allied Ideals*, 1918; *Americans*, 1922) and his essays on American values (*The Genius of America*, 1923). Sherman also earned professional acclaim for his study of Matthew Arnold (1917) and his overview of recent literature (*On Contemporary Literature*, 1917). From his post in Urbana-Champaign, he became what would later be termed a public intellectual. During the 1920s his essays on press censorship, prohibition, and other controversial issues appeared regularly in the *Atlantic Monthly*, *The Nation*, and many other popular magazines.

Stuart Pratt Sherman became one of the youngest members of the American Academy of the Arts and Letters when he was elected to the group in 1923. The following year the *New York Herald Tribune* appointed him editor of its literary supplement, "Books." During Sherman's tenure there, "Books" became a central forum for literary debates, and the Illinois professor regularly moderated discussions of modern literature. As head of a rapidly growing and influential English Department who was also in demand as a literary critic, Sherman was at the top of his career when he died suddenly in a boating accident on Lake Michigan in the summer of 1926.

Sherman was a pivotal figure in the history of modern literature. His criticism introduced the American public to new authors and new ideas, and his teaching and departmental leadership helped establish literary studies as a central feature of the modern research university. His career put an end to the idea that the arbiters of national taste would be confined to the East Coast or limited to a small group of editors. His success made it clear that in the new century, new voices and new constituencies would wrestle for attention and influence.

### Sources

The University Archives holds significant material on Sherman's life and achievements. For an overview of his career at Illinois, see Bruce Michelson, "American Literature in the Cornfields: Stuart Pratt Sherman and J. Kerker Quinn," in Lillian Hoddeson, ed., *No Boundaries* (Urbana: University of Illinois Press, 2004), 88–101.

# Ruth Maslow Lewis and Oscar Lewis
## Giving Voice to the Voiceless

Susan M. Rigdon

> If we had a keen vision and feeling of all ordinary human life, it would be like hearing the grass grow and the squirrel's heart beat, and we should die of that roar which lies on the other side of silence.
> —George Eliot, *Middlemarch*

When Oscar Lewis (1914–1970) and Ruth Maslow (1916–2008) met in their native New York in the early 1930s—he a City College of New York undergraduate and she still in high school—radical change was in the air. Financial institutions had failed, the Great Depression was deepening, the number of jobless and homeless was growing, Hitler was on the ascent, and war in Europe seemed likely. Campuses were aboil with political activity, and Oscar and Ruth were part of it. For them all the world was open to critique against a new set of moral and political standards. It was the job of their generation to make that critique and change the world.

They married in 1937 and left graduate school as they entered—penniless—with no clear idea how, together, they could make a difference. They had trained in different disciplines and jobs were scarce. To help Oscar complete his doctorate in anthropology, Ruth (who had completed a master's degree in education at Columbia Teacher's College) postponed further studies and began teaching blind and deaf students. Oscar's undergraduate work on the social structures and economies of small communities, class stratification, and mobility had a very different focus from Ruth's studies at Brooklyn College with Solomon Asch, a founding figure in social psychology. There were points of convergence, however, because Oscar did much of his graduate coursework with Ruth Benedict, a leading figure in the subfield of culture and personality, and the person for whom he had abandoned history for anthropology, almost solely on the basis of her personal qualities. When the United States entered World War II, the Lewises

Ruth Maslow Lewis and Oscar Lewis. Photo courtesy of Susan Rigdon.

moved to Washington. With Benedict's help, Oscar began a series of government jobs, beginning as a propaganda analyst at the Department of Justice and ending at the Bureau of Agricultural Economics (1944–1946). In 1943 Oscar accepted a position with the Department of the Interior as U.S. representative to the Inter-American Indian Institute in Mexico City. Ruth's training in psychology was a crucial factor in the appointment—even though she was never employed or paid by Interior—because a secondary part of Oscar's job was to organize the Mexican side of a cross-national study of American Indian personality led by Commissioner of the U.S. Bureau of Indian Affairs John Collier and his wife, University of Chicago anthropologist Laura Thompson. They were looking for another husband-wife team to join the project, and with the Lewises they had both a psychologist to administer the projective tests and an anthropologist to identify an appropriate research site and do the background research.

There were many husband-wife teams in anthropology at the time, each with its own dynamic. The way Oscar and Ruth's collaboration evolved was not by design; they simply gravitated toward their strengths as their projects widened and deepened. Although a community study of Tepoztlán—the village chosen as their research site—was not part of their assignment, Oscar saw an opportunity, assembled a field staff of anthropology students, and quickly established himself as an omnivorous and indefatigable data gatherer. That set a pattern in which Oscar planned and ran the investigations—although Ruth did write the field guide for the Tepoztlán staff—and wrote up the ethnographic and archival data. Ruth administered the personality tests, constructed personality profiles, interviewed women and children, and edited all the written material. Taking the family as "a mirror of the culture," they began developing their family-study method.

It turned out that Ruth had a gift for editing household observations and life histories into narratives that could stand alone. Small portions of their first family histories were integrated into the larger community study, *Life in a Mexican Village: Tepoztlán Restudied* (1951), and together they wrote (but never published) the first of their stand-alone family studies, a portrait of two Tepoztecan families. This was the first of several jointly authored pieces, but after Oscar entered academic life—he joined the Anthropology Department at the University of Illinois in 1948—almost all subsequent work appeared under Oscar's name alone. In addition to *Life in a Mexican Village*, the best known of his books were collaborations with Ruth: *Five Families* (1959), *The Children of Sánchez* (1961); *Pedro Martínez* (1964), and *La Vida* (1966). The fieldwork Oscar did alone or in collaboration with others, as in India, produced lesser-known titles but included some of his best academic writing (see, for example, "Group Dynamics: A Study of Factions within Castes").[1] By the 1960s the couple was spending less time together in the field than working separately in their areas of specialization, yet in a way that one contribution could not be separated from the other. Recognizing theirs was a professional as well as personal partnership, Oscar called it "a double marriage."[2] Ruth described it as "a tightly woven tapestry."[3]

*Five Families* was the couple's first attempt at writing up field data for a general audience. The families were from Tepoztlán and Mexico City and represented different income levels, types of household organization, and family dynamics. The manuscript was assembled by inserting dialogue from taped and hand-recorded interviews into household observations taken down in longhand, augmented with descriptive detail from other field data. This combination of personal narrative and social science reporting Lewis called "ethnographic realism" to distinguish it from literary realism. *Five Families* was given a "setting" and a "cast of characters" and was illustrated by their friend Alberto Beltrán, a noted member of the Taller de Gráfica Popular who would later become a political cartoonist for several Mexican publications. The wonderfully evocative pen-and-ink drawings Beltrán made at field sites were first used in *Life in a Mexican Village* and would be used again in *Pedro Martínez*. Lewis often spoke about "capturing" his informants, as if in a snapshot or series of photographs, and Beltrán's drawings portrayed informants in tableau-style poses that complemented the Lewises' scenic-inspired editing.[4]

*Five Families* also contained Lewis's first statement about the existence of a "culture of poverty," a subculture he said was shared by some of the poorest people in capitalist societies, one perpetuated in families over generations through cultural agencies and with "distinctive social and psychological consequences for its members." Early versions of the thesis gave primacy to the social consequences of deep poverty, especially the way in which the urban poor were marginalized in class-stratified societies, while the later versions—following a research trajectory toward the inner life of the individual—placed increasing emphasis on the psychological *consequences* of poverty and untreated mental illness as a *contributing* factor to the low incidence of upward mobility. By the late 1950s the Lewises were regularly consulting with members of the Mexican Psychoanalytic Institute, including Drs. Erich Fromm, Emmanuel Schwartz, and Carolina Luján. Luján was an influential consultant on every subsequent project, but local psychologists and psychiatrists were hired as

"The way Oscar and Ruth's collaboration evolved was not by design; they simply gravitated toward their strengths as their projects widened and deepened."

well to administer and analyze projective tests. (In Cuba an Academy of Sciences psychologist was forced to suspend testing because security officials there regarded it as a form of intelligence gathering.)

The Lewises' intention was to follow *Five Families*, with a separate volume devoted to each family. *The Children of Sánchez* was the first of these, and it was their first experiment in using overlapping, often conflicting, individual voices to tell a family's story with no commentary or third-person narrator. From the day it appeared in print, *Sánchez* was received as a work with something to say to a general readership about the "crime of poverty." Margaret Mead called it "one of the outstanding contributions of anthropology—of all time;" while the Spanish director Luís Buñuel said it would be the "pinnacle" of his career to make a film that was true to the book. Fidel Castro called it "revolutionary" and "worth more than 50,000 political pamphlets." In her *New York Times* review, the literary critic Elizabeth Hardwick wrote that Lewis had "made something brilliant and of singular significance, a work of such unique concentration and sympathy that one hardly knows how to classify it." *Sánchez* made *Time* magazine's list of best books of the decade. It was translated into many languages, adapted for stage and screen, and has never been out of print.[5]

The vividness of the family's first-person testimony, however, produced critics as well, some of whom thought it too frank and detailed in its description of poverty and family life. This was nowhere more true than in Mexico, where critics, inspired by nationalist sentiment (or xenophobia, as defenders of the book such as novelist Carlos Fuentes charged), were enraged by a foreigner "exposing" Mexico's poverty, as if it were some carefully guarded national secret. In 1964, when the first Spanish-language edition was published, opponents petitioned Mexico's attorney general to file criminal charges against Lewis and his publisher for obscenity and defamation of the Mexican people and government. Lewis was called an FBI agent, and Jesús Sánchez's characterizations of party-dominated unions as useless and of government officials as being on the payroll of drug traffickers were said to have been "put in his mouth" by a foreigner. There can be little doubt that what most upset those in Mexico who tried to suppress the book were the ability and willingness of poor people to describe their lives and to express their anger at politicians.

In roundtable debates, television programs, and newspaper and periodical articles, critics and defenders argued the book's merits and issues of government censorship. The *London Times* called it "one of the stormiest public intellectual debates Mexico has known." With sales of the book suspended pending a decision from Mexico's attorney general, copies were selling on the black market for three to four times the list price. Meanwhile, Sánchez became "Mexico's most celebrated family," and the book earned a wide audience in the United States. In April 1965, Mexico's attorney general handed down a decision dismissing the charges and allowing the book to remain in circulation.[6]

After the initial reaction to *Sánchez*, both within the United States and abroad, the Lewises knew they had found the way to make a difference with their work—letting the poor speak for themselves. Although they often referred to the oral histories as stories, they treated them more as evidence in narrative form. Providing a forum for the poor to describe their lives in their own words was a means to educate and provoke in a way that might make people want to pay attention and, in Ruth's words, "not just shove things under the rug." Elaborating on their goals, she said: "We hoped that these intimate life histories would arouse understanding and sympathy and would help bridge the great gap between the poor and the rest of society. That was how the material affected me; it was an antidote to stereotypical thinking and left me with a deep feeling of respect, even of awe, for our informants—for their courage and humor and for their ability to struggle and to share in the face of extreme poverty."[7]

Although the way *Sánchez* was put together may seem to follow Kipling's conviction that "if history were taught in the form of stories, it would never be forgotten," the method the Lewises used to collect the material was not that of a novelist or storyteller. Studs Terkel, for example, one of America's best-known oral historians, said his approach to interviewing was to treat it not as an inquisition but as an exploration of the past so that "the gentlest question is the best one, and the gentlest is, 'And what happened then?'" If the Lewises had worked in this way, it would give some credence to those critics who dismissed their efforts in the belief that the key to "writing" a book like *Sánchez* was finding good informants, recording them on tape, and then opening a little trap door and letting the words fall out on the page.

Although they chose, as Ruth described it, "to publish their informants' words in a literary format that was meant to read like fiction," the Lewises saw themselves as social scientists. They and their field assistants did not go into a community and simply talk to people. They worked from a battery of more than a dozen questionnaires, redesigned for each field site, gathering data on household budgets, material culture, kinship networks, and residential, job, and health histories—all bolstered by psychological tests, analyses, and interviews with members of from three to five generations in a family, as well as with ex-spouses, partners, and neighbors. After each taped interview was transcribed, whoever was working with a specific informant would go back into the field with a new list of questions (often written by Ruth as she pieced the material together) to fill holes or fix inconsistencies in informants' accounts or chronology. By comparison, Studs Terkel, whom the Lewises knew personally and admired, was a conversationalist.

In 1964 *Pedro Martínez* became the second of the *Five Families* to appear as a stand-alone study. It was the result of twenty years of intermittent work with a Tepoztecan family whose members were singly and collectively, in terms of language and willingness to share, nowhere near the quality of informants that the Sánchez family were, nor a fraction as controversial. Nevertheless, *Pedro Martínez* is arguably the best piece of anthropological reporting the Lewises achieved together. They accomplished it through patience and the depth of their familiarity with the village, local culture, and individual family members, even though their personal ties to the Martínez family were less intimate and intense than those with the Sánchez family.

Oscar Lewis in Puerto Rico. Photo courtesy of Ken Heyman.

Although *Pedro Martínez* did receive some effusive critical praise—Michael Harrington called its form of anthropological reporting "one of the greatest intellectual achievements of the post-war era"[8]—it found nowhere near the international readership that *Sánchez* did. In his review Carlos Fuentes called it "literature as statement, as the ground upon which the twin trees of history and personality grow. For the life of Pedro Martínez is a striking example of the dramatic clash between history and personality in the underdeveloped world. . . . In [his] world life is besieged, pressed and devoured by history."[9] Fuentes echoes the tone of the book's introduction, which Oscar rather reluctantly laced with personality assessments from his colleagues at the Mexican Psychoanalytic Institute, but he also unintentionally described how the work resulted from the interweaving of the Lewises' in-

terests and skills—Oscar always coming back to history, Ruth always to the individual psyche.

Instead of moving on to the other three of the *Five Families*, Oscar wrote a proposal for extended research in Puerto Rico and New York City, partly in response to criticism that he should study poverty in his own country. The purpose of the work, then, was to compare poverty cultures, not to explore Puerto Rican culture, as some believed. The project began in San Juan with a field team surveying one hundred households in four different kinds of poor neighborhoods, then moved on the following year to survey fifty related households in New York City. After the initial round of census taking and interviewing, the research was narrowed to six extended families in one of San Juan's poorest and most notorious barrios—La Esmeralda (a pseudonym)—and with some of their relatives who had migrated to New York, Miami, and New Jersey. Publication of the first of the family studies, *La Vida*, spurred another round of attacks, although nothing like the media frenzy that sustained the Mexican campaign against *Sánchez*. But again, there were assemblies on university campuses, roundtables—some televised—and numerous newspaper and magazine articles both attacking and defending *La Vida*'s depiction of life in La Esmeralda and its focus on a family, some of whose members worked as prostitutes and pimps. One Puerto Rican legislator even gave testimony before the U.S. Senate claiming Lewis had "slandered" his culture.

By this time the controversy over the "culture of poverty" thesis was peaking (it has never gone away). The introductions to both *Sánchez* and *La Vida* had contained expanded discussions of the concept, and an article-length version appeared in *Scientific American* in 1966 as well. When *Sánchez* was published, most readers had focused on the family itself as the Lewises had hoped, not on sociological concepts. The debate began after the publication of *The Other America* (1962) in which its author, Michael Harrington, who knew of it from *Five Families* and *Sánchez*, applied the thesis to poverty in the United States, although in ways Lewis had not intended. Harrington claimed poverty itself was a culture, whereas Lewis said that 70 percent to 80 percent of the poor people he studied were *not* living in a poverty subculture; he applied the term only to those at the very bottom of the income ladder who also were socially and politically marginalized. But Harrington, a man of the Left like Lewis, saw the utility in the culture of poverty's structural explanation of poverty for his cause of democratic socialism.

It was through Harrington's role as an adviser to the Kennedy and Johnson aides who wrote the legislative program known as "the war on poverty" that the concept entered the public debate over poverty policy in the 1960s. However, according to the aides who wrote the legislation, the concept played virtually no role in their deliberations.[10] And Lewis himself was never involved in the policy process. However, he became a consultant to Head Start, participated in Daniel Patrick Moynihan's seminars on race and poverty, engaged in a public dialogue with Senator Robert Kennedy about the causes of poverty in America, lectured around the country on the culture of poverty, and gravitated toward the status of public intellectual.[11]

Despite the continuing controversy over the frank portrayal of life in La Esmeralda, *La Vida* won the National Book Award for nonfiction in 1967, and the Puerto Rican project staggered on with a minimal staff until 1970, when funding expired. The second and longest of the Puerto Rican family studies was still in press in 1969 when the Lewises moved on to Cuba. After eight years of trying to get permission to do field work on the island, Oscar finally succeeded in arranging a personal meeting with Fidel Castro in 1968. Castro gave verbal approval to three years of open-ended research on the understanding that Oscar would train a group of Cuban students in field methods. The overall subject of the research, "Culture Change in a Revolutionary System," was divided into a number of subprojects, including one meant to explore whether a poverty subculture that Lewis claimed could evolve and be sustained only in highly stratified capitalist societies would disappear in a system that required social and economic integration. In June 1970, just sixteen months after the field work had begun, the Cuban foreign minister called Lewis to his office and rescinded his research permission. The same day security police searched the Lewises' residence and office and confiscated all field data, including their only copies of the previous three months of tapes and transcriptions. After the Lewises left the country, one informant was imprisoned, possibly others.[12]

Oscar Lewis had taken at face value Castro's promise that he would be free to carry out his research in an open-ended manner. An admirer of the revolution, of Castro specifically, and a life-long socialist, Lewis was stunned—although given the audacity of his reach, he was perhaps the *only* person stunned—by the government's reversal. He died six months after leaving Cuba and spent most of that time trying to recover lost material, win freedom for

> "Sixteen months into the projected three years of field work the Cuban Foreign Minister called Lewis to his office and rescinded his research permission."

the one informant he knew to be in prison, and convince the Cuban government to reinstate his research permission. He did not live to hear Raul Castro publicly charge him (but not Ruth) with being a spy in 1972, an act perhaps precipitated by Ruth Lewis's decision to publish the field data as planned.

Ruth succeeded her husband as director of the Cuba project and spent the next eight years bringing it to conclusion.[13] She worked intermittently over the next decade preparing their field papers for archival deposit and editing unpublished Puerto Rican field data. In 1988, in recognition of her uncredited contributions to her husband's publications, the University of Illinois awarded her an honorary doctorate of humane letters. She outlived her husband by almost thirty-eight years and was still affiliated with the Anthropology Department when she died at age ninety-two.

It was no doubt in part because he received his greatest public attention during the politically volatile 1960s that Lewis was surrounded by political controversy throughout the last decade of his life. He had long been a target of anthropologists who believed it was their obligation to protect their informants by not revealing anything that might draw a critical gaze on them individually or on their communities. He and Ruth could have taken to heart Emily Dickinson's caveat: "Tell all the truth but tell it slant," but they did not. They did what they could to maintain informants' anonymity, but they never saw the point of prettying up the very injustices and suffering they wanted readers to see and understand.

The Lewises' informants spoke quite differently about their involvement in the work than their critics did. Both Jesús and Manuel Sánchez boasted about the utility of their participation in the research; Manuel in fact called his identity as one of the children of Sanchez, his Social Security. He said that by participating, his family had made a contribution to the world and that he no longer felt like "a worm crawling across the face of the earth." Thirty years after Lewis began his survey of the Casa Grande, the block-long, one-story complex that housed the Sánchez family and seven hundred others sustained severe earthquake damage. A resident told a *Boston Globe* reporter covering its 1986 demolition, "We were known

world-wide, but it's all over now." His comment echoed Manuel's claim that *Sánchez* had put their little part of Mexico City on the map.[14] Mexican President Miguel de la Madrid confirmed the Casa Grande's place in Mexico's modern urban history by attending ceremonies for the opening of the new housing complex built at the site.

In December 2014 the Mexican periodicals *Excelsior* and *Cultura Reforma* ran articles marking the centennial of Oscar Lewis's birth, the latter describing him as one of the twentieth century's most important writers on Mexico. The only work cited was *Sánchez*, which, except for its introduction, was, of course, not "written." In a 1963 interview, Lewis attributed the literary qualities assigned to the book solely to the talent of the Sánchez family to express themselves. "If I could have written a book like *The Children of Sánchez*, I would never have been an anthropologist. . . . [But] I am an anthropologist, first, second, and third. I am only an anthropologist."[15]

The book's impact in Mexico was so significant that Lewis is much more likely to be regarded there as a Mexicanist, not the comparativist he was, having worked among the Northern Piegan in Alberta, Canada, and American farmers in the West and in Texas (*On the Edge of the Black Waxy*, 1948), as well as in India, Spain, Cuba, Puerto Rico, and New York City. In the introduction to *Anthropological Essays*, Lewis claimed (just months before his death) that "the precise recording of the social facts of poverty and inequality in peasant villages and . . . urban slums, and their destructive effects on human beings, is in itself a revolutionary act," an idea he seems to have borrowed from Castro's description of the impact of *Sánchez* in Mexico. Ruth Lewis said it is perhaps better characterized as "a progressive act." In the end she said, their work "aroused social conscience, and that's all we ever hoped to do."

## Notes

1. This appeared in several versions in India and as a chapter in Oscar Lewis, *Village Life in Northern India* (Urbana: University of Illinois Press, 1958). Although Ruth was with him in India, she had two young children to care for and, like Oscar, did not know Hindi. The village study he did there was completed with

the assistance of Indian graduate students and did not involve the collection of life histories or taped material of any kind.

2. Letter, Oscar Lewis to Ruth Lewis, January 20, 1964.

3. Letter, Ruth Lewis to Oscar Lewis, April 5, 1968.

4. The Gutiérrez family day was adapted as a television play, with Ben Gazzara, and shown on New York Educational Television's *Camera Three*. The University of Illinois Archives has a copy of the program.

5. In order, these quotes are from Margaret Mead, letter to Jason Epstein, February 28, 1962; letter from Luís Buñuel to Oscar Lewis, February 6, 1966; Fidel Castro to Oscar Lewis, personal conversation in Cuba, March 1968; Elizabeth Hardwick, "Some Chapters of Personal History," *New York Times Book Review*, August 27, 1961, 1; *Time* magazine's best-of-decade list, December 26, 1969, 56.

6. A summary of the legal case and of the national discussion that followed, including statements made by Carlos Fuentes and others, can be found in *Mundo Nuevo*, September 1966. The text of the attorney general's decision—Preliminary Investigation no. 331/965—was published as an appendix to the 3rd–5th editions of *Los Hijos de Sánchez* and in *Mundo Nuevo*, September 1966.

7. From a speech delivered by Ruth Lewis at a reception at the University of Illinois president's house when accepting an honorary doctor of humane letters degree in 1988.

8. Michael Harrington, "The Voice of Poverty Speaks for Itself," *New York Times Book Review*, May 3, 1964, 3.

9. Carlos Fuentes, "A Life," *New York Review of Books*, June 25, 1964, 3.

10. Michael Gillette, *Launching the War on Poverty: An Oral History* (Oxford University Press, 2010).

11. The conversation with Kennedy, taped at his home in New York City, appeared in *Redbook*, September 1967. The original tape is in the University of Illinois Archives. Papers from the Race and Poverty Seminar were published by Basic Books in two volumes in 1969: Daniel P. Moynihan, ed. *On Understanding Poverty*, and James L. Sundquist, ed. *On Fighting Poverty*.

12. The Lewises knew of only one Cuban informant convicted and sent to prison for his participation in their project. Ruth Lewis helped him and his family get U.S. entry visas in 1979. However, several years after Ruth's death one of their Cuban field assistants claimed other informants were arrested days after the Lewises' departure from the country. She provided no numbers or details. See Maida D. Donate, "Oscar Lewis: Proyecto Cuba," parts 1 and 2, June 30 and July 4, 2011 (available at www.cubaencuentro.com).

13. Oscar Lewis, Ruth M. Lewis, and Susan M. Rigdon, *Four Men* (1977); *Four Women* (1978); and *Neighbors* (1978) (Urbana: University of Illinois Press); see also Douglas Butterworth, *The People of Buena Ventura* (Urbana: University of Illinois Press, 1980).

14. Phillip Bennett, "Storied Symbol of Poverty Is Gone," *Boston Globe*, August 20, 1986.

15. Interview by Elena Poniatowska, *Siempre* (supplement), June 19, 1963. Translated from the Spanish by the author. Poniatowska, one of Mexico's best known feminists, had worked briefly as an editorial assistant to the Lewises.

## Sources

Lewis's doctoral dissertation and most of his major articles were reprinted in *Anthropological Essays* (Random House, 1970). For more comprehensive coverage of Lewis's career, the evolution of the culture of poverty concept, selected correspondence, and a complete bibliography, see Susan M. Rigdon, *Culture Facade: Art, Science, and Politics in the Work of Oscar Lewis* (Urbana: University of Illinois Press, 1988). The raw field data used for major publications can be found in The Oscar and Ruth Maslow Lewis Papers (record series 15/2/20) in the University of Illinois Archives. The collection also contains more than half of Lewis's professional correspondence but none of his personal letters, to which I had access. I also used interviews I taped with Ruth Lewis in 1986–87, which are not part of the archival collection.

# Thomas K. Cureton

## The Father of Physical Fitness

*Rafal Ciolcosz*

Thomas Kirk Cureton (1901–1992) came to the University of Illinois in 1941, just as the United States was entering World War II. Trained as an engineer, Cureton was fascinated by the mechanics of the human body—a field which would later be called "kinesiology." In addition to his interest in human movement, Cureton loved sports and exercise; he was an avid swimmer and cross-country runner.

The young professor quickly applied his scholarly interests to the burgeoning war effort. He began to study the physics of human movement and to analyze physical fitness from a scientific perspective. His research soon produced results. In 1943 Cureton published *Warfare Aquatics*, an instructional guidebook that became a staple text for training courses. As the war progressed, he focused on the impact of regular exercise on human health and longevity, and he nurtured the idea of a research laboratory devoted to improving athletic performance. Cureton established his laboratory (the first of its kind in the United States) in 1944. Soon he was producing results that proved people could reduce their cholesterol levels through exercise and improve physical stamina by maintaining a healthy diet.

Cureton was the first researcher to use a "heartometer" (a forerunner of modern heart monitors) to monitor subjects during fitness experiments. His most widely publicized findings demonstrated that forty-five minutes of strenuous walking or jogging, done three times a week, would significantly improve blood circulation and extend individual life expectancy. Cureton headed the Physical Fitness Department at the University of Illinois for twenty-five years and traveled widely to publicize his views. He served on the President's Council on Physical Fitness under five U.S. Presidents. When he retired in 1969, he continued to pursue his research and to win multiple world records in masters swimming competitions. He lived to see his research findings adopted by the public and become a part of everyday American life.

### Sources

Cureton's findings were summarized in his book *The Physiological Effects of Exercise Programs on Adults* (Springfield, Ill.: Thomas, 1971). The University Archives holds material on the history of physical education at the university, as well as biographical information on Cureton (in its faculty files).

Cureton at work in his laboratory using the ergometer

# Timothy Nugent

## "Wheelchair Students" and the Creation of the Most Accessible Campus in the World

Leslie J. Reagan

"How many of you paraplegics are missing the boat as far as a college education is concerned, simply because you don't know of a school equipped to serve wheelchair students?" Raymond Crigger asked his fellow veteran-paraplegics in 1948. "There is one, ideally suited to your needs." That ideal school, he announced with great enthusiasm in *Paraplegia News*, was his own: the University of Illinois—at Galesburg. After its launch in Galesburg, the first university program dedicated to the success of students with disabilities soon moved to the Urbana campus, and by 2015 the program (renamed "DRES"—Disability Resources and Educational Services) was serving thousands of students. The vision and dedication of one man, Tim Nugent—together with the persistence of the

university's disabled students—was largely responsible for this remarkable program.

In 1948 admitting people with disabilities, specifically "wheelchair students," to the state's flagship university and treating them like any other student on campus seemed strange and questionable. It was also groundbreaking. The Special Rehabilitation Program developed a set of technologies: ramps, curb cuts, wheelchair design, accessible buses, and architecture. But the inventiveness and passion of the program that Nugent created accomplished something even more important: it made accessible design and policies *commonplace*, first on the University of Illinois campus and, eventually, across the nation and in many parts of the world. For that reason, the

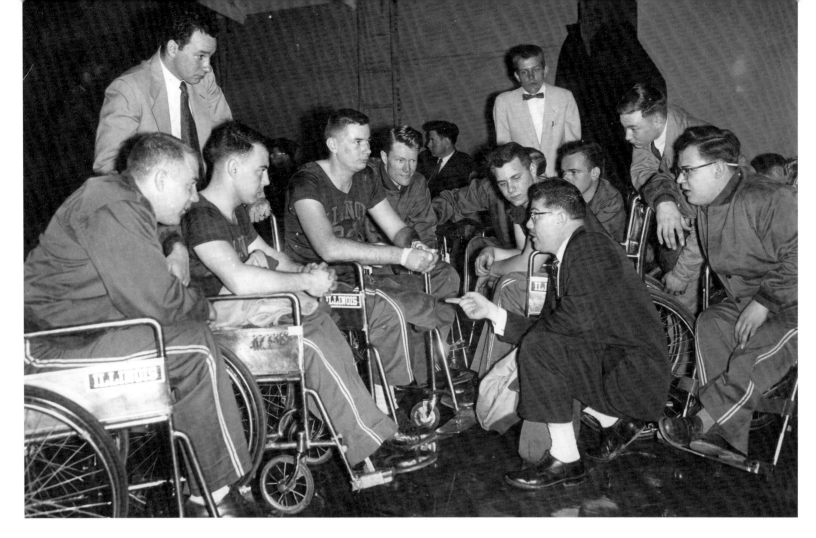

Tim Nugent and the Illinois "Gizz Kids"

program's most important innovations were social and cultural. Nugent created a climate that welcomed disabled students and a program that drew them into the campus mainstream while providing spaces where a separate community of their own could nurture and encourage them.

Historical records reveal a man brilliant at designing a program that would survive, who fought to prevent its destruction at crucial junctures, and who worked eighteen hours and more each day—frequently sleeping in his office—in order to ensure that students with disabilities had everything they needed to attend college, live independently, and succeed. At the same time, Nugent produced and managed the representation of people with disabilities at the University of Illinois, and those repre-

sentations deliberately obscured the discrimination and difficulties that the program and its students encountered. Like Nugent, the disabled students subscribed to a mid-century ideal of making themselves normative and downplayed their disabilities. The image and reputation of students with disabilities as independent, intelligent, socially integrated, and successful were, in the eyes of both Nugent and the students themselves, essential for their individual success. The program's institutional survival depended as well, Nugent knew, on the students' independence and social success.

It was the active involvement of students with disabilities that created and perpetuated the university's innovative program. Tim Nugent regularly credited students and, from the beginning, recognized that the disabled students had educated him and influenced the program's directions. Indeed, Nugent recorded that it was thirty-year-old Harold "Hal" Scharper, the first veteran and "paraplegic" to enroll at Galesburg, who had encouraged campus leaders to admit more disabled veterans like him. At Scharper's urging, the school pursued the idea. Soon, eight veterans who used wheelchairs and several disabled nonveterans enrolled. The post–World War II GI Bill brought the veterans to college; the Veterans Administration also agreed to reimburse the university hospital for rehabilitation services, and by September 1948 Tim Nugent, a twenty-four-year-old University of Wisconsin college athlete, doctoral student, and World War II veteran, had been hired to design and run the new rehabilitation and vocation program. Disabled students actively pushed the university to make the innovations it did, and they co-produced the program with Nugent. In contrast to students in later decades, students in the 1940s and 1950s did not generally proclaim their demands publicly. Instead, they sought to prove their normality and independence, display their abilities, fit in with able-bodied people and culture, and thereby win over those who feared and stigmatized people with disabilities.

The phrase "the program moved" may suggest an automatic transfer of students and their program from a closing branch of the university to the main campus, but in fact the move from Galesburg to Urbana-Champaign was a victory achieved by Director Nugent, the program's allies, and the disabled university students themselves. To the surprise of students and faculty, Illinois Governor Adlai Stevenson announced the sudden closing of the Galesburg campus in May 1949; he planned to turn the campus, which had originally been an army medical hospital, into a facility for the elderly. Shocked at the sudden closing of

> "The inventiveness and passion of the program that Nugent created did something even more important: it made these innovations *commonplace*, first on the university campus and eventually, across the nation and many parts of the world."

the ideal, completely accessible campus, the program tried to reverse the governor's decision. Finally, Nugent decided he and his students should visit him in Springfield.

As Nugent later recalled, he called up "the gang," and they organized themselves among a dozen or more "paraplegic driven cars" and drove straight to the governor's mansion. Having been "forewarned," however, as the story went, the Governor sneaked "out the back door." The caravan of cars then drove to the capitol—with city policemen saluting the veterans at every corner—and into the circular driveway reserved for the governor. Newspapers across the state covered the spectacle under headlines such as "Crippled Students Fight College Closing" and "Vets in Wheel Chairs Descend On Mansion." National papers took note, too. Although this protest failed to keep the university branch at Galesburg open, it succeeded in making the program for "wheelchair students" visible to the general public and to veterans in particular. Although the University of Illinois had not agreed to a transfer of either Galesburg's students or the program to its main campus, under the pressure of national publicity, veterans' organizations (including the American Legion, Disabled Veterans of America, local veterans' groups, and the VA), students, parents, and Tim Nugent, George Stoddard, president of the University of Illinois, changed his mind and agreed to admit all of the Galesburg students to the Urbana campus.

At the start of the 1949 fall semester, the *Daily Illini* reported on the "14 paraplegics" along with three thousand incoming freshmen. These new students, unlike the other three thousand, had their bodies explained to the entire campus: they were introduced individually, by name, age, major, and reason for the paralysis that "forced [them] to use wheelchairs." The article is matter-of-fact in tone, yet the fact that the student newspaper introduced each student with a disability and discussed their physical and medical conditions reveals that disabled bodies were not granted privacy but were presumed to be an appropriate topic for general discussion. The article underscores how bizarre these students appeared to the majority of the campus population and what a truly revolutionary innovation the new program represented.

The *Daily Illini* did not mention the demonstrations or pressures that had produced the new program. A few months after protesting at the governor's mansion, Galesburg's wheelchair students had gone to Urbana to visit and to demonstrate that they could get around campus. They appropriated nearby construction boards and built a ramp to Lincoln Hall. Two of the most adept wheelchair students, Hal Scharper and Jack Chase, rolled up and down the steep ramps. This was a demonstration in more ways than one: a political protest, but without picket signs or chants; an exhibition of their skills and their ability to get around campus; and a show for anyone who happened to see it. They proved that their bodies deserved to attend the University of Illinois at Urbana. The following June, at the end of the program's first year in Urbana, Scharper, a talker, basketball player, PR man for Delta Sigma Omicron (DSO, the disabled students co-ed service fraternity), and a key leader in the effort to bring "wheelchair students" to the university, died unexpectedly following an appendectomy. In recognition of Scharper's significance, the students created two awards in his name. Today, they are combined as the Harold Scharper Award, presented annually to a disabled student to honor his or her academic achievements and public service.

Although the flat landscape of central Illinois fostered the conversion of the Urbana-Champaign campus into the most accessible campus in the world, the university did not initially welcome the students and their program with open arms. In fact, over the years Nugent found some elements of the campus to be quite "vicious and destructive." Even after the program had a presence on campus, funding for the program and its permanence remained vague. Indicative of the marginalization of the people and the program—and perhaps expressing a hope that they would go away—the university first housed the program and the male students in old, dusty, unheated

Hal Scharper. Photo courtesy of the College of Applied Health Sciences.

army surplus shacks. In general, the administration and the faculty greatly disappointed Nugent. They doubted whether the wheelchair students belonged at the university, questioned their intelligence, and charged that they were "distracting, demoralizing," and a liability. In Nugent's view the campus administration failed to fund the program adequately and also fought needed changes in the physical plant. When a new provost wanted to combine the program with offices addressing mental health, Nugent recalled, "I had a big fight with him. . . . I said, 'Look, I've been fighting all these years to prove these people *weren't* mentally handicapped' . . . we had a big blow-up."

But hostility, both open and covert, did not stop Nugent or the disabled students. Rather, it inspired them to insist that university authorities and faculty accept their presence on campus. The Office of the Dean of Women, for example, refused to rent women's dorm rooms at Lincoln Hall to disabled students because "they objected to putting a ramp in," Nugent recalled. "[First,] they said it would cost $10,000 and second, it would destroy the looks of the building because Lincoln Hall was a brand new building." After much arguing, Nugent decided, "[I'm going] to call their bluff." He approached the father of Shirley Sayers, the one "wheelchair woman" who would be transferring from Galesburg, and asked if he would be willing to help him with his plan. "Yeah, . . . I want my daughter to go to school there," Sayers replied. Nugent asked him, "Would you make out a $10,000 check for me made out to the University of Illinois for their ramp? I know they won't use it." When the father agreed, Nugent reported, "I went to the Dean's Office and I presented the check to them and they were embarrassed and they built the ramp and it cost about $250." The women would be in a brand new beautiful building with a ramp while the men remained in their substandard tar-paper shacks. When the first class arrived at the Urbana campus, six classroom buildings had new ramps; several others were already accessible. Students who used wheelchairs received elevator keys for other buildings. If a student registered for a class located in an inaccessible room, Nugent got the class moved to an accessible building. And he repeated that exercise every semester.

As a result of relentless lobbying by Nugent and the students, the campus became a model of innovative architectural design. By the early 1950s the university required that all new construction be built to accommodate people with disabilities—nearly twenty years before a federal law extended this requirement to public buildings across the nation. In 1955 the Rehabilitation Center reported that forty buildings on campus had been ramped and that "at least ten buildings are accessible to wheelchair students without ramping. Four buildings are connected by underground tunnels [and] all new buildings, including the new College of Law, are being built to accommodate wheelchair students." Two nearby campus churches also built

ramps. Yet at the same time, Nugent and the students fought for years to get ramped sidewalk curb cuts across campus. Whenever existing sidewalks required repairs, however, the university's Department of Operations and Maintenance agreed to make the cuts to accommodate wheelchairs. In frustration, Nugent and a group of students then went out late one night and broke curbs with sledgehammers, forcing the university to "repair" them with curb cuts. In 1951 the program could boast of two new buses donated by Greyhound and rebuilt by Carmont Blitz Corporation in Chicago with "wheelchair lift[s]" and other newly designed technologies able to carry multiple passengers using wheelchairs. "Wheelchair students," the *Daily Illini* reported, "get a free 'elevator ride' from the ground to the floor of the bus by the way of a 'lift.'" Nugent developed allies and good friends who made major donations like this—repeatedly—to create an accessible world for the disabled students at Illinois.

As other colleges and towns realized that they needed to address their inaccessible buildings and campuses, they looked to the University of Illinois and turned to Nugent for guidance. Nugent served on a state disabilities commission. In 1959, with a small grant from the Easter Seal Society, he and the Rehabilitation Center researched optimal ramp incline and developed the first standards for the American National Standards Institute (1961). Those standards became the basis of the Uniform Federal Accessibility Standards (UFAS) of 1973 (governing public buildings) and the Fair Housing Amendments Act (FHAA) of 1988.

While Nugent planned to make the physical space of the Urbana campus ready for its new "wheelchair students," he also devised a plan to get the incoming students ready for the university. Nugent created "Functionality Week," otherwise known as "Hell Week." Many of the disabled students came to hate Nugent during these weeks. The orientation program (originally two weeks) had been designed to ensure that every student in the rehabilitation program could function independently on campus and succeed in class with the same workload as ordinary students. Nugent believed (and insisted) that people in wheelchairs were completely capable of doing what everyone else did, and he was determined to make it so. His view challenged the medical truths of the time that expected people with spinal cord injuries to live a few months to three years at most. Doctors typically advised minimal exertion, regular rest throughout the day, and twenty-four-hour attendants.

The orientation program tackled the physical aspects of independence and the educational requirements for success at Illinois. If students had attendants or parents pushing their wheelchairs, Nugent declared this had to stop if they wanted to attend the university. Those who disagreed were sent packing. No one was allowed to be (or appear to be) dependent. New students thus would spend Functionality Week developing the strength to push their own chairs (much heavier than today's lightweight models) across campus and up ramps. Some had never attended to their own personal care. "I had never once dressed myself from start to finish," recalled one woman. "I would get up at 4:00 in the morning to catch the bus at 8:25. It took me that long to get dressed on my own that whole first six months." She had been an athlete before her car accident and was thrilled to find the university and to join its bowling and swimming teams. Her doctors had told her she would "always need a 24-hour attendant"; forty years later she still took pleasure in remembering the day she drove by one of the doctors and "peeled rubber" in her "hot" black '63 Plymouth convertible. She showed him how completely wrong he had been. "Tim" seemed "mean," in those first weeks, many students later recalled, but these same students later relied on him, counted him as a friend, and sang his praises. Finally, Functionality Week tested their college readiness. Because schools frequently barred disabled students, many had been educated at home or in hospitals and had never experienced the give and take of a typical classroom. Nugent realized that some had been undereducated as a result or needed "training" in note taking, studying, and test taking in the unfamiliar educational environment.

"The DSO and its publications aimed to change popular thinking about disabilities and to inspire people with disabilities around the world to pursue their aspirations."

Student independence was also essential for the preservation of the program. Although he "never discussed" it with the students, Nugent later explained, "I was protecting the program from the adverse attitudes on campus. I didn't want anybody to say, 'Hey, this guy's not able to do it; this guy's failing.' So I was perhaps a little more rigid than I was in subsequent years because I had to make sure that nobody could . . . find fault in the conduct of our students." It should be noted that failure and poor conduct in the eyes of those who doubted this social experiment meant not only academic failure but *also* failure to move without assistance around campus.

Nugent also quickly created a brand new service fraternity, the Disabled Student Organization (or Delta Sigma Omicron [DSO]), and supported related student publications in order to foster the self-expression and independence of disabled students. In a society that routinely excluded people with disabilities from social events, sports teams, and clubs, Nugent conceived of the DSO as a way to guarantee that every student in his program enjoyed the full college experience. Students edited, wrote, and produced *Sigma Signs*, an annual magazine that became known around the world among professionals working in rehabilitation services and people with disabilities, as well as a short-lived student newspaper. Started in 1950, *Sigma Signs* provided student-written columns on current issues, an annual report of events in the program, sports reports (with a spotlight on wheelchair basketball), announcements of awards, names of students who made the honor roll, lists of graduates, and notes on alumni. The program distributed the magazine around campus and to its alumni and to every rehabilitation center, orthopedic school, and VA hospital in the country. The Eisenhower administration even distributed it globally as part of its anticommunism program and read excerpts from it on Voice of America. President Eisenhower cited Nugent for his "distinguished service . . . [to] the physically handicapped" in 1956.

Wheelchair basketball cheerleaders, 1950s

around the world to pursue their aspirations. *Sigma Signs* reported on students' jobs, marriages, and PhDs. It emphasized their physical abilities and prowess through sport, thus reinforcing the masculinity of the male students, and with photos of the wheelchair basketball players and cheerleaders, it also underlined their gender normativity. It advertised—to students, alumni, parents, university administrators, faculty, and the world—the success of the disabled students and of the Illinois program.

Sports were a fundamental feature of the therapeutic program that Nugent invented. Indeed, one student remarked in 1950 that the rehabilitation program was "50 percent sports." Nugent's philosophy of rehabilitation and education for the veteran paraplegics was that they needed physical activity. First, physical activity and specifically sports were "absolutely necessary" for good health, for blood circulation, and to avoid kidney and bowel complications; second, the disabled men needed it for recreation, social interaction, and emotional stability. Finally, Nugent's expertise was in rehabilitation and physical education, and he was a member of his college football and track teams. Nugent's belief in the value of athletics also grew out of his own childhood experiences with a minor heart condition and his insistence on joining in sports. In the first year at Galesburg, students could participate in wheelchair bowling (Nugent and the students created the ramp that made the game possible), swimming, and wheelchair basketball.

The DSO became a space for students to socialize, plan events, and, equally crucial for the program's survival in Nugent's eyes, to represent the successes of people with disabilities to the wider campus community. The DSO and its publications aimed to change popular thinking about disabilities and to inspire people with disabilities

World War II veterans invented wheelchair basketball, and most of the teams were associated with VA hospitals. In 1948 Nugent and the DSO formed the first university team (also made up primarily of veterans) and invited other teams to the first national wheelchair basketball tournament, held in Galesburg. As a result of that tournament, the teams founded the National Wheelchair Basketball Association in 1949 and named Nugent its first commissioner, an office he held for twenty-five years. In the next decade, the program added wheelchair square dancing, tennis, track and field, football, baseball, and archery to its offerings.

Sports—particularly wheelchair basketball—met other goals besides physical therapy. Indeed, wheelchair basketball became central to the identity of the Illinois program and proof of the ability and normality of people with disabilities. For Nugent and the students, the exhibition games broke down barriers and discrimination against "the handicapped" by showing (off) their abilities. The team played games in public and toured nationally and internationally. In exhibition games, the team played against able-bodied high-school teams or local firefighters, who, "for the first time in their lives [sat] down in chairs to play basketball." As a former Gizz Kid (as the men had named themselves after the "gizzmo" on their urinal bags) recalled, "One of them invariably hits the hand rims too hard and flips on to his back" (which provoked laughter from their own fans). Soon enough, the Gizz Kids were zooming around making baskets and occasionally letting the home team catch the ball. The local stars, whom everyone had assumed would beat the pitiful wheelchair team, had become "the underdogs." The alum also recalled glancing at the "local high school paraplegic, the one who rolled a tractor over on himself a year ago." He had been "slumped over" before the game began, but the team saw him "sitting up a little taller now." They knew that night that they had made "another tear in that [1950s] tangle of prejudice and ignorance."

Nugent personally coached the Gizz Kids; they appeared often in media coverage of the program and enjoyed a privileged status within it. Exhibition games showed off the team and were intended to show off the abilities—both physical and intellectual—of the disabled students.

Through games, the DSO raised money to support the teams and to donate to disability-related organizations. The team (exclusively male; there was no women's team until 1970) and the accompanying cheerleaders proved to the public that they were skilled and athletic. At the same time, the sweaty, fast play of basketball, players who made baskets in regulation-height hoops from a chair, and cheerleaders in skirts and letter sweaters who cheered and executed routines, demonstrated the masculinity and femininity of the students. In addition, as Coach Tim Nugent always informed the press and the crowds, the disabled students all received good grades, graduated, and went on to well-paying jobs, averaging $5,000 per year in 1959 (more than $40,000 in 2015 dollars). Printed game programs listed students' majors, degrees, and jobs.

Many students, like Frederick Fay, found the program "liberating" and a source of inspiration and independence. Fay, who later became a national disabilities rights activist, recalled seeing the Illinois campus for the first time in 1962: "When I went to visit, it was so accessible, it was fantastic." He credited his awareness of disability rights activism to Nugent, who, on day 1 of their orientation, told students of the Springfield protest. At the same time, Nugent encouraged Fay to organize and talk to people to win the changes he wanted. "Nugent," Fay recalled, "brought this can-do philosophy and this spirit of competition to the campus that was really refreshing."

But students also had grievances. Every year new students complained bitterly during orientation week about Nugent's demands that they push their own wheelchairs across campus and about the other physical and educational training. In the 1970s, though, problems arose around sexism in sports and prejudiced attitudes toward people with disabilities. The Gizz Kids had always been a men-only group, and Nugent balked at the idea of a women's wheelchair basketball team. Nonetheless, in 1970, several students, together with their able-bodied friends, formed a women's basketball team and named it the "Ms. Kids." Like people with disabilities elsewhere at that time, Illinois students protested their segregation from able-bodied students and the "paternalistic" attitudes they encountered at the university and in the Rehabilitation Center itself. Blind students in particular charged that attitudes at the center were "among the worst in the nation." One blind student reported being steered toward work in a "sheltered workshop"—places known to offer only low-paying, dead-end positions and to treat blind adults as incapable, childlike, and in need of custodial care. In other cases, students' private medical information had become "gossip" among center staff. Others criticized the dependency created by the center: it "extend[ed] itself into the social sphere" to such a degree that students with disabilities befriended each other and rarely associated with able-bodied students. Students proposed deemphasizing the traditional "Functional Training Week," receiving academic advising in academic departments rather than from the center, and expanding the support staff. As one student put it, "We've become too big for one man."

In the 1990s, prejudices among the students with disabilities surfaced as a problem, particularly among the athletes. The primary tension on campus, according to students and alumni, was between the "paras," who played basketball, and the "quads," who played quad rugby. Both had spinal cord injuries, but paraplegics had more function and full use of their upper bodies and, because "they're closer to being able-bodied," seemed to be insulted by any association with quads or other severely disabled students. A year later, however, paras and quads socialized together and no longer made mean cracks. More quads on the track team who trained with paras and for rugby had broken down barriers because the paras had come to see the quads as "real athletes." This was a very masculine system of appraisal and approval, one that left out students who did not lean toward sports. DSO, which might have served as a place where students with different disabilities got to know and appreciate each other's unique capacities and personalities, had grown weak.

In the 1950s and 1960s the DSO had created community through not only sports but also through picnics, dances, shows, and more, and a number of disabilities rights activists of the 1970s and 1980s came from this community at the University of Illinois. Functionality Week had ended in the 1970s, not just because students objected to the segregation it produced; new federal laws required that disabled students be treated exactly like every other student. Ironically, the growing emphasis on equal treatment contributed to a decline in the disabled students' sense of community. By the 1990s the DSO consisted mostly of student athletes who were required to go to its meetings. A few students organized events and wrote for *Sigma Signs*, but they struggled to attract their peers and to develop a strong commitment among disabled students to each other and to the service fraternity's original purposes to promote "the social and recreational welfare of . . . all handicapped people everywhere" and higher education for people with disabilities. By the twenty-first century, the organization's magazine (like so many other print periodicals) had disappeared.

Yet the University of Illinois is still known internationally as the most accessible campus in the world for students with disabilities, as the source of innovative accessible design and technologies, and as the home of internationally recognized disabled athletes. Tim Nugent's ideas, personality, and most of all his belief in the independence and abilities of people with disabilities made this reputation possible. He, the students, and their allies created an accessible world on the campus in Urbana. They showcased the university and the independence and success of the wheelchair students and worked to expand the accessible environment and welcoming atmosphere to people with disabilities across the country and the globe.

Tim Nugent nevertheless rejected the idea that he was a "visionary." In his view, he did what needed to be done in order for disabled GIs to enjoy the benefits of higher education. The architectural and social barriers to people in wheelchairs struck him as injustices—and cruel injustice could enrage him and bring out, as he said of himself, the "fiery redhead" Irish in him. At the core of Nugent's philosophy was a passionate belief in the rights of disabled people to higher education and to respectful treatment as social equals—and that it was his job to make it happen.

Nugent was an organizer. He was an administrator, but in a position at a temporary, branch campus that was never wanted at the university's main campus, working with people who were treated as social outcasts. He believed in the program and the people. He knew how to be diplomatic and when to demonstrate. He knew how to make friends on campus and off, and how to cultivate long-time friends (now called "donors") to keep the program alive. He was a brilliant organizer who turned a small program into a permanent—and celebrated—feature of the flagship campus. He succeeded because he was driven, magnetic, demanding, diplomatic, and at times angry and infuriating. Nugent always encouraged the students to make the program their own, to reach for their highest goals, and at the same time to see a larger mission of making education and the world accessible to "all handicapped." He had told the members of DSO in 1953, "In union is strength." He hoped that they would always remember the larger mission and work together. "I am proud to have worked with Delta Sigma Omicron since its beginning," he wrote. "I pledge myself to its service whenever called upon in any capacity." T. J. Nugent, counselor and administrator, twenty-nine years old, pledged his service to disabled students. Those were no idle words, and he was never an idle man. He did exactly that for the next thirty years and beyond, well past his retirement in 1985.

## Sources

The University of Illinois Archives in Urbana, Illinois, is a rich source of material about Tim Nugent, the Rehabilitation Education Program he built, and related subjects. Most helpful are the Timothy J. Nugent Papers, the Leon Dash Papers, and Delta Sigma Omicron Records, much of which the Archives has digitized and made available online. For secondary sources on rehabilitation education at the University of Illinois, see Lindsey Patterson, "Points of Access: Rehabilitation Centers, Summer Camps, and Student Life in the Making of Disability Activism, 1960–1973," *Journal of Social History* 46, no. 2 (2012): 473–99; *Expanded Horizons: A History of the First 50 Years of the Division of Rehabilitation-Education Services at the University of Illinois*, compiled by the Commemorative Book Preparation and Publication Committee (Champaign: Roxford DT, 1998); and Steven E. Brown, "Breaking Barriers: The Pioneering Disability Students Services Program at the University of Illinois, 1948–1960," in *The History of Discrimination in U.S. Education*, edited by Eileen H. Tamura (New York: Palgrave MacMillan, 2008), 164–92. For a superb history of disabilities in the United States, see Kim E. Nielsen, *A Disability History of the United States* (New York: Beacon, 2012). I thank University of Illinois and DRES alum Mike Rembis, now director of the Center for Disability Studies and associate professor of history at the University of Buffalo, for sharing his insights about the program and for helping me to understand that because of Tim Nugent, the University of Illinois is known as "the most accessible campus in the world."

# Renée and Henry Kahane

## Exploring Language's History and Structure

*Kelsey Reinker*

When pioneering linguists Henry (1902–1992) and Renée Toole Kahane (1907–2002) first met in Berlin at the end of the 1920s, an academic career in the American Midwest for

Renée and Henry Kahane

either of them would have seemed unimaginable. Henry, the son of Austrian Jews, had earned his doctorate at the University of Berlin and had stayed on as a departmental assistant in classical philology. Renée Toole was a linguistics graduate student from Cephalonia, an island off the coast of Greece. Her ancestors were from Greece, Italy, and Ireland, but she and Henry fell in love and were married in 1931. History then intervened. The Nazis came to power, expelling Jews from German universities. Henry and Renée fled, first to Italy and then, in 1939, to the United States.

Henry taught initially in Los Angeles, but in 1941 he and Renée relocated to Urbana-Champaign. Henry received a professorship and taught French, Italian, Portuguese, and classics at the University of Illinois full time, while Renée soon became an instructor in Spanish and held a series of part-time positions that enabled her to teach and do research.

Although hired as language instructors, the Kahanes were primarily interested in linguistics, the scientific study of languages, a field experiencing a revolution in the first decades of the twentieth century. Their collaborative approach was unique. In his scholarship Henry took a broad structuralist perspective, while Renée preferred to examine the precise relationships among a language's dialects. American structuralists analyze different levels of a language (sounds, words, syntax [grammar], and semantics [meanings], for example) as they contrast and combine with other units as used by current speakers. Dialectologists like Renée on the other hand, examine dialect variations *within* a language, such as ethnic and regional differences generated by the geographic location of speakers. Together, the Kahanes made enormous contributions to cultural and historical linguistics. They wrote widely on the history of Greek and Latin and traced linkages between those languages and other Mediterranean tongues. Their research showed in fine detail the connections between this linguistic history and the intellectual roots of western society. Their historical work—together with their later interest in the process by which children develop language skills—established them as founding figures in modern American linguistics. In 1984 Henry was elected president of the Linguistic Society of America.

Throughout their careers, the Kahanes found the Urbana-Champaign campus an ideal place for their work. The wide array of languages taught at the university provided them with a ready set of intellectual colleagues and collaborators. This collegiality inspired Henry to found and lead the Program in Linguistics in 1960, and then to persuade the university to launch a Department of Linguistics in 1965 (one of the first of its kind in the United States). Henry later wrote that he called on administrators regularly to lobby for support for linguistics research. He recalled that they were unmoved and would "throw me out the door," but he insisted that he never gave up, adding: "I would come back through the window."

## Sources

The University Archives holds the papers of Renée and Henry Kahane. A collection of essays on their career was published in *Romance Philology* 15, no. 3 (1962).

# Alta Gwinn Saunders
## The Invention of Business English

Carol Spindel

At the turn of the twentieth century, typewriters, carbon paper, and Gregg shorthand were changing the way business was transacted. Since a business owner no longer had to write every letter by hand, correspondence proliferated, businesses grew larger, and new jobs were created for white-collar workers. In 1900 the Illinois legislature mandated classes to prepare students for careers in business and allocated funds to the University of Illinois for this purpose. Professor of economics David Kinley, who became the first dean of the College of Commerce and, later, president of the university, was put in charge of the new program. One of the classes that resulted was Rhetoric 10: Business Writing.

Although high school business classes were common, Rhetoric 10, first taught in 1902, was the first American collegiate class in business writing. Thomas Arkle Clark, a professor of rhetoric, taught the class for eleven years, although he preferred to handwrite his own letters, eschewing dictation and the typewriter as too impersonal. Nor did he believe women should write business letters; the female mind, according to Clark, lacked the necessary logic. In 1909 Clark became the first dean of men, not only at Illinois but in any American university. In this capacity his business letters were brief notes summoning male students to his office for pointed interrogations.

In 1903 sixteen-year-old Alta Gwinn and her three sisters moved from their small town of Oakland, Illinois, to Urbana, where they bought a house at the edge of the University of Illinois campus. Both their parents had passed away, and the four girls were determined to stay together while they pursued their respective educations. The eldest, Avis, managed their household at 806 South Goodwin Avenue. (In 1919, 806 S. Goodwin was changed to 606 S. Goodwin.) Alta, second, enrolled at the university. She was the scholar of the family, "talented and ambitious for learning." The two younger sisters, Ethel and Edith, attended Urbana High School and then followed Alta to the university, as did Avis, once the others were launched. "The home of the Gwinn girls" was described as a hospitable place where their friends loved to gather for conversation, meals, and slumber parties. Remarkably, all four sisters graduated from the university and went on to have professional careers.

As a student, Alta majored in English, was inducted into Phi Beta Kappa, Mortar Board, and Alethenai, the literary society for women, and served as secretary of the YWCA. Beyond her studies and her sisters, her deepest commitment was to the chapter of Delta Gamma fraternity she helped found at Illinois. Her three sisters followed her into Delta Gamma and the sorority became their extended family. Once their chapter was established, the Delta Gammas had their eye on a spacious brick house for sale at the corner of West Nevada and South Mathews Streets, just across the street from the Music Building and a block from the home of the Gwinn sisters. To raise funds, the young Delta Gammas rented a second-floor space on Green Street between Sixth and Wright Streets and opened the Green Teapot Tea Room. After a year of hard work they sold the tea room and used the money as a down payment on the house with white columns, where the Iota Chapter of Delta Gamma still resides today.

After graduation Alta accepted a position as principal at Ridge Farm High School in nearby Vermilion County. She returned to the University of Illinois to study English and philosophy, wrote her master's thesis on Horace Walpole's 1764 Gothic novel *The Castle of Otranto*, and received her master of arts degree in 1910. She traveled to England to do research in the British Museum and the Bodleian Library and attended Columbia University in the summer of 1913. In 1914 she married fellow Illinois student Thomas Earle "Tony" Saunders of Ridge Farm, Illinois. Described as "dapper and suave," Saunders managed the Flat Iron Department Store in Urbana, which

Alta Gwinn Saunders

occupied the first two floors and basement of a triangular flatiron building designed by Joseph Royer at the merger of Springfield Avenue and Main Street in Urbana; Alta worked as his assistant. But in 1919 Tony left, and in 1922 Alta was granted a divorce.

In 1918 Alta applied for a job at the University of Illinois to teach Business Writing. When the College of Commerce and Business Administration was created in 1915, Business Writing remained in the Department of Rhetoric and Oratory, which also included composition, public speaking, and journalism. Alta had already taught Rhetoric 1: Rhetoric and Themes, the introductory writing class, but she needed credentials in business. To Dean N. A. Weston she wrote:

My business experience, since I was fifteen, has been such as any girl would have who helped to manage the domestic economy of a household without a father and mother at its head. Since my marriage, I have participated in Mr. Saunder's [sic] work as Manager of the Flat Iron Store Company, giving my entire time to his business for two years; organized Delta Gamma Building Corporation; served as its president; originated, financed, and equipped the Tea Room on Green St.; acted on its board of directors; administered an estate; and had some experience in buying and selling stocks and bonds.

My work in the Flat Iron Store Company was the daily correspondence of considerable volume necessary in a department store with thirty employees and doing a business of over $125,000.00 a year. It required a knowledge of buying, selling, advertizing, credits and collections, and particularly the writing of collection letters. The Presidency of the Delta Gamma Building Corporation involved buying real estate, borrowing money, collecting notes, and paying notes. As administratrix, I had to collect notes, and sell real estate.

My early environment and recent business experience have given me a knowledge of both the agricultural and the trade class of people.

I hope you deem this experience sufficient to round out my qualifications, through academic training and teaching, to teach Rhetoric 10.

Yours very sincerely,
Alta Gwinn Saunders

Alta was hired as an instructor in the department of Business Organization and Operation, but since the courses remained in the Department of English, she held appointments in two different colleges. She taught Business Writing and a class on writing reports, Rhetoric 22: Summarizing and Abstracting. These practical courses were in high demand, in part because of the influx of World War I veterans enrolling at the university.

With her colleague H. L. Creek, Saunders published her first book on business writing in 1920, an anthology of readings about business. *The Literature of Business* (Harper and Brothers) contained fifty-two excerpts or short articles taken from a wide-ranging selection of speeches, books, and periodicals. They included works written by their fellow teachers of business writing, but their choice of other authors was diverse: John Ruskin, Herbert Spencer, Theodore Roosevelt, Robert Louis Stevenson, and John D. Rockefeller, placed alongside his strongest critic, the muckraking journalist Ida Tarbell. Subjects ranged from business education to ethics to how to increase the "pull" of your sales letters through scientific management. The book also included a bibliography and short biography of each author.

In 1925 Macmillan published Saunders's second textbook, *Effective Business English: As Applied to Business Letters and Reports*. By this time she was associate professor of English in charge of courses in Business Writing. *Effective Business English* emphasized basic principles of clear, concise writing and provided many models, both good and bad, of actual business letters. The same year, Saunders published (through the University of Illinois Supply Store) a booklet for Illinois students applying for teaching jobs in elementary and secondary schools, titled *Your Application Letter*. For a good application letter, her prerequisites were a good education, an attractive personality, and common sense; assuming those, she recommended the four components of the sales letter: contact, persuasion, conviction, and clincher. She also offered advice about stationery, salutations, headings, and length, and she ended with this advice:

> In closing it seems worth while to add a personal word. Act with dignity, for you have something of which to be proud. Certainly no one is going to place a higher value upon your ability than you yourself place upon it. On the other hand, the more you can look at yourself objectively, the more you will know what is possible for you. If you think it worth while to apply for a position, use all your intelligence and ingenuity to get it. The world is just as much yours as it is any one's else and for most people success depends upon concentration, combined with intelligent and persistent effort.

In 1929 Saunders published a third textbook, with co-author Chester Reed Anderson, titled *Business Reports: Investigation and Presentation* (McGraw-Hill), which focused on methods of collecting and presenting data. She

The College of Commerce

is listed as first author of each textbook on which she collaborated. *The Literature of Business* was reissued in five editions, the other two textbooks in two.

The University of Illinois was the recognized center of this new field of business education. The courses in business writing were under the rubric of Business English, a division of the English Department that Saunders supervised. Rhetoric 10, which was not open to freshmen, had an enrollment equal to one-fifth of the three upper classes, and her lectures were broadcast regularly on the campus radio station. Her textbooks were widely adopted nationally and even internationally. During the summers, she worked as a business consultant. With her capable hands and enterprising spirit, she had turned her expe-

rience teaching composition, her brief foray into business as her husband's assistant, and her sorority fundraising and real estate experience into a successful career in an emerging field she was helping to create.

A skillful networker, Saunders joined and served as a leader in local and national organizations, professional, social, and cultural alike. She also became a sought-after speaker for business associations in general and those organized specifically by and for women. Perhaps it was slightly easier for a woman to become prominent in a field that was inventing itself as it went along than in a more traditional academic discipline. The university appreciated her national visibility, and she was promoted to full professor in 1938.

In 1935 the leaders in the field of teaching Business English decided to organize an association. Saunders served on the organizing committee; her colleague, co-author, and friend C. R. "Andy" Anderson of Illinois was chosen as chairman. In May 1936 sixty-six charter members agreed to pay the Depression-era dues of two dollars per year, and a year later the organization incorporated under the name American Business Writing Association. Saunders served as vice president for the Middle West region and as a member of the board of directors. All who describe the early days of the organization emphasize its friendliness; it was a supportive network whose small meetings felt like family reunions. C. R. "Andy" Anderson became the first executive director and served until 1956. Two other Illinois professors followed him, Francis W. Weeks (1957–1984) and Robert D. Gieselman (1984–1980).

In 1967 the organization changed its name to the American Business Communication Association (in 1985 the name changed again to the Association for Business Communication, or ABC). From its creation in 1937 to 1980, the association was headquartered in the Department of English at the University of Illinois. By nurturing teachers, developing curricular materials, and fostering research, ABC has been essential to the development of the field now called business communication. In 1941 Saunders was elected the organization's fourth president, the first woman to serve in that role.

While Saunders was founding and organizing the most important organization in her field, the Association of American Business Writing, she also became editor of the national monthly magazine of Delta Gamma, *The Anchora*. As editor from 1935 until her death, Saunders solicited articles from prominent alumnae on travel, the arts, and current affairs, and she herself wrote a monthly column. She also served on the board of directors of the University of Illinois Alumni Association in 1939 and 1940 and as vice

president from 1939 to 1941. She continued to update and issue new editions of her textbooks. The introduction to the fifth "contemporary" edition of *The Literature of Business* (1946) began, "We are living in a revolutionary world." The nearly all-new selections included pieces by economist Friedrich Hayek and former Secretary of Commerce and Vice President Henry A. Wallace.

Saunders was admired for her wit and charm, and in 1937 she published a little book on conversation with the plainspoken Midwestern title *How to Become an Interesting Talker*. Her advice about being a good listener and choosing a subject that includes everyone is still useful eighty years later. She relished verbal combat, as long as it was "never bitter or acrimonious." "There is no finer compliment," she writes, "if it is genuinely felt on both or all sides, than that revealing little sentence, 'We had a really good talk!'"

During World War II, Saunders represented the University of Illinois at a conference on what women could do to aid the war effort. She wrote about the experience in an article for *The Anchora*, explaining in great detail how college women could determine the most suitable and useful way, given their qualifications, to contribute to an allied victory.

When asked to list her hobbies, Saunders always replied "travel." On June 16, 1948, she visited her sister Ethel in Evanston. The following day she boarded a luxurious United Airlines DC-6 for New York. She intended to meet with her editor about the third edition of *Effective Business English* and then to go on to Swampscott, Massachusetts, for the seventy-fifth annual Delta Gamma Convention. The plane crashed near Mount Carmel, Pennsylvania, killing all forty-three people aboard. The University of Illinois community, preparing for commencement ceremonies, was shocked and saddened. When the news arrived at the Delta Gamma Diamond Jubilee Convention, "All Convention delegates were stunned and an aura of gloom cast over the meetings." A subsequent issue of *The Anchora*

"At the time of her death, Alta Gwinn Saunders was sixty-one years old, one of only a handful of women who had attained the rank of full Professor at the University of Illinois."

bemoaned the loss of Saunders's "rare combination of beauty, wit, good sound sense, and devotion to Delta Gamma" and announced the formation of a memorial committee to establish a fitting tribute.

At the time of her death, Saunders was sixty-one years old, one of only a handful of women who had attained the rank of full professor at the University of Illinois. She had been a founder and leader of the emerging field now known as business communication. Her memorial service was held in Smith Music Hall, across the street from the Delta Gamma house. University of Illinois President George D. Stoddard wrote in a condolence note to her sister, "She was known everywhere and everywhere admired."

When the Pennsylvania Avenue Residence Halls, the first coeducational dormitories at Illinois, were opened in 1962, one of the four was named Saunders Hall, in honor of Alta Gwinn Saunders.

## Sources

The personnel file of Alta Gwinn Saunders in the University of Illinois Archives, record series 2/5/15 Staff Appointments File, includes her work applications and the letters quoted above. Her books are in the University of Illinois Library. *Champaign News-Gazette* and *Urbana Courier* obituaries and articles, and her marriage and divorce records, can be found in the Champaign County Historical Archives at the Urbana Free Library. Articles from *The Anchora* are cited here courtesy of Delta Gamma Fraternity archivist Marilyn Ellis Haas.

### General Sources on Business Communication

Adams, Katherine H. *A History of Professional Writing Instruction in American Colleges: Years of Acceptance, Growth, and Doubt.* Dallas: Southern Methodist University Press, 1993.

Locker, Kitty O. "The Role of the Association for Business Communication in Shaping Business Communication as an Academic Discipline." *Journal of Business Communication* 35, no. 1 (January 1998): 14–49.

Weeks, Francis W. "The Teaching of Business Writing at the Collegiate Level, 1900–1920." In *Studies in the History of Business Writing*, edited by George H. Douglas and Herbert W. Hildebrandt (Urbana: Association for Business Communication, 1985).

### Newspaper Articles and Obituaries

"Faculty Woman Heads Group." *Daily Illini*, September 30, 1941.

"Mrs. Saunders, UI Professor, Dies in Pennsylvania Air Crash." *Daily Illini*, June 19, 1948.

Obituaries for Alta Gwinn Saunders. *Champaign News-Gazette*, June 18, 1948, and June 20, 1948.

"People's Forum: Visits with Mrs. Saunders 11 Days before Tragedy and Recalls Family of Sisters." By C. C. Burford. *Champaign News-Gazette*, June 27, 1948.

Winant, Marguerite. "In Memoriam: Tribute to Alta Gwinn Saunders." *The Anchora*, November 1948.

Winship, Olive Sprague. "The Gwinn Sisters," *The Anchora*, November 1948.

### Works by Saunders

"As the Editor Sees It: College Women and the War." *The Anchora*, January 1943.

*Business Reports, Investigation and Presentation.* New York: McGraw-Hill, 1929.

*Effective Business English as Applied to Business Letters and Reports.* New York: Macmillan, 1925.

*How to Become an Interesting Talker.* New York: Droke, 1937.

*The Literature of Business.* New York: Harper, 1920, 1923, 1928, 1937.

*The Literature of Business: Contemporary.* New York: Harper, 1946.

*Your Application Letter.* Urbana: University of Illinois Supply Store, 1925.

# Shozo Sato

## Reinventing Kabuki Theater

*Nicholas Hopkins*

Shozo Sato at work on a kabuki production

Shozo Sato's (1933–) contributions to the performing arts have spanned a long, path-breaking career. A professor of art and design at the University of Illinois for fifty years, Sato gained international attention for his adaptation of classic Western theater plays into Kabuki performances. In the process, Sato produced a new, hybrid genre of performance that blurs the boundaries between classical Western and Japanese theaters.

Sato, a native of Japan, came to Illinois in 1964 as an artist-in-residence. With the opening of the Krannert Center for the Performing Arts in 1969, he shifted his attention from visual arts to theater production. In 1978 he and a student cast performed *Kabuki Macbeth* at Krannert. The performance generated positive reviews in Champaign County and went on to win three of Chicago's Joseph Jefferson Awards, for best production, director, and costuming. The success of *Kabuki Macbeth* brought Sato (and the university's theater program) to the attention of drama producers and critics across the country.

Sato's next production, *Kabuki Medea* (1982), played at the Berkeley Repertory Theatre, Chicago's Wisdom Bridge Theater, and the Natal Performing Arts Center in Durban, South Africa, winning awards in each city. A *Chicago Tribune* critic was captivated by the play's "boldly painted makeup and richly colored costumes . . . and chorus, as well as elaborate puppets and hand props." He added that the drama transported audiences "from a joyous wedding celebration to an underwater battle with a sea monster, to the ritual murder of Medea's two children."

After his first production, Sato embarked on more than two decades of remarkable, creative work. He directed Kabuki productions of Western classics (*Othello*, *Romeo and Juliet*, *Macbeth*, and plays by Euripides) and operas (*Madame Butterfly*) and toured as far afield as India, Germany, and Japan. Sato's productions were more than adaptations. Under his direction, classical performances were given new choreography, set design, and lighting, and at times the dialogue was revised to fit the classic Japanese settings. The productions reflected Sato's dedication to detail in costume design, set construction, and choreography. He also reimagined classic Kabuki performances, revising dialogue, shifting the gender of lead characters, and punctuating performances with original turns.

Sato's artistic innovations have extended beyond theater. He has published works on calligraphy, flower arrangement, Sumi-e (ink wash) painting, cross-cultural studies, and the art of the traditional Japanese tea ceremony. Much of this activity has emanated from Japan House on the Illinois campus, where he served as founding director. In 2003 the Japanese government awarded Sato its first-ever Cultural Achievement Award, citing his international dissemination of traditional Japanese culture.

### Sources

The University Archives houses an extensive collection of materials related to Professor Sato's life and career. Chicago critic Richard Christenson's review of *Kabuki Medea* appears in the *Chicago Tribune*, January 12, 1983.

# John Bardeen
## Citizen of Science

Vicki McKinney and Lillian Hoddeson

In 1950, theoretical physicist John Bardeen was thinking of leaving Bell Labs. William L. Everitt, dean of the College of Engineering, and Francis Wheeler Loomis, head of the Physics Department, seized the moment. Neither department alone had the resources, but by early 1951 they had together created a package they hoped would be enough to lure Bardeen to Illinois. Fortunately, Bardeen, despite his reputation as a brilliant theorist, did not expect special treatment. His greatest desires were a supportive environment in which to pursue his science, a pleasant social community for himself and his family, opportunities to make practical contributions outside of academia, and a decent golf course or two.

After World War II, the University of Illinois had become one of the nation's most productive centers of engineering research. Led by physicist Louis Ridenour, who became dean of the graduate college in 1947, the university began to seek out physicists who would enhance and complement the College of Engineering. By the spring of 1951, a small but robust group was in place, including Frederick Seitz, Robert Maurer, James Koehler, David Lazarus, Dillon Mapother, James Schneider, and Charles Slichter. They established Illinois as a world-class solid-state research center, the very field in which Bardeen was most interested. Solid-state physics—later known as many-body theory—was a brand new field in the early 1930s when Bardeen was a graduate student. He was at the vanguard of an effort to understand the behavior of systems with many interacting particles, behaviors that could not be explained with existing quantum mechanical

John Bardeen in the classroom

device underpinning what became known as the Information Age. They had been looking for a way to amplify electrical signals without using vacuum tubes. The tubes were bulky, fragile, and expensive. In order to make telephones, radios, and television cost effective, and therefore accessible to more people and businesses, Bell Labs needed a more efficient way to manipulate electrical signals. Semiconductors, with their unusual conduction properties, offered possibilities. Bardeen's comprehensive theoretical understanding of the behavior of solid materials nudged the research forward, and his suggestions came alive under Brattain's skilled hands. Their work paid off in December 1947, when the team demonstrated the world's first transistor. Over the next decade, that clunky prototype evolved into a small, sturdy, and energy-efficient device that could be easily mass produced. It would make vacuum tubes obsolete and inaugurate a technological sea change on par with the Industrial Revolution.

To his surprise, Bardeen suddenly found himself cut off from the team's semiconductor research. William Shockley, like Bardeen a brilliant and highly trained theoretical physicist, was the semiconductor group leader and Bardeen and Brattain's direct supervisor. He had made the original suggestion that initiated the research leading to the transistor. While Bardeen and Brattain persisted in the slow-moving, day-to-day process of brainstorming and experimentation, Shockley had lost interest in favor of more glamorous projects. He therefore was not directly involved in their discovery. Stung by his failure to invent the device himself, Shockley reacted badly. He aggressively inserted himself into the team's subsequent research, planning to invent the next (commercially viable) version of the transistor himself and relegating Bardeen and Brattain to dead-end problems.

Bardeen found himself in an impossible situation, his efforts to contribute blocked by his own supervisor. Although Bardeen's modesty and easy tolerance was legendary among his friends, he was also known for his strong work ethic. He quickly tired of Shockley's machinations. At age forty-three, Bardeen would not sit back while there were scientific puzzles yet to solve. Since his graduate studies in the early 1930s, he had been partic-

theories. He and his friend Fred Seitz had been graduate students together at Princeton University, and it was Seitz who encouraged him to come to Illinois. Bardeen thought that he may have found just what he had been hoping for—a dual appointment in physics and engineering with talented and congenial colleagues. Illinois had the right research environment, including opportunities for travel and networking, funding for equipment and experiments, access to top-notch students and postdoctoral fellows, and the research freedom that had lately been consuming his thoughts. His present job at Bell Telephone Laboratories in New Jersey had become stifling.

At Bell, Bardeen and his friend Walter Brattain, an experimental physicist, had invented the transistor, the

ularly fascinated by the question of superconductivity, the startling absence of electrical resistance in certain metals and alloys when cooled to temperatures near absolute zero. But at Bell Labs there was not much interest in superconductivity.

There was no shortage of opportunities for a physicist of Bardeen's caliber. When he quietly made it known to a few friends—including his old friend Fred Seitz from the University of Illinois—that he was considering leaving Bell Labs, more than one job offer materialized. Although there were some advantages to industry or government work, Bardeen's heart was still in academia. He had grown up in Madison, Wisconsin, where his father had been the founding dean of the University of Wisconsin's medical school. Bardeen's university years, first at Wisconsin and later at Princeton, Harvard, and the University of Minnesota, had been the most stimulating times of his life.

Bardeen accepted the University of Illinois job offer, and by the fall 1951 he and his wife Jane had found a spacious new home on a large, pie-shaped lot in Champaign. Jane had plenty of room for her gardening and occasional entertaining. The children—Bill, Jim, and Betsy—found playmates and room to roam, as well as excellent educational opportunities. Bardeen discovered the Champaign Country Club within easy walking distance from the house. He promptly joined, earning a reputation as both a good golfer and a pleasant companion. Over the years, the club provided him with exercise—he usually walked the eighteen holes rather than riding a cart—camaraderie, and both physical and psychological challenges.

That fall, Bardeen taught his very first course on transistors and semiconductors. Nick Holonyak, an electrical engineering student, sat in. Although some students found Bardeen's minimalist lecture delivery hard to follow, Holonyak was electrified. He switched thesis advisors so that he could work in Bardeen's newly established semiconductor lab, the Electrical Engineering Research Laboratory (EERL). Under Bardeen's guidance, Holonyak augmented his remarkable skill in the laboratory with an equally sharp theoretical mind. The EERL would be home to a series of outstanding researchers and the setting for many breakthroughs in semiconductor physics and en-

gineering. Although Bardeen gradually relinquished control of the EERL, he continued to follow semiconductor research closely.

Bardeen attended conferences and visited physics labs around the world. In 1953 he went to a meeting of the International Union of Pure and Applied Physics in Japan. There he met two Japanese scientists, Michio (George) Hatoyama and Makoto Kikuchi, with whom he formed lifelong friendships. Both men would come to occupy key executive positions in Sony Corporation's research and development organization, where Bardeen was a frequent and honored guest. The Japanese conference was the first of many memorable trips.

At Illinois, Bardeen finally had the freedom and the resources to devote himself fully to the gnarly theoretical question that had been tugging at him since he was a graduate student. Experimentally discovered by Heike Kamerlingh Onnes in 1911, superconductivity—the absence of electrical resistance—occurs when certain metals and alloys are cooled to near absolute zero temperatures. The very best scientific minds—Hans Bethe, Richard Feynman, Felix Bloch, Niels Bohr, Herbert Fröhlich, and others—had tried and failed to produce a verifiable explanation for the phenomenon. Bardeen set himself the goal of being the first to explain superconductivity on a first-principles quantum mechanical basis.

The physicist began, as always, by conducting a review of the literature and dividing the problem into smaller "sub-problems." His comprehensive literature review was published in the 1953 *Handbuch der Physik*, a major review encyclopedia. Over the course of nearly one hundred pages, Bardeen offered a detailed analysis of both theoretical and experimental research and identified what he believed to be the crucial

"Their work paid off in December 1947, when the team demonstrated the world's first transistor. Over the next decade, that clunky prototype evolved into a small, sturdy, and energy-efficient device that could be easily mass produced."

elements of any workable theory of superconductivity. At the same time, he developed a working list of related problems that he thought would have to be solved along the way. All of these subproblems could be elaborated experimentally as well as theoretically, providing checkpoints to ensure that he was heading in the right direction.

This ability to confirm or expand upon theory through experimentation was critical to the way Bardeen worked. He was skeptical of any theory that did not demonstrably agree with the way that materials behaved in the real world. Unlike many theorists, Bardeen enjoyed working closely with experimentalists, often literally side by side, just as he had worked with Walter Brattain to invent the transistor. James Bray, one of Bardeen's later theory students, learned from him that "it was very important for theorists to immerse themselves in experimental data and be guided by that."

Bardeen was instrumental in bringing a number of outstanding scientists to the University of Illinois. He sought and found students and postdoctoral fellows who would complement and supplement his own knowledge, and whom he would teach, guide, and encourage, modeling his own method of scientific collaboration and accomplishment. For example, when he decided that he needed to know more about the new field theory formalism in order to apply it to problems in superconductivity, he asked David Bohm, one of its developers, to recommend someone to bring the new techniques to Illinois. Bohm suggested David Pines, and thus began a successful collaboration and friendship between Pines and Bardeen that would span nearly four decades. When Pines accepted a job offer at Princeton a few years later, Leon Cooper came to Illinois as Bardeen's postdoc in much the same way that Pines had arrived. Robert Schrieffer, a bright young graduate student, came to Illinois from MIT. With Bardeen's approval, Schrieffer boldly decided to work on superconductivity for his doctoral thesis. Bardeen would lead Cooper and Schrieffer into a scientific adventure inconceivable for most aspiring young scientists.

Bardeen fostered a relaxed atmosphere and exhibited a paternal regard for his students and postdocs. Working collaboratively, often with other colleagues in the department, Bardeen, Cooper, and Schrieffer were in and out of one another's offices all the time. Bardeen and Cooper shared an office, where they often worked quietly in companionable concentration. Cooper later recalled "parties and camaraderie." Knowing that other physicists were also closing in on superconductivity, the team worked hard, but there was a warm collegiality pervading the effort.

It had never been a foregone conclusion that a superconductivity theory would come together, but Bardeen's persistence, his confidence, his encyclopedic knowledge, and his ability to foster teamwork gave the younger men confidence as well. With Cooper's innovative "Cooper pairs" breakthrough in 1955, they thought they were getting close. But by the fall of 1956, Cooper and Schrieffer were becoming discouraged. Schrieffer, especially, needed to finish a successful doctoral thesis before graduating and moving on with his career.

Just then, the team got an unexpected boost. Word spread that the Nobel Prize in physics had been awarded to Bardeen, Brattain, and Shockley for the transistor. Celebration ensued, complete with a noisy surprise party for the overwhelmed Nobel laureate. Buoyed by Bardeen's recognition, the younger scientists renewed their efforts. The final breakthrough was made by Schrieffer shortly after Bardeen returned from Stockholm. Under Bardeen's calm direction, they worked feverishly to complete what became known as the Bardeen-Cooper-Schrieffer, or BCS, theory of superconductivity in the spring of 1957. The BCS theory almost immediately began to receive experimental confirmation, igniting more research into the phenomenon. Today, superconductors are widely used in medicine, where magnetic resonance imaging (MRI) is an important diagnostic tool. MRI technology, for which Paul Lauterbur, another University of Illinois scientist, earned a Nobel Prize, depends on creating an extraordinarily powerful magnetic field. The production of the magnetic field re-

> "It had never been a foregone conclusion that a superconductivity theory would come together, but Bardeen's persistence, his confidence, his encyclopedic knowledge, and his ability to foster teamwork gave the younger men confidence."

quires so much energy as to be cost prohibitive, but superconducting coils made the technology cost effective enough for use in medical centers around the world.

The BCS theory was undoubtedly worthy of a Nobel. Bardeen worried that his young collaborators would not get the recognition he felt they deserved; the Nobel committee had never awarded two prizes in the same field. He was therefore deeply relieved when the award came in 1972, long after Cooper and Schrieffer had gone on to distinguished careers in other places. Once again, there was great celebration in Urbana-Champaign, among not only Bardeen's university family but also his country club friends and other well-wishers.

Bardeen's influence extended beyond his students, colleagues, and postdocs. Even as he was fully engaged with his own scientific interests, he made time to reach out to industrial laboratories. Always adamant about the importance of open communication among scientists and engineers, he supported the creation of the Midwest Electronics Research Center, where scientists from industry and academia could interact. He sometimes traveled with Paul Coleman, an engineering colleague, to industrial labs where they fostered connections that would benefit both industry and the university. Coleman liked to joke that when he went alone, "we'd talk to the janitor," but if Bardeen also went, "we'd go in and talk to the president."

Bardeen informally visited his friends at Sony and Bell Labs as often as he could. He also enjoyed a longstanding relationship with Xerox, first as a consultant and later as a member of the company's board of directors. Just as his own desire for research freedom had contributed to his decision to come to the University of Illinois, Bardeen insisted that all science progressed better in an open environment. He encouraged Xerox and other companies to offer their scientists as much freedom as possible to "participate fully in the scientific community." Scientists were most productive when they could select their own research problems, publish their results, attend scientific meetings, visit universities, and, perhaps, take an occasional sabbatical "to get refreshed."

The University of Illinois ultimately benefited from Bardeen's long associations with industry when the Sony Corporation endowed a $3 million chair in Bardeen's name.

John Bardeen and prototypes of his equipment designs

Appropriately, the first Bardeen Chair of Electrical and Computer Engineering and Physics was awarded to his former student and long-time colleague, Nick Holonyak. After working in industry for a few years, Holonyak had returned to Illinois in 1963 for the remainder of his illustrious career. A brilliant and prolific scientist, Holonyak invented the LED (light-emitting diode) and the laser diode, a ubiquitous component of cellphones and other devices.

Bardeen's stature as a scientist inexorably brought him into public service. He served on the President's Science Advisory Committee (PSAC) for Presidents Eisenhower and Kennedy. During his tenure, the committee was instrumental in laying the groundwork for the National Aeronautics and Space Administration (NASA), encouraging a nuclear test ban treaty, and strengthening American science education. He also participated in more local concerns, such as a panel at University High School, where he emphasized the value of a broad scientific education. In 1962 he and Jane attended a sparkling dinner at the White House honoring forty-nine Nobel laureate, as well as some other distinguished guests, including astronaut John Glenn, poet Robert Frost, and author John Dos Passos. President Kennedy quipped, "I think that this is the most extraordinary collection of talent, of human knowledge, that has ever been gathered together at the White House—with the possible exception of when Thomas Jefferson dined alone."

Bardeen especially enjoyed the role of scientific ambassador to other countries. He participated in scientific delegations to China and Russia when those countries were still largely closed to Americans. Delighted with the opportunity to meet scientists whose work he had only been able to read in translation, if at all, he enjoyed their face-to-face conversations and became good friends with scientists from around the world. He often played a key role in setting up exchanges and visits of individual scientists and students, an important cross-fertilization for both the individual and the hosting institution.

Bardeen's world had expanded into realms of influence that he could never have imagined. Reserved and laconic, he did his best to respond appropriately to the many invitations and accolades: though he was aware of the importance of his work, they somehow still pleased and surprised him. During his forty years at Illinois, he received the National Medal of Science, the Franklin Medal, and the Medal of Freedom, the nation's highest civilian award. *Life* magazine named him one of the twentieth century's one hundred most influential Americans. He was inducted into the National Inventors Hall of Fame, joining Alexander Graham Bell and Eli Whitney. In 1988 he even received the Lomonosov Award, the Soviet Academy of Science's highest honor. Of all the great honors, the Nobels and the medals and the prizes, one of Bardeen's favorite awards came from his adopted community: the key to the city of Champaign. He was the first University of Illinois faculty member to be given this honor, and for Bardeen there was "nothing more gratifying than being recognized by your friends and neighbors."

Bardeen never gained the public notoriety of an Einstein or Feynman, for he never sought the limelight. Yet his quiet genius contributed to technologies that brought profound changes in the second half of the twentieth century. For Bardeen, scientific progress always came before ego, and he was the consummate team player. His influence rippled out from his modest Urbana office into laboratories across the country and around the globe. The Nobel Prizes and other honors marked his scientific achievements. For those who knew him, Bardeen's generous spirit, his lifelong advocacy of research freedom and shared knowledge, and the example of his own collaborative style may have left the most enduring legacy of all.

## Sources

The most comprehensive account of John Bardeen's life and career is *True Genius: The Life and Science of John Bardeen*, by Lillian Hoddeson and Vicki McKinney Daitch (Washington, D.C.: Joseph Henry, 2002). The largest and most important collection of Bardeen papers is at the University of Illinois, in both the University Archives and the physics archive in Urbana. Oral history interviews regarding Bardeen's life are in the UIUC Department of Physics collection. The American Telephone and Telegraph (AT&T) archive in Warren, N.J., holds documents and notebooks related to the discovery of the transistor. Hoddeson's co-authored work with Michael Riordan, *Crystal Fire: The Birth of the Information Age* (New York: Norton, 1997) tells the story of the initial invention and subsequent development of transistor technology.

# Carl Woese

## The Discovery of a Third Domain of Life

*Steven Lenz and Nicholas Hopkins*

Carl Woese (1928–2013) received a bachelor's degree in math and physics from Amherst College in 1950. Despite his fascination with physical phenomena, however, Woese opted to explore the relationship between physics and the world of living things. He completed his graduate work at Yale University just as scientists were becoming aware of the role of the genetic code in the evolution of life. Marked by an independent turn of mind, however, Woese chose to explore the origins of the genetic code itself rather than to study its operation in living cells as had Nobel laureates James Watson and Francis Crick. He pursued this curiosity through postdoctoral work at Yale and the General Electric Research Laboratory in Schenectady, New York, and brought it with him to the University of Illinois, where he was recruited to the faculty (and immediately tenured) in 1964. Woese would remain in Urbana-Champaign for the rest of his career.

Woese's research revolutionized the field of biology. For centuries it had been an article of faith that all life could be broken down into two kingdoms—bacteria, and larger, more complex organisms such as plants and animals, which are called eukaryotes. Initially, Archaea had been classified as bacteria, but Woese, after studying cultures that originated in the stomach of a campus cow, determined that they had distinctive gene structures and metabolic pathways that set them apart. They constituted a third branch of life. Woese first published his findings in 1977, but they remained controversial for decades. Because his ultimate goal was an understanding of the deep history of evolution, Woese focused on Archaea's distinctive internal mechanics and their relationship to other life forms. Despite the public debate over the classification of Archaea, his principal concern

Carl Woese. Photo by Richard Hildwein. Courtesy of the University of Illinois Archives.

continued to be the exploration of how molecular and genetic structures could illuminate the course of evolution.

In the last decade of his life Woese's focus on genetic structures also contributed to the horizontal gene transfer hypothesis, an instrument for explaining the development of life forms across the three domains of living organisms. He argued that typical Darwinian "vertical" evolution only begins after the development of the three domains of life. By contrast, Woese asserted that patterns of horizontal transfer indicated that early organisms would trade their own genetic information with each other.

The impact of Carl Woese's innovative ideas has been felt in fields as diverse as evolutionary biology, bioinformatics, biochemistry, medicine, and ecology. By the end of his career, his single-minded pursuit of some of the most difficult questions in biology had won him a MacArthur Fellowship and, in 2003, the Crafoord Prize in Biosciences, awarded by the Royal Swedish Academy of Sciences to mark accomplishments in scientific fields not covered by the Nobel Prize. Woese received the Crafoord Prize (and a $500,000 award) from the King of Sweden in Stockholm.

## Sources

Press coverage of Woese's career and achievements is extensive. See, for example, "Theory Fills in the Gap before Darwin," *USA Today*, June 18, 2002; William Yardley, "Carl Woese Dies at 84; Discovered Life's 'Third Domain,'" *New York Times*, January 1, 2013; "Carl Woese; Biologist Whose Discovery of a Third branch of the Evolutionary Tree Was Initially Greeted Skeptically," *London Times*, February 1, 2013.

# Clarence Shelley
## The Campaign to Diversify the University

Joy Ann Williamson-Lott

The history of black students at the University of Illinois at Urbana-Champaign is a complicated one that involves discrimination, racism, protest, and resilience. Because the African American community maintained an unwavering belief in the importance of education, colleges and universities have long been important battlegrounds for black liberation efforts. Black students across the nation became the battering rams—and in many ways the vanguard—of the struggle for equal education. From the late 1960s through the early 1970s, in particular, black students helped redefine the goals and tactics of the struggle and demanded change, respect, and equity. Black students at the University of Illinois were at the forefront of that struggle and changed the face of the university and the nature of student experiences forever.

The battle to change the University of Illinois was not an easy one, particularly since the institution was located in Champaign County, which predominantly resembled southern states in its attitude toward and treatment of African American residents. For instance, large Ku Klux Klan meetings took place throughout the county, including a mass rally at a park in Urbana in 1924. Klan sentiment and hostility was not wholly embraced by white residents, but the cities of Champaign and Urbana established firm patterns of educational and residential segregation early in the twentieth century. By the 1930s a combination of federal housing programs, restrictive covenants, and bank lending policies led to the creation of all-black areas and a dual housing market in the twin cities. Residential segregation patterns also created ed-

Black Chorus, 1973. Photo courtesy of Student Life and Culture Archives at the University of Illinois Archives.

ucational segregation patterns, so that in Champaign, most black students attended all-black or predominantly black elementary schools through the twentieth century. By the late 1960s, blacks still had higher rates of living in deteriorated housing, unemployment, and infant mortal-

ity, and had median family incomes that remained about half that of whites.

The University of Illinois was established and evolved in this context. The first African American man would not graduate from the university until 1900, the first African American woman until 1906. African American undergraduate enrollment slowly climbed throughout the first part of the twentieth century. Their numbers rose from two in 1900 to sixty-eight in 1925, 138 in 1929, and 148 in 1944. Though their numbers multiplied, never did they amount to more than 1 percent of the student population until the late 1960s. In 1966, UIUC could count only ninety-three black freshmen. The next academic year it counted fifty-nine.

Consequently, African American students at Illinois experienced discrimination on and off campus. In the mid-1930s, a university report found that some professors refused to give black students higher than a grade of C. Black men were kept off the basketball team so as not to offend the university's southern competitors. Barred from living in residence halls, black students not living in black Greek fraternity or sorority houses had no option but to live with black families in the North End of Champaign, quite a distance from campus. The campus did not open residence hall housing to black students until 1945.

Despite these barriers, African American students made themselves a part of the campus and took advantage of university life. A few participated in established university organizations, including the glee club, literary societies, and the student newspaper, the *Daily Illini*. Others created parallel organizations to those established by the university or white student groups. In the early 1930s black students formed Cenacle, an honorary society for black students that sponsored plays with black student actors and a book exhibit in the university library featuring black authors. In 1938 black students published the *Scribbler*, "the official voice of the Negro students enrolled in the University of Illinois," and discussed the segregation in Champaign, the debate over voluntary segregation, as well as lighter subjects. In the early 1950s students celebrated Negro History Week with invited speakers, movies, and plays. In this way, black students created social and extracurricular outlets for their artistic interests, social welfare, and racial consciousness. Like blacks in general, black University of Illinois students demanded to be seen *and* heard.

In the mid-twentieth century, black students and their white campus allies demanded positive change on and off campus. Black student alienation, coupled with a growing racial consciousness associated with the Black Power movement, was transformed into activism. In October 1967, black undergraduate and graduate students formed the Black Students Association (BSA). The new organization adopted the motto "We hope for nothing; We demand everything" and linked itself to the Black Power movement. Leaders declared that the BSA would promote solidarity and unity among black students, celebrate and disseminate the positive aspects of black culture, and provide a training ground for political organization and leadership. It soon became the organization through which black students would force the university to recognize and act on black issues. BSA members and sympathetic administrators would play a leading role in diversifying the campus over the next several years.

## Launching the Special Educational Opportunity Program

Responding to public pressure from BSA, white faculty and student allies, and a newly formed interracial Champaign organization called Citizens for Racial Justice, the campus leadership created the Special Educational Opportunities Program (SEOP) in the summer of 1968. Originally intended to include two hundred students, administrators increased the number to five hundred in response to the urgency created by Dr. Martin Luther King Jr.'s assassination in April. Even with that increase, black students still constituted only 3 percent of the undergraduate population. (In 1970, there were just over one million African Americans in Illinois.) Nevertheless, by admitting such a large number of students, SEOP became one of the largest programs in the nation initiated by a predominantly white university to enroll low-income black high school students.

Clarence Shelley was recruited and appointed dean of the program in July 1968. Born and raised in Detroit,

Michigan, Shelley received his bachelor of arts in English and taught English and speech at a Detroit high school for several years before returning to Wayne State University, his undergraduate alma mater, for a master's in educational psychology. Shelley then became a counselor in Wayne State's Higher Education Opportunity Program, where he began his professional focus on diversifying higher education and improving the quality of students' experiences. In his role, Shelley worked with several local high schools to disseminate information about admissions requirements, financial aid, and tutoring. He also worked with students at Wayne State to increase their retention and success rates. Shelley's success in Detroit—which came just as racial tensions were reaching a breaking point in that city—won him wide recognition.

"Black students created social and extracurricular outlets for their artistic interests, social welfare, and racial consciousness. Like blacks in general, black Illinois students demanded to be seen *and* heard."

The Detroit Committee for Student Rights, for example, recognized him for his outstanding achievements in recruiting and retaining African American students at Wayne State. His wealth of experience and knowledge of what was then the very new field of minority recruitment made him the perfect candidate to become the director of the SEOP at the University of Illinois.

According to a UIUC press release issued at the time, Shelley was expected to "supervise campus-wide services to help Negro students achieve academic success" at Illinois. To do so, he focused on all facets of the institution. He pushed staff and faculty to be accountable for student success in and out of the classroom. He pushed black students to treat their education seriously and helped them create ways to sustain themselves scholastically and socially. He pushed colleges and departments to devise policies and programs that would increase student opportunity and success. Without any other staff or resources, Shelley was the go-to person for all things diversity related on campus.

Clarence Shelley

The university scrambled to respond to Shelley's recommendations and to accommodate and enroll the SEOP students. The first order of business was orienting the new recruits to campus. To facilitate this process, the SEOP participants were invited to arrive in Urbana-Champaign one week before other incoming students in the fall of 1968. During that time they and members of BSA lived in Illinois State Residence Hall (ISR), a new and highly coveted dormitory on Green Street. As the SEOP students arrived, it became clear that many tasks remained undone. A number of the new arrivals had not taken the appropriate tests for course placement, others did not have room assignments for the coming semester, and others were still awaiting the details of their financial aid packages. Administrators assured students that the remaining housing and financial aid issues would be resolved either during New Student Week or in the first few weeks of school. On the last day of orientation, campus administrators instructed the SEOP students to move into their permanent room assignments. The general student body was arriving for the beginning of the new academic year, and—awkwardly—many returning students, the majority of them white, expected to move into their previously assigned rooms in the popular ISR building.

A number of female SEOP students were dissatisfied with the size and condition of their permanent rooms. Because of overcrowding, several women were placed temporarily in hall lounges until adequate space could be found for them. In addition, several SEOP recruits suddenly learned that the financial aid packages campus recruiters had promised them (perhaps prematurely) were nonexistent. Many of the new students reacted angrily to these revelations, but SEOP director Shelley and the campus housing staff urged them to remain calm. Shelley also warned the group that they would face disciplinary action if they did not vacate their rooms at ISR.

Word of the negotiations between campus administrators and the SEOP students spread across the black student community, and many, including BSA members among the returning students, began to assemble in the South Lounge of the Illini Union (the student union building) to consider taking action in protest. Though clearly agitated, the students remained calm. At midnight on September 9, while most students remained in the lounge, a group of administrators met with the BSA officers to discuss a course of action. The students refused to leave. Many chose to stay for the sake of unity and to support the women protesting their room assignments. Other women remained because they simply were afraid to walk home so late at night. When rumors of a growing police presence outside the Illini Union spread among the protestors, many students reported they were afraid they would be injured by billy clubs and dogs. Some later recalled being coerced into staying at the Union by BSA members, nonstudents, and older students. Some students simply fell asleep.

Administrators, according to Clarence Shelley, "were trying to decide what to do, arrest them, make them leave, or let them sit all night until they got tired." The decision to arrest the students was not an easy one, but Chancellor Jack Peltason felt compelled to take action. "As much as one hates to call the police the alternative was to let them stay there for a week," Peltason declared. "Then the State will be breathing down our neck, the program will be in trouble, and everybody will say, 'you shouldn't have done it.' So, let's clean it up."[1] The police moved in quickly, and the students, after being assured they would not be injured, left peacefully. By the early morning hours of September 10, the UIUC campus was labeled by the media as the scene of the first student "riot" of the 1968–69 academic year, with almost 250 black students, most of them freshmen, arrested.

The arrests caused a backlash against SEOP on the campus and across the broader Urbana-Champaign community. Letters to the editor in both the student newspaper (the *Daily Illini*) and the Champaign community paper (the *News-Gazette*) chastised the SEOP students for their actions. The *Chicago Tribune*, under the headline "Negroes Riot at U of I: Negroes Go on Rampage after Row," painted a particularly vivid and grossly inaccurate image of the student sit-in. The article estimated the damage at $50,000, a figure far exceeding official estimates. It also offered a false representation of the financial assistance students received, which increased resentment toward SEOP participants: "The students, most of them Negroes from Chicago and East St. Louis—but some of them from as far away as Philadelphia—were to receive free tuition and free room and board." A *Tribune* editorial published the same day went further, using racist imagery to describe the sit-in. The editorial described how "black students and outside supporters went ape" and "swung from chandeliers in the lounges of the beautiful Illini Union." The author lamented that these "slum products" responded to the benevolence of the university and Illinois taxpayers "by kicking their benefactors in the groin." A similarly hostile letter sent to Clarence Shelley called the students " black apes," "black pigs," "dregs of society," and "hoodlums."[2]

On the other hand, defense of the arrested students came from many directions. Black alumni in Chicago organized the Concerned Alumni of Illinois to support the students' grievances. Led by Chicago Aldermen A. A. Rayner and William Cousins Jr., the group requested a meeting with Dean Clarence Shelley and Chancellor Jack Peltason and sponsored a rally in Chicago to support the students. They did not defend the damages that had occurred at the Union (though they pointed out that reports of destruction had been grossly exaggerated), but they did support the students' grievances and were interested in the kind of disciplinary action that would be taken against them. The National Students Organization sent a telegram to UIUC students decrying police conduct on the night of the arrest. The Illinois Graduate Student Association protested the arrests as well.

The arrests also fostered a strong sense of community among the SEOP students and became a unifying catalyst for activism. As Clarence Shelley stated, "A lot of kids who wouldn't have been active spent all their time trying to get even for [the arrests]." With this newly energized and politicized group, black students reaffirmed their connection to the Black Power movement sweeping the nation in the late 1960s and found themselves a place in it. Their mobilization helped transform the UIUC campus.

## Changing the Campus

Black students barreled forward despite the calls from administrators and despite state and federal officials urging them to remain quiet and simply pursue their education on campus. The BSA organized a number of strategy meetings during the fall of 1968, and by February 1969 the organization was ready to engage the university in a process of reform. The BSA launched its campaign by issuing thirty-five demands. These ranged from requests that charges be dropped against participants in the sit-in, to hiring more black staff and faculty, to increasing the number of black graduate students, to increasing the wages of janitorial and food service staff (black and white), to working with the black Champaign community residents in ameliorating racist policies and practices in housing, hiring, and education in the local area. Certain demands—for instance, that the university hire five hundred black professors by 1972—were improbable. However, even outlandish demands highlighted areas for university improvement, and concerned administrators, especially Jack Peltason and Clarence Shelley, worked to improve the situation. In particular, the newly created Faculty-Student Commission on Afro-American Life and Culture, a committee appointed by Peltason that

> "The arrests . . . fostered a strong sense of community among the SEOP students and became a unifying catalyst for activism."

The staff of the Irepodun, the yearbook sponsored by the Black Student Association and African American Cultural Center, 1972. Photo courtesy of Student Life and Culture Archives at the University of Illinois Archives.

included Shelley as a member, worked toward operationalizing some of the more feasible demands.

For example, the campus Afro-American Cultural Program opened in the fall semester of 1969. The center became the cultural and artistic hub for black-oriented activities on campus. While all students were welcome at the new center, the black students' sense of ownership there, together with separatist sentiment of the times, meant that, practically, only black students and black Urbana-Champaign residents used the cultural center facility to its fullest. The center sponsored several culturally focused workshops, including a writer's workshop where students read, learned about, and wrote poetry and essays; a dance workshop where students learned and performed African dances; and manhood/womanhood workshops where issues of gender roles and male/female relationships were discussed. Often, workshop participants would showcase their talents in shows or publications.

The center became the campus locus of the creation and exultation of black culture and the black aesthetic

and was extremely popular with black students. Many considered it a haven from the hostile academic and social atmosphere of the campus. According to former student Jeffrey Roberts, "It was a place you could go and you didn't feel like you were being beat-up on by the university. Every place else you went had such a negative situation. At least for that hour you were at the cultural center you felt like you were in a positive situation where people were reinforcing whatever needs you had."

Members of the UIUC community had made individual attempts to initiate black-centered courses before the SEOP program began, but there was no coordinated effort to organize an African American Studies program until the 1969–70 academic year. According to Clarence Shelley, institutionalizing the black experience in an academic course helped allay black student concerns and frustration on campus. Shelley applauded the efforts and commented, "I think more than any other single activity on campus this program has been responsible for the intellectual and cultural growth of the SEOP students for experiences in light of the social and political pressures to which they have been subjected."

In 1972 a new academic entity, the Afro-American Studies and Research Program, became an institutional reality, with Walter Strong, a graduate student in political science, serving as director. By the late 1970s the Afro-American Studies and Research Program had emerged as a viable new interdisciplinary academic effort. The struggle to put the program on solid footing continued until early in the twenty-first century, when, under the leadership of Chancellor Nancy Cantor, African American Studies began to appoint its own faculty. The program became the Department of African American Studies in 2008.

The black student movement also left a more student-centered legacy on campus. Though nearly fifty years have passed, various events and organizations initiated by students in the Black Power era still exist. Since many black students continue to feel alienated from the larger campus community, these events and organizations provide meaning and acceptance. Black Mom's Day celebrations—begun in the wake of the SEOP program—are still held the same weekend as the university's Mom's Day celebrations. Other activities from that era continue to thrive. These include Black Homecoming, which involves social events and the recognition of returning alumni. In addition, the Black Chorus has grown from its founding with four students to more than one hundred members and continues to perform in churches and educational institutions across the state of Illinois. The first dinner to recognize black SEOP graduating seniors, held in 1972, was later transformed into the Black Congratulatory Ceremony, a more personal event for black graduating seniors, graduate students, and professional students and

their families held as part of the university graduation ceremonies each spring. (Similar ceremonies are now organized as well for Latino/a, Asian American, and Native American students.) The Central Black Student Union still offers an alternative to the university-sponsored student government and a vehicle for students to communicate concerns regarding residence hall living and student life. In recent years, a campus "Black Lives Matter" group has also been formed. It maintains a presence on social media as well as in student affairs. In all of these ways, black students continue to remind the academic and student community of the historical and ongoing need for such organizations and events on campus and the institution's special responsibility to educate black students by supporting their academic work as well as acclimating them to campus and providing a voice for them in the campus community. These concerns are a powerful echo of the goals set forth by BSA almost fifty years ago.

Clarence Shelley retired from the University of Illinois in 2001. During his time at Illinois he served as associate dean of students, dean of students (for eleven years), and associate vice chancellor for student affairs—the first black person to hold any of those positions. Even in retirement he continued to serve the institution as a special assistant to the chancellor. As a tribute to his long and productive career and his tireless efforts to diversify the campus and foster success for all students, Shelley received the Chancellor's Medallion, only the third ever awarded, in 2002. Vice Chancellor for Student Affairs Pat Askew outlined the long list of Shelley's contributions to the University of Illinois but called special attention to his steadfastness in helping the institution weather the tumult of late 1960s and early 1970s. As she stated during the ceremony, "This

> "Black students continue to remind the academic and student community of the historical need for such organizations and events on campus and the institution's special responsibility to educate black students, by supporting their academic work . . . and providing a voice for them in the campus community."

University owes a great debt to Clarence Shelley for having the wisdom and fortitude to face the situation and persist in bringing change."

Shelley himself remembered the late 1960s and early 1970s as a unique time in university history that has had far-reaching consequences. Students have never regained the kind of decision-making power they held in the middle to late twentieth century, but administrators are now much less likely to ignore their concerns. He also believes that the black student movement made the campus more adaptive. Administrators learned how to react to different pressures without the luxury of time and think in new and innovative ways about the nature of higher education. He credits black students with precipitating institutional change that had not previously been entertained: "I have no doubt it was the students and their presentation that made the difference." Indeed, black students pushed the envelope.

Black students during the Black Power era provided a benchmark for change at UIUC. Their time there was short and often intense, but they were able to influence educational policy and programs in ways that no students had done previously or have since. With students and administrators forced into a closer relationship than had existed, black students created space for dialogue on black student issues and concerns. Their dedication ensured that long-lasting changes came out of their collaboration with administrators on different reform initiatives. Their accomplishments demonstrate the power of a social movement within an institution. For Clarence Shelley and many others, "the legacy is about the possibilities,"—the possibilities for change, the possibilities for compromise, and the possibilities for growth.

## Notes

1. Quoted in Williamson, *Black Power on Campus,* 86.
2. See Williamson, *Black Power on Campus,* 90.

## Sources

The one major published work on the subject is Joy Ann Williamson, *Black Power on Campus: The University of Illinois, 1965–1975* (Urbana: University of Illinois Press, 2003). Major archival collections, including oral interviews with former students, administrators, and community members conducted by this author, are in the Student Life and Culture Collection at University of Illinois at Urbana-Champaign.

# PART TWO

# WORLD-CHANGING INVENTIONS

Created and Nurtured on the
University of Illinois Campus,
Then Spread to the World

# Affordable Higher Education

James R. Barrett

From its origins in 1867 as the Illinois Industrial University, the University of Illinois intended to provide the children of the state's common people—"farmers and mechanics"—with the highest quality education at the lowest possible cost. Depending on financial conditions and the level of state support, this has often been a struggle, and the university has embraced a range of financial aid programs as it tried to maintain accessibility to Illinois's flagship institution. By the early twenty-first century, however, these efforts fell short of fulfilling the institution's original goals. As a consequence, the university reached a crisis point.

The Morrill Act (1862), which provided federal support for the establishment of state universities to offer higher education at low or no cost to its citizens, represented a remarkable achievement. It gave birth to mass democratic education at the college and university level; applied the results of this education to the state's economic development; and provided upward social mobility for tens of thousands of students who took advantage of these opportunities. The act explicitly declared the purpose of these universities would be to provide practical education for the children of the "industrial classes"—the states' farmers and manual workers. Historian Allan Nevins called the law, which for the first time committed federal resources to higher education, "a profession of faith in the midst of Civil War" and "an embodiment of the whole democratic dream of the time."[1] In the post–World War II period, the dramatic expansion of higher education at relatively low tuition rates revolutionized not only edu-

ILLINOIS
Industrial University,
URBANA, CHAMPAIGN CO., ILL.

This ~~New~~ State University is now in the _fourteenth_ ~~eleventh~~ year of its progress. It already ranks in numbers and appointments among the first institutions of the country. Its Faculty embraces 25 Professors and Instructors. It has an attendance of about 400 students. Its Buildings, ~~15 in number, embrace two large College Buildings, a large Mechanical and Military Building, a large Chemical Building, including five Laboratories, Veterinary Hall, Green House, etc. Its~~ Library, Scientific Collections, and Scientific Apparatus have been provided by the State on a scale of unusual magnitude.

THE UNIVERSITY EMBRACES FOUR COLLEGES, AS FOLLOWS:

## College of Agriculture.
## College of Engineering.
## College of Natural Science.
## College of Literature.

These Colleges are sub-divided into 14 separate Departments or Schools, affording 14 distinct Courses of Study.

The aim of the University is to unite Practice with Study in all Departments where this is possible, and thus to make Education thoroughly practical, without sacrificing its solid and liberal character.

FALL TERM OPENS SEPTEMBER 11th; WINTER TERM JANUARY 2nd, 1878.

TUITION FREE.—A small fee charged for entrance and incidentals. Open to persons of both sexes, over 15 years of age. For conditions of admission send for circular. Address,

J. M. GREGORY, Regent,
CHAMPAIGN, ILLS.

An early handbill advertising the university

cational levels but also economic development, scientific and technological research, and the creative arts. It is not too much to say that access to institutions like the University of Illinois at Urbana-Champaign created a new, better-educated American society.

Not everyone benefited. Opportunities in higher education opened only gradually for students of color; few African American students attended the university before the 1960s. As late as 1967, in the midst of the civil rights movement, only 372 of 30,400 students on campus were African American. (According to the U.S. Census, the state in 1970 was home to just over one million African Americans.) Data also suggest that the student body at Illinois always included large numbers of relatively elite students, and it is likely that this segment of the student body has increased over the years.[2] As late as the end of the nineteenth century, however, about two-thirds of the student population derived from the "industrial classes."[3] Low tuition rates provided generations of white- and blue-collar youth, those who have literally built the state and its economy, with outstanding educations and a path up in the social structure through much of the late nineteenth and twentieth centuries.

Tuition at Illinois was extremely low and in some cases free for much of its early history. The university's first class (1868) paid $15 per year for in-state students and $20 per year for those from out of state. Those studying in the agriculture, polytechnic, and military departments paid no tuition at all.[4] Tuition remained at $15 per year throughout the 1870s and below $25 per year from 1880 through 1916. Even as they began to rise from that point on, the relatively low rates facilitated a system in which students could pay their own way, through summer employment and part-time employment, often on campus, during the school year.[5] By the World War I era both the YMCA and YWCA operated employment bureaus where undergraduates could secure jobs in businesses around campus, and during the Depression thousands of students secured work through the National Youth Administration.[6] Beginning in the mid-1960s, thousands of students financed their educations in part through the Federal Work-Study Program established in 1964 under the Economic Opportunity Act.

Accessibility to the university has remained a vital concern, and African American students have been particularly vocal on the issue. In 1968, in the wake of massive protests following the assassination of Dr. Martin Luther King Jr., for example, the university launched the Special Educational Opportunities Program, or Project 500, under whose auspices 565 additional African American and Latino students were admitted for the fall semester. Protests by minority students continued, and their proportion of the student body on the campus did continue to rise until the early twenty-first century, when high costs led to a decline.[7] Student protests in 1968 and over the course of the three decades that followed also led to the establishment of ethnic studies programs and cultural houses and, gradually, to a relatively more diverse student body.

In the last decades of the twentieth century, the issue of accessibility made tuition increases a volatile subject. When Governor Richard B. Ogilvie proposed a 70 percent tuition increase in the spring of 1977, four hundred students turned out to protest, but, in fact, the rates had remained low for most of that decade. The tuition increase of $90 per year for in-state tuition in fall of 1977 was the first in five years. By the 1980s, however, tuition was increasing sharply—up 31 percent for freshmen and 46 percent for upperclassmen from 1982 to 1983, and more than doubling from $1,104 to $2,070 between the 1983–84 and 1988–89 academic years. By 1988 Illinois was the second-most-expensive university in the Big Ten, and student trustee Robert Scott Wylie feared that "we're pricing ourselves out of reach of most of the middle class." In the early 1990s, state cuts lead to even more substantial increases.[8] The most dramatic increases, however, came in the early twentieth-first century, as state support for the university declined sharply. This included an increase from $7,042 in 2005–06 to $11,104 in 2011–12. The cost of four years of tuition, room and board, and fees passed the $100,000 mark for in-state students in 2012–13.[9]

Students have employed various forms of financial aid to keep up with the rapidly increasing cost of an education at the University of Illinois. The GI Bill, which provided tuition aid for veterans and their children, underwrote a sharp expansion of the student population at Illinois and elsewhere in the postwar era.[10] In fall 1947, 11,296 GIs were on campus, and as late as 1956, when Korean War veterans were replacing those who had served in World War II, the figure was still over 3,600. In the end, 22,000 veterans received degrees from UIUC during this time period. In addition, financial aid (almost unknown early in the century) allowed thousands of first-generation

college students to enter the University of Illinois, and enrollment expanded enormously from the late 1940s through the 1970s. By 1953 Illinois was the second largest university in the United States, with an enrollment of 18,592: by 1973 it had reached 33,857.[11]

During most of the years when enrollment was expanding most dramatically, the net tuition paid by students increased only modestly: union, corporate, state, federal, and university financial aid allowed families to keep up with such increases. Their efforts helped extend the possibility of a high-quality Illinois education to thousands of working-class youth. In 1964, for example, the State of Illinois provided almost $4.8 million in various forms of aid, while the state's universities and colleges offered about $2 million in scholarships. By 1972 the *Chicago Tribune* estimated that, thanks to these scholarships, just under half of the students in the state's universities paid no tuition at all.[12]

Throughout the late twentieth century, the university tried to match each tuition increase with a proportional increase in financial aid. In 1967–68, 18,448 awards totaled just over $10 million and then rose steeply through the 1970s. Total aid at the Urbana-Champaign campus rose from $42,152,856 in the 1972–73 academic year to $77,511,023 in 1982–83, but the character of aid had begun to shift.[13] The amount of aid coming through student loans doubled in the early 1980s and has continued to make up an increasingly larger proportion of aid in recent years. The campus struggled to maintain an admission standard based on demonstrated achievement and ability rather than on a family's ability to pay, but as increases in scholarship funding declined and the state withdrew support, the task grew harder.

By the early twenty-first century, the balance between rising tuition and rising financial aid became nearly impossible to sustain. State support dropped by 25 percent between 2003 and 2013, and the university, despite a robust fundraising effort, was forced to balance its budget largely through tuition increases. Nearly 100 percent of the increase in the budget for fiscal year 2014, for example, came

> "Tuition at Illinois was extremely low and in some cases free for much of its early history."

Student workers at the university, ca. 1950

those from China represented a substantial proportion of this increase. While the university has maintained close China ties over much of its history, the number of Chinese students has risen dramatically in the past few years. In fall 2014 the university enrolled nearly five thousand students from the Peoples' Republic, the highest number of any university in the country. Since these students pay much higher tuition ($31,000 to $38,000) compared with that of in-state students ($15,600 to $20,600), their tuition and fee dollars help to offset the decline in state support.

Aside from the sometimes complicated matter of helping a very large number of overseas students to integrate and adjust to life and academic work on a huge American campus, the increasing reliance on international students has presented a number of challenges and remains a tenuous strategy even from the perspective of the budget. In the case of Chinese students, for example, a severe economic downturn, as the country began to experience in 2015, or an abrupt change in government policy regarding study overseas could cause a sudden drop in applications. Likewise, as Chinese universities expand and improve in disciplines with the greatest demand, interest in the University of Illinois and other high quality institutions could well diminish.

More important, perhaps, in terms of Illinois students' access to affordable higher education, the financial benefits of the turn to international students come with social costs. And the resulting change in student demographics speaks directly to the university's mission as established under the Morrill Act. As late as 2006, 89 percent of UIUC students came from in state; by 2014 that percentage was down to 71.7 percent. The proportion of African American students has fallen as the number of international students has risen. By 2014 they accounted for about 5 percent of students on campus. (African Americans, meanwhile, make up 15 percent of the state's population.) There may be many reasons for these declines, but one of them is certainly a drop in the "yield" on offers

from a large tuition increase. Revenue from tuition was now almost twice as high as income from state support. By 2013, however, university administrators had concluded that they could not continue to balance the budget by simply raising tuition. Substantial increases in tuition and fees could and apparently did have the effect of excluding some students who met the academic standard but simply could not afford the increasing costs. Other talented students who might otherwise have come to Illinois were leaving the state for institutions where even the nonresident tuition was lower than in-state costs at the university, or for private institutions that offered lavish financial aid packages. At the same time, the demographics of the student body began to change as Illinois became even more socially elite than it had already been. Administrators struggled to respond. The tuition increase for the 2013–14 academic year was the lowest in eighteen years.[14]

One response to this funding crisis has been a striking increase in the proportion of international students on campus. As of 2014, the university ranked second in the country for the number of international students, and

of admission for in-state students, and this is driven at least in part by rising costs. Many families with qualified students have trouble meeting costs and are turning to out-of-state institutions for their educations.[15] Increasing costs are likely one reason that the number of transfer students from community colleges has risen in recent years; families and individual students aim to reduce costs by completing general education requirements at lower-cost institutions. (In 2015 more than twelve hundred community college transfer students were admitted to the University of Illinois.) Rising costs seem also to be reshaping student academic interests. Forced to rely increasingly on loans to finance their studies, many students facing the prospect of large debts are inclined less toward social science, arts, and humanities courses and majors and more toward those that seem to offer the best prospects for postgraduation employment and earnings.

The University of Illinois at Urbana-Champaign continues to offer thousands of students from a wide range of backgrounds the opportunity for an outstanding university education, but for many, this opportunity appears to be in jeopardy. The welter of statistics raises a blunt but extremely important question that brings us back to the university's original mission: Will the University of Illinois remain accessible to the sons and daughters of the state's farmers, workers, and other common people, or will it become primarily a socially elite institution due to increasing tuition costs and the lack of state support?

## Notes

1. Allan Nevins, *The Origins of the Land-Grant Colleges and State Universities: A Brief Account of the Morrill Act of 1862 and Its Results* (Washington, D.C.: Civil War Centennial Commission, 1962), 26. See also Nevins's *The State Universities and Democracy* (Urbana: University of Illinois Press, 1962).

2. J. Gregory Behle, "Educating the Toiling People: Students at the Illinois Industrial University, Spring 1868," in *The Land-Grant Colleges and the Reshaping of American Higher Education*, edited by Roger L. Geiger and Nathan M. Sorber (New Brunswick, N.J.: Transaction, 2013), 73–94; J. Gregory Behle and William E. Maxwell, "The Social Origins of Students at the Illinois Industrial University, 1868–1894," *History of Higher Education Annual* 18 (1998): 93–109.

3. Winton U. Solberg, *The University of Illinois, 1867–1894: American Intellectual and Cultural History* (Urbana: University of Illinois Press, 1968), 234.

4. Solberg, *University of Illinois*, 234 and 111.

5. "Survey of General Tuition and Incidental Fees and Estimated Annual Student Costs Urbana-Champaign Campus [1994]," University Archives Reference File, 1963–, record series 35/3/65, Tuition, University of Illinois Archives.

6. *Daily Illini*, July 1, 1920, October 29, 1920, and October 14, 1938, Illinois Digital Newspaper Collection, UIUC Library, accessed November 23, 2015.

7. See Joy Ann Williamson, *Black Power on Campus: The University of Illinois, 1965–75* (Urbana: University of Illinois Press, 2003), and Williamson's essay in this volume (ch. 1.16).

8. *Daily Illini*, April 11, 1977, Illinois Digital Newspaper Collection, UIUC Library, accessed August 24, 2015; *Chicago Tribune*, April 22, 1983, and July 15, 1988.

9. "Historical Tuition Data" [2015], Office of Public Affairs, University of Illinois at Urbana-Champaign, http://public affairs.illinois.edu/surveys, accessed March 24, 2015. Since tuition rates have varied by class over the past several years, I have used the rate for entering freshmen in order to be consistent.

10. *Daily Illini*, October 5, 1955, Illinois Digital Newspaper Collection, UIUC Library, accessed August 24, 2015.

11. *Daily Illini*, March 25, 1953, Illinois Digital Newspaper Collection, UIUC Library, accessed August 25, 2015; *Farmers' Weekly*, January 4, 1973, Illinois Digital Newspaper Collection, UIUC Library, accessed August 25, 2015.

12. *Chicago Tribune*, February 23, 1964, and February 14, 1972.

13. University of Illinois, *Report of Financial Aid to Students, 1967–68*, December 1968; University of Illinois, *1982–83 Annual Report of Financial Aid to Students*, June 1984.

14. *Daily Illini*, November 5, 2013, http://www.dailyillini.com/article/2013/11/top-ui-administrator-university-cant-afford-to-significantly-raise-tuition, accessed August 25, 2013.

15. Elizabeth Redden, "The University of Illinois at China," *Inside Higher Education*, January 7, 2015, https://www.insidehighered.com/news/2015/01/07/u-illinois-growth-number-chinese-students-has-been-dramatic, accessed August 1, 2015; "When 10% of Frosh at a Flagship Are from China," *Inside Higher Education*, August 4, 2015, https://www.insidehighered.com/quicktakes/2014/08/04/when-10-frosh-flagship-are-china, accessed August 25, 2015.

# Sound on Film

*Alexis Clinebell*

Joseph Tykociner (1877–1969) made numerous contributions to the world in the field of electrical engineering. Tykociner was instrumental in advancing aspects of radio, radar, and zetetics (a field defined by Tykociner as the study of all human knowledge and culture), but his most memorable accomplishment was recording the first example of sound associated with film. Trained as an electrical engineer, Tykociner was part of the London-based Marconi Company team that sent the first radio signal across the Atlantic in 1901. Following this achievement Tykociner worked for both the Polish and Russian governments on radio designs before Ellery B. Paine, head of the University of Illinois Electrical Engineering Department, recruited him in 1921.

In his first year on campus Tykociner stunned the engineering world with a demonstration of the first sound recorded on film. In a short "talkie," his wife Helena said "I will ring" and then hit a bell. Professor Paine then read the Gettysburg Address. Despite the attention focused on Tykociner, many other faculty members participated in his achievement. In addition to suggestions and advice from his fellow electrical engineering colleagues, Tykociner received the crucial photoelectric cell used in the projector that showed his film from Jakob Kunz, a theoretical physicist. Tykociner submitted a patent application for his design on February 1, 1923, but disputes over ownership and patent controls with university president David Kinley delayed approval of the patent until 1926. That lapse in time allowed a competitor to nose ahead of Tykociner and prevented his design from being adopted for commercial use. Nevertheless, Tykociner is considered the "father" of sound on film.

Tykociner remained on the faculty at Illinois until his official retirement in 1946. He and his students continued to develop new products (his innovative antenna design was a significant contribution to radar technology), but he never again garnered the attention he received in 1922 when Helena had delivered "I will ring."

## Sources

For a profile of Tykociner see John B. McCullough, "Joseph T. Tykociner: Pioneer in Sound Recording," *Society of Motion Picture and Television Engineers* 67, no. 6 (August 1, 1958): 520–23. The University Archives also holds all of Tykociner's personal papers.

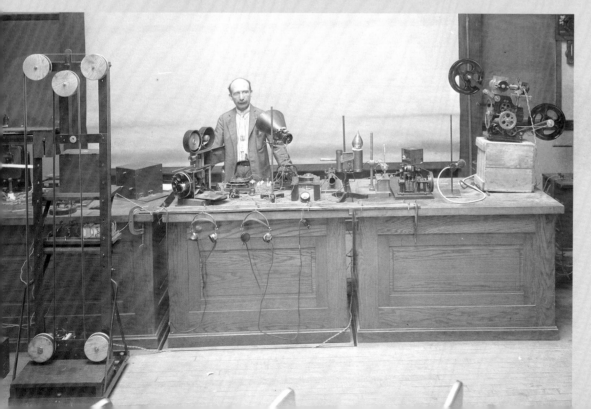

Professor Tykociner and his sound projector

# Inventing Professional Architecture

Bryan E. Norwood

In June 1922, almost two decades after becoming the first black graduate of the University of Illinois School of Architecture, Walter T. Bailey wrote to the program's first graduate and long-time leader Nathan C. Ricker, saying, "If I have made any success at all during the eighteen years of professional practice it has been due to my following the advice you gave."[1] The inclusion of "professional" in Bailey's description of his work is not surprising; it speaks to a fundamental goal that university-based architectural education assumed in its first decades of development and maintained to the present. Since Benjamin Henry Latrobe's attempts at the beginning of the nineteenth century to make "professional" (a term which was routinely used in connection with law and medicine) a fundamental descriptor of American architectural practice,

the term has been used to denote the learned and ethical character of the architect's work. It is this term, perhaps more than any other, that has guided the development of architectural practice in the United States over the past two centuries. The rise and eventual dominance of university-based architectural education over all other paths to the modern architectural profession—a process in which the University of Illinois was heavily involved—is an integral part of this discrete conquest.

When Ricker completed his studies in 1873, he was the first graduate not only of the University of Illinois architectural program but of any university-based architectural program in the United States. However, graduates from the Massachusetts Institute of Technology were only months behind, and eighteen additional ar-

1. Fisher.    4. Parkman.    7. Young.    10.
2. Braucher.  5. Dunaway.    8. Burt.     11. Barnes.
3. Peterson.  6. Clark.      9. Hannsen.  12. Shattuck.

ARCHITECTURAL DRAFTING ROOM.
UNIVERSITY HALL
1888.

Architectural drafting room, 1888

chitectural programs would spring up by the turn of the century. These early years of professional architectural education were marked by a search for the correct model of knowledge. What must the architect know? For Ricker, who shortly after graduating had returned to take charge of the University of Illinois's architecture program (and where he continued to teach until 1916), the search focused primarily on identifying a model of architectural education suited to a part of the country with a rapidly growing demand for buildings of all kinds, but especially for a new architectural type: the skyscraper.

By the middle of the twentieth century, the University of Illinois's architecture program had become one of the largest and most productive in America. American architectural education was entering a new phase, one in which the rapid influx of returning GIs would transform architectural education into a nationally organized project. The department held a conference in 1949 to address this new demand on architectural education, asking the question of what traits and abilities would be necessary for the professional practice of architecture in the second half of the twentieth century.[2] The formidable figure of Turpin C. Bannister presided over the conference's con-

versations. He had just taken over as head of the Department of Architecture and was about to become a key member of a committee organized by the American Institute of Architects (AIA), the profession's premier organization, that would complete a sweeping study of the profession and professional education. The committee's report, *The Architect at Mid-Century*, it is important to note, claimed not to focus merely on "architectural education" but rather on "education for professional practice of architecture." By midcentury, the pattern that would dominate architectural education and consequently professional architecture had been firmly established. Thanks to the efforts of Nathan Ricker and other pioneers, university-based architectural education was considered foundational to the formation of a sizeable professional practice. The model developed at Illinois and other pioneering programs would provide the profession with a consistent body of knowledge and manage the flow of practitioners into the professional field across the United States.

## A Foundation of Technical Proficiency: Education and Credentials

While the sociological and historical definitions of professionalism are many, most point to some combination of expert knowledge, an ethical code, and gatekeeping methods such as schooling, licensing laws, and professional associations. The question of what the exact character of these various professional institutions should be for architects has been a difficult one, as American architects have long struggled to define a precise area of distinct expertise to be defended, particularly as their practice developed in the nineteenth century in relation to builders and engineers. The model for forming a distinct kind of architectural knowledge destined to become the most prominent in the early twentieth-century universities would be that of the design studio (*atelier*) used at the French École des Beaux-Arts. Beginning with the architect Richard Morris Hunt's residency in Paris during the 1840s and 1850s, Americans attended the École (as they called it) at an increasing frequency up through the early decades of the twentieth century. These students brought back ideas (which did not always reflect the total educational mission of the École) about the fundamentality of design and composition in architectural knowledge. Architectural expertise was to be found primarily in the principles of formal composition—such as proportion, arrangement, scale, and axial relations of basic building elements—and character worked out through the medium of drawing. Studio-based education sought to impart these fundamentals. The architecture school at MIT, for example, founded under the guidance of William Ware (who had trained in the atelier of Hunt) was strongly influenced by this model.[3]

The foundations of architectural expertise at the University of Illinois were somewhat different. Rather than a primarily French model, Ricker looked toward a German polytechnic one. One of the preconditions for Ricker's employment as head of the architecture program at the University of Illinois was that, after his graduation in the spring of 1873, he would travel to Europe for six months of further learning, and Ricker chose to spend several of these months at the Bauakademie in Berlin rather than the far more common École des Beaux-Arts. This choice was shaped by the substantial influence of German architectural culture on the Chicago-based architects, most notably the polytechnic-trained Swiss architect Harold M. Hansen, from whom Ricker learned as a student at the University of Illinois, as well as by the university's early commitment to engineering education.[4]

In the first decades of the program at the University of Illinois, courses in design and composition only made up a small percentage of the coursework. Instead, mathematics and physics, geometrical and architectural drawing, the history of architecture, and technical subjects such as materials, mechanics, and construction occupied the most substantial portions of the curriculum. In fact, Ricker for a number of years delayed any design-studio classes until the final year of a student's career, prefer-

ring to emphasize competence in safe and economical construction. Only a gifted few, he thought, would ever be able to move past these basic abilities to pursue the true art of architectural design.[5] The early curriculum of the architectural program at Illinois was thus aimed at meeting the Midwest's functional need for technically proficient, professional architects at a time of rapid industrialization and urban growth.

This focus on technical proficiency squared with the aims of the first credentialing law for architects, which was passed in Illinois in 1897.[6] Ricker had joined forces with his friend Dankmar Adler, the engineering and business-oriented partner of the famed Chicago architect Louis Sullivan, to get the Illinois licensing law passed (something that architects in Illinois and other states had been pushing for since the 1880s). The licensing law, via the process of a three-day examination, attempted to ensure the architect's adequate knowledge about building materials and structure, construction supervision, and mechanical systems (plumbing, heating, and ventilation), as well as his or her ability to make "a preliminary study of a problem" through planning, design, and architectural rendering.[7] The necessity of these credentialing laws was justified to the Illinois State Legislature as important for the health and safety of the general public. Licensing was not primarily a measure of artistic skill; it was measure of necessary competence.

Under the licensing law a state board would regulate access to the title of professional architect. Ricker himself sat on the board from its inception until his retirement from the university in 1916, as the law stipulated that one of the board's five members would be an educator from the University of Illinois. Licensing was initially to be acquired by taking an exam, but Ricker in 1898 was able

> "The early curriculum of the architectural program at Illinois was thus aimed at meeting the Midwest's functional need for technically proficient, professional architects at a time of rapid industrialization and urban growth."

A student aesthetic from the 1880s

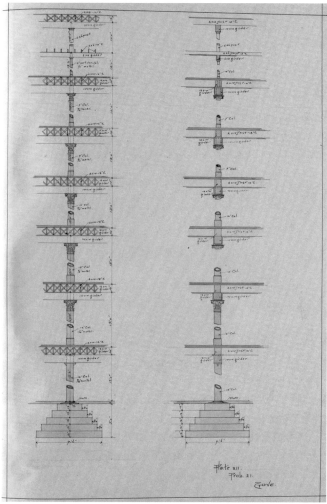

A student technical drawing from the 1880s

to establish the University of Illinois diploma (along with proof of adequate practical experience) as adequate in lieu of the exam, a privilege extended to graduates of other schools in 1902. The university was thus established as a key instrument for assuring the state that a professional architect had the proper technical skills.

## The Polytechnic Dilemma: Design and Construction

From the start of the architectural program at the University of Illinois, Ricker and his colleagues puzzled over the relationship between technical competence and the aesthetics of architectural design. The program's earliest curriculum stated that its aim was to provide education for those aspiring to the "profession of Architect and Builder," conflating two practices that self-styled architectural professionals since Latrobe had often been at pains to distinguish. While builders were technically proficient, they most often worked from pattern books and copied existing works of architecture when they built. The architect, in contrast, Latrobe and others argued, acted as

an intermediary between client and builder by producing drawings of the proposed project. Further, because professional architects would know the fundamental principles of design, they would be able to produce unique buildings that nonetheless exhibited proper character and style.

Only a few years into its existence, the School of Architecture's curriculum acknowledged the distinction between architect and builder by redefining the existing four-year course as being for the "profession of Architecture" and establishing a separate one-year program for master builders. At the same time, rapid developments in steel and high-rise construction techniques in nearby Chicago (swiftly rebuilding after the devastating fire of 1871) had vastly increased the demand for individuals with technical knowledge of construction. The builder, if he or she were to participate in the management of the construction of these large projects, could no longer be educated through a bit of schooling and apprenticeship. In 1891, the builder's course was thus converted into a parallel four-year course in "architectural engineering," a term that Ricker himself seems to have coined.[8] As the 1891–92 catalog noted, this course was "intended for those students preferring the mathematical and structural side of architecture to its artistic side, and for those who wish to acquire a thorough knowledge of iron and steel construction as it is now executed in architectural structure." Architectural education was divided between a program that emphasized design and one that emphasized the technical aspects of the structure of buildings.

But if the technically focused architectural engineer was to be educated in a distinct program and perhaps even enter a distinct profession, where would design fit into his or her training? And how much technical education should be required for the design-oriented architect? Fiske Kimball, the influential architectural historian and museum director best known for establishing architectural education at the University of Virginia in the 1920s and later leading the Philadelphia Museum of Art, taught at the University of Illinois for the single academic year, 1912–13. In a paper on the school, written while he was living in Urbana-Champaign, Kimball noted that the division of the architecture and architectural engineering programs was a fundamental characteristic of the school and that the school, since its beginning, had a stronger affinity for the approach of architectural engineering: "The science has been really better established than the art," he observed.[9] Nonetheless, in the view of Ricker and his colleagues, these two programs should be properly understood as two aspects of a large, integrated project. While the architectural program aimed at "thoughtful and beautiful" design, architectural engineering aimed at "scientific determination and verification of structural methods." That is, "the subjects studied must be largely the same, but the emphasis and method of treatment are and should be different."[10] Architects and architectural engineers both studied architecture, but the former approached it as an issue of design and aesthetics (in other words, as an art) and the latter an issue of measurable structural adequacy (as a science).

Architectural engineering faced a series of existential crises starting in the late 1910s, as the distinction of engineering fields (such as structural, mechanical, and civil) and architecture was being further articulated. Disagreements between architecture and engineering over control of particular courses in the architectural engineering curriculum erupted at the University of Illinois, as at many other schools.[11] Architecture departments that had been founded in engineering schools across the country (as Illinois's had been) began fighting to form their own separate divisions within the university. In addition—and perhaps more important—architectural engineering would come to have an increasingly difficult time finding a proper method for credentialing.[12] Architectural engineering graduates were not going to be licensed as pure engineers (they had their own programs), but many questioned whether architectural licensing boards were fit to judge the technical competence of an architectural engineer. If architectural engineering was the science, and architectural design the art, could their two types of knowledge be measured by the same standard?

"Disagreements between architecture and engineering over control of particular courses in the architectural engineering curriculum erupted at University of Illinois, as at many other schools."

## History: The Foundation of Professional Architectural Knowledge

The distinction of the architecture and architectural engineering programs was softened in the 1931 curricula, the same year the architecture program shifted from the College of Engineering to the newly formed College of Fine and Applied Arts. The department began to offer

The Ricker Architecture Library. Reproduction rights granted courtesy of the University of Illinois at Chicago, University Library.

a single degree in architecture with different "options": design, construction, and general. The curricula for these options began as one and then slowly diverged in upper years. This shift toward specialization internal to architecture would, however, not provide a simple solution to the dilemma that fractured architecture between a technical and a design discipline, between a science and an art.

The architect has for more than two millennia often been described as a well-rounded generalist, a person versed in a variety of subjects who could bring all these issues together in one of the most fundamental of human acts: building shelter. And at the Department of Architecture's 1949 conference on the future of architectural education, several of the discussants took just such a position on the practice and the future of the architectural profession. What was primarily needed from the schools,

they said, was general, well-rounded architectural education; specialization was something that would naturally develop once an individual entered the practice. But how could one give definition to the broad education that the architect needed?

Ricker taught the architectural history courses throughout his tenure at the school and consistently held that the library in the architecture school was fundamentally important. Concerned about the lack of quality texts—technical, historical, and aesthetic—available to his students, Ricker translated numerous volumes from French and German (more than thirty completed in his lifetime).[13] The vast majority of these texts were historical, and his devotion to this task only became more fervent later in his life. One of Ricker's publications was even a short treatise on how to expand the architectural area of the Dewey decimal system, and his "Syllabus of the History of Architecture," which he used in teaching for a number of years, is organized by this system of classification. The library and historical education were fundamentally intertwined.

Nathaniel Curtis, who taught briefly at Illinois but is best known for his book *Architectural Composition* and his founding role in the architectural school at Tulane University, wrote a short text while teaching at Illinois, "The Ricker Library: A Familiar Talk to Students of Architecture in the University of Illinois," that aimed to convince students of the primary importance of reading and of the posthumously named library. The Architecture Department had noted in a 1914–15 report that "the Architectural Library is the laboratory for the department," and Curtis echoed this conception of the lab when he said that while architecture students in Europe had the great works of architectural history immediately available to them, in America this kind of knowledge could simply not be gained from the exterior field.[14] The library was the place American students must spend time learning the history of their profession.

Of course, establishing a relation to architectural history through study did not simply determine the form of architecture a student would produce. Two of the most well-known students of the program, Henry Bacon (attended 1884–85) and Walter Burley Griffin (graduated 1899), went on to produce wildly different types of architecture. Bacon, most famous for his design of the Lincoln Memorial in Washington, D.C., worked with the historical forms of classical styles. Griffin, who worked with Frank Lloyd Wright and who, with Marion Mahony Griffin, designed the Australian capital city of Canberra, no doubt felt more of the influence of Ricker's technical training at the University of Illinois as he attempted to participate in the modern break from the historical styles of the past. Nonetheless, both the attitudes—working with or break from—are rooted in an understanding that what one does is necessarily related, by repetition or disjunction, to history.

In remarks at the 1949 conference, Rexford Newcomb, the founding dean of the College of Fine and Applied Arts, took a tangential route into this question of fundamental professional architectural knowledge that would underlie any specialization. Lawyers and doctors, two of the most successful modern professions, he said, had developed a certain social consciousness. Architects had not. He described a need for architects "to detach themselves from their technical subjects and see the common theme running through their various fields so that" they could form "an integrated understanding of their world, their relationships to their own and other families, their place in the body politic, and their responsibilities as citizens of a democracy."[15] A holistic understanding of the profession of architecture required one to see the place of architecture in the broader world. Newcomb's way of answering this need—through education in architectural history—followed in the footsteps of his teacher and mentor Ricker. As Newcomb had written of his history classes thirty years earlier, "The student . . . learns to see that architecture is a primal necessity and also a mental or spiritual satisfaction, that it is a perfect index to the life and thought of a people."[16]

By the mid-twentieth century, the path to professional architecture through university-based education had been

Student architectural sketches

firmly established, and its hybrid technical and artistic character owed a great deal to the pioneering architecture educators at the University of Illinois. The architecture library became one of the main gateways to expertise in this profession. While the binding of the system of professional architectural knowledge to the library as much to the drafting room was certainly not a new idea, it was one that the University of Illinois gave particular importance in the American university context. It was in the library, this intellectual laboratory full of texts and drawings, histories and plans, that the student and aspirant to the profession—immersed in the works and theories of great architects of the past and present—could find their profession's clandestine knowledge, a knowledge that was more than mere building.[17]

## Notes

1. Letter from W. T. Bailey to Nathan Clifford Ricker, June 7, 1922, in "Golden Anniversary Greetings, 1872–1922," Nathan C. Ricker Papers, 1875–1925, box 1, University of Illinois Archives.

2. "Conference on Architectural Design Proceedings," February, 1949, box 1, University of Illinois Archives.

3. Gwendolyn Wright, "History for Architects," in *The History of History in American Schools of Architecture, 1865–1975*, edited by Gwendolyn Wright and Janet Parks (New York: Temple Hoyne Buell Center for the Study of American Architecture, Princeton Architectural Press, 1990), 20.

4. Paul Kruty, "Nathan Clifford Ricker: Establishing Architecture at the University of Illinois," in *No Boundaries: University of Illinois Vignettes*, edited by Lillian Hoddeson (Urbana: University of Illinois Press, 2004), 5–6; Roula Mouroudellis Geraniotis, "German Architectural Theory and Practice in Chicago, 1850–1900," *Winterthur Portfolio* 21, no. 4 (1986): 293–306.

5. Roula Geraniotis, "The University of Illinois and German Architectural Education," *Journal of Architectural Education* 38, no. 4 (1985): 17.

6. Paul Kruty, "A New Look at the Beginnings of the Illinois Architects Licensing Law," *Illinois Historical Journal* 90, no. 3 (1997): 154–72.

7. The examination schedule is reproduced in Kruty, "A New Look," 162.

8. Andrew Saint, *Architect and Engineer: A Study in Sibling Rivalry* (New Haven, Conn.: Yale University Press, 2007), 451.

9. Fiske Kimball, "University of Illinois: The Department of Architecture; Development, Conditions, Ideals" (Urbana, 1913), 6. A copy can be found in box 14, folder "Annual Reports #1 (1910–15)," Architecture Department Subject File, 1910–1959, University of Illinois Archives. Fiske Kimball, "American Architectural Schools: The University of Illinois," ca. 1913, box 112, folder 2, Fiske Kimball Papers, Philadelphia Museum of Art, Archives.

10. Kimball, "Development, Conditions, Ideals," 5.

11. Correspondence in folder "Architectural Engineering," box 1, Architecture Department Subject File, 1910–1959, University of Illinois Archives.

12. "Conference on Architectural Design Proceedings," 12.

13. Christopher J. Quinn, "Nathan Clifford Ricker: Translator and Educator," *Arris* 11 (2000): 40–54.

14. Nathaniel Cortlandt Curtis Papers, Manuscripts Collection 5, box 10, folder 4, Louisiana Research Collection, Howard-Tilton Memorial Library, Tulane University.

15. "Conference on Architectural Design Proceedings," 48.

16. Department of Architecture Annual Report, 1918–19, box 14, folder "Annual Reports #2 (1915–20)," Architecture Department Subject File, 1910–1959, University of Illinois Archives.

17. I would like to thank Paul Kruty for comments on an earlier draft of this essay.

## Sources

Nathan Ricker's papers and a number of his translations are in the University of Illinois Archives, and the Ricker Library of Architecture and Art contains a full set of Ricker's translated texts. Other archival material can be found in the Architecture Department Subject File, the Conference on Architectural Design, and the Ricker Centennial File.

Key texts on Ricker and the early years of the University of Illinois include Roula Geraniotis, "The University of Illinois and German Architectural Education," *Journal of Architectural Education* 38, no. 4 (1985): 15–21; Christopher J. Quinn, "Nathan Clifford Ricker: Translator and Educator," *Arris* 11 (2000): 40–54; Paul Kruty, "Nathan Clifford Ricker: Establishing Architecture at the University of Illinois," in *No Boundaries: University of Illinois Vignettes*, edited by Lillian Hoddeson (Urbana: University of Illinois Press, 2004), 3–14; and Alan K. Laing, *Nathan Clifford Ricker 1843–1924: Pioneer in American Education* (Champaign: Building Research Council, 1973).

Rexford Newcomb's papers reside at the University of Illinois Archives. The preface to *The Midwest in American Architecture*, edited by John S. Garner (Urbana: University of Illinois Press, 1991), ix–xv, provides a short biography of Newcomb.

Fiske Kimball's papers at the Philadelphia Museum of Art contain material related to his brief time at the University of Illinois, as do the Nathaniel Cortland Curtis Papers in the Louisiana Research Collection at Tulane University.

Additional information on the context of licensing laws can be found in Paul Kruty, "A New Look at the Beginnings of the Illinois Architects Licensing Law," *Illinois Historical Journal* 90, no. 3 (1997): 154–72, and Sibel Bozdoğan Dostoğlu, "Towards Professional Legitimacy and Power: An Inquiry into the Struggle, Achievements and Dilemmas of the Architectural Profession through an Analysis of Chicago, 1871–1909," PhD diss., University of Pennsylvania, 1982.

The context of professionalization in architecture is dealt with at length in Mary N. Woods, *From Craft to Profession: The Practice of Architecture in Nineteenth-Century America* (Berkeley: University of California Press, 1999).

# The Hillel Foundation

## The Invention of University Diversity

*Nicholas Hopkins*

Jewish students and faculty have not always been welcome at the University of Illinois. Even though there had been a Jewish community in Champaign County since before the Civil War, campus leaders generally believed, as Dean of Men Thomas Arkle Clark wrote in 1920, that "this is a Christian country, established along Christian traditions and Christian principles." The university's duty, Clark believed, was "to uphold these traditions and maintain these principles, even when they may be opposed by foreigners or by those who would wipe out all our Christian traditions."

Given this attitude, it is not surprising that Benjamin Bing, who graduated in 1888, was the only student to identify himself publicly as Jewish prior to 1895. Jewish students, "foreigners," and others who did not fit Clark's definition of who belonged at Illinois faced enormous challenges: how to make a place for themselves within the campus community and, more important, how to raise the university's definition of itself from a parochial one rooted in religion and nationalism to a more universal view that would be more compatible with the academic pursuit of truth. The creation of the Hillel Foundation in 1923 was one answer to this question.

The first Jewish student group at the University of Illinois, *Ivrim* (a Hebrew word meaning "Hebrews"), was organized in 1907 by Isaac Kuhn, a successful Champaign clothier who had studied for his bar mitzvah at the Hebrew Union College (Reform Jewish seminary) in Cincinnati. A prominent local businessman, Kuhn was active in B'nai B'rith and sought out ways for young Jewish people in the community to connect with their heritage. While Ivrim was a student group, it

Hillel members collect food for war refugees, ca. 1950

also reached out to Jewish community members (such as newly arrived Jacob Zeitlin of the English Department, the first Jewish member of the faculty) and found many supporters on campus. (Campus Catholics—similarly dismissed in the past by the university's Protestant leadership—had organized a similar student group two years earlier.) Ivrim reorganized itself as a chapter of the national Menorah Society in 1912 and concentrated on the promotion of Jewish learning, but the campus community remained indifferent to its presence. Champaign County lacked a full-time rabbi, and campus facilities such as the library and tennis courts were routinely closed on Sundays.

This situation changed dramatically in 1923 when Benjamin M. Frankel, a newly ordained rabbi from Peoria, accepted a half-time appointment as rabbi for Sinai Temple in Champaign (where Kuhn was a leading member). Six feet four inches tall and a magnetic speaker, Frankel reached beyond his congregation to engage Jewish students. He quickly became convinced of the need for a Jewish religious and social community on campus, and he established the Hillel Foundation to meet that need. Named after a first-century sage, Hillel championed Jewish culture and religion. Rejecting the goal of assimilation, Frankel and his colleagues offered religion classes, organized forums on public issues affecting Jewish Americans, and sponsored a magazine aimed at students. Hillel won the sponsorship of Jewish community leaders in Chicago as well as Jewish service organizations, most prominently, B'nai B'rith. At the urging of the organization's leaders, including Isaac Kuhn, B'nai B'rith awarded Frankel $25,000 in 1924, both to support his work at Illinois and to establish a Hillel branch at the University of Wisconsin. The next year at the B'nai B'rith central convention, Frankel persuaded the group to incorporate Hillel into its organization. This step triggered a $1 million grant that would be used over the next five years to expand Hillel to universities in Ohio, Michigan, and Southern California.

With Hillel's establishment at Illinois and at peer institutions across the Midwest, Jewish culture and Jewish students would become an active and visible part of campus and university life. Using the tradition of religious activism on campus to its advantage, the Hillel Foundation took its place alongside Methodist, Catholic, and other Christian organizations that had previously established themselves. Hillel also joined these groups in offering credit-bearing classes to students. Rabbi Frankel's efforts created a space for Jewish students and Jewish culture at Illinois. More important, Hillel put into practice the idea that public universities are not defenders of "Christian principles" but are communities where all people and the ideas they offer, regardless of their origin, should be welcome.

## Sources

Winton U. Solberg, "The Early Years of the Jewish Presence at the University of Illinois," *Sources: Religion and American Culture: A Journal of Interpretation* 2, no. 2 (Summer 1992): 215–45. The University Archives also holds a collection of the campus publication, *Hillel Post*.

# Clarence W. Alvord

## The Illinois Historical Survey and the Invention of Local History

Robert Michael Morrissey

I n 1918 a reporter from the *New York Times* visited the fourth floor of Lincoln Hall on the University of Illinois campus to witness for himself the cutting edge of historical scholarship. In a suite of five rooms, a staff of researchers, along with five or six typists and other "busy persons," were working away at their desks, searching through vast storage rooms, sorting through tall stacks of materials. Although the reporter noted that they could have been mistaken for employees of "a big insurance office" with their "filing cases and card indexes and typewriters and dictaphones," in fact these people were professors, graduate students, and research associates of the Department of History. To the *New York Times* reporter, who was accustomed to thinking of historians as solitary individuals laboring with piles of dusty books, the activity taking place on the top floor of Lincoln Hall was remarkable. It was, one of the researchers declared, "a history laboratory," or even "a history factory."[1]

But the "up-to-date" offices of the historians in Lincoln Hall were just part of what made them so impressive. For in addition to their innovative and collaborative *methods*, the *Times* reporter noted, these historians were exploring an unusual and revolutionary *subject* of study. Rather than the conventional topics U.S. historians were pursuing at the time—European civilization, the American Revolution, nineteenth-century nation building—these historians were studying local history, applying all of their innovative methods to a nearly comprehensive study of Illinois and the Midwest. Their project had various components. First, they were assembling a massive archive

Clarence Alvord

of primary materials related to the history and culture of the state. These first-person accounts and documents were subsequently edited, annotated, and published as the *Illinois State Historical Collections*. Second, they were editing the *Mississippi Valley Historical Review*, a new scholarly journal dedicated to gathering and publishing the latest historical research focused on the West (a term which referred at that time to all of the territory west of the Appalachians). Third, they were compiling a six-volume, comprehensive history of the state of Illinois that they planned to release as part of the celebration of the first hundred years of statehood: the *Centennial History of Illinois*. And finally, many of the individuals on the team were writing their own monographs on the history of the state and region. Their intention was to demonstrate the national significance of events taking place in the North American interior. All of these efforts were being carried out using the latest "scientific" methods of historical scholarship. Their publications were meticulously researched and sourced, and their investigations led them far beyond the papers of elite leaders to explore evidence related to the economy, family life, race relations, and technology. Their approach neatly mirrored the rapidly professionalizing historical enterprise that was appearing at major universities in both Europe and the United States.

At the helm of these many projects was Clarence W. Alvord (1868–1928), an American historian whose hugely productive career at the University of Illinois lasted from 1901 until 1920. As the *Times* reporter noted, "The vision and initiative that built up this office, the judgment and tact that keep it going, the kindliness and genial humor that make it the pleasantest work place on the campus—belong to Clarence W. Alvord." Other American historians of Alvord's generation have gained greater celebrity, especially the Wisconsin historian Frederick Jackson Turner, who is remembered today as the author of the "frontier thesis," the idea that America was shaped by westward expansion. But while Turner urged Americans to pay attention to regional patterns in our history and particularly to recognize the significance of histories that occurred away from the Eastern Seaboard, Alvord and his colleagues at Illinois created an entirely new historical infrastructure for telling the history of the early West. From their busy hive, which they called the "Illinois Historical Survey," Alvord and his colleagues helped to reshape the understanding of what history is, even as they set new standards for historical scholarship and archival practice.

Although Alvord was celebrated by the *Times* as the true star of local history in 1918, the university's rise to eminence in the history profession was powered by several people working in an important moment in the development of American higher education, as well as the history discipline more specifically. It began in 1894, when Evarts B. Greene (1870–1947) became the first full-time instructor in history at the university. As a graduate of Harvard and a veteran of postgraduate study in Germany, Greene certainly had adopted the "scientific" mission that characterized the newly professionalizing discipline of history at the end of the nineteenth century, which was to understand "the past as it really was." But in the University of Illinois Greene found a campus where liberal and humanistic study was still undeveloped in favor of more practical education. As one overview of the early years of the History Department at Illinois tells it, this was a time when campus tours for prospective professors were as likely to feature Illini Nellie, "the world champion Brown Swiss cow," as they were to feature a stop at the library.

A son of missionaries, Greene was prepared for a career in proselytizing, and he earnestly embraced the challenge of bringing the serious academic study of history to Illinois. As part of his efforts, he worked to develop the fledgling historical institutions in the state. The Illinois State Historical Library had been founded in 1889 to preserve and publish materials about the history of the state. In 1899 Greene helped create the Illinois State Historical Society. These new institutions were part of a wider trend of historical organizations founded in the midwestern states to promote historical work, education, and commemoration. The most sophisticated efforts were in Wisconsin, where Lyman C. Draper and Reuben Gold Thwaites had been collecting and publishing historical documents and collections since the mid-nineteenth century. Emulating this kind of activity, the Illinois State Historical Library published the first volume of its *Collections* in 1903.

While important, these beginnings of historical work in Illinois were not so significant to a wider academic conversation outside the state. The first products of the Illinois State Historical Library were what professional academic historians of that time would have termed antiquarian and amateurish. Soon, however, forces converged to transform these humble beginnings into one of the most important historical projects in America. Having served previously as president of Northwestern University, Edmund J. James was already a member of the board of trustees of the Illinois State Historical Library when he became the University of Illinois's president in 1904. The following year, hearing of the discovery of old French documents in St. Clair and Randolph Counties, he appointed a thirty-seven-year-old history instructor, Clarence W. Alvord, to check them out.

This assignment could not have been more fortuitous for Alvord, who was at the time languishing in a kind of professional stall. Born in Massachusetts, Alvord had graduated from Williams College, taught briefly at Phillips Andover Academy, and then moved to Berlin, where he was trained in the new scientific history. Returning to the United States, Alvord began doctoral studies at the University of Chicago but left this pursuit for a job at the University Laboratory High School in Urbana, today's "Uni High." Greene soon tapped him to be an instructor of European and Renaissance history at the university, a job which was probably no match for his ambition as a researcher. Sending Alvord on the archival reconnais-

sance in 1905, James may have recognized Alvord's potential, or he may have chosen Alvord simply because he had the language skills to make sense of the old French documents. Regardless, Alvord's trip to St. Clair County changed both his career and the practice of history at the University of Illinois.

Alvord realized that the documents in the archives of Randolph and St. Clair Counties were significant windows into the earliest colonial history of the Midwest. They made up one of the most extensive collections of colonial records from any colonial region in the United States outside the original thirteen British colonies. He quickly publicized his discovery and its significance to various audiences—the American Historical Association, the Chicago Historical Society, and, of course, the Illinois State Historical Library and Society. All of this impressed James and Greene, who were instrumental in getting Alvord a job as editor of the fledgling Illinois Historical Collections. With new purpose, Alvord completed his doctorate in history at the University of Illinois in 1908 and was promoted to assistant professor. In 1907 he published the first of his many edited volumes in the *Illinois Historical Collections*, an edition of the old French records he had found in 1905 in southern Illinois. As his colorful introduction to this volume makes clear, he had found his calling. As a true scientific historian, he would "tell the story as it is narrated by those who took part in these events" and "remain uninfluenced by prejudice for or against either parties or men."[2] Over the next few years he would totally immerse himself in this work, taking the fledgling history enterprise begun at the Illinois Historical Society and State Library and transforming it into something unique and remarkable at the university.

Alvord was indeed a visionary. In 1907 he wrote an essay outlining his plan for a comprehensive historical initiative for the state. This would involve, as he put it, "systematic labor of many minds working along well-planned

> "Alvord realized that the documents in the Randolph and St. Clair County archives were significant windows into the earliest colonial history of the Midwest."

lines for a number of years." The biggest immediate need for the "scientific" historian was to assemble sources, particularly for the colonial period, which were scattered in archives in France, Britain, Spain, and other far-flung locales. As Alvord wrote, "Strange it is, that although we can lay our hands on all the material for the history of the landing of the Pilgrim fathers in any good library, there is not a man who knows all the sources for the story of an event of equal importance, the conquest of the Northwest by George Rogers Clark."[3] In 1909 the ambition to collect all relevant materials for Illinois history was realized in the founding of the Illinois Historical Survey, with Alvord as the director. Alvord quickly scaled up the ambitions of the *Illinois Historical Collections* project. He organized the assembly and editorial work necessary to publish fourteen new volumes of the series between 1907 and 1920, and he maintained this rapid pace of publication by sending copyists and researchers to libraries in Washington, D.C., Paris, Seville, and London to gather more documents. Though only a small fraction of documents in its collection would ever be published, the "survey" now provided for history what other newly formed agencies—the Illinois Natural History Survey and Illinois Geological Survey, for instance—provided for other subject areas in the state: a center for serious and comprehensive study.

Alvord also hired assistants locally to manage his growing projects. Solon Buck, a recent PhD from Harvard, was teaching at Indiana University when Alvord hired him to his staff. Theodore Calvin Pease had earned his doctorate from the University of Chicago. Both Buck and Pease would go onto distinguished academic careers: Buck eventually became the first archivist of the National Archives in Washington, D.C., and Pease would publish widely on the history of Illinois and teach at the university until 1948. Meanwhile, research associates and Alvord's own graduate students also assisted the work of the survey. These included Clarence E. Carter, Paul C. Phillips,

> "Alvord's cosmopolitanism and broad vision helped him to see the project of 'local history' in a wider national and even transnational context."

Wayne E. Stevens, and Louise Phelps Kellogg. In addition to those he hired, Alvord collaborated with newly arrived faculty members at Illinois. Among many university faculty members who contributed to the work of the Illinois Historical Survey were historians and economists Charles Cole, John Mabry Mathews, Charles Manfred Thompson, and Ernest Ludlow Bogart.

Alvord and this team brought an important and completely new and professional sensibility to the work of local history. A native of the East, Alvord must have had no particular passion or concern for the history of Illinois when he began his work assembling and publishing historical documents. In fact, he was downright resentful of the kind of antiquarianism that characterized the work of many historical societies, charging that most of their work was "worthless," consisting of "personal recollections of the burning of the First Congregational Church, or of a corn-husking bee of olden times."[4] Alvord's ideal of "scientific history" would go far beyond such "mental children." The key for him was to tie—as Turner had done a generation earlier—the history of midwestern locales to broader themes in human experience. Alvord's cosmopolitanism and broad vision helped him see the project of "local history" in a wider national and even transnational context. "The situation of Illinois, historically and geographically considered," he wrote, "makes it a component part of three distinct and important regions and has joined its fate with the commercial and political development of four great powers. Its history can only be written as a part of the history of the St. Lawrence valley, the Old Northwest, and the valley of the Mississippi. At one time or another France, England, Spain, and the United States have possessed or sought sovereignty over it. It is this pivotal position of the territory, now known as the state of Illinois, which makes its history so well worth the serious consideration of students and which prevents the subject from being merely local and antiquarian."[5] Although the project of the Historical Survey and the *Illinois Historical Collections* was state history, Alvord never accepted the state's boundaries as the limits of his work, and he was always careful to place his local subjects in the widest possible context.

For Alvord, as for many professional historians of the period, the most important context for understanding

Illinois in the early twentieth century was undoubtedly as part of "the west." Frederick Jackson Turner's 1893 address, "The Significance of the Frontier in American History," had argued against the assumption that American culture was an inheritance from European traditions as well as the idea that midwestern societies derived from political and social developments on the East Coast. Turner posited that American culture derived from Americans' encounter with the "free land" of the West. For people like Alvord this idea provided a wholly new way of thinking about the development of American culture and exceptionalism. This framework gave Alvord an organizing principle to guide all of his projects on Illinois and western history.

The state history projects in Illinois were not unique. Following Wisconsin's lead, a number of government agencies and university history departments across the Old Northwest were simultaneously engaged in similar projects of collecting and publishing historical materials in the early 1900s, and a generation of newly professionalized historians were at work in these institutions. In 1907 many of these people came together at a conference in Omaha. Fueled by Turner's arguments about the significance of their region in American history and increasingly alienated from the East Coast–dominated American Historical Association, they founded the Mississippi Valley Historical Association (MVHA), the first national scholarly society devoted exclusively to American history. Alvord was a key figure in this movement, and he became the second president of the organization in 1908. The Illinois historian remained prominent in the organization. In 1913 Alvord founded the group's new scholarly journal, the *Mississippi Valley Historical Review*. An immediate rival of the more general *American Historical Review*, Alvord's journal was headquartered at the Illinois Historical Survey, making it yet another in his suite of projects.

Of all of Alvord's many achievements, the *Mississippi Valley Historical Review* has had the widest and most lasting legacy. The MVHA is now known as the Organization of American Historians, the preeminent professional organization for historians of the United States. It boasts thousands of members who travel to its annual meetings from schools and universities in all fifty states as well

as from overseas. Both its membership and the extent of its programming rival those of the American Historical Association, the umbrella group that represents all professional historians in the United States. In addition, Alvord's journal, renamed the *Journal of American History* in 1964, is widely recognized as the journal of record in American history. It annually publishes original scholarly articles and hundreds of book reviews covering all aspects of the American past.

But if these are the most important legacies of Alvord's work, they were probably not, in his view, the most important projects of his career or of the "history laboratory" that he had assembled. In 1913 Alvord was tapped by the Illinois Centennial Commission to organize, edit, and co-author a six-volume, comprehensive history of Illinois from the colonial period through its first hundred years. As Alvord told an associate, this would be a landmark piece of scholarship and would "make the reputations of a great many men that are connected with it."[6] Indeed, Alvord had an almost utopian vision for what this project would be—"a history of Illinois that would be one of the greatest contributions to the knowledge of humanity ever produced."[7]

As in all his other projects, in the centennial history Alvord relied on two things: collaboration and relentless hard work. He delegated each of the volumes to a different Illinois scholar. Alvord himself wrote the volume on Illinois colonial history; Buck wrote *Illinois in 1818*; Pease wrote *The Frontier State;* Cole wrote *Illinois in the Era of the Civil War;* Illinois economists Bogart and Thompson wrote *The Industrial State;* and Bogart and Mathews wrote the concluding volume on the generation leading up to the centennial in 1918. Pease also wrote a brief one-volume history of Illinois to synthesize the whole.

Organizing this project on a tight deadline produced many challenges. It is no surprise that the *Times* reporter

"In 1913, Alvord was tapped by the Illinois Centennial Commission to organize, edit and co-author a six-volume, comprehensive history of Illinois from the colonial period through its first hundred years."

who visited Alvord in 1918 described the Illinois Historical Survey as a busy hive of activity. Missing from this description, however, was the fact that much of the *Centennial History* project ran far behind schedule. Occupied with other projects, most of the authors of the volumes received immense help from research associates—particularly women who were largely barred from faculty positions. These included Louise Phelps Kellogg and Frances Helen Relf, who drafted major parts of the history but who received little credit for their work.

Even as it ran past the deadline, the centennial project took a major toll on Alvord himself. With all of his commitments, Alvord took to working late into the night, drinking pots of coffee and smoking cigars at his desk in Lincoln Hall. Having just finished his two-volume study *Mississippi Valley in British Politics*, a major study which was awarded the Loubat Prize for the best work on American history, Alvord needed a break. Instead, he only increased his pace. Still, by 1918, the deadline for the project, only one volume had been published, and Alvord himself was only beginning to write his own. As John Hoffmann has noted, all of this work severely compromised Alvord's health.[8]

The *Centennial History* was finally finished by 1920, a couple of years after the centennial itself. This embarrassment was compounded by some controversies that broke out as the books found their readership. First, some readers cried foul over what they considered anti-Irish sentiment in one passage of Buck's volume, a reference to "drunken, profane, and worthless Irishmen." This was a quotation, not Buck's own sentiment, but since he inserted it uncritically into his narrative, some took offense. In the ensuing controversy, some critics also questioned whether the authors paid enough attention to Catholics in another volume of the history. As editor, Alvord defended the authors involved but was frustrated when political forces and what he called "special interests" interfered in his ideal of unbiased "scientific history." The supposedly anti-Irish line was edited from the commercial version of the text.[9]

Fortunately for Alvord, these controversies were mostly overshadowed as reviewers praised the work. In 1922 Columbia University historian Dixon Ryan Fox wrote a review of recent state histories in which he expressed appreciation nearly as warm as Alvord's original utopian ambitions, calling the *Centennial History* a substitute for "the great American novel."[10]

By the time of this review, Alvord had left Illinois for a new job at the University of Minnesota. Pease continued the work of the survey, and some of the finest volumes of the *Collections* were published under his direction and with the help of his partner, Marguerite Pease, through the 1940s. The Turnerian moment passed, and some of the energy for state and regional history was eclipsed by new trends—political history, social history, cultural history. But Turner, Alvord, and their successors had permanently altered the focus of American historians. Scholars of course continued to view European culture as a major influence on America, but they would no longer ignore the fascinating and complex history of the continent's local communities.

The Illinois Historical Survey continued its active program of collecting materials relevant to the history of the state. In 1939 it gained independence from the State Historical Library and became a part of the Graduate College, and in 1966 the survey moved from Lincoln Hall to the library, where it remains to this day as an independent unit.

Alvord spent only a few years at Minnesota before moving to Europe, where he died in Italy in 1928 at age sixty. As his health declined, Alvord had turned to new writing projects—a book on the American Revolution, and popular articles for magazines such as H. L. Mencken's *American Mercury*. Like other members of the generation that had witnessed World War I, he often expressed doubts regarding the inevitable "progress" that he had argued lay at the heart of the intellectual project of "scientific" history. In one essay titled "Musings of an Inebriated Historian," Alvord revealed uncertainty about whether history had any underlying patterns or coherence at all. This was an existential crisis common to many historians of Alvord's day.

But what Alvord never doubted—at least not in print—was the value of the local history project that he had helped pioneer. Walking through the stacks at the Illinois History and Lincoln Collections (the former Illinois Historical Survey) today, it is not hard to imagine the great excitement and activity that went into collecting and using these materials in the first decades of the twentieth century. Of course it remains a vital collection for scholars and students, thanks primarily to the stewardship of Librarian John Hoffmann. But it is also a monument to Alvord and a generation of historians who put local history—and the University of Illinois—at the forefront of the historical profession in the United States.

## Notes

1. "Up-to-Date Methods."
2. Alvord, *Cahokia Records*, x.
3. Alvord, "Future of Research," 252.
4. Alvord, "Planning," 218.
5. Alvord, "Future of Research," 251.
6. Alvord quoted in Hoffmann, "History," 58.
7. Alvord, *Illinois Country*, iii.
8. Hoffmann, "History," 65.
9. Ibid., 71–79.
10. Fox, "State History II," 118.

## Bibliography

Alvord, Clarence Walworth. *Cahokia Records, 1778–1790*. Collections of the Illinois State Historical Library; Virginia Series. Springfield: Trustees of the Illinois State Historical Library, 1907.

———. "Changing Fashions in History." *American Mercury* 9 (September 1926): 71–76.

———. "The Future of Research in Illinois History." *Educational Bi-Monthly* 1 (February 1907): 251–56.

———. "Historical Science and the War Guilt." *American Mercury* 11 (July 1927): 324–26.

———. *The Illinois Country, 1673–1818*. Chicago: Loyola University Press, 1920.

———. "Musings of an Inebriated Historian." *American Mercury* 5 (August 1925): 434–41.

———. "Planning the Publication Work of Historical Agencies." *Annual Report of the American Historical Association* 1 (1915): 217–23.

———. "The Relation of the State to Historical Work." *Minnesota History Bulletin* 1, no. 1 (February 1, 1915): 3–25.

———. "Review of Turner, The Frontier in American History." *Mississippi Valley Historical Review* 7, no. 4 (March 1, 1921): 403–7. doi:10.2307/1886214.

———. "The Science of History." *Popular Science* 84 (May 1914): 490–99.

———. "The Study and Writing of History in the Mississippi Valley." *Mississippi Valley Association Proceedings*, 1907.

Buck, Solon J. "Bibliography of the Published Works of Clarence W. Alvord." *Mississippi Valley Historical Review* 15, no. 3 (December 1, 1928): 385–90. doi:10.2307/1892437.

———. "Clarence Walworth Alvord, Historian." *Mississippi Valley Historical Review* 15, no. 3 (December 1, 1928): 309–20. doi:10.2307/1892432.

Dargan, Marion. "Clarence Walworth Alvord." In *The Marcus W. Jernegan Essays in American Historiography*, edited by William Thomas Hutchinson, 323–39. Chicago: University of Chicago Press, 1937.

Fox, Dixon Ryan. "State History I." *Political Science Quarterly* 36, no. 4 (December 1, 1921): 572–85. doi:10.2307/2142384.

———. "State History II." *Political Science Quarterly* 37, no. 1 (March 1, 1922): 99–118. doi:10.2307/2142321.

Hoffmann, John. "A History of the Centennial History of Illinois, 1907–1920." In *Selected Papers in Illinois History, 1982*, 57–78. Springfield: Illinois State Historical Society, 1984.

Lauck, Jon K. "The Prairie Historians and the Foundations of Midwestern History." *Annals of Iowa* 71, no. 2 (2012): 137–73.

Ross, Earle D. "A Generation of Prairie Historiography." *Mississippi Valley Historical Review* 33, no. 3 (December 1, 1946): 391–410. doi:10.2307/1898052.

Sutton, Robert. "Introduction." In *The Illinois Country, 1673–1818*, by Clarence Walworth Alvord. Sesquicentennial History of Illinois, vol. 1. Urbana: University of Illinois Press, 1987.

University of Illinois (Urbana-Champaign campus). Department of History. *University of Illinois Department of History, 1894–1954: Opportunities for Research and Graduate Study*. Urbana, Ill., 1954.

"Up-to-Date Methods of Illinois Centennial Historian." *New York Times*, July 14, 1918.

Wunder, John R. "The Founding Years of the OAH." *Newsletter of the OAH* 34, no. 4 (November 2006).

# Beyond Women's Studies

*Kristen Allen*

Women students and faculty were a minority when the University of Illinois campus first opened 150 years ago; they still are in 2016. But that has never prevented women from learning, researching, expressing their views, or expanding the horizons of the university despite dismissive attitudes and the many barriers placed in front of them. Women students, staff, and faculty created spaces and found ways to develop their intellects and interests and to change the university. One of those spaces was created in the 1970s, in the form of the Women's Studies Program.

In the middle of the twentieth century, the university issued *Illini Wise*, a special handbook for freshman women to help them adjust to college. Really, it was a book of rules designed to govern the manners and sexuality of female students. It stipulated that women (but not men) would be subject to a curfew requiring them to be in their housing halls by 10:30 P.M. on school nights and 1:00 A.M. on Fridays and Saturdays. Similarly, school officials were often unsure whether women cheerleaders should be allowed to travel with university teams to distant locations for sporting events—even after they signed waivers releasing the university from responsibility for their safety. Such paternalism paralleled practices around the country. Furthermore, as a 1951 report from the American Council for Education made clear, some questioned educating women at all: the council declared that women belonged in the home (despite a labor shortage) and that women's education should focus exclusively on their domestic responsibilities.

As the postwar era unfolded, the situation began to change. Women opposed the university's paternalism. Many called for more personal freedom on campus and in 1958 some proposed a separate women's student government. The first proposal failed, but the second gained a wider following. As was the case in so many other aspects of campus life, the 1960s brought calls for change from many quarters, including from women who objected to the tradition of separate rules and regulations based on gender. Curfew hours were abolished first for senior women and later for their younger peers. At the same time, feminist staff and faculty tackled the structural inequalities that women faced on campus.

In 1970 the campus administration created the Committee on the Status of Women, composed of leaders of the women's studies movement, including Joan Huber (professor of sociology), Marianne Ferber (professor of economics), and Paula Treichler (later professor of the Institute for Communication Research, Medicine, and Gender and Women's Studies). The committee wrote equal-employment guidelines, made recommendations for the enforcement of the ban on workplace discrimination based on sex, and evaluated affirmative action programs. The committee also conducted research on discrimination in graduate admissions, financial aid, hiring practices, and salaries. It found that in 1972, male professors were paid on average 20 percent more than female professors ($21,043, compared with $17,586). Especially important, the committee helped end the university's anti-nepotism rule, which prevented the hiring of those related by marriage or third-degree blood and had long been used to explain why professors' wives with doctorates were hired as instructors and adjuncts but not in permanent tenure-track positions.

The committee later wrote guidelines to address and combat sexual harassment, and it hosted workshops about this newly illegal behavior. In the twenty-first century, the

Poet Laureate of Illinois Gwendolyn Brooks (far left) joins other participants at the National Women's Studies Association meeting on campus in 1986. Photo courtesy of the Department of Gender and Women's Studies.

committee produced studies that showed the persistence of gender inequity in faculty salaries, fought for equal wages for women, and raised the issues of reproductive-health insurance benefits and childcare on campus. Between 2009 and 2011 the co-chairs of the provost's Gender Equity Council, Kathryn Anthony (Architecture) and Gale Summerfield (Women and Gender in Global Perspectives), focused attention on inequality in the built environment. The council funded the design and construction of the gender-friendly universal design podium, which is built for speakers ranging in height from 4'2" to 7', wheelchair users, and both left- and right-handers. The council also sought gender equity in bathroom design and lactation rooms that met legal requirements.

Women's Studies emerged from this atmosphere of activism and change. Female students, staff, adjunct faculty, and the handful of female faculty created new organizations, classes, and speaker series, which laid the groundwork for the academic program that soon emerged. Nina Baym (English), for example, taught one of the first Women in Literature courses in the country. In another setting, students packed into the Allen Hall dormitory every "Monday at 8" beginning in 1972 to hear speakers on "Women's Liberation: General Perspectives and Practical Skills." The first workshop in this five-year series was on rape and included the local prosecutor and a victim-witness who discussed why their particular case had failed. Paula Treichler, administrator of the Allen Hall Unit One program, held a doctorate, but as a woman and a male professor's partner, she could not obtain a tenure-track position on campus. Feminists at the university sponsored a major conference on feminist theory in 1978 with internationally known radical theologian Mary Daly as the keynote speaker, and in 1982 the National Women's Studies Association held its national conference in Urbana.

These outspoken feminist leaders—Joan Huber, Marianne Ferber, Paula Treichler, Cheris Kramarae (Speech Communication), and Beth Stafford (University Library)—soon began to work for the creation of an academic program in women's studies. The Office of Women's Studies was established in 1978, and Huber served as the office's first director. That office sponsored two core courses, Introduction to Women's Studies in the Humanities and Introduction to Women's Studies in the Social Sciences, and called on established departments to create other courses focusing on the experiences and achievements of women. The University of Illinois program was quite similar to women's studies efforts at peer institutions. Courses analyzed sex roles, gender inequality and women's work, feminist theory, and women and health, and called for greater attention to women's experiences and perspectives throughout history. Like most other large public institutions, Illinois had no full-time faculty who specialized in women's studies and no prospect of hiring new professors with that specialty. Nevertheless, existing faculty offered women's studies courses, and the Office of Women's Studies advertised recommended courses, issued a newsletter, and sponsored presentation of new research through the lunchtime Feminist Scholarship Series.

The official landscape changed dramatically in 1986 when the university formally established a Program in Women's Studies that was authorized to offer an undergraduate minor and to hire its first full-time staff members. (A graduate minor was established in 1993.) This was completed under the direction of Berenice Carroll, who had already been teaching courses in women's studies. She also was active in the community, participating in antiwar groups and the establishment of the women's crisis shelter, A Woman's Place, in Urbana. Soon the program welcomed its first faculty member, Mary Loeffelholz, an expert in

nineteenth-century American poetry. Loeffelholz, like many of the program's early faculty, was hired jointly by Women's Studies and another academic program—in her case, English. This initial appointment was quickly followed by additional faculty appointed in English and psychology. Today there are fourteen "core" faculty members in the department and an additional fifty-one "affiliated" faculty who research and teach in the field but have full-time appointments in other departments. In the 1990s many of the faculty and students began to chafe under the program's name, "Women's Studies," finding it too restrictive for what the field and its inquiry had become. In 2003, under the leadership of Kal Alston (Educational Policy Studies), the program's first African American director, the program renamed itself the Program in Women's and Gender Studies and launched a major in the field. In 2010 Gender and Women's Studies (GWS) became an academic department.

As the Women's Studies program took root, feminist faculty and students turned increasingly to exploring the differences and disagreements among women rather than treating all women as essentially the same. They actively sought to de-center white, middle-class, and American/European women. The breadth of expertise on campus about cultural life in all quarters of the globe deepened this scholarly turn. In 1983 the university hosted a conference, "Common Differences: Third World Women and Feminist Perspectives." Many international feminist scholars and activists, including women of color and from Third World countries, convened to discuss how gender, class, and race are intertwined and to hear the perspectives of women from the Global South. Other similar gatherings occurred thereafter. Illinois faculty began producing new knowledge on women's experiences beyond North American to include Russia, Germany, the Middle East, Tanzania, Brazil, and Central America.

A collective interest in investigating the idea of gender rather than focusing solely on "telling women's stories" developed as well in the 1980s and 1990s. Research on gender coincided with the embracing of new theories and interdisciplinary approaches as scholars asked how gender is defined, how it is experienced, and what it means across the entire range of human experience. Professors in many different disciplines began to pursue new research and offer new courses on the social construction of gender roles and identities. Topics varied greatly, ranging from economics to politics to fertility, sex roles, and even women's folklore. A growing group of engaged faculty members produced cutting-edge research, but the Office of Women's Studies still had no tenure-line teaching staff of its own.

As it grew first into a program and later an academic department, Gender and Women's Studies has followed a remarkable arc of innovation. Pressed by student demand as well as changes in society beyond the campus, faculty members brought women's concerns into the curriculum, but their efforts were always enriched by the large and diverse university community in Urbana-Champaign. Because women's studies was neither a traditional discipline nor a department, it was always interdisciplinary. Scholars from a wide array of fields not only contributed to the growth of the program—and later the department—but also argued for expanding women's studies to consider broad questions of gender and sexuality and their construction as well as the enduring social concerns involving race, cultural difference, and international and cross-cultural communication. As the scope of the program flourished, its staff and faculty developed new opportunities to support and enrich the lives of students on campus.

Among its many contributions to student life and to the growth of gender, women, and sexuality studies, GWS-sponsored talks and symposia have exposed the campus to superb research produced by University of Illinois scholars and outside experts. These have included a symposium, "Family, Gender and Law in a Globalizing Middle East and South Asia" (2004), lectures about Israeli women (2005), a town hall meeting to discuss the impact of recent Supreme Court decisions on the rights of women as well as of lesbian, gay, bisexual and transgender people. The department has also sponsored talks and panels on "Race Relations 101" (2006); the Latina/Latino community; and the Black Lives Matter movement (2015–16). In its relatively short history, the Gender and Women's Studies Department has supported creative, award-winning scholarship; taught courses about topics that were taboo fifty years ago; and helped to make the University of Illinois more equitable. The department and its students, staff, and faculty continue to address the issues that generated its founding while simultaneously challenging themselves, society, and the university campus community to examine how inequality and injustice are created and sustained and how they might be dismantled.

## Sources

The University Archives holds the records of the Committee on the Status of Women as well as numerous documents related to the program, then department, of Gender and Women's Studies. Published material on women at the university is scarce, but interested readers should consult the departmental website, http://www.gws.illinois.edu, for basic information.

# John Laughnan
## Sweet Corn Revolution

William F. Tracy

And pray what more can a reasonable man desire, in peaceful times, in ordinary noons, than a sufficient number of ears of green sweet corn boiled, with the addition of salt?

—Henry David Thoreau, *Walden*

There is no substitute for the man who can observe and who lives so closely with his material that he can recognize a lucky break when he sees it.

—Henry A. Wallace, the founder of Pioneer Hi-Bred and Vice President of the United States

Until an inspiration from Illinois revolutionized sweet corn, it was mainly a regional favorite unknown outside of the United States and Canada. Old-fashioned sweet corn, based on a gene called *sugary1* (*su1*), originated in the northeastern United States in the early 1800s and in that region became a summer favorite. Starting in the 1860s, sweet-corn canneries sprang up in the Great Lakes states and in New England, and people throughout the country could enjoy sweet corn year round. But, for the most part, fresh sweet corn remained a local delicacy, available principally at roadside stands in August in the northern and mid-Atlantic states. Sweet corn's limited availability was a consequence of the fact that it wasn't very sweet and, more important, that it lost what little sugar it had very quickly, especially under warm conditions. Sweet corn thus remained a product to be consumed in the north, with its cooler summers. Sweet corn didn't change much for the next century until an idea and a lot of hard work by Professor John Laughnan of the University of Illinois's Department of Botany changed a local specialty into one of the most popular vegetables in the world.

In the early 1950s Professor Laughnan was studying the phenomenon of genetic linkage in his favorite model organism, maize (*Zea mays*). The specific chromosomal linkage he was studying was an extremely tight one between the genes *a1* (*anthocyaninless1*) and *sh2* (*shrunken2*). In addition to the tightness of their linkage, these two genes had the advantage of being easily seen and counted on the cob when the grain was mature (see photo on p. 117).

A quick look at Professor Laughnan's bibliography shows that from 1946 through 1955 he published sixteen papers in the leading genetics journals, fourteen on the structure and genetics of the *a1* locus. The two other papers reveal the kernel of the idea that revolutionized sweet corn and made it an international favorite. In 1953 in the journal *Genetics* Professor Laughnan published "The Effect of the *sh2* Factor on Carbohydrate Reserves in the Mature Endosperm of Maize." Deep in this decidedly scholarly article on the biochemistry of kernel carbohydrate composition lay a rather unusual phrase: "the kernels are unusually sweet and have a pleasant malty flavor." The second article not on *a1* was in the decidedly nonscholarly publication, *The Canner*. In this 1954 report to the canning industry, Laughnan discussed some very favorable taste-test results and the principal advantages of higher sugar and longer shelf life of *sh2*. This was the beginning of supersweet sweet corn, an innovation that shook the vegetable world.

Before we continue the story of supersweet corn, it might help to know more about Professor Laughnan and how his background may have informed his discovery. John R. Laughnan was born in 1919 on a farm in Irish Valley, Wisconsin, one of the many small valleys bisecting the Driftless area of southwestern Wisconsin. In 1919 the bottoms of these valleys were dotted with small dairy farms with lush pastures and woods on the steep hillsides. John's dad died when he was an infant, and the family moved into Sauk City, a village on the Wisconsin River. As a boy, John worked in a sweet-corn cannery in Baraboo, Wisconsin. Hot, hard work it was at that time, performed primarily by hands and horses.

Laughnan went to the University of Wisconsin and received his bachelor of science in plant sciences in 1942. At Madison, John was influenced by Aldo Leopold, one of the early thinkers in ecology of wild lands, and R. A. Brink, a leading maize geneticist. Brink saw something special in Laughnan and told him about an opportunity to do graduate work in genetics with Lewis J. Stadler at the University of Missouri. Missouri had strong genetics programs in maize, wheat, and *Drosophila*, with numerous faculty and students who later became well known for their research achievements. After his time at Missouri, Laughnan went on to a postdoctoral study at Iowa State

Professor Laughnan at work in an experimental plot

University, an academic position at Princeton University, and a fellowship at the California Institute of technology. At all of these places John worked with leaders in maize genetics and breeding, among them Edgar G. Anderson, Albert E. Longley, Barbara McClintock, George H. Shull, and George F. Sprague.

In 1948, Laughnan was hired as an assistant professor of botany at the University of Illinois and with the exception of a brief stint at Missouri spent the rest of his career there. He was hired to do basic research in genetics with the model system of his choice and to teach courses in botany and genetics. While he did research with *Drosophila*, maize genetics was his passion. Laughnan excelled at research, was a highly regarded teacher and mentor, and also spent time as department head. Like most maize geneticists, he logged countless hours in the cornfields, observing his favorite plant.

In the early 1950s Laughnan was fully engaged in teaching and leading a productive research program on genetic linkage. Among his many genetic stocks was one that he received from E. B. Mains. This stock had the *sh2* allele tightly linked to *a1*, which blocked the ability of the kernel (and plant) to make purple pigment. As the story goes, John popped a dry *sh2* kernel into his mouth, actually not a rare thing for corn people to do, and found it to be surprisingly sweet. This observation precipitated a brief shift in his research to the study of the biochemistry of starch synthesis in the maize endosperm, the energy storage tissue in cereal grains. Among his conclusions found in the 1953 *Genetics* paper were the following: "sh2 endosperms store less starch than normal (starchy) and su1 endosperms but in regard to sugars, exhibit approximately ten-fold and four-fold increases over normal (starchy) and sugary types respectively; most of this is due to sucrose." He correctly predicted that in the starch biosynthesis pathway *su1* gene acts after *sh2*. He suggested also that *sh2* would be desirable for the sweet-corn industry because of its initially higher sugar content and expected longer shelf life. As it turns out, traditional sweet corn based on the *sugary1* (*su1*) gene only has 5 percent to 15 percent sugar at the fresh eating stage. Even more import-

ant, traditional sweet corn rapidly loses what little sugar it does have—a 50 percent loss in the first twenty-four hours after harvest. This characteristic puts the farmer, the shipper, and the grocer in a very difficult position as they rush to deliver a high-quality product to consumers.

Laughnan knew that commercial sweet-corn breeders probably didn't read *Genetics*, so he published the brief 1954 report in the trade magazine *The Canner*, highlighting the fact that canners would no longer have to add cane sugar to the can, a realization that must have come from his experience during the many hot summers he spent in the canning factory. In *The Canner* article, he also said that "representatives of a considerable number of experiment stations and private companies have expressed their enthusiasm over the possibilities which this new finding offers. Soon they will be actively engaged in introducing the new shrunken factor into preferred sweet lines."

As a faculty member of the Department of Botany, with responsibilities in teaching and basic research, Laughnan had gone above and beyond the call of duty. Not only had he done the basic research on the *sh2* gene, but he had also reached out to the industry to explain the implications and importance of this innovation. No doubt he believed his work on *sh2* was done. However, he soon realized that the sweet-corn breeders had little interest in adopting what they saw as a disruptive technology.

At this point, perhaps, most faculty would have shaken their heads at the shortsightedness of the sweet-corn breeders, maybe uttered a few choice words, and gone back to the lab bench and classroom. Undoubtedly, Laughnan did all those things, but also he nearly single-handedly turned his observation into a commercial reality. He did this because he was convinced his findings would vastly improve the delivery of corn to the public. He proceeded without special funding for the work and

"At room temperature old fashioned sweet corn loses 50% of its sugar in 24 hours making it difficult to market to distant consumers. Supersweet maintains its sugar levels for up to five days at room temperature."

while still doing his day jobs—teaching, research, and department administration.

Laughnan began a breeding program in which he crossed the *sh2* allele into the inbreds that were the parents of the leading *su1* hybrids of the day, Golden Cross Bantam and Iochief. The parents of Golden Cross Bantam were P39su1 and P51su1; those of Iochief were Ia5125su1 and Ia453su1. During the breeding program he incorporated the *sh2* allele and removed the *su1* allele and created P39sh2, P51sh2, Ia5125sh2, and Ia453sh2. This breeding program needed at least seven breeding generations, but using winter breeding nurseries in Florida to get two generations per year, he was able to develop the new lines in four or five years.

After developing the new inbreds, Laughnan needed to make enough hybrid seed for farmers and seeds people to evaluate eating quality and agronomic performance (yield, disease resistance, and standability). Finding still no commercial interest in *sh2*, Laughnan rented land and planted hybrid seed production blocks that he and his sons managed. In addition to the standard practices of planting, fertilization, weed control, and harvest, they detasseled the female rows so that the female inbreds would be pollinated only by pollen from the male inbreds. The hybrid seed was then packaged up and offered free of charge to home gardeners, who received it enthusiastically. John was also able to have some of the corn commercially canned and frozen.

In a 1961 *Seed World* article Laughnan announced that supersweet versions of the *su1* hybrids Golden Cross Bantam and Iochief would be available for planting in the spring of 1961 through Illinois Foundation Seed Inc. (IFSI). The supersweet Iochief was the better of the two hybrids and was named Illini Chief. Seed of Illini Chief, however, was difficult to produce on a commercial scale, and IFSI worked with Crookham Seed Company of Caldwell, Idaho, to develop a three-way hybrid using one of the inbreds Laughnan had developed for supersweet Golden Cross (P39sh2) and the two parents of Illini Chief. Seed of this three-way hybrid, (Ia453sh2 x P39sh2) x Ia5125sh2, could be produced commercially, and the hybrid was named Illini Xtra Sweet. Illini Xtra Sweet was the first supersweet hybrid, and it is still sold today.

An ear of corn showing the tight genetic linkage of the sh2 allele (wrinkled kernels) and the a1 allele (white kernels). Photo courtesy of Cold Springs Harbor Laboratory Press.

But the story doesn't end here. Illini Xtra Sweet was the first sweet corn to gain popularity outside North America. IFSI, under the leadership of Floyd Ingersoll, began marketing Illini Xtra Sweet in Japan under the name Honey Bantam. Honey Bantam was wildly popular and created the Japanese sweet corn market. Direct descendants of Laughnan's Illini Xtra Sweet are now grown on every continent with arable land and are the foundation for worldwide trade worth billions of dollars. Sweet corn's popularity is booming around the globe and Laughnan's supersweet innovation is the root of it all.

As you'll recall, old-fashioned sweet corn is not very sweet, only 5 percent to 10 percent sugar. And most lovers of old-fashioned sweet corn will remember it most fondly only when it's been coated with copious amounts of butter and salt. Supersweet sweet corn is about 35 percent sugar by dry weight (although there is less sugar in an ear of supersweet than a typical apple) and quite edible without butter and salt. Incidentally, while sweeter than *su1* corn, supersweet corn has more protein per calorie consumed. But most important, supersweet greatly improves shelf life and processing ability. At room temperature old-fashioned sweet corn loses 50 percent of its sugar in twenty-four hours, making it difficult to market to distant consumers. Supersweet, however, maintains its sugar levels for up to five days at room temperature. This characteristic, of course, is invaluable for long-distance shipping and the grocery-store trade. Supersweet corn also makes a more desirable canned product that does not require added sugar or salt. It also improves both frozen and canned product by having a pleasant crunchy texture; it is not mushy.

Professor Laughnan created a new crop with new qualities that in turn created new markets in every part of the globe. He did this in the face of a skeptical industry, and he did it in a very short time, while keeping up with his full-time professorial duties. Perhaps more important, his new sweet corn brings pleasure (and nutrition) to people around the world.

A bit of cost accounting is order. Presuming Laughnan's salary and plant genetic infrastructure were provided by the university, the additional cost of development of supersweet corn was probably about $10,000 in 2015 dollars. Compare this to a modern genetic engineering program that attempts to create a crop with a new characteristic: the cost is in the tens of millions of dollars. A final figure is worth noting, too: Professor Laughnan never received a penny for this thought.

## Sources

The literature cited in this essay is listed below. The most accessible general treatment of supersweet corn is the 1997 article in *Plant Breeding Reviews*, also listed below, by the author. The best overviews of sweet corn and its history are Walter A. Huelsen's *Sweet Corn* and William F. Tracy's "History, Breeding, and Genetics."

Andrew, Robert H., and Joachim H. von Elbe. "Processing Potential for Diallel Hybrids of High Sugar Corn." *Crop Science* 19 (1979): 216–18.

Boyer, Charles D., and Jack C. Shannon. "The Use of Endosperm Genes for Sweet Corn Improvement." *Plant Breeding Reviews* 1 (1984): 139.

Coe, Ed. "John R. Laughnan: Over 40 Years of Contributions to Genetic Concepts: Genetics from A to Zea in Three Score and Ten." *Maydica* 34, no. 3 (1989): 167–72.

Creech, Roy G. "Carbohydrate Synthesis in Maize." *Advances in Agronomy* 20 (1968): 275.

Evensen, Kathleen B., and Charles D. Boyer. "Carbohydrate Composition and Sensory Quality of Fresh and Stored Sweet Corn." *Journal of the American Society for Horticultural Science* 111 (1986): 734–38.

Galinat, Walton C. "The Evolution of Sweet Corn." *Massachusetts Agricultural Experiment Station Bulletin* 591 (1971).

Garwood, D. L., F. J. McArdle, S. F. Vanderslice, and J. C. Shannon. "Postharvest Carbohydrate Transformations and Processed Quality of High Sugar Maize Genotypes." *Journal of the American Society for Horticultural Science* 101 (1976): 400–404.

Goldman, I. L., and William F. Tracy. "Kernel Protein Concentration in *sugary1* (*su1*) and *shrunken2* (*sh2*) Sweet Corn." *Horticultural Science* 29 (1994): 209–10.

Huelsen, Walter August. *Sweet Corn*. New York: Interscience, 1954.

Laughnan, John R. "The Effect of *sh2* Factor on Carbohydrate Reserves in the Mature Endosperm of Maize." *Genetics* 38 (1953): 485.

———. "Super Sweet: A Product of Mutation Breeding in Corn." *Seed World* 13 (January 1961): 18–19.

———. "What's Ahead for Sweet Corn." *Canner* 82 (March 1954): 15–17.

Marshall, S. W., and William F. Tracy. "Sweet Corn." In *Corn: Chemistry and Technology*, 2nd ed., edited by Paul E. Ramstad and P. White, 537–69. Minneapolis: American Association of Cereal Chemists, 2003.

Showalter, R. K., and L. W. Miller. "Consumer Preference for High Sugar Sweet Corn Varieties." *Proceedings of the Florida State Horticultural Society* 75 (1962): 278–80.

Smith, O. S., K. Hoard, F. Shaw, and R. Shaw. "Prediction of Single Cross Performance." *ASTA Corn and Sorghum Research Conference Proceedings* 51 (1996): 67–74.

Steffensen, Dale M. "Dedication: John R. Laughnan, Maize Geneticist." *Plant Breeding Reviews* 19 (2000): 1–13.

Tracy, William F. "History, Breeding, and Genetics of Supersweet Corn." *Plant Breeding Reviews* 14 (1997): 189.

Tracy, William F., Sherry R. Whitt, and Edward S. Buckler. "Recurrent Mutation and Genome Evolution: Example of *sugary1* and the Origin of Sweet Maize." *Crop Science* 46 (2006): S49–S54.

# Remarkable Animals

## Illini Nellie and Big Al

*Nicholas Hopkins*

The University of Illinois has been the site of many agricultural advancements. But while the Morrow Plots are a campus landmark that commemorates the university's role in expanding corn production, the public is less aware of the parallel story of livestock development. In 1930 the university's record-setting Brown Swiss cow Illini Nellie became famous for her milk output. She began giving milk in 1930 and averaged 93.5 pints of milk per day for the next ten years. Nellie's world records for both milk and butterfat content made her somewhat of a celebrity. She was often displayed on the main quad for visiting politicians and other celebrities of the period. Nellie died in 1940 and was buried in front of the Purebred Dairy Barn under a commemorating plaque and boulder. More than seventy years later she continues to be a symbol of agricultural advancement at the University of Illinois and her lineage continues to give milk.

More recently, animal sciences researchers have turned from breeding and nutrition to engineering. In 1994 Professor Matthew Wheeler announced the birth of Big Al, a transgenic pig named for the milk-producing alpha-lactalbumin gene. The new resident of the Animal Science Laboratory had been produced by injecting genes from a Holstein cow into numerous pig embryos. Al's appearance on campus was the outgrowth of work performed in conjunction with the National Animal Genome Research Program, a national effort at mapping the genomes of the most common agricultural animal species.

Matthew B. Wheeler and Gregory T. Bleck set out to improve milk production in a line of Chinese pigs that produced more piglets than usual but not enough milk to feed the litter. To accomplish this, the researchers transplanted

Illini Nellie

the alpha-lactalbumin gene of a Holstein cow into the ovum of Big Al's mother. The embryo that produced Big Al was the only one of the entire batch (more than six thousand embryo injections) to undergo the gene transfer successfully. Al was the first piglet to have inherited the Holstein's milk-producing gene. His descendants (as of this writing

One of the university's
record-setting pigs
from a century ago

in their seventeenth generation) have thrived. His offspring gain weight faster than pigs without the alpha-lactalbumin gene and produce up to 70 percent more milk. Wheeler and his colleagues later extended their work with Big Al by replicating the gene transfer process they pioneered. This new line will diversify the alpha-lactalbumin positive swine gene pool and undertakes to bring a breed of larger pigs into the livestock market. The birth of Big Al and similar pigs promises to continue the university's role in expanding agricultural production and increasing the food supply across Illinois, the United States, and the world.

## Sources

The University Archives holds primary materials on the life of Illini Nellie. For information on the Big Al project see Matthew B. Wheeler, "Production of Transgenic Livestock: Promise Fulfilled," *Journal of Animal Science* 81 (2003): 32–37.

# "2 + 2 = green"

## Innovation in Experimental Music
## at the University of Illinois

David Rosenboom

The easiest thing to call it was music.
—John Cage[1]

Amid the transdisciplinary mind-fields uniting everything with everything that typified the hard-to-match postwar mid-twentieth century tsunamis of creative imagination that littered our cognitive beaches with infinite possibilities, a center of musical innovation of rare magnitude in scope and lasting influence erupted from fertile midwestern prairie soil in the School of Music and its Experimental Music Studios (EMS) at the University of Illinois in Urbana-Champaign (UIUC). So rich was this rainforest of ideas and influences that legends and stories about it persist and even show up in fiction. To Peter Els, the young composer seeking epiphanies linking music and biochemistry in Richard Powers's striking page-turner *Orfeo*, "That self-inventing outpost on the edge of the endless cornfields felt like a new Vienna."[2]

Indeed it was! It was a time when the range of ideas about what music could be was experiencing inflation, like a musical Big Bang.

Such centers of creativity generally emerge when the right confluence of energetically curious people and organizations mix and collide. And it wasn't only the UIUC School of Music scene that fueled this expansion. It was the mix of experimental composer-performers around EMS, founded in 1958 by the pioneering composer (and chemist) Lejaren Hiller, the innovative thinkers at the legendary Biological Computer Laboratory (BCL), and kindred spirits across campus working in computer science, engineering, psychology, literature, and linguistics. These creative individuals would meet at concerts, talks, happenings, festivals, film showings, and parties, and in seminars, labs, and pubs. Their energy and inventiveness was responsible for triggering a surge of creative action in a town where, frankly, there wasn't much else to do.

The term "experimental music" can invoke complex associations and controversial musings. It did not originate at Illinois. The "American experimental tradition" in music dates back to the late nineteenth and early twentieth centuries, with composers like Charles Ives, Charles Seeger, Ruth Crawford, and John Cage.[3] Broadening this to include the Americas, particularly Mexico with Julián Carrillo and Conlon Nancarrow (then an expatriate American composer living in Mexico City) and in France with Pierre Schaeffer's *musique expérimentale*,[4] reminds us that it is nearly impossible to assert with certainty that any specific "first" could be the absolute genesis of a historical movement.

Each tributary feeding the river of music we call "experimental" brings its own particular definition and contextualization. Composer-scholars such as Christian Wolff and Michael Nyman have described the setting that encouraged this movement in the mid-twentieth century, but the career of Lejaren Hiller suggests how national and international forces came to be focused on Urbana and Champaign.[5] Trained in chemistry and music both inside and outside Princeton University and having worked for E. I. DuPont de Nemours and Company, Hiller came to the UIUC chemistry faculty in 1952, where he found greater intellectual freedom and flexibility than in industrial chemistry. By the mid-1950s he was teaching an array of courses in chemistry while continuing his studies in music composition and analysis. Eventually, this cross-disciplinary mixing led Hiller to develop groundbreaking ideas for computer music. Before pursuing that subject more, though, it may be interesting to pause and examine a chemistry textbook that Hiller and his colleague from Rutgers University, Rolfe H. Herber, wrote and published in 1960, *Principles of Chemistry*.[6]

> "New notions about expectation, prediction, and surprise associated with elements in time-based musical forms arose from this *artscience* matrix."

This text underscores the authors' sense of urgency that the teaching of chemistry must evolve to introduce general principles of chemical systems. In the book's preface the authors write, "In particular, the formerly successful presentation of chemical facts unrelated by fundamental underlying principles is no longer adequate for students in the physical sciences, engineering, and related fields."[7] Hiller and Herber emphasized that it was crucial for students to move from the rote learning of chemical properties to engage with the dynamics of chemical change. One senses, therefore, even in this undergraduate chemistry text, hints of ideas that would later unfold in fields that investigate the dynamics of self-organizing systems.

These attitudes and hints of evolving thinking appear throughout the text, a particularly intriguing example being how concepts about chemical equilibrium, entropy and probability, information theory, statistics, and thermodynamics are presented as general organizing principles in physical and perhaps other kinds of systems. Later, Hiller applied these ideas, particularly those associated with information theory and probabilities, to analyzing extant musical literature and in generative systems for musical composition.[8] Hiller was also instrumental in bringing a translation of the influential 1958 landmark text by Abraham Moles, *Théorie de l'information et perception esthétique*, to the University of Illinois Press.[9]

*Principles of Chemistry* emphasized the new ways of thinking about entropy that were developing around information theory as it had become known in the mathematical theory of communication.[10] That new way of thinking about order and disorder and how to measure quantities of information contained in a system, especially in relation to constraints placed on the freedom of choices among possibilities for arrangements of parameters in sequential configurations of that system, was pushing ideas forward in both the sciences and the arts. Ultimately, new notions about expectation, prediction, and surprise associated with elements in time-based musical forms arose from this *artscience* matrix.

In the mid-1950s a particular aspect of Hiller's work on probabilistic processes in chemistry, known as restricted random walks, clearly suggested musical applications. With his collaborator Leonard Isaacson he soon produced

*Quartet No. 4, for Strings, The ILLIAC Suite*, using programs for algorithmic music composition that ran on UIUC's original ILLIAC I computer (later sold for $67 worth of electronic scrap). The four movements of *The ILLIAC Suite*, labeled *Experiment I, II, III*, and *IV*, chronicle the evolution of what musicians think of as "music theories," from monody through multipart counterpoint, diatonic and chromatic harmony, to post-tonal twentieth-century systems and stochastic techniques. In the hands of musicians, these "theories," far from being predictive (as is customary in the sciences), are usually employed as tools for analysis. Hiller turned them around to make them prospective generative tools. His algorithms followed contrapuntal and harmonic conventions from random starting points to resolutions via restricted random walks, which generated numbers that were later transcribed into musical notation. In the spirit of Hiller-style *experimental music*, none of the resulting notes were changed to suit his musical taste. The outcomes of the experiments remained unbiased, and what was heard was purely the result of algorithmic compositional models unfolding. This procedure identifies one clear meaning of *experimental music*.

The University of Illinois Composition String Quartet recorded *The ILLIAC Suite* for its first distributed release.[11] *The ILLIAC Suite* enraged tradition-bound listeners, who were challenged by difficulties in interpretability born from the conceptual paralysis of ironclad musical presuppositions. As one would anticipate, Hiller's ideas and compositions were also controversial within and around the School of Music. The extraordinary systems theorist Heinz von Foerster, who formed BCL at Illinois in 1958, addressed the problem of interpretability in a pioneering book, *Music by Computers*,[12] which he edited with James Beauchamp, a prolific engineer-theorist who had helped to develop EMS.

In an essay in *Music by Computers* von Foerster attempted to explain the new sounds coming from experimental musicians this way:

> If sounds are uninterpretable, they are called "noise." "Noninterpretability" is a concept however; hence "noises" may well be used in a symbolic way on a higher level of symbolization. The proposition

2 + 2 = green

is uninterpretable on the level of mathematical discourse. This proposition is not even false; it is pure mathematical nonsense, "mathematical noise." We cannot deny, however, that by its very form of nonsensicality this proposition generates a specific frustration in the search for its meaning, which is precisely the meaning it carries with it.

At this point of the discussion it may have become sufficiently clear that the search for the necessary and sufficient conditions under which sounds will be interpreted as "music" is doomed to fail. This failure is, by all means, not due to a semantic opacity of the term "music." The search is doomed by an intrinsic property of cognitive processes which permit the operators of conceptualizations to become concepts themselves.[13]

Many feared that electronics and computers would bypass performers. "But what, alas, will be the fate of interpreters?" wrote one reviewer in the *New York Times*.[14] Near-violent reactions took place against *The ILLIAC Suite* and other music that pushed the boarders of preconception. Those reacting so strongly were often wearing mental shackles placed on them by the deleterious segregation of composers from performers that had grown out of the progressive iconizing of "composition" in Western Euro-American music during the previous two hundred to three hundred years.

Undaunted by his critics, Hiller continued his work with computers and music. Over the next few years he implemented an astonishing range of new applications, from algorithms for composition to computer-controlled music typewriters, to sound synthesis, and more.[15] Hiller was also instrumental in bringing other music experimentalists to UIUC, including John Cage, with whom he collaborated to produce *HPSCHD*, in which the ILLIAC II computer was used to implement an array of chance procedures derived from the *I Ching*. The data

> "*The ILLIAC Suite* enraged tradition-bound listeners, who were challenged by difficulties in interpretability born from the conceptual paralysis of ironclad musical presuppositions."

David Rosenboom, Salvatore Martirano, and Mary Ashley, 1976.
Photo courtesy of David Rosenboom.

generated was used to construct a huge assemblage of musical and visual materials, which were presented in the work's premiere at the University of Illinois Assembly Hall on May 16, 1969. The work has been restaged only a few times since then and remains a monument of computer-assisted multimedia composition.[16]

It was in Hiller's graduate seminar on contemporary music that this author first met John Cage and heard reinforcing language about the breadth of human experiences and ideas we could call music. It was in Kenneth Gaburo's graduate seminar on systems theory that interdisciplinary collisions sparked lasting trajectories for materializing them. Gaburo, another experimental music innovator among UIUC's faculty in the 1960s, forged a kind of meta-theater by melding his compositional methods with linguistics, graphical notations, and multimedia. In his seminar, each student delved into a chosen topic and presented results for lively discussions, sometimes lasting for hours. The discourse reflected fertile influences among composers and seminal figures at BCL, especially systems thinkers like Heinz von Foerster, Francisco Varela, Humberto Maturana, W. Ross Ashby, and others.[17] So important was Maturana's work on the neurophysiology of cognition that Gaburo republished a key Maturana

paper in his own catalog of experimental music scores and writings;[18] and later, a seminal collection of von Foerster's writings, *Observing Systems*, appeared.[19] Both of these publications still inspire experimental composers.

Herbert Brün was another composer who bridged the School of Music and EMS with BCL. He co-taught courses with Heinz von Foerster and expanded the range of cybernetic thinking in music at UIUC. He also developed innovative techniques for computer synthesis of sound, especially presaging what is now widely known as granular synthesis, and ways to represent computer composition with graphics.[20] Also influential in this musically interdisciplinary mix were Charles Osgood and his colleagues at the university's Institute of Communications Research. In particular, Osgood led investigations into how individual human beings develop their own internal semantic landscapes, thereby stimulating new ideas for experimental music. A tool relatively new to musicians, the semantic differential opened doors to many applications for multidimensional scaling that found their way into important studies in music perception, particularly with respect to the perception of timbre, the tunings of pitch complexes, and a variety of other musical elements and structural parameters responsible for articulating musical forms.[21]

UIUC's Allerton House in Monticello provided a retreat for important gatherings in the arts, sciences, and humanities. In 1955 it was the scene of a working conference for the Committee on Linguistics and Psychology of the Social Science Research Council on the subject of content analysis. The meeting produced a book, *Trends in Content Analysis* (1959), that caught the attention of some experimental composers.[22] These statements explored methods for both qualitative and quantitative analysis of content in human expressive media, identifying *kinds* of content imbedded in expressive products and finding ways to make revelatory "content-descriptive observations" in a wide range of media. Experimental composers and musicians found inspiring concepts and questions in this interdisciplinary work. For example, how might these ideas be used to better understand the roles of musical notation, transcription, recording, and what we now refer to as interactive media?

Many of these lines of influence became interwoven back in Gaburo's self-organizing seminar. It was an unforgettable class for many young experimental composers, myself included. Students heard Gaburo speak about "incipient theory" and a wordplay performance, *Extraction*, demonstrating ideas about how incipient mental associations evolve into defining relationships among differentiated conceptions.[23] We investigated information theory and neurolinguistics, along with surveying composers' writings on current composition techniques. For me, seeds were planted, which, along with influences from Salvatore Martirano, Hiller, and others, would eventually grow into the formulation for what I call *propositional music*.[24]

In 1962 Gaburo founded the New Music Choral Ensemble, a group that programmed works (often by Illinois composers) that pushed the boundaries of vocal music. The group performed compositions by Will Ogdon, Charles Hamm, Arthur Maddox, Gary Grossman, and Gaburo himself, along with a mixture of prominent European and American innovators like Luigi Nono and Charles Ives. A particularly influential Gaburo work from that time was his Fromm Foundation commission, *Antiphony III (Pearl White Moments)* for 16 singers, electronic and pre-recorded sound (1963), which was presented on the Smith Music Hall stage on March 5, 1967, during the Festival of Contemporary Arts that took place at UIUC in alternate years and drew an international audience.[25]

The magnetism of Gaburo's ideas was profound. A notable example from the early days was his influence on the late composer Harley Gaber, who enrolled at Illinois as a freshman in the fall of 1961 and studied with Hiller and Gaburo. Though not widely known, Gaber, who went on to study composition in Rome and to establish an international reputation, emerged in the 1970s as a celebrated composer of highly original music composed with extraordinary attention to minute details of execution and also a precursor to music exploring suspended time and consciousness.

Gaburo and his colleague Ben Johnston helped to facilitate the work of critically important American experimental composer, instrument builder, and explorer of microtonal music and corporeal theater Harry Partch, who had come to UIUC in the late 1950s. Johnston and Gaburo embraced Partch's work. Johnston, in particular, developed his own approach to microtonal music theory and produced a prodigious body of compositions employing alternative tuning systems highlighted by his phenomenal series of ten string quartets. One of the earliest to be recorded was String Quartet No. 2,[26] and by now many others are also available.[27] Gaburo later produced a version of Partch's dance satire, *The Bewitched*, and wrote about that work and the nature of its physicality.[28]

Along with emerging interests in alternative systems of tuning, there was a fascination with general principles of proportionality and the perception of proportionally related forms in music. Performances of Ben Johnston's *Knocking Piece* for two players using chime hammers on the interior surfaces of a piano highlighted this in a dramatic way. The two players must articulate independent and continuously modulating, proportional time references among the musical meters that each one performs. (Johnston derived these proportions from the harmonic ratios relating the pitches in his *A Sea Dirge*.) Each performer, and listeners alike, must maintain independence of their internal mental rhythmic contexts as each one shifts in turn. During a memorable performance I witnessed in Smith Recital Hall, a dramatic augmentation occurred when a chime hammer struck a high string inside the piano that snapped, slinging shrapnel over the audience and into the balcony. Fortunately, no one was hurt, and many were so engrossed in the music they didn't even notice. Ben Johnston continued to develop advanced approaches to microtonal music theory and proportional metric systems for many years, and Bob Gilmore has collected his writings in a volume from University of Illinois Press.[29]

Like most American centers for mid-twentieth-century music, UIUC felt the weight of the European avant-garde. Among various lines of influence were those from the

> "Along with emerging interests in alternative systems of tuning, there was a fascination with general principles of proportionality and the perception of proportionally related forms of music."

aftermath of serialism (non-tonal, twelve-tone composition with serialized pitch classes). At UIUC, though, this quickly became generalized to mean combinatorial thinking applied to any sonic objects or elements of musical form that may be active in a particular musical context, not just pitch classes. With respect to pitches, Salvatore Martirano, a composer who had come to the University of Illinois in 1963, developed a system of "magic squares," square arrays of groups of notes that could be combined along rows, columns, diagonals, and internal squares to produce tone rows with important combinatorial qualities. These rows also had certain harmonic qualities that contributed to a signature "Martirano sound." Seminal early Martirano pieces like *Underworld* (1965) for four actors, computer-generated tape, and ensemble, and *Ballad* for singer and ensemble exhibited this sound. Being experimentally inclined, Martirano also composed with ordered collections of other sound objects (for example, in *Underworld*), electronic sounds, and various kinds of laughing and wailing. Even such diverse works as his piano solo, *Stuck on Stella* (1979), exhibited thinking about collections and permutations of sounds, in this case "permutations of everything you can do with seventh chords."[30]

Experiencing Martirano's *Underworld* and Hiller's experiments helped tip my decision toward enrolling as a composition student at UIUC in the 1960s. Studying with Martirano included engaging in regular, long discussions that continued for many years, until his passing in 1995. While studying with Martirano, I worked on extending combinatorial techniques and combining them with grand-scale proportional structures made with long time durations, lengths of segments in a work, durations of notes and phrases, rhythms, pitches, locations and movements of sounds in space, degrees of freedom in musical notation, and the colors of lights illuminating performers. While at Illinois, I composed a work with these techniques called *A Precipice in Time* (1966) for two percussionists, alto saxophone, piano-celeste, cello, and Sound Rotator.[31] It was written for percussionists William Youhass and G. Allan O'Connor, who premiered it in Smith Music Hall on May 5, 1967, under the working title *The Thud, Thud, Thud of Suffocating Blackness*.

On July 20, 1969, an extraordinary concert took place in Gregory Hall Auditorium. The Rockefeller Foundation had provided funding for a summer program in contemporary music. This concert was presented during that program and simultaneously with the Apollo 11 spaceflight's descent into the Sea of Tranquility on Earth's Moon. Video monitors surrounded the audience displaying CBS reporter Walter Cronkite's emotional narration as the first steps by a man were taken on the Moon's surface. The concert featured the Moon in its programming. Edwin London conducted Schoenberg's *Pierrot Lunaire*, musicologist-composer Charles Hamm made an arrangement of Franz Joseph Haydn's Overture to *Il mondo della luna* in which all the musicians played instruments they had never learned how to play, and other works by Neely Bruce, Charles Ives, Mauricio Kagel, Ben Johnston, James Cuomo, and Erik Satie–John Cage–Arthur Maddox were performed. The Ron Dewar Quartet played jazz. Artist William Wegman—then at UIUC and later to become famous for using Weimaraner dogs in art pieces—offered "Gift Presentations," plastic bags given to audience members or placed under their seats containing instructions for actions to perform at various times during the evening. Other happening-like things took place. There were films by Ron Nameth, dancers, and handicrafts; Carl Volkers played "Interpretations from the History of Recorded Sound" on tape. In the middle of this, Salvatore Martirano and I played the first of what over subsequent years became a series of live electronic music duets.[32] This one was called *B.C.–A.D. (The Moon Landing)*.

By this time Martirano had begun to imagine ways in which compositional thinking, even compositional methods, could be imbedded inside digital logic circuits. Physical processes in computation and music were linked. Indeed, such physical processes themselves could be thought of *as* composition. I had also been developing unique electronic circuits for music, especially some that produced nonlinear dynamical behavior—much later to be known by the "pop" term *chaos*.[33] It had also been clear to me that what we had experienced with compositional software, which at that time could run only on slow and cumbersome, large computers, could someday run on fast

UNIVERSITY OF ILLINOIS SCHOOL OF MUSIC
URBANA-CHAMPAIGN CAMPUS

### NEW SOUNDS IN MUSIC

A Series of Seven Concerts

### CONCERT No. 5

GREGORY HALL AUDITORIUM, SUNDAY, JULY 20, 1969, 8:00 P.M.

*Note:* Due to the unusual nature and length of the concert, events will begin at the approximate timings indicated below.

8:00 P.M. — Television coverage (network and closed circuit) begins and continues throughout the program until the lunar landing.

8:10 P.M. — Overture to *Il mondo della luna* . . FRANZ JOSEPH HAYDN-
CHARLES HAMM

THE CONTEMPORARY CHAMBER PLAYERS

Salvatore Martirano, *violin*      David Rosenboom, *flute*
Thomas Howell, *violin*            Arthur Maddox, *oboe*
Howard Smith, *violin*             Cheryl Fippen, *clarinet*
Robert Quade, *viola*              Eric Jensen, *horn*
William Brooks, *viola*            Jon English, *bassoon*
James Cuomo, *cello*               Ben Johnston, *trombone*
Carol Deak, *bass*
Edwin London, *conductor*

8:20 P.M. — *Pierrot Lunaire, Op. 21* . . . . . . . . ARNOLD SCHOENBERG

Marilyn Coles, *voice*                  David Rosenboom, *violin and viola*
Thomas Howell, *flute and piccolo*      Eric Jensen, *cello*
Robert Quade, *clarinet and bass clarinet*   Arthur Maddox, *piano*
Edwin London, *conductor*

9:05 P.M. — *Au clair de la lune* for tape . . . . . . . . . . . . NEELY BRUCE

9:35 P.M. — *He Is There* . . . . . . . . . . . . . . . . . . . . CHARLES IVES

THE INELUCTABLE MODALITY
Edwin London, *conductor*

9:45 P.M. — *Antithese* for performer with electronic
and public sounds . . . . . . . . . . . . . . . . . . . . MAURICIO KAGEL
Tom Rickman, *actor*

9:57 P.M. — Recipe for Flutist . . . . . . . . . . . . . . . . . BEN JOHNSTON
Thomas Howell, *flute*

10:17 P.M. — B.C.-A.D. . . . . . . . . . . . . . SALVATORE MARTIRANO and
DAVID ROSENBOOM

---

11:00 P.M. — Dominic James present

*More Feathers* . . . . . . . . . . . . . . . . . . . . music: JAMES CUOMO
lyrics: DANIEL HANKS

"Prologue," "Scene I"
CAST (in order of appearance)

Laverne . . . . . . . . . . . . . . . . . . . . . . . . . . . . . Marilyn White
Maxine . . . . . . . . . . . . . . . . . . . . . . . . . . . . . . Diane Tasca
Patti . . . . . . . . . . . . . . . . . . . . . . . . . . . . . . . Carol Rubin
Vittorio di Fiasco . . . . . . . . . . . . . . . . . . . . . . . Gene Kelly
Rex Dentalworth . . . . . . . . . . . . . . . . . . . . . . . . Gary Gardner
Bubbles Cheery . . . . . . . . . . . . . . . . . . . . . . . . Deborah Cuomo

"Those Old Stock Pavilion Blues" or "Will The Big Bands Ever
Feedback?" for four prepared jazzmen and two-channel
tape, played in three movements without interruption
. . . . . . . . . . . . . . . . . . . . . . . . . . . . . . . . . JAMES CUOMO

Allegro, Collage, Tango

THE DOMINIC JAMES QUARTET
Ron Dewar, *tenor saxophone*
James Cuomo, *tenor saxophone*
Bob Witmer, *bass*
Charles Braugham, *drums*

11:45 P.M. — *Socrate* . . . . . . . . . . . . . . . . ERIK SATIE-JOHN CAGE-
ARTHUR MADDOX

Peter Takacs and Arthur Maddox, *pianos*

12:20 A.M. — Selections by the Ron Dewar Quartet

THE RON DEWAR QUARTET
Ron Dewar, *tenor saxophone*
Jon English, *trombone*
Bob Witmer, *bass*
Charles Braugham, *drums*

THROUGHOUT THE EVENING:

Interpretations From The History of Recorded Sound in sixteen sides for
single-channel tape . . . . . . . . . . . . . . . . . . . . . . CARL VOLKERS

Nellie Melba (1901); Sarah Bernhardt (1904); Vasella's Band (1910); En-
rico Caruso et al. (1911); Victor Light Opera Company (1914); Harry Lauder
(1918); Beethoven-Toscanini (1915); Pryor's Band (1920); Beethoven-
Richard Strauss (1925); Sergei Rachmaninoff (1928); Rudy Vallee (1930);
University of Illinois Band (1930); Edward VIII (1936); Wagner-Fürtwangler
(1939); The Andrews Sisters (1940).

Films by Ron Nameth
Gift Presentations by William Wegman
Dancing by Mary Fulkerson, Nicolas Aneskiewitch, Priscilla Simpson, Ashley T.
Tetroski, Bill Fold
Clay balls — Shambana Society for the Prevention of Handicrafts

The *Time Schedule* is a guide, the absolute accuracy for which the management
cannot be held responsible.

(RELAX AND ENJOY!)

---

INELUCTABLE MODALITY
a new music lyric ensemble

| Sopranos | Tenors |
|---|---|
| Jean Geil | William Brooks |
| Phyllis Hurt | Richard Dohrmann |
| Joanne Lacquet | Fred Henzelin |
| Patricia Sentman | Robert Newell |
| Linda Vickermann | |

| Altos | Basses |
|---|---|
| Esther Carpenter | Ray Jackendoff |
| Becky Keyes | Robert Quade |
| Roberta Poellein | Larry Watts |
| Sandra Winslow | |
| Joan Luchsinger | |

NEXT CONCERTS

Gregory Hall Auditorium, Thursday, July 24, 1969 — 8:00 P.M.
Gregory Hall Auditorium, Sunday, July 27, 1969 — 8:00 P.M.

Program for the 1969 "Moon Landing" concert in Gregory Hall. Photo courtesy of David Rosenboom.

and accessible small processers; and we would be able to imbed these processors running compositional software inside electronic instruments and *play* them. In other words, whole compositional models could eventually be *played* and even used in structured improvisations. Indeed, this futuristic dream eventually did come true, and musicians now regularly employ such practices.

Both Martirano and I were interested in live performance with electronics; in July 1969, in Martirano's garage, we soldered together duplicate sets of my circuit for voltage-controlled, nonlinear frequency division, coupled those to an experimental setup with patchable and reconfigurable, modular digital logic systems that both of us had been working with previously, added digital-to-analog converters and some of my analog computer circuits to produce cycling control-voltage envelopes, and performed

*B.C.—A.D. (The Moon Landing)* simultaneously with the first human Moonwalk.

Martirano and I followed this event with our own individual lines of work in live electronic performance. I pursued intensive projects in biofeedback and the arts[34] and extended musical interface with the human nervous system.[35] Spurred on by emerging models for interactive, self-organizing systems, I also worked on what were then called "intelligent" electronic instruments, partly because they also drew inspiration from ideas in artificial intelligence.

Martirano's subsequent direction with electronics evolved through several versions of what became the legendary Sal-Mar Construction, an extraordinary example of a composer's personal composing models being imbedded in circuitry. Watching "Sal's" performances with the Sal-Mar, which he often titled *Look at the Back of My Head for a While*,[36] included the fascination of seeing someone set up musical worlds on a large control panel containing 291 touch-sensitive, binary switches with indicator lights, none of which were labeled, and listening to twenty-four-channel spatialized sound emanating from an array of speakers that had been strategically suspended prior to the performance in ways intended to complement the architecture of each venue.[37] Actually, Martirano regarded the Sal-Mar Construction as a composition in itself. For some time he resisted representing the Sal-Mar with recordings, which he considered to be mere snapshots of particular moments in the Sal-Mar's life. The "composition" included the construction and everything it produced, from the first moment it was powered on to its last. (The Sal-Mar Construction has now been restored, with all buttons labeled, and is on display at the university's Sousa Archives and Center for American Music.)[38] Martirano continued inventing systems for Sound and Logic, the name he gave to a software tool he later developed for composing. Sound and Logic found its applications in generating data for various electronic instruments—this included the Kyma system, a very powerful electronic music system that also had its origins at UIUC[39]—and for use in instrumental compositions.

> "For many decades, a rich musical atmosphere fueled by inventions in electronic instrumentation, theoretical work in computer music, and experimental composition enveloped EMS."

For many decades, a rich musical atmosphere fueled by inventions in electronic instrumentation, theoretical work in computer music, and experimental composition enveloped EMS. A very important experimental composer and theorist, James Tenney, came to Illinois, earning a master's degree under Hiller in 1961. Tenney built a white-noise generator as part of his coursework and produced the first version of his seminal theoretical work on form and perception in twentieth-century music, *Meta ╪ Hodos*. Tenney's writings have now been collected and published in a foundational theoretical book from the University of Illinois Press, *From Scratch*.[40] The Sound Rotator enabled a real-time performer to position and move sounds in space. Another stand-out EMS invention was the Harmonic Tone Generator, developed in 1964 by James Beauchamp, who held appointments in both electrical engineering and music. Throughout his career Beauchamp has been a prolific researcher and developer of many powerful computer music techniques, especially for sound synthesis, instrument tones analysis, sound spectrum analysis, and other areas. At Illinois he was always available with innovative devices and ideas. The Harmonic Tone Generator employed a unique, nonlinear method for generating harmonics of a fundamental frequency, which were voltage controlled. Its musical qualities attracted many composers, and a collection of examples appeared on a record released in 1967.[41] (The Harmonic Tone Generator also now resides in UIUC's Sousa Archives and Center for American Music.)

Edward Kobrin, another innovative composer, developed his unique HYBRID system for sixteen-channel spatial sound distribution in 1971. Kobrin also collaborated with Ben Johnston on computer tools for composition with microtonal music. International conferences in computer music began to grow in the 1970s (UIUC hosted one in 1975), and the music world in general became more accepting of computer music and the broad interdisciplinary nature of music computation. Nevertheless, the University of Illinois music community retained a radical aura that added to the feeling of excitement on campus.

In 2008 Scott Wyatt, a UIUC composer who served as director of EMS for several decades and was instrumental in the continuous modernizing and updating of the studios, celebrated this era of innovation by spearheading the production of a broadly representative, four-CD compendium, containing forty-six examples of music created by composers associated with EMS, and who utilized its inventions over a half-century of its history.[42]

Innovation and invention in experimental music at Illinois was also evident outside the arena of technology. Among these conceptual innovations were "extended techniques" in playing musical instruments and new directions in musical notation. Exploring extended techniques for wind and percussion instruments was a particularly vigorous pursuit. For example, legendary flutists Patrick Purswell and Thomas Howell encouraged new compositions employing precisely articulated multiphonics and special effects. Composers were able to write these effects into groundbreaking scores. Two striking examples were Burt Levy's *Orbs with Flute*[43] and William Brooks's ear-opening *Poempiece I: whitegold blue*, which was scored with both sound and text fragments.[44] Levy's piece, though not widely known, is an extraordinary example of effective systematic composition with extended techniques. It was a highly influential score at the time and was well studied by other composers wishing to explore these methods. Brooks's piece mingled linguistic composition with an expanded palette of sound objects for the flutist. Thomas Howell eventually produced a huge compendium of extended techniques for the flute, a kind of catalog of multiphonics and other effects with information about how to write them in scores and how to produce them on the instrument, a guide for both performers and composers.[45]

New percussion techniques were everywhere, especially since composing for multi-instrument solo and ensemble percussion had grown increasingly popular. Jack McKenzie's Illinois percussion studio was therefore another hub for experimental music. McKenzie was also a composer who had written an engaging array of percussion music, founder of the music school's Contemporary Chamber Players, founding member of the Percussive Arts Society, and a former student of the university's legendary percussion guru, Paul Price. I remember well the day in early 1967 when percussionist G. Allan O'Connor, who performed many works by UIUC experimental composers, brought in new percussion mallets made from Super Ball® synthetic rubber, which enabled an entirely new spectrum of percussion sounds, from sustained sizzles and roars to rapid-fire bursts of impulses. The Wham-O Toy Company had just produced the Super Ball® in 1965. I immediately wrote Super Ball® percussion mallets into my quartet for percussion, *To That Predestined Dancing Place*, which premiered at UIUC soon thereafter. Now, Super Ball® mallets are standard equipment for contemporary percussionists.

Extended techniques for the voice and vocal ensembles were also a hot topic. Kenneth Gaburo's New Music Choral Ensemble fueled this in the 1960s, and after Gaburo's departure Edwin London's Ineluctable Modality vocal ensemble kept the ball rolling. Others, particularly William Brooks (who had been a member of the New Music Choral Ensemble) and later, Jacqueline Bobak (then a UIUC doctoral student, now a faculty member in the Herb Alpert School of Music at California Institute of the Arts) continued to take things further.

In the arena of new musical notation, during the 1960s and 1970s practically the entire experimental community at Illinois was putting forth new ways of making musical scores, new ways of regarding notation as the delicate interface between musical ideas, performance practices, and documentation. Others had set the stage for this. Pierre Schaeffer, the seminal French experimentalist, had written in 1952, "Now, in its concrete as in its abstract aspect, contemporary music is limited in its development by the very means of 'making music' and 'writing music down.'"[46] At Illinois, pianist Virginia Gaburo's *Notation (a lecture to be performed by solo speaker to attentive audience)* was an illuminating treatise about the dynamical roles of notation in music. She wrote, "Meaning takes place in the mind. The sensibly perceivable symbol acts as a stimulus to mental activity" and "musical notation need not be merely inscribed musical sound—a translation with attendant losses and gains of possible indicators of meaning: nor need it be inscribed directions for the production of sound—a contract."[47] This thinking was far from what had unfortunately become all-too-common stilted methodologies of conservatory-oriented pedagogues.

Ear-opening extended instrumental techniques and new directions in notation literally blasted out from Salvatore Martirano's Experimental Orchestration class, which gave young composers opportunities to try things out with numerous experimental ensemble configurations

> "Ear-opening extended instrumental techniques and new directions in notation literally blasted out from Salvatore Martirano's Experimental Orchestration class . . ."

along with full orchestra. Musicians were extensively exploiting ingenious new graphical techniques for musical notation. While working with Martirano in 1966–67, I developed a systematic approach to composing with degrees of freedom in notation, beginning with standard Western notation and progressively stripping away layers of specificity until what remained constituted directions for structured improvisation. The "degrees" were arranged on a scale so that they could be used in ordered arrays much like musical notes. *Melodies of Freedom*, arrayed with these scales of notation, could be composed in this way.

Eventually and predictably, it appeared to some that experimental music, as it became more widely accepted, was increasingly being subsumed inside the usual and traditional, concert-hall cultural milieu. (Some even started calling it "classical contemporary music.") This growing acceptance actually irritated some of the younger, more radically inclined, experimental composers of the late 1960s. They began to feel that even the creative community at Illinois was becoming a bit too set in its ways and not paying enough attention to the latest experimental directions in music and multimedia. News from the New York "Downtown Scene," as represented by composers and artists like La Monte Young, Nam June Paik, the Velvet Underground, and Andy Warhol's Factory, had arrived, as had awareness of West Coast developments in rock music, which was clearly crossing genres with "classical contemporary" and non-Western music, and goings on at places like the Fillmore Auditorium and the San Francisco Tape Music Center.

It seemed to many that a more confrontational expression was necessary. As a consequence, on March 17, 1967, during a Festival of Contemporary Arts concert in Smith Music Hall, featuring important works by Lucien Goethals, Bernard Rands, Iannis Xenakis, and György Ligeti, the Composition String Quartet—the same ensemble that had recently recorded *The ILLIAC Suite*—challenged audience, faculty, and festival planners by also presenting a stirring, rock-style performance of a string quartet by Michael von Biel. The piece was scored primarily with carefully structured noises instead of pitched sounds. To this the performers had added specially designed lighting, costumes, cheering groupies, balloons, and stream-

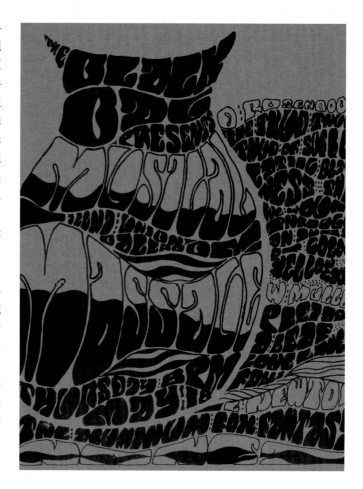

Poster for the 1967 Black Bag concert. Photo courtesy of David Rosenboom.

ers. Many in the audience applauded enthusiastically, but some music faculty and concert planners were less enthusiastic. While a few critics were outraged, others supported the performers' right to make creative choices.

The student experimental music community at UIUC in the 1960s was an extraordinarily entrepreneurial bunch. That may explain why so many went on to achieve prominence in their respective contemporary music fields. Following the official 1967 Festival of Contemporary Arts, a group of students staged their own mini-festival in the ballroom of the Illini Union, called The Black Bag Presents Musical Massage—media ecologist Marshal McLuhan's influence was already evident—complete with West Coast–inspired balloon lettering on the posters. The performances featured new pieces by William Mullen, Lynn

William Duckworth's group performing music by David Rosenboom.
Photo courtesy of David Rosenboom.

David Newton, myself, and others. They combined music with multimedia, theatrics, electronics, and compositions blending rock music and improvisation. The group was pushing on the future's wall. Whatever the nature of controversies that various flavors of experimental music could create, Illinois remained a place of opportunity and a fertile environment for musical innovations spanning an extraordinary range of interests, ideas, and cultural contexts.

The community of experimental music innovators with links to Illinois is too large to enumerate. Space does not permit doing justice to all the important and nurturing faculty, staff, and students, but any list should at least include John Garvey, violist with the Walden Quartet and director of the Illinois Jazz Band; James Campbell, tireless

recording expert and technology advisor; Jaap Speck, another skilled technologist; Soulima Stravinsky, an astonishing pianist and teacher; Neely Bruce, composer-pianist; the late composer-trombonist William Duckworth (later a pioneer in internet-enabled composition); and Eric Lund, a composer of acoustic and electroacoustic music who continues to teach composition at the university.

An extraordinary group of women composers and researchers also emerged from the simmering musical soup at Illinois. Maggi Payne is an innovative composer of electronic music; Mary Ellen Childs is a composer and multimedia artist who founded the ensemble CRASH; Carla Scaletti is a composer of music inspired by phenomena of nature and a developer of computer music instrumentation; and while at UIUC composer Insook

Choi pursued pioneering, multimedia human-computer interface work in Beckman Institute's full-immersion interactive environment, The Cave.

Another comment from Richard Powers's *Orfeo* captures the creative vigor of the University of Illinois music community in the mid-twentieth century and beyond: "Not since *ars nova* in the fourteenth century or the development of sonata-allegro form at the end of the eighteenth had there been a better time to be a beginner."[48]

## Notes

1. I heard John Cage speak these words in Lejaren Hiller's graduate seminar in the fall of 1965 after a performance-lecture Cage had just given during the School of Music's regular Tuesday convocation required of all students, in which, as I recall, Cage made carrot juice (or something similar) with contact mikes amplifying his apparatus while delivering a talk. Afterward, a fellow seminar student had asked something like, "But Mr. Cage, can you call this music?"

2. Richard Powers, *Orfeo* (New York: Norton, 2014), 90. Powers mentions many UIUC experimental music composers in this novel.

3. David Nicholls, *American Experimental Music 1890–1940* (Cambridge: Cambridge University Press, 1990).

4. Pierre Schaeffer, "Vers une Musique Expérimentale," *La Revue Musicale* 236 (Paris: Richard-Masse, 1957): 18–23; Carlos Palombini, "Pierre Schaeffer, 1953: Towards an Experimental Music," *Music and Letters* 74, no. 4 (November 1993): 542–57.

5. Christian Wolff, "Experimental Music around 1950 and Some Consequences and Causes (Social, Political, Musical)," *American Music* 27, no. 4 (Winter 2009): 424–40; Michael Nyman, *Experimental Music* (London: Cassell and Collier Macmillan, 1974). See especially Nyman's interesting essay on the term "experimental music" in chapter 1 of his book.

6. Lejaren A. Hiller Jr. and Rolf H. Herber, *Principles of Chemistry* (New York: McGraw-Hill, 1960).

7. Ibid., v.

8. Lejaren Hiller and Calvert Bean, "Information Theory Analyses of Four Sonata Expositions," *Journal of Music Theory* 10 (Spring 1966): 96–137; Lejaren Hiller and Ramon Fuller, "Structure and Information in Webern's Symphonie, Op. 21," *Journal of Music Theory* 11 (Spring 1967): 60–115.

9. Abraham Moles, *Information Theory and Esthetic Perception* (Urbana: University of Illinois Press, 1966).

10. Lejaren A. Hiller Jr. and Rolf H. Herber, *Principles of Chemistry* (New York: McGraw-Hill, 1960), 578–79; Claude E. Shannon and Warren Weaver, *The Mathematical Theory of Communication* (Urbana: University of Illinois Press, 1964). This document was first published in 1948 in the *Bell System Technical Journal*. Note the number of references herein to innovative work published by the University of Illinois Press, which established itself early on as a leading academic publisher.

11. Lejaren Hiller, Leonard Isaacson, and Robert Baker, *Computer Music from the University of Illinois*, LP Heliodor H/HS 25053 (New York: MGM, 1967), later released as *Quartet No. 4 "Illiac Suite"* on Lejaren Hiller, *Computer Music Retrospective*, LP WER 60128 and CD WER 60128-50 (Mainz, Ger.: Wergo, LP 1986 and CD 1989). I was violinist on this recording. The later release also contains a variety of other pieces by Hiller and various collaborators, notably including John Myhill. Myhill, a mathematician famous for his work in mathematical logic, which he also applied in areas of music theory and algorithmic composition, spent time at UIUC before eventually settling, along with Hiller, at the State University of New York at Buffalo for their later careers.

12. Heinz von Foerster and James W. Beauchamp, eds., *Music by Computers* (New York: Wiley, 1969). This book also contains important chapters by UIUC experimental composers Herbert Brün and Lejaren Hiller.

13. Ibid., 8–9.

14. Howard Taubman, "Play It Again, I.B.M.," *New York Times*, November 14, 1966.

15. James Matthew Bohn, *The Music of American Composer Lejaren Hiller and an Examination of His Early Works Involving Technology* (Lewiston, N.Y.: Mellen, 2004).

16. For a recording of HPSCHD see *Cage and Hiller: HPSCHD/ Johnston: String Quartet No. 2*, LP record H-71224 (New York: Nonesuch, 1969) and a later remastered version, *HPSCHD [for harpsichords and computer-generated sound tapes]*, EMF 038 CD (Albany, N.Y.: Electronic Music Foundation, 2003).

17. See the BCL website, http://bcl.ece.illinois.edu.

18. Humberto Maturana, "Neurophysiology of Cognition," *Lingua Press Collection Two Catalogue November 1977* (La Jolla, Calif.: Lingua, 1978), also published in Paul L. Garvin, ed., *Cognition: A Multiple View* (New York: Spartan, 1970), 3–23.

19. Heinz von Foerster, *Observing Systems*, 2nd edition (Seaside, Calif.: Intersystems, 1984).

20. Herbert Brün, *SAWDUST Computer Music Project*, CD EMF 00644 (Albany, N.Y.: EMF, 1998); Arun Chandra, ed., *When Music Resists Meaning: The Major Writings of Herbert Brün* (Middletown, Conn.: Wesleyan University Press, 2004).

21. Charles E. Osgood, George J. Suci, and Percy H. Tannenbaum, *The Measurement of Meaning* (Urbana: University of Illinois Press, 1957).

22. Ithiel de Sola Pool, ed., *Trends in Content Analysis* (Urbana: University of Illinois Press, 1959).

23. Kenneth Gaburo later published "Extraction" as part of a personal paper-play mini-book series, now considered a rare item.

24. David Rosenboom, "Propositional Music: On Emergent Properties in Morphogenesis and the Evolution of Music," in *Arcana, Musicians on Music*, edited by John Zorn (New York, Granary/Hips Road, 2000), 203–32.

25. I gleaned much of this information on Gaburo-related events and some others from UIUC School of Music concert programs, programs from Salvatore Martirano's legendary Round House concerts, notes and scores Gaburo and others gave me at various times, and files containing notes, concert programs, posters, and other documents in my personal archives. Martirano's Round House (where he lived in Urbana for a time in the 1960s) was one of the best places to go to hear new experimental music. For example, one program from a concert that took place there on March 12, 1966, lists five world premieres by Gordon Binkerd, Phil Winsor, Herbert Brün, Salvatore Martirano, and Kenneth Gaburo, four Urbana premieres by Ralph Shapey, Will Ogdon, Luigi Nono, and Anton Webern, and another work by Ben Johnston.

26. For an early example, see *Cage and Hiller: HPSCHD/ Johnston: String Quartet No. 2*, LP record H-71224 (New York: Nonesuch, 1969).

27. Ben Johnston, *String Quartets 1, 5, and 10*, CD 80693 (New York: New World, 2011); Ben Johnston, *String Quartets 2, 3, 4, and 9*, CD 80637 (New York: New World, 2006). I am aware of an ongoing project by the Kepler Quartet to release all the Johnston quartets that still remain unavailable.

28. Kenneth Gaburo, "In Search of Partch's Bewitched: Part One—Concerning Physicality" (copy of manuscript Gaburo inscribed and gave to me, 1983), later published in *Harry Partch: An Anthology of Critical Perspectives*, edited by David Dunn (New York: Harwood Academic, 2000, and Routledge, 2013).

29. Ben Johnston, *"Maximum Clarity" and Other Writings on Music*, edited by Bob Gilmore (Urbana: University of Illinois Press, 2006).

30. In 1979 Martirano wrote significant portions of *Stuck on Stella* while visiting my home in Piedmont, California, and using my piano for composing. This quote is from personal conversations with Martirano during that time. He was probably referring to "seventh chords" as they emerge from emphasizing "octatonic" scales. For a recording see *Salvatore Martirano, O, O, O, O, That Shakespeherian Rag*, CD 80535-2, (New York: New World, 1998).

31. For a recording see *The Virtuosos in the Computer Age—I*, CDCM Computer Music Series, vol. 10, CD CRC 2110 (Baton Rouge, La.: Centaur, 1991).

32. For two examples see David Rosenboom and Salvatore Martirano, *B.C.–A.D. (The Moon Landing)* (1969) on David Rosenboom, *Roundup Two, Selected music with electro-acoustic landscapes (1968–1984)*, two-CD set, 001 (Japan: Art into Life, 2012), and Salvatore Martirano and David Rosenboom, *B.C.—A.D. II* (1977) on David Rosenboom, *Life Field*, CD TZ 8091 (New York: Tzadik, 2012). Note: *Life Field* also contains Rosenboom's work *Pocket Pieces* for flute, viola, alto saxophone, and percussion, which he wrote while studying composition with composer Gordon Binkerd at UIUC; it premiered on a Student Composition Recital, April 28, 1966, at 1203 W. Nevada, Urbana, and was performed again on a Convocation Program in Smith Recital Hall along with his *Trio* for clarinet, trumpet, and string bass on May 19, 1966.

33. David Rosenboom, "'B.C.–A.D.' and 'Two Lines': Two Ways of Making Music While Exploring Instability in Tribute to Salvatore Martirano," *Perspectives of New Music* 34, no. 1, (Winter 1996): 208–26.

34. David Rosenboom, ed., *Biofeedback and the Arts: Results of Early Experiments* (Vancouver: Aesthetic Research Center of Canada, 1976).

35. David Rosenboom, *Extended Musical Interface with the Human Nervous System: Assessment and Prospectus*, Leonardo Monograph No. 1 (San Francisco: International Society for the Arts, Sciences and Technology, 1990), 1997 revised edition available for download at http://www.davidrosenboom.com/media/extended-musical-interface-human-nervous-system-assessment-and-prospectus.

36. Salvatore Martirano, "Look at the Back of My Head for A While" (1974), on *The Composer in the Computer Age—V, A Salvatore Martirano Retrospective: 1962–92*, CDCM Computer Music Series, Vol. 22, CD CRC 2266 (Baton Rouge, La.: Centaur, 1995).

37. For an informative though not complete technical picture of the Sal-Mar Construction, see Sergio Franco, *Hardware Design of a Real-Time Musical System*, PhD diss., UIUCDCS-R-74-677 (Urbana: Department of Computer Science, University of Illinois, 1974).

38. On April 1, 2004, I gave a lecture-demonstration-perform-

ance, *The Sal-Mar Construction of Salvatore Martirano*, with the restored instrument in Smith Music Hall during a conference presented by UIUC's Division of Musicology, School of Music, *New Directions in the Study of Musical Improvisation*, organized by Gabriel Solis, William Kinderman, and Bruno Nettl (chair).

39. Kyma was developed by Carla Scaletti, also an accomplished composer, and Kurt Hebel after they had worked on innovative projects at UIUC's CERL (Computer-based Education Research Laboratory) and its IMS (Interactive Music System) in the 1980s. Scaletti and Hebel eventually went on to found Symbolic Sound Corporation, based in Urbana-Champaign, which still develops Kyma systems and serves as a focal point for a worldwide community of electronic music practitioners and Kyma developers.

40. James Tenney, *From Scratch: Writings in Music Theory*, edited by Larry Polansky, Lauren Pratt, Robert Wannamaker, and Michael Winter (Urbana: University of Illinois Press, 2015).

41. *Electronic Music from the University of Illinois*, LP record HS-25047 (New York: Heliodor/MGM, 1967).

42. *In Celebration of the 50th Anniversary of the University of Illinois Experimental Music Studios (1958–2008)*, four-CD set EMS-2008 (Urbana: University of Illinois School of Music, 2008).

43. Burt Levy, *Orbs with Flute* (Cincinnati, Ohio: Apogee, 1966).

44. William Brooks, "Poempiece I: whitegold blue," *Lingua Press Collection Two Catalogue November 1977* (La Jolla, Calif.: Lingua, 1978).

45. Thomas Howell, *The Avant-Garde Flute: A Handbook for Composers and Flutists*, The New Instrumentation, vol. 2 (Berkeley: University of California Press, 1974).

46. Pierre Schaeffer, *In Search of a Concrete Music*, translated by Christine North and John Dack (Berkeley: University of California Press, 2012), 118.

47. Virginia Gaburo, *Notation (a lecture to be performed by solo speaker to attentive audience)* (La Jolla, Calif.; Lingua, 1977).

48. Powers, *Orfeo*, 96.

Blue Waters, one of the most powerful supercomputers in the
world, was made possible by the combined support of the State
of Illinois, private donors, and the National Science Foundation.
It is the latest version of a series of revolutionary computers that
began on campus with the creation of ILLIAC I in 1952.

Kimiko Gunji, professor emeritus of Japanese arts and culture and former director of Japan House, performs a tea ceremony. Continuing the legacy of its founding director, the artist and actor Shozo Sato, Japan House and its surrounding gardens promote cultural understanding by hosting tea ceremonies, community classes, cultural events, and courses for students in the College of Fine and Applied Arts.

Pursuing the goal of determining optimum growing conditions for the nation's agricultural food supply—a goal established when the Morrow Plots were first cultivated in 1876—researchers at the SoyFACE (Soybean Free Air Concentration Enrichment) Plots analyze the effects of atmospheric change on the productivity of soybeans and other crops.

Daniel Shike (Department of Animal Sciences) provides instruction on the U of I South Farms. Faculty and students in the College of ACES routinely extend the research findings that produced the breakthroughs represented in part by its most famous achievements: Illini Nellie and Big Al.

By vastly expanding the library's ability to house the materials in its care while keeping them within reach of scholars, the university's high-density storage facility has enabled it to sustain President Edmund James's vision of maintaining one of the world's largest research collections on the Urbana-Champaign campus.

Multifaceted theatrical collaborations such as *Kama Begata Nihilum* demonstrate that the idea of bringing together a range of artistic disciplines in a single building—something Herman and Ellnora Krannert suggested as they helped launch the Krannert Center for the Performing Arts—continues to pay rich dividends.

The four Nevada Street units—the Department of Asian American Studies, the Department of African American Studies, the Department of Latino/Latina Studies, and the American Indian Studies Program—hold recognition ceremonies like this one to honor graduating students and their families.

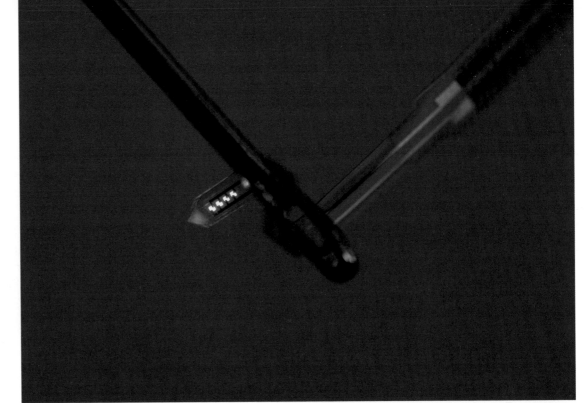

Recent innovations in LED technology have built on Professor Nick Holonyak's pioneering research into the potential of semiconductors to emit light. Today's LEDs can literally dance on the head of a pin.

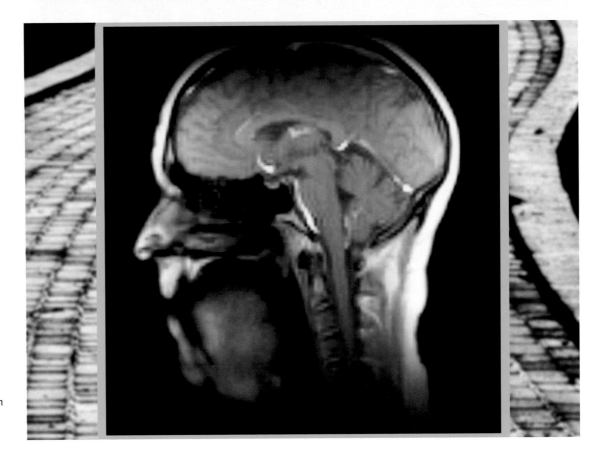

Superfast MRI techniques developed by faculty in the Beckman Institute's Bioimaging Science and Technology Group (including Zhi-Pei Liang, professor of electrical and computer engineering, and Brad Sutton, associate professor of bioengineering) improve upon the innovations in medical diagnostics initiated by Illinois Nobel laureate Paul Lauterbur. They demonstrate as well the ongoing—endless—process by which major innovations can continue to benefit humanity.

In 2014 Spike Lee came to Champaign for the twenty-fifth-anniversary screening of his film *Do the Right Thing* at that year's Ebertfest. Illinois alumnus Roger Ebert was an early advocate of both Spike Lee and *Do the Right Thing*, giving the film a rave review despite public criticism of the film's unapologetic examination of racism in America. Pictured from left to right: Odie Henderson (a contributor to RogerEbert.com), Michael Phillips (film critic for the *Chicago Tribune*), Chaz Ebert (cofounder and producer of Ebertfest), and Spike Lee.

Today, the Experimental Music Studio continues to redefine the limits of music by elaborating on the innovations first developed during the "musical Big Bang" that occurred on the Illinois campus during the decade of the 1960s.

The Department of African American Studies' enduring commitment to enriching the campus community continues through its support of innovative courses in many units, including the Department of Dance. Recently, C. Kemal Nance (shown above) and Cynthia Oliver have offered courses that help students explore issues of race and gender through the medium of African and African American dance.

Named for Timothy Nugent, founder of the university's Division of
Disability Resources and Educational Services, this residence hall
fulfills this pioneering educator's vision. A combination of singles,
doubles, specially accessible rooms, and dedicated support services creates a uniquely diverse living community available to all.

Timothy Nugent's mission to improve accessibility to higher education continues with the Beckwith Residential Support Services, which offers campus housing and basic assistance for students with physical disabilities. The program also reflects Nugent's determination to create a sense of community and enthusiasm among all of the university's students.

Installed on the west plaza of the Institute for Genomic Biology, Darwin's Playground is an artistic expression of the constantly evolving field of the life sciences. Reminiscent of clay figures, Tony Tasset's piece reveals the power of genetic engineering to shape and enhance life.

The University Library is expanding into the digital world with projects that increase humanities researchers' access to resources. This equipment facilitates the mass digitization of archive materials via two projects: Illinois Harvest Digitization, and the Open Content Alliance Mass Digitization.

Emma Mercier (Department of Education) at IDEALL (Illinois Digital Ecologies and Learning Laboratory) with a multitouch table designed for collaboration in classroom settings. Mercier's work focuses on computer-supported collaborative learning and how technology influences group interactions and learning in classroom contexts.

Founded in 1968 as Project 500 got underway, the University of Illinois Black Chorus has long been directed by Professor of Voice Ollie Watts Davis. Under her leadership the group—now more than one hundred strong—performs and records its music for a wide audience.

The Department of Gender and Women's Studies promotes scholarship that bridges disciplines in the arts, humanities, and social sciences. Professor Ruth Nicole Brown represents a recent example of this effort. She has explored how Black girls have been marginalized in academic life. Her writing and public outreach, including the organization Saving Our Lives Hear Our Truths (SOLHOT), have helped these young women to reimagine their own belonging in society.

# The Beginning of Public Broadcasting

*Kristen Allen*

Wilbur Schramm came to the University of Illinois from the University of Iowa in 1947 to establish the Institute of Communications Research. His work with the War Information Office during World War II had convinced him that communications technology could be a powerful force for public education and drew him into research on the role of modern communications in the shaping of public opinion. As the war ended and the nation returned to "normal," Schramm feared that the expansion of commercial radio and the rapid advance of televised entertainment would imperil the potential of publicly supported educational broadcasting to improve the lives of everyday Americans.

Eager to tackle this looming problem, Schramm persuaded John Marshall of the Rockefeller Foundation to support a meeting of twenty directors of educational broadcast outlets, mainly members of the newly formed National Association of Educational Broadcasters (NAEB), at the university's conference center at Allerton House in Monticello, Illinois. After two separate meetings, the group produced a strategic plan for the future. They declared that educational broadcasting should broaden its audience by developing programming for people of all backgrounds and education levels. They added that educational outlets should expand their audiences, train new staff, and develop collaborative programming. The conferences also produced a system for sharing educational radio programs.

As Illinois and other university-based broadcasters implemented these ideas, they developed networks for circulating programs within regions and producing jointly developed projects. Soon, more than one hundred educational stations around the country began receiving tapes of program recordings from the NAEB headquarters in the basement of Gregory Hall. This network formed the basis for the national broadcasting networks National Public Radio (NPR) and the Public Broadcasting Service (PBS), which emerged in 1970 following the passage of the Public Broadcasting Act. (Schramm and the NAEB played a vital role in lobbying for passage of this new law.) It is fair to say that the inspiration for both NPR and PBS was born at Allerton House under the guidance of Wilbur Schramm.

## Sources

Schramm's Allerton House conference is discussed in Robert B. Hudson, "Allerton House 1949, 1950," *Hollywood Quarterly* 5, no. 3 (Spring 1952): 237–50. Information on the creation of PBS can be found in Laurence A. Jarvik, *PBS: Behind the Screen* (New York: Forum, 1997). For NPR, see Michael P. McCauley, *NPR: The Trials and Triumphs of National Public Radio* (New York: Columbia University Press, 2005). The University of Illinois Archives also contains information on the Allerton conferences, WILL radio and television, and Schramm.

"Book Talk," an early public radio program

# Joseph McVicker Hunt
## The Invention of Early Childhood Education

Elizabeth H. Pleck

In 1951 Lyle Lanier, the dynamic new chair of the Psychology Department at the University of Illinois, set out to recruit nationally recognized scientists and leaders of the profession to Urbana-Champaign. At the top of his list of possible new faculty was Joseph McVicker Hunt, then age forty-three, whom Lanier invited to head up his department's counseling and clinical psychology doctoral program. Lanier had come to Illinois from New York University and had known Hunt for many years. Lanier had asked Hunt to teach a graduate course in psychological research methods at NYU. In New York City Hunt had been director of a research unit within a social welfare agency.

Hunt was committed to a model of training that would prepare clinical psychologists both to counsel individual patients and to engage in research. He had come a long way from the Nebraska farm where he had grown up and from Lincoln, Nebraska, where he had married his college sweetheart and taken up a first job selling life insurance. By the time he answered Lanier's call, Hunt had become a leader of his profession, renowned for his experimental cognitive research based on hoarding behavior in rats, and had served as the president of the American Psychological Association. (Hunt was also an advocate of social justice. At the 1951 APA conference in Washington, D.C., he and other leaders responded to black members who complained of discriminatory treatment by successfully proposing a resolution establishing a boycott on future conventions in the city. The hotel hosting the convention claimed the charges of racial discrimination were fabrications created by subversives and Communists, but President Hunt rejected those claims. He insisted that the complaints were valid and that his organization would continue to fight against all forms of discrimination.)

At Illinois Hunt quickly grew restless with teaching graduate courses in psychotherapy and Freudian theory. Recognizing that individual psychotherapy reached few people and could not address large-scale social problems such as racial discrimination or poverty, Hunt looked for theory and practice that could "bring a major share of the children of the persistently poor into the mainstream of our society."[1] He believed that closing the educational gap between poor and middle-class children was the most effective way of accomplishing that goal. Hunt soon secured funding from the Russell Sage Foundation for a review of empirical research about the effects of early childhood experiences on all aspects of the psychological development of adults; he wanted to sort through diametrically opposed claims about effective parenting practices. After writing several hundred pages about the history of childrearing in Western thought to show how prevalent beliefs shaped societal goals for childrearing, he opted instead to write about how the child's environment influenced IQ.

At the time the prevailing psychological wisdom was that an individual's IQ was fixed, based on the child's genetic inheritance. It was believed that parents and schools had little or no opportunity to raise a child's IQ scores. The title of the book Hunt eventually wrote, *Intelligence and Experience* (1961), summarized his essential argument, that rich and stimulating early childhood environments could substantially boost a child's intelligence. Hunt argued that the human brain processed information much like a computer. When the information processing system was working well, it generated "intrinsic motivation" for more learning ("learning begets learning"). Hunt believed that genetic inheritance set the limits of intelligence, but that parents and teachers, rightly trained, could assist the child in reaching the upper limits of his or her potential. To reach that upper limit, the instructor had to find "the match," the optimum learning environment in which the child reacts to new things, sounds, and experiences with spontaneous interest and joy. The trick was finding activities that were just a little beyond

Professor Hunt at work

the child's abilities—something not too frustrating but not boring, either. Throughout his career Hunt repeated his claims that the average person's IQ could be boosted by twenty to thirty points, that the IQs of the mentally handicapped could be raised in the proper environment, and that the upper limit of growth in the IQ was about eighty-five points.[2]

Hunt grounded his optimism in the cognitive theories of Swiss psychologist Jean Piaget. From observing his own children Piaget described specific stages in an infant's physical and mental development. Each stage was marked by mastery of distinct features of motor and cognitive development; these stages were central in getting the child ready to speak. To Piaget children were not simply sponges soaking up adult instructions, they were thinking beings. The more the infant was challenged, the more he or she would want to touch, grab, see, hear, make noises, and learn. Hunt believed the Montessori method of early childhood education, supplemented by teaching language skills, was the instructional method that best implemented Piaget's ideas. To Hunt the early-twentieth-century Italian educator Maria Montessori solved "the problem of the match" by allowing the child to choose activities that interested him or her and proceed at a deliberate speed, thus making use of the child's "intrinsic motivation" to learn. "Don't push, but don't hold back, either," would remain his advice about early childhood education.

In the early 1960s Americans were discovering persistent poverty and racial discrimination in a largely affluent nation. Books like Michael Harrington's *Other America* (1962) and the ongoing struggle for civil rights and racial equality persuaded policymakers at all levels that society needed new tools to help those who had been excluded from postwar prosperity. Poor children, especially minority children, had tested as having lower IQs than middle-class children and often did poorly in school. Hunt claimed the reason for racial and class differences in IQ scores was not heredity but the child's limited contact with the world of sounds, words, and objects, compounded by parents and caregivers who rarely answered children's questions and failed to talk extensively with them. To Hunt such children were "culturally deprived," arriving at school already behind in their skills and motivation to learn and falling further behind with every passing grade. Following Piaget, the Illinois psychologist argued that the early years of childhood represented the most opportune time to intervene on behalf of the child because it was then that intellectual development could be most rapid.

Hunt's ideas and optimism were also a perfect match for the activist era that produced Lyndon Johnson's War on Poverty. Hunt was not the father of Head Start (several claimed that title), but he was an influential expert who can be credited with providing the intellectual legitimacy for it. In fact, all the initial Great Society antipoverty programs were aimed at adults; by the summer of 1965, Head Start, a smattering of federally funded programs for early childhood education, was added to the mix. Head Start became a full-year program by the end of the year. It would retain its popularity over the decades and become the major federal program promoting the educational development of poor children in the pre-kindergarten years.

Hunt's clearest influence in the years just prior to the launching of Head Start was in his role as an advisor to a pilot program run by two psychologists, Martin and Cynthia Deutsch in Harlem. Martin Deutsch invited Hunt to an academic conference at Columbia University in 1962 to deliver an address about the importance of early childhood education in overcoming the "cultural deprivation" of poor children. Hunt's article, based on his conference paper "The Psychological Basis for Using Pre-School Enrichment as an Antidote for Cultural Deprivation," was widely reprinted. Even more than *Intelligence and Experience*, this article became the intellectual blueprint for the Deutsch program in Harlem and for other pre–Head Start educational experiments.

In 1965 Joseph Califano, President Lyndon Johnson's chief domestic aide, traveled to several universities to seek feedback regarding Head Start. He was met with a uniform response: by the time a child enrolled in the program (typically at age five), it was already too late. Rather than appointing a task force of government officials and administrators, Califano sought the recommendations of distinguished academics. He asked Joseph Hunt to serve as chair of the White House Task Force on Early Childhood Education.[3] The Hunt Task Force consisted of social workers, pediatricians, psychiatrists, and distinguished academics, including Hunt's colleague from Illinois, anthropologist Oscar Lewis, who worried, like Hunt, about the "cultural deprivation" of poor children.

Hunt wrote the task force's report, which stated that "the need of infants and children deserve top priority in Government." He drew heavily on his own published research in articles and in *Intelligence and Experience* in making the case for the benefits of an enhanced educational environment in early childhood. The report, *A*

*Bill of Rights for Children* (1967) called for expansion of Head Start as well as new programs that offered expanded children's programs in the public schools. (The panel proposed "Project Follow-Through," compensatory public education that would extend through the third grade.) The group also called for an extension of programs to younger children through neighborhood Parent and Child Centers and the creation of an institutional anchor for all of these efforts in a newly established Office of Children (which President Johnson endorsed and President Nixon established in 1972).

*A Bill of Rights for Children* was not narrowly focused on the education of the child. It emphasized instead parental involvement in government programs, free healthcare for poor children, a guaranteed annual income, daycare, and family planning. Despite the emphasis on massive federal funding in this list of proposals, Hunt characteristically added a note of caution, common for academic experts. He suggested experimental programs should begin "in a limited fashion" so as to avoid "imposing nation-wide an untried pattern." Shorn of Hunt's diffidence, the recommendations of the task force were incorporated in LBJ's message to Congress in 1967 and his Special Message to Congress on Children and Youth the same year. In these messages the president referred to "recent studies" that "confirm what we have long suspected. In education, in health, in all of human development, the early years are the critical years."[4]

Because of his academic standing and role as the author of this report, Hunt was appointed to the National Advisory Board of the Children's Workshop, which was developing a new program for preschool children to be broadcast on public television. The workshop was designing a children's television program to entertain young children through animation, puppets, and songs while teaching them the alphabet and their numbers. Although it was understood that the program would reach children from all backgrounds, the emphasis was on holding the attention of an inner-city child. After several years of research *Sesame Street* was first broadcast on public television in 1969 and became an immediate hit. As a member of the advisory board, Hunt defended *Sesame Street* from the occasional educational critic, commented on instructional methods used in the program, reacted to specific programs, and pressed for segments of phonics education to teach reading.

In 1969, only three years after Head Start had begun, the psychologist Arthur Jensen of the University of California published a lengthy review of studies about the inheritability of IQ in the *Harvard Educational Review*. A small section of the article, titled "Is Intelligence Fixed?" took aim at the new conventional wisdom, derived from Hunt's *Intelligence and Experience*, "that there was no such thing as fixed intelligence." Evaluation studies showed that early Head Start programs had failed to increase children's IQ and that whatever gains children derived from the program evaporated by third grade; Jensen claimed the reason for these results was the genetic difference in IQ between black and white children. Since intelligence was mainly inherited, he argued, it could not be changed by any form of compensatory education.

Hunt noted that Jensen's findings had been discussed at a Nixon administration cabinet meeting and may have contributed to a reduction in funding for early childhood education. As to Jensen's review of the literature, Hunt told a reporter, "What Jensen says is a half-truth and a very dangerous half-truth."[5] In a rejoinder to Jensen published in a subsequent issue of the *Harvard Educational Review*, Hunt admitted that Head Start IQ gains of

> "*A Bill of Rights for Children* was not narrowly focused on the education of the child. It emphasized instead parental involvement in government programs, free health care for poor children, a guaranteed annual income, day care, and family planning."

The Early Childhood Education Laboratory

neighborhood Parent and Child Centers in infancy and continued through the first three elementary grades.

By the early 1960s Hunt and his colleagues in the university's Psychological Development Laboratory had turned their attention to the learning patterns of infants. Hunt believed that the earlier infants received the proper cognitive stimulation, the sooner they would be able to learn to talk and develop other crucial mental abilities. In collaboration with a former graduate student, Ina Uzgiris, he developed a set of scales for assessing an infant's ability to achieve the key breakthrough of memory (knowing that a toy exists, even if it has been hidden under a blanket) along with six training films that illustrated various other breakthrough moments. As part of the White House task force, Hunt had been the leading advocate of federally funded neighborhood parent-child centers—infant care centers to train low-income mothers in how to stimulate their infant's cognitive development. Separate from Hunt, professors and their graduate students in the College of Education had been developing such a program training welfare mothers in Urbana-Champaign. Hunt, along with Earladeen Badger, an Illinois PhD who had helped pioneer the Urbana project, made the parent-child program at Mt. Carmel, Illinois, a model for other centers across the country.[6]

In addition to the parent-child centers, Hunt also believed his ideas could be useful in orphanages. For most of their history, orphanages offered little cognitive stimulation. Even in the 1960s, a mobile hanging above the infant's crib was an unknown feature of an orphanage's environment. In 1956, Hunt's long-time friend and colleague, psychologist Wayne Dennis, had come across an orphanage in Tehran where the vast majority of children were not walking, even at age four, and could not speak. With Dennis's introduction Hunt began research at the Orphanage of the Queen Farah Pahlavi Charity Society in 1966. Babies there often had glum faces and barely moved; often thirty or forty babies in cribs were cared for by two or three attendants. Hunt's Tehran research included a successive series of interventions in the care of infants; the most important of these was a program to train caretakers to respond when the infant cooed or babbled. They would encourage staff, for example, to stimulate the baby

poor children faded quickly but claimed that the program had been oversold and that Americans were naïve and impatient if they expected a summer or a single year of early childhood education to overcome deep deficits in learning and motivation. All along he had worried that Head Start was using the wrong educational method in teaching children of the poor. He believed that War on Poverty director Sargent Shriver and LBJ had chosen to emphasize providing poor children with medical care and instruction heavy on social and emotional development at the expense of boosting intellectual development. To catch up with middle-class children, poor children, Hunt claimed, needed cognitive stimulation that began at

to make sounds and then to respond to the words of the caregiver ("Now I am washing your *ear*"). In 1966 Hunt made his first of six trips to Tehran.

As a result of Hunt's new methods of care, the Iranian babies were soon making happy faces, perking up in response to sound, smell, and touch, and learning to crawl and speak a few words in Farsi. As a consequence, more found permanent homes with adoptive families. By 1978, the year the Shah went into exile, the University of Illinois was evacuating personnel from its Tehran Illinois Research Unit. Hunt admitted in a letter to an American colleague that he mistakenly thought the violence in the streets of Tehran was simply a young people's revolt. He wrote letters of recommendation for a former student and director of the program, Khossrow Mohandessi, who wanted to find an academic post in the United States, but to no avail. Mohandessi was executed in Tehran in 1982.[7]

After his retirement in 1974 Hunt continued his research in infant development, often collaborating with former graduate students. He was a frequent lecturer and keynote speaker at conferences and universities on many continents. He also took singing and piano lessons and on Sundays could be heard in the choir of the Unitarian Universalist church. His wife Esther, who died sixteen months before he did, was president of Champaign County Planned Parenthood Association and, as the mother of a University High student, headed a committee recommending improved programs and facilities there.

A scholar's contributions are defined by the times he lives and, when popular and innovative, can outlast him. Most psychologists would now dismiss Hunt's central research contribution, the malleability of IQ, as entirely too optimistic. The demise of the Great Society and the results of the revolution in Iran curtailed many of the educational programs Hunt advocated. His most enduring legacy lives on not in the realm of his own research or that of his students but in two of the early childhood educational programs he supported, Head Start and Sesame Street.

## Notes

1. J. McVicker Hunt, *The Challenge of Incompetence and Poverty* (Urbana: University of Illinois Press, 1969).

2. It is interesting to note that Hunt formulated his ideas about cognition and education during a decade when a number of researchers at the University of Illinois had become fascinated with digital computers and the ways computers could model and even duplicate the working of the human brain.

3. Hugh Davis Graham, *The Uncertain Triumph: Federal Education Policy in the Kennedy and Johnson Years* (Chapel Hill: University of North Carolina Press, 1984), 137–45.

4. Lyndon B. Johnson: "Special Message to the Congress Recommending a 12-Point Program for America's Children and Youth," February 8, 1967. Online by Gerhard Peters and John T. Woolley, *The American Presidency Project*, http://www.presidency.ucsb.edu/ws (accessed March 2, 2015).

5. J. McVicker Hunt, "Has Compensatory Education Failed? Has It Been Attempted?" *Harvard Educational Review* 39, no. 2 (Summer 1969): 278–300; J. McVicker Hunt, "Reflections on a Decade of Early Education," *Journal of Abnormal Child Psychology* 3, no. 4 (1975): 31; "Is Intelligence Inherited," *European Stars and Stripes*, May 14, 1969.

6. Gary Metz, "Successful Local PCC Programs Receiving National Recognition," *Daily Republican-Register*, December 28, 1972.

7. Letter from J. McV. Hunt to Dr. Lionel Maldonado, Khossrow Mohandessi File, 1972–1982, box 37; Memo from Marty Marsh to George Brinegar, et al., November 12, 1982, box 37, J. McVicker Hunt Papers, 1926–1991, University of Illinois Archives.

## Sources

Hunt's papers are at the University of Illinois Archives: J. McVicker Hunt Papers, 1926–1991. The closest thing to an autobiography is an article Hunt published, "A Professional Odyssey," in T. S. Krawiec, ed., *The Psychologists*, vol. 2 (New York: Oxford University Press, 1974), 134–202. In an otherwise scholarly remembrance, Hunt's student Ina Uzgiris provided some personal recollection in I. C. Uzgiris, "Joseph McVicker Hunt: 1902–1991," *American Journal of Psychology* 105, no. 3 (1992): 471–76.

# Samuel Kirk

## The Birth of Special Education

*Nicholas Hopkins*

Samuel A. Kirk (1904–1996) was a pioneer in the study of children with special learning needs, both those who have difficulty in school and those who are specially gifted academically. Kirk established much of the scientific rationale for special education programs and popularized the idea among educators and psychologists. He helped shift his discipline away from viewing learning problems as genetically determined and toward an understanding that took into account social factors and the effect of innovative educational strategies. During his long career, Kirk published more than one hundred studies of the learning process and created the university's Institute for Research on Exceptional Children. Kirk also contributed to the formulation of national policy in the area of special education and helped frame the landmark Children with Specific Learning Disabilities Act of 1969.

Kirk's passion for teaching began early. The son of Lebanese immigrants, he eagerly gave reading lessons to farmhands on his parents' North Dakota farm. He studied philosophy at the University of Chicago but shifted to a graduate program in clinical psychology when he moved on to the University of Michigan. One reason for this change of course was Kirk's early experience working at the Oaks School in Chicago in the 1920s. There he taught boys with behavioral disorders and cognitive deficiencies. "My first experience in tutoring a case of reading disability was not in a school, was not in a clinic, was not in an experimental laboratory," he declared, "but in a boy's lavatory." After receiving his doctorate in clinical psychology from Michigan, Kirk served for more than a decade

Professor Kirk administering a reading test

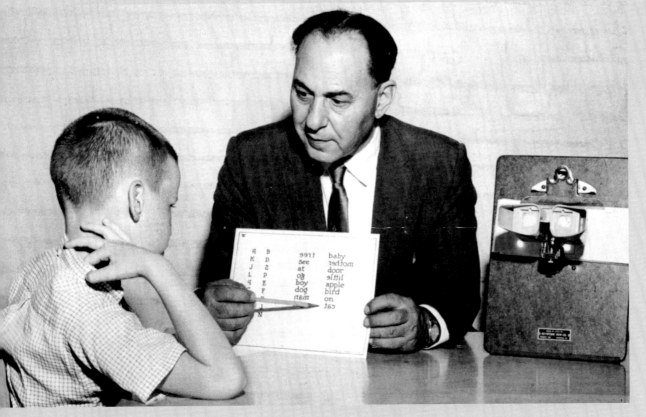

as the director of the teaching program at Milwaukee State Teachers College. He came to Illinois in 1947 and immediately set about developing a curriculum and research program focused on special education curricula.

Adopting approaches from many disciplines, Kirk studied learning disabilities and exceptional children, observing blind and deaf children, as well as immigrant children and those with speech impediments. Kirk believed his discipline could benefit more from new "technologies of evaluation" than from narrowly focused standardized tests that focused on discrete skills. His new evaluation techniques drew on principles derived from education, linguistics, psychology, sociology, and statistics, and culminated in 1961 with the unveiling of the Illinois Test of Psycholinguistic Abilities, which measured language, memory, and cognitive abilities in young children from diverse backgrounds.

Soon after his arrival in Urbana-Champaign, Kirk proposed the creation of an institute to study the learning processes of exceptional children. Its program was to be interdisciplinary and would draw together researchers from a variety of departments on campus as well as educational experts employed by the State of Illinois. He envisioned using the institute to improve special education curricula and to help coordinate clinical facilities across the state.

University administrators supported Kirk's ideas. University of Illinois president George Stoddard argued that the proposed institute would coordinate the research of a wide array of scholars and serve as a link between researchers and public officials responsible for the education of handicapped and otherwise disabled children. The Institute for Research on Exceptional Children was established in 1952 with Kirk as its founding director. The new organization focused on three major research areas: developing a statistical profile of exceptional children of all kinds, creating learning assessment tools for children with specific learning needs, and producing and testing specialized school programs. During the next ten years the university awarded thirty-five doctoral degrees to students who had been affiliated with the institute and had secured an impressive roster of external supporters and funders.

Directing the first research unit devoted to gifted-child learning and one of the largest programs studying learning disabilities thrust Kirk into the national policymaking arena. Politicians and government officials consulted with him frequently and recruited him to participate in major projects, such as a 1962 study of Soviet special education programs. Later that same year Kirk received one of the first International Awards in Mental Retardation from the Joseph P. Kennedy Jr. Foundation. In 1964 the president appointed him the first director of Division of Handicapped Children and Youth in the Department of Education's Office of Education.

Kirk applied the same rigor to policymaking as he did to research. He also supported the growth of grassroots organizations that advocated educational support for students with special needs. These efforts achieved notable success, with the passage of the 1969 Children with Specific Learning Disabilities Act. The law grew directly out of Kirk's scholarship (supporters claimed it took the term "learning disabilities" from one of his conference papers). With the passage of this law, all federal education programs began including programs for special education; children with special needs would have a right to receive service appropriate to their condition. Today it is difficult to imagine a time when these accommodations were not available. Kirk's advocacy made mental handicaps a classroom focus rather than something to ignore. Moreover, his exploration of learning in settings of special need opened new pathways for teaching children who come to school from every part of the learning spectrum.

## Sources

The University Archives holds primary materials on Kirk's work and career, as well as the planning of the IREC (see RS 39/1/11). For an overview of Kirk's scholarship see Samuel A. Kirk, *The Foundations of Special Education*, edited by Gail A. Harris and Winifred D. Kirk (Arlington, Va.: Council for Exceptional Children, 1993).

# The Invention of MRI

Katherine Skwarczek

At four o'clock on the morning of October 6, 2003, Professor Paul C. Lauterbur of the University of Illinois Chemistry Department was awakened by a telephone call. Across the Atlantic, Professor Peter Mansfield of the University of Nottingham was also being summoned by telephone, though his call came at a slightly more conventional time. The scientists were being informed that they were co-winners of the Nobel Prize in the category of Physiology or Medicine, in recognition of their discoveries concerning magnetic resonance imaging, otherwise known as MRI.[1] "My first comment was, 'There goes my day,'" the *Champaign News-Gazette* reported Lauterbur's having said. His wry response was a premonition of the myriad congratulations and celebrations that were about to flood in that day from friends, family, and professional colleagues, as well as the entire University of Illinois at Urbana-Champaign campus (although the festive mood did not keep Lauterbur from meeting with his students as planned later that day).[2]

The 2003 Nobel Prize in Physiology or Medicine recognized the different but complementary work that both Lauterbur and Mansfield had done in making magnetic resonance imaging not only possible but also indispensable to modern medical practice and research. Paul Lauterbur's key insight, which first occurred to him in 1971 while he was a professor at the State University of New York at Stony Brook, was in imagining how to create detailed images of complex objects, especially the interior of the human body. Lauterbur's idea was to apply magnetic field gradients—deliberate variations in the magnetic field—to produce a two-dimensional (or even three-dimensional) spatial image. As MRI technology began to gain momentum in the 1970s and 1980s, Lauterbur eventually moved to the University of Illinois, where he could pursue his research as head of the Biomedical Magnetic Resonance Laboratory (BMRL). The Beckman Institute's modern Biomedical Imaging Center is the successor to the BMRL.

Meanwhile, Peter Mansfield had approached the problem of magnetic resonance imaging from a different angle, envisioning magnetic field gradients as creating a kind of diffraction pattern when applied to solids. Beginning in the early 1970s, Mansfield also developed new ways of capturing and mathematically analyzing MR images, including refining slice selection and developing a means of speeding up the MRI process via echo planar imaging. A professor of physics at the University of Nottingham for most of his career, Mansfield also spent two years as a postdoctoral researcher at the University of Illinois at Urbana-Champaign, a stay that he described as "invaluable."[3]

## MRI: Science and Technology

Since the groundbreaking work carried out by scientists such as Lauterbur and Mansfield in the 1970s, MRI iconography has become familiar to patients the world over: a large cylindrical tube enclosing a subject lying supine on a retracting table, with doctors and technicians monitoring computers nearby. The MRI scanner consists of several components, the most easily recognizable of which is a large magnet.[4] Described by many as "the most significant medical diagnostic technique of the [twentieth] century" (as University of Illinois chancellor Nancy Cantor declared on hearing the Nobel news[5]), MRI scanners have become ubiquitous in hospitals, clinics, and imaging centers.

It took some time for the techniques being developed by scientists in the 1970s to coalesce into the MRI scans we know today. As Lauterbur said of his achievement, "It's not an overnight thing. Lots of things have to come together to make it practical."[6] Once the research floodgates were opened, however, there was a rush to develop scanners that could image the entire human body for clinical purposes. In her biography of Lauterbur, Joan

NOBEL WINNER PAUL LAUTERBUR: A LIFE REMEMBERED

# UI LOSES SCIENCE PIONEER

Lauterbur's Nobel honor was the central feature of this memorial published in the local newspaper at the time of his death. Photo courtesy of the University of Illinois Archives and the *News-Gazette*

Dawson described the early 1980s as a period of "such an explosive growth in MRI that it was difficult to keep track of imaging methods,"[7] a growth propelled by both academic researchers and medical imaging companies. MRI sales exploded: as of 2010, more than 12 million MRI scans are performed annually in the United States,[8] and the number of MRI scans performed in the United States tripled in the first decade of this century. An MRI scanner can provide a clinician with a spatially resolved and detailed image of a patient's interior anatomy, soft tissues, and organs, such as the kidneys and spinal cord. This type of imaging is particularly suitable for brain scans and for identifying neurological diseases and brain cancers. Although MRI scanners are more expensive and more time consuming compared to X-rays and CT (computed tomography) scans, they do not use ionizing radiation.[9]

MRI scanning technology and imaging techniques are continually evolving to meet new diagnostic and research needs. Open MRI scanners are being developed and used as an alternative to the original closed, confining cylinder, while functional MRI (fMRI) uses the BOLD (blood oxygenation level dependent) contrast imaging discovered by Dr. Seiji Ogawa to view the brain "in action." At the Beckman Institute, for instance, the researchers at the Cognitive Neuroimaging Lab are currently using fMRI to study age-related differences in memory processing.[10]

> "His idea was to purposefully place objects in varying, nonhomogenous magnetic field gradients because the measurements of different resonance frequencies could be translated to position, resulting in an image."

MRI has such a strong hold on our cultural imaginary of what medical imaging and diagnostics "looks like" that it can be difficult to remember that it began its theoretical life in an altogether different place, in the physical principles of atomic nuclei.[11] Physicists have long known that certain atomic nuclei, including hydrogen (found in water, and thus profusely in the human body), function as "tiny magnets" and therefore can be manipulated if placed in a strong magnetic field.[12] In the 1930s, I. I. Rabi found a way to measure the spin and other magnetic properties of these nuclei (the spin is what aligns with the magnetic field). In the following decade, both Edward Purcell and Felix Bloch discovered that while under the influence of a strong magnet, these nuclei can be made to "resonate" with the application of electromagnetic waves that match their resonance frequency.[13] Hence the name for this phenomenon: nuclear magnetic resonance, or NMR.

The story of MRI thus began with NMR. When physicists learned in 1950 that nuclear spin is also influenced by chemical bonds, NMR began to attract the interest of chemists, who could now use it to examine molecular structure. NMR studies were an exciting new field at the University of Illinois at this time as well. One of the pioneers of chemical NMR was Illinois chemistry professor Herbert Gutowsky, who gave a seminar at the Mellon Institute in 1952–53 that inspired Lauterbur's own interest in NMR.[14] The stage was then set for both physicists and chemists to take the next step and apply NMR to medical use.[15] When they eventually did so in the form of imaging, NMR became known more widely as MRI.[16]

## Paul Lauterbur

Paul Lauterbur first learned of NMR in 1951 when he began working for a division of the Dow Chemical Company. Originally from a small town near Dayton, Ohio, Lauterbur had just graduated from Case Institute of Technology (now Case Western) with a degree in chemistry when he accepted a job with Dow in its Mellon Institute laboratories in Pittsburgh, where he began studying the properties of natural and silicone rubber. As a Mellon fellow, Lauterbur was also able to enroll in graduate courses at the University of Pittsburgh. Drafted during the Korean War, he managed to continue working with NMR as an army scientist when the base needed someone to operate a newly purchased NMR machine.[17] Lauterbur later continued his work at Mellon and his graduate studies at the University of Pittsburgh, completing his doctorate in 1962 and eventually joining the Chemistry Department at SUNY–Stony Brook as an associate professor.

Lauterbur's September 1971 discovery that magnetic resonance could be used to produce images came as the result of a peculiar set of circumstances.[18] Lauterbur's main insight was to turn what seemed like a weakness of NMR—the difficulty of maintaining a homogenous magnetic field—into a strength. His idea was to purposefully place objects in varying, nonhomogenous magnetic field gradients because the measurements of different resonance frequencies could be translated to positions, resulting in an image. In short, his imaging technique assigns "magnetic Zip Codes to the atomic nuclei" in the object.[19] The story goes that the epiphany came to Lauterbur as he was eating a hamburger in a restaurant, and he immediately ran out to buy a notebook to record and date his ideas.[20] He submitted his discovery of what he termed zeugmatography (from the Greek word for joining), and the images he had generated of microtubes of $H_2O$ against $D_2O$ (heavy water), to *Nature*. Ironically, the journal initially rejected it, publishing it in 1973 only after Lauterbur added a brief description of possible applications of the technique.[21]

Although the name zeugmatography did not catch on, the principles of MRI certainly did, and Lauterbur continued to work with MRI for most of the rest of his career, publishing 278 articles on the subject between 1972 and 2000.[22] In 1985, Lauterbur, recently remarried, and his wife Joan Dawson, whose work in physiology also used NMR spectroscopy,[23] left Stony Brook for new positions at the University of Illinois. Lauterbur was attracted to the university's strengths in computational technology as well as the opportunity to be affiliated with a medical school, which he believed was necessary for his research.[24] Dawson recalled that the postdoctoral fellows, students, and staff of the new Biomedical Magnetic Resonance Laboratory became the "BMRL family," in part due to their closeness and their enthusiasm. At its height, Dawson later reported, the BMRL "had between forty and fifty affiliated faculty and students." But they also faced some disappointments. Lauterbur was not always able to obtain all of the laboratory and scanning equipment that he had hoped for or hoped to access, and in 1994 a highly publicized project funded by the National Science Foundation to build a 4 T shielded whole-body MRI ended when the magnet failed.[25]

Still, some projects were a success; Lauterbur worked on a project with Zhi-Pei Liang, once his postdoctoral fellow and now a professor of electrical and computer engineering at Illinois, in which they developed a method of constructing real-time images of a beating heart while using only limited data, a technique still being explored today. After the 1994 setback, Lauterbur drew closer to the Chemistry Department, where he held a joint appointment. He had already begun contemplating a shift in his research, an examination of the origins of life and

Professor Herbert Gutowsky discusses his work on radio frequency spectroscopy with his Illinois chemistry colleagues, ca. 1967

the chemical origins of biology in the "prebiotic stew."[26] Unfortunately, illness during the last few years of his life slowed his progress on that project. Lauterbur passed away in Urbana on March 27, 2007.

## Peter Mansfield

Peter Mansfield first encountered NMR when he began studying physics at Queen Mary College, University of London. Born in London and with a childhood disrupted by World War II evacuations, Peter Mansfield's earliest interest in science had been in rocketry. After spending several years working at the Rocket Propulsion Department within the Ministry of Supply and catching up on his studies, Mansfield began his undergraduate degree in physics in 1956. One of the university's readers in physics, Dr. Jack Powles, had organized an NMR group, and Mansfield's third-year project was to measure the earth's magnetic field by building an NMR spectrometer.[27]

Mansfield continued NMR studies of solids as a graduate student. After completing his doctorate, he accepted a postdoctoral position at the University of Illinois, working with physicist Charles Slichter on the NMR of metals. He and his wife Jean sailed to the United States in 1962 and stayed in Urbana for two years. Though initially intimidated by some of the illustrious physicists who were now his colleagues, Mansfield later wrote that "in Urbana itself we were made very welcome."[28] In 1964 the Mansfields returned to England and Peter Mansfield accepted a position in physics at the University of Nottingham, where he continued his work on multipulse NMR spectroscopy and spin echoes in solids.

In his autobiography, Mansfield described the moment when he first made the leap from NMR to imaging: during a midmorning coffee break in the department tea room, he and several colleagues discussed research plans for their new computerized spectrometer, and it occurred to Mansfield that "it might be possible to carry out experiments using a magnetic field gradient in combination with the line narrowed experiments that we had already achieved. If we could apply a sufficiently large gradient . . . we ought to be able to see the actual atomic structure in these materials, at least theoretically, in what amounted to an NMR diffraction experiment."[29] While Mansfield introduced the mathematical elegance of k-space notation and performed his experiment on solids instead of liquids, like Lauterbur, the result was noticeably similar: Mansfield had also generated an image using magnetic field gradients.

After a sabbatical year spent in Heidelberg, Mansfield presented his work at a conference in Krakow in 1973, where a commentator pointed out the resemblance of his method to that of Paul Lauterbur, whose seminal paper had just appeared in *Nature*.[30] Comparing his work to Lauterbur's convinced Mansfield to switch from imaging solids to easier liquid (biological) specimens. In addition, he focused his attention on improving slice selection and on speeding up imaging time by using a line scanning technique instead of Lauterbur's projection reconstruction method.[31] Mansfield also patented his group's work, again unlike Lauterbur, who had been unable to interest the university in pursing a patent for his initial MRI techniques. In 1976 Mansfield's research group succeeded in creating the first human NMR image: a "picture" of his student Andrew Maudsley's index finger.

In 1976 Mansfield introduced what was to become another key technique in MRI: echo planar imaging. EPI takes advantage of spin echoes to acquire an entire line or plane of data at once, making for faster and more dynamic imaging.[32] According to Kevles, "a variation of this approach would eventually trigger a second revolution in magnetic resonance scanning."[33] The 1980s were a "golden period" for Mansfield; with a pause in the departmental squabbling that had sometimes marred the academic atmosphere in the past, Mansfield and his group were able to focus completely on developing EPI and medical applications of high-speed imaging. Honored with a knighthood in 1993, Mansfield retired from teaching in 1994 to focus on research activities at the university and on General Magnetic, the imaging company he had founded.[34]

## Continuing Research

Although Lauterbur and Mansfield shared the Nobel Prize for their work on MRI, other researchers were also making significant breakthroughs. In the mid-1970s, Swiss scientist Richard Ernst successfully applied Fourier transform mathematics (a method he had devised earlier with Weston Anderson) to two-dimensional MRI imaging.[35] Several British researchers also quickly picked up on the new imaging possibilities, including another group within Mansfield's department at Nottingham, led by Raymond Andrew. Waldo Hinshaw and others in Andrew's group produced several particularly detailed MR images, including a human wrist and a well-known image of a lemon that graced the cover of *Nature* in December 1977.[36] Yet another British team was lead by John Mallard at the University of Aberdeen in Scotland.

All of this intense work in the 1970s led to some feelings of competition, some of it quite acrimonious, especially in the case of Raymond Damadian. A research physician working at the SUNY Downstate Medical Center, Damadian published a paper in 1971 arguing that cancerous tissues had different NMR relaxation times than healthy tissues. The following year, he applied for a patent for a full-body NMR scanner that could detect cancerous tissues. Several years later he even built such a scanner and managed to image an entire human body.[37] In her biography of Lauterbur, Dawson conceded that while Damadian's work was important, "to the point that [Lauterbur] conceived of MRI as a result of watching a repetition of Damadian's experiments," she concluded that his innovation was not imaging, and not MRI.[38] Nonetheless, Damadian continues to believe that he and his work were overlooked, particularly by the Nobel committee, and he has lobbied hard to assert what he feels are his claims to priority in the invention of MRI.[39] Perhaps the most unfortunate effect of this controversy is that it has tended to overshadow more meaningful and more significant aspects of MRI's history.

## Where Did MRI Come From? And Where Does It Lead?

Is MRI a history of people? Of ideas? Of technology? Of institutions? In "Technology Is Society Made Durable," French philosopher and sociologist of science Bruno Latour claims that a "first principle" of any study of innovation in science and technology is "the fate of a statement is in the hands of others."[40] Seen through this Latourian lens, MRI has indeed been transported and transformed in hands far beyond those of its original developers. In fact, as the debate over whom to honor for its invention has swirled through the academic world, it is also evident that exactly whose "hands" first held the "statement" that became MRI is equally uncertain and even unclear. The story of MRI is a stunning illustration of Latour's insight. Without minimizing the enormous intellectual and physical efforts mounted by the extraordinary scientists who developed it, the location of MRI's "invention" and ultimate significance remains elusive.

At the University of Illinois's Beckman Institute, for instance, Professor Zhi-Pei Liang continues with the real-time cardiac imaging research he began with his mentor and friend Paul Lauterbur.[41] His research group is also developing new technology for molecular imaging as well as high-resolution imaging to provide earlier and better diagnostic information. While Liang looks forward to the medical contributions that future generations of MRI technology can make, he is also mindful of MRI's past. Liang emphasizes that MRI is part of a much larger narrative of biomedical imaging that began with Roentgen's discovery of X-rays in 1895 and continues in our own time.[42] This past appears also to be MRI's future, at least as predicted by Liang and others pursing the "integrative imaging" theme at the Beckman Institute: MRI pursued not as a sole imaging technique but as part of a larger array of imaging innovations, all working in concert.

## Notes

1. "The Nobel Prize in Physiology or Medicine 2003," Nobel prize.org, http://www.nobelprize.org/nobel_prizes/medicine/laureates/2003.

2. Jodi Heckel, "Two with Ties to UI Win Nobel," *News Gazette*, October 6, 2003; Digital Surrogates from Topic Files ca. 1957–2009, University of Illinois Archives, University of Illinois, http://www.archives.library.illinois.edu/erec/University Archives/3901018/Topic Files/N-Z/Nobel Prize.pdf. The excitement at the University of Illinois doubled the next day when the Nobel committee informed Professor Anthony J. Leggett that he was one of the winners of the award in physics for his work on superconductivity and superfluidity.

3. "Sir Peter Mansfield—Biographical," Nobelprize.org, http://www.nobelprize.org/nobel_prizes/medicine/laureates/2003/mansfield-bio.html.

4. Most clinical magnets used for body MRI today are superconducting, and while strengths vary, 1.5 Tesla is considered optimal, though stronger magnets of 3 T are also being used. Magnets used for research can be even more powerful. See Christopher G. Roth, *Fundamentals of Body MRI* (Philadelphia: Elsevier Saunders, 2012), PDF e-book.

5. Heckel, "Two with Ties."

6. Ibid.

7. M. Joan Dawson, *Paul Lauterbur and the Invention of MRI* (Cambridge, Mass.: MIT Press, 2013), 131.

8. Marcus E. Raichle, "Images of Body and Brain," in *A Century of Nature: Twenty-One Discoveries that Changed Science and the World*, edited by Laura Garwin and Tim Lincoln (Chicago: Chicago University Press, 2003), 193.

9. Richard B. Gunderman, *X-Ray Vision: The Evolution of Medical Imaging and Its Human Significance* (Oxford: Oxford University Press, 2013), 145, 144.

10. "Cognitive Neuroimaging Laboratory," University of Illinois, http://cnl.beckman.illinois.edu.

11. Bettyann Holtzmann Kevles, *Naked to the Bone: Medical Imaging in the Twentieth Century* (Reading, Mass.: Helix, 1998), 200.

12. Dawson, *Lauterbur*, 38.

13. Kevles, *Naked to the Bone*, 176.

14. Ibid., Dawson, *Lauterbur*, 39, 40–41. For more on Gutowsky's work in NMR, see Jiri Jonas and Charles P. Slichter, "Herbert Sander Gutowsky," in *Biographical Memoirs*, vol. 88, edited by National Academy of Sciences (Washington, D.C.: National Academies Press, 2006). Also available online at http://www.nasonline.org/publications/biographical-memoirs/memoir-pdfs/gutowsky-herbert.pdf.

15. Kevles, *Naked to the Bone*, 176.

16. Gunderman, *X-Ray Vision*, 142.

17. Dawson, *Lauterbur*, 36, 44.

18. Ibid., 1. The circumstances were these: During the summer of 1971, a small company called NMR Specialties, which had been improperly managed and was near bankruptcy, hired Lauterbur to be its president and chief executive officer in a last-ditch effort to save the company. In fulfilling his duties to the company, Lauterbur happened to witness a postdoctoral fellow using the company's labs to confirm the research of Raymond Damadian, a medical doctor working for the SUNY Downstate Medical Center in Brooklyn, who had recently published an article claiming to have used NMR signals to detect cancerous tissue.

19. Ibid., 4.

20. Images of the "Notebook" are available in Dawson, Appendix A. The original notebook and additional Lauterbur papers are located in the Paul C. Lauterbur Collection, Chemical Heritage Foundation Archives, Philadelphia, Penn.

21. P. C. Lauterbur, "Image Formation by Induced Local Interactions: Examples Employing Nuclear Magnetic Resonance," *Nature* 242 (1973): 190–91.

22. Dawson, *Lauterbur*, 122.

23. "Paul C. Lauterbur—Biographical," Nobelprize.org, http://www.nobelprize.org/nobel_prizes/medicine/laureates/2003/lauterbur-bio.html.

24. Dawson, *Lauterbur*, 146.

25. Ibid., 157–59, 167–72.

26. Ibid., 164, quote on 190.

27. "Sir Peter Mansfield—Biographical."

28. Peter Mansfield, *The Long Road to Stockholm: The Story of Magnetic Resonance Imaging—An Autobiography* (Oxford: Oxford University Press, 2013), 68, 73.

29. Ibid., 88.

30. Ibid., 109–10.

31. "Sir Peter Mansfield—Biographical."

32. Kevles, *Naked to the Bone*, 183; Dawson, *Lauterbur*, 129.

33. Kevles, *Naked to the Bone*, 183.

34. Mansfield, *Stockholm*, 135, 169.

35. Kevles, *Naked to the Bone*, 186.

36. Dawson, *Lauterbur*, 123–25. For an expanded history of MRI development outside of Europe and the United States, see Amit Prasad, *Imperial Technoscience: Transnational Histories of MRI in the United States, Britain, and India* (Cambridge, Mass.: MIT Press, 2014).

37. Gunderman, *X-Ray Vision*, 143; *Naked to the Bone*, 178.

38. Dawson, *Lauterbur*, 108–9.

39. For two sides of this controversy, see Jeff Kinley and Raymond Damadian, *Gifted Mind: The Dr. Raymond Damadian Story, Inventor of the MRI* (Green Forest, Ark.: Master, 2015), and Donald P. Hollis, *Abusing Cancer Science: The Truth about NMR and Cancer* (Chehalis, Wash.: Strawberry Fields, 1987).

40. Bruno Latour, "Technology Is Society Made Durable," *Sociological Review* Supplement 38 (1991): 103–31, 105–6. doi: 10.1111/j.1467-954X.1990.tb03350.x.

41. "Liang Develops New Generations of MRI Technology," Coordinated Science Lab, University of Illinois, January 6, 2015, https://csl.illinois.edu/news/liang-develops-new-generations-mri-technology.

42. For a book-length treatment of this very claim see Kevles, *Naked to the Bone*.

## Sources

Press materials, including those from the *News-Gazette*, can be found in the digital University Archives of the University of Illinois library. Information about the current research undertaken at the Beckman Institute can be found on its website, http://beckman.illinois.edu. Biographical information about the Nobel laureates is available from three key sources: M. Joan Dawson's biography, *Paul Lauterbur and the Invention of MRI* (Cambridge, Mass.: MIT Press, 2013), Peter Mansfield's autobiography, *The Long Road to Stockholm: The Story of Magnetic Resonance Imaging* (Oxford: Oxford University Press, 2013), and the Nobelprize.org website, parts of which are published by the organization in the book series *Les Prix Nobel / Nobel Lectures / The Nobel Prizes.*

# Nick Holonyak Jr.

## The Development of LED Lights

*Steven Lenz*

In 1946 Nick Holonyak Jr. left his immigrant parents and the small southern Illinois town of Glen Carbon to begin his studies in Urbana-Champaign. He would remain there until he received his doctorate in electrical engineering in 1954. At Illinois, Holonyak fell under the spell of physicist John Bardeen, the inventor of the transistor. The young graduate student was fascinated by the potential of the transistor and other semiconductor devices to revolutionize the development of electronic processes. Holonyak was particularly curious about the potential of semiconductors to emit light.

Holonyak soon moved to Bell Labs and, later, to the General Electric Advanced Semiconductor Laboratory where in 1962 he entered the race to develop the first semiconductor laser. He lost that race to his colleague Robert Hall, but soon afterward he announced that he had developed the first *visible* semiconductor laser. Holonyak's laser was unique. It relied on new materials (called III-V alloys), which led the young engineer to produce the first visible spectrum red LED (light-emitting diode) light. In addition to the novel nature of this light source, Holonyak argued that LED would use less energy than incandescent lights, last longer, and generate less heat. In addition, the fact that LED lights could also be engineered in a wide variety of sizes meant that over the succeeding years they would be attached to every manner of device, from tiny electronics to automobiles and outdoor advertising.

Holonyak returned to Illinois in 1963. He brought with him the spirit of competition that had motivated him at Bell Labs and GE, and his laboratory produced dozens of new inventions over the ensuing decades, most recently the transistor laser, a device which emits both light and

Nick Holonyak Jr.

electrical signals, and promises to increase dramatically the speed of broadband communications.

### Sources

For a profile of Holonyak, see Laura Schmitt, *The Bright Stuff: The LED and Nick Holonyak's Fantastic Trail of Innovation* (Champaign: Premier Print Group, 2012). See also "Absent at the Creation: How One Scientist Made Off with the Biggest Invention since the Light Bulb," *Washington Post*, April 6, 1997.

# Mosaic
## The First Point-and-Click Internet Browser

Jimena Canales

Point, click, and scroll. Are these natural ways of signaling, communicating, and navigating? Or are they advanced *cultural techniques* used to navigate our networked world? You probably point, click, and scroll while browsing the Web with Safari, Firefox, or Chrome. You may have previously used Netscape and Explorer. You might remember Mosaic—the first widely used point-and-click interface to the internet.

Before the development of Mosaic, most users could only access the internet with a command-line computer interface, usually by typing instructions after the small blinking cursor following the "unix%:" prompt. Today, your *browser* probably appears as an *icon* on the *desktop* of your computer or laptop. It is usually the first *window* you open from the *operating system* to access a *Website*

on the *internet*. This innovative arrangement, now the standard one in most personal computers, was the product of a complex series of events and negotiations that involved the University of Illinois, federal officials, private investors, lawyers, students, and computer programmers. At some point in 1994, it seemed like computers and the internet might abandon its democratic roots and move in an entirely different direction.

Interfaces are strange entities. In one sense, they are quite new. The modern meaning of the word "interface," referring to "a means or place of interaction between two systems," dates only as far back as the 1960s and is tightly connected to the increased use of computers. But in another sense, interfaces have always been around. Handles, knobs, keys, windows, and screens we routinely use to step into or peer into different worlds can be considered interfaces. Through them, we can gain access to a portal, cross a threshold, or simply peer into a different space while at a safe distance. Often, interfaces are the places were "flesh meets metal" but their benefits reside in removing any sense of contact so that interactions are as seamless as possible.[1] Interfaces are generally overlooked: a good one is defined by its very unobtrusiveness (its *user-friendly* quality). Although interactions through interfaces have long played prominent roles in fairytales and myths, it is only recently that contemporary scholars have started to focus on them in order to fully understand social and material relations around us. Why?

Interfaces are often needed to begin an action. We employ them to set off a chain of related effects somewhere else. Through them we feel like free agents, as subjects exercising our wills. Interfaces stand guard at the door of history, permitting us to boldly venture into the future or to hold back if we do not dare. Consequences follow. Interfaces can transform minor movements (left or right, up or down, open or close, click or unclick) into decisive actions. But they are also what make us feel less free. In his analysis of film, the philosopher Stanley Cavell described watching movies as a predominantly masochistic pastime because of how we permit others to live life for us. In comparison, trolling and so-called "click activism" appear to have a uniquely sadistic component.

In fairy tales, interfaces appear at key turning points in the storyline, when seemingly minor actions can lead to entrapment or liberation. The spell is broken only after we smash the glass, spill the potion, or look behind the curtain. Today we can shut down the browser and admire the http code traffic. We can see every request and response taking place between our computers and many others.

What are the origins of this innovation? Who invented Mosaic?[2] Marc Andreessen, a computer science undergraduate at the University of Illinois is generally acknowledged as "author of the Mosaic Web browser."[3] This attribution is hardly controversial. Standard accounts of Andreessen's invention were detailed in numerous publications ever since the new browser emerged as the "hot product" of the 1990s.[4] But back then, attributions of the invention of Mosaic to a single individual were also

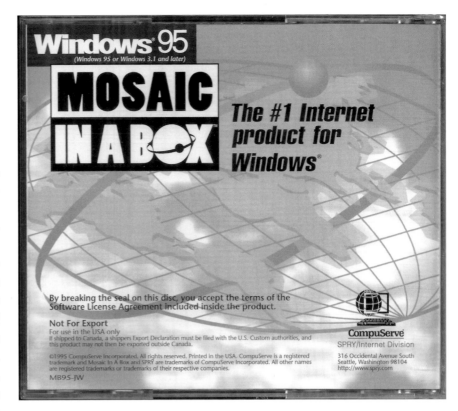

The container for the Mosaic software.
Photo courtesy of Jimena Canales.

understood as a commercial strategy, essential for the task of transforming innovative software into a successful business product. The National Science Foundation (NSF), the European Organization for Nuclear Research (CERN), the National Center for Supercomputing Applications (NCSA), and the University of Illinois all played critical roles in the Mosaic story.

In December 1993 the *New York Times* introduced Mosaic to the world with an article that made no mention of Andreessen. Instead, the news identified NCSA director Larry Smarr, project coordinator Joe Hardin, and their team as responsible for offering a powerful new software for free.[5] A year later (1994) computer programmer Eric Bina was inducted to the Hall of Fame at the WWW (World Wide Web) Awards ceremony as the person who "wrote most of the code for Mosaic."[6] *GQ* magazine even labeled Andreessen as an imposter.[7] If Andreessen was not the inventor of Mosaic, then who was?

To install Mosaic In A Box

**1.** Insert the disc in your CD-ROM drive.

**2.** In Windows Program Manager, choose **Run** from the File menu.

**3.** In the Command line box, type **d:\setup**, where *d* is the letter representing your CD-ROM drive, and press **Enter**.

**4.** Follow the instructions on your screen.

MOSAIC IN A BOX

MB95 CDW

Windows 95
*or Windows 3.1 and later*

The #1 Internet product for Windows®

CS
102350-01

CompuServe
SPRY/Internet Division

Mosaic software on CD. Photo courtesy of Jimena Canales.

The history of Mosaic is a whodunit mystery with an unexpected finale, one that leads us to reconsider the category of "inventor" in the age of high-tech venture capital. During the Enlightenment, the philosopher John Locke explained how the word "person" was "a *forensic* term, involving praise and blame, and a capacity to obey laws." Extending his insights to our times, the history of Mosaic makes us consider how the category of person has become a commercial term, leaving us unsure whom to blame, praise, or call to obey the law.

## Whodunit

What is Mosaic? In 1994, *Time* magazine described it as "a kind of onscreen control panel that enables you to drive through the Web by pointing and clicking your electronic mouse."[8] It was a tool that "gives the Internet what the Macintosh gave the personal computer: a navigation system that can be understood at a glance by anybody who can point and click a mouse."[9] Its use was exploding. The first "academic" prototype had attracted more than 3 million users in 1993.[10] Back then, nobody was making any money from it—yet.[11]

The Silicon Valley entrepreneur and venture capitalist Jim Clark saw an opportunity. How could he transform a freely available product created by a group of individuals working for public institutions into a commodity that a private corporation could sell? The University of Illinois asked him to pay a licensing fee. After all, the program had been produced as part of a campus project. Clark refused.[12] What if Clark could argue that the product was not the university's in the first place? The Bayh-Dole Act (1980) had only recently changed the rules of the game with regard to intellectual property rights from federally funded projects at universities.[13] The law spelled out how universities could profit from inventions they had sponsored. Would this legal provision apply to a widely shared computer code that could be easily copied, pasted, and even rewritten?

The arguments that soon erupted were delicate ones: the funding for the project that created Mosaic at Illinois had come from NSF grants. But did NSF own this new product? Did Illinois? Did anyone? These questions became more complex when it became apparent that, as a student working on the project, Andreessen had simply "looked around the Internet and discovered that he didn't have to start from scratch." Insiders knew that he had used "an existing code base available from CERN," which "meant that his work could progress very quickly."[14] He had made $6.85 an hour working at the university, he had just received his degree, and he was looking for an opportunity. He was more than happy to talk to Clark.[15]

The invention and ownership of Mosaic quickly became an intellectual-property issue. Clark moved fast. From a temporary office at the University Inn, he interviewed and hired students who had worked on Mosaic and organized them into a new company named Mosaic Communications Corporation.[16] Smarr, who managed hundreds of employees and projects as director of the National Center for Supercomputing Applications (NCSA), and who considered Clark a friend and supporter of the university, was shocked. Clark was raiding his center. Clark viewed the situation quite differently: he was merely hiring recent graduates. Students (and Smarr) should be grateful.[17] Hard feelings spread rapidly across the Urbana-Champaign campus, even reaching the programmers' hangout at Espresso Royale coffee shop, "where late-night brainstorming sessions had first shaped the software that would transform the computer world."[18]

Tensions came to a head at the Second World Wide Web conference (October 1994), where participants witnessed a "family feud" in which Smarr publicly chastised "people who take and don't give back to the community."[19] Twenty companies were paying a licensing fee for it. Ten million copies of NCSA Mosaic had already been licensed, but Clark did not like the terms offered to him.[20] When Andreessen and his team "tried to attend the conference press briefing, an NCSA spokesman blocked the door and refused to admit them because they weren't official vendors."[21]

What is in a name? After seeing that the University of Illinois was considering "potential legal moves" against Mosaic Communications, Clark struck the first blow.[22] He sued the University of Illinois in U.S. District Court in San Jose, California. His legal team argued that "NCSA was a fumbling, short-sighted organization that wasn't sure what Marc had created, and where it fit inside their organization."[23] Clark promoted Andreessen as boy genius and managed his public persona to reinforce his lawsuit.[24] The former student's university colleagues were not pleased. Andreessen soon quickly "drew resentment from insiders after articles credited him with the original idea."[25]

The attacks on Andreessen backfired. The University of Illinois eventually won back the name "Mosaic" and was awarded $2.7 million in settlement payments. Clark's Mosaic Communications Corporation was ordered to rewrite the code for their browser. Clark was unfazed. He announced that this rewrite "was relatively easy to do because it [the original] was done by a bunch of amateur students."[26] The company also had to find a new name for itself and for its browser. They agreed on Netscape. (It had originally been "code-named Mozilla—a monster to destroy Mosaic."[27]) The Illinois alumnus was now alienated from his alma mater: "You go to school, you do research, you leave and they try to cripple your business—is this the way you want to be treated?" Andreessen asked right after the settlement. "Had I known this would happen, I would have gone to Stanford," he concluded.[28]

## For Profit or Against?

The line between innovation and grand theft started to blur. The two Janus sides of science, one where it is meant to serve the public good, the other where it is used for profit and for the benefit of the few, once again competed. The philosophy of Clark and Andreessen clashed starkly against that of Tim Berners-Lee, the English computer scientist who is generally acknowledged as the inventor of the World Wide Web at CERN. Berners-Lee had dreamed of an open world of shared knowledge instead of profitability. But as in every good drama, the two opposing parties needed each other. The Web needed a browser just as much as a browser needed the Web: "The combination of Tim Berners-Lee's Web protocols, which provided connectivity, and Marc Andreessen's browser, which provided a great interface, proved explosive. In twenty-four months, the Web has gone from being unknown to absolutely ubiquitous."[29] Users quickly noticed that "there are two ages of the Internet—before Mosaic, and after." With both, the growth of the internet seemed unstoppable: "Last year there were a handful of these Mosaic 'sites'; today [1993] there are more than 10,000, including such blatantly commercial ventures as the California Yellow Pages and the Internet Shopping Network."[30]

Fights over the ownership of the Mosaic invention quickly became intertwined with fights over the history of Mosaic. In publications produced and published by Mosaic Communications Corporation, Clark and associates described Andreessen as sole "creator and architect of NSCA Mosaic—which he conceived and designed while

> "Fights over the ownership of the Mosaic invention quickly became intertwined with the fight over the history of Mosaic."

still a student working at the University of Illinois."[31] Clark's genius, in turn, was due to "recognizing the vast potential of what Andreessen had created." While he described Andreessen as the "young pioneer," other collaborators were relegated to the role of "engineers who worked with Andreessen." Clark and Andreessen were a Batman-and-Robin "one-of-a-kind team . . . enthusiastic and driven on the one hand, experienced and industry savvy on the other." At the height of the first dot-com bubble and right before its impending crash, Netscape was bought for $4.2 billion by AOL (America Online). It was one of the first companies to go public without ever making money.

## Enter Microsoft

In August 1994 the university, eager to make money from projects originally supported by NSF, reached an agreement with Spyglass Inc. to become their licensing agent for Mosaic. Spyglass had been created by the university to commercialize innovations created on campus, and several Spyglass engineers were students at UIUC. Profits soon exploded: "It appeared that Spyglass had struck gold with Mosaic." At the end of 1994 Microsoft bought a license for $2 million for the rights to include Mosaic-based technology in its new Internet Explorer product that would soon be included in the Windows 95 operating system. And the bonanza only increased, as "by the end of 1995, the company was pulling down $20 million annually in licensing revenue alone."[32]

In times of war, coding can be used to foster or prevent our ability to comprehend, navigate, and conquer desired territory. When the Russians invaded Czechoslovakia in 1968 they found it impossible to use their maps because resistance fighters had torn the road signs from their posts along the highways.[33] Computer codes can be manipulated in similar ways. What if Mosaic could be adapted to per-

> "Berners-Lee and his colleagues managed to gain an advantage. Netscape was forced to retreat and rewrite its codes. Attempts to privatize the Web had failed."

mit only certain computers access to the internet and to specific regions of it, but not to others? When the leaders of Netscape saw that Bill Gates appeared to be lining up with Spyglass and the university, they tried a different strategy. A browser could defend itself from the competition by choosing which network extensions would catch on. Competing browsers would be unable to read sites created with different, incompatible specifications. Clark and Andreessen started creating an alternative to the HTML markup language developed by Berners-Lee and used by most of internet. They also started convincing some of the most popular content providers to switch to their standard. If their strategy worked, then Netscape's edge would reside in its capacity to read these vendor-specific Web pages, while Mosaic and Explorer would not. The university and Microsoft would be stuck with useless maps like Russian tank commanders had back in Czechoslovakia. The result would be what Clark had wanted all along: "The Net on the Net."[34] If it became dominant enough, Andreessen and Clark's browser could theoretically have an effect on which underlying operating systems clients would choose. It could even make operating systems completely obsolete. Microsoft could be vulnerable.

Berners-Lee and many others were horrified by the idea that access to particular sites and areas of the internet would be potentially cut off and that users would see only what their browsers allowed them to access. He left CERN to found the World Wide Web consortium (W3C) to ensure the long-term growth of the Web. In response to the development of unique proprietary standards by Netscape and others, it placed its weight on a Netscape-incompatible HTML standard for its 4.0 version. Berners-Lee and his colleagues managed to gain an advantage. Netscape was forced to retreat and rewrite its codes. Attempts to privatize the Web had failed.

Eventually, Microsoft pulled the plug on Spyglass, Netscape, and others by giving away Explorer for free. Spyglass started losing money by the millions. The period that has come to be known as the "Browser Wars" came to a rapid end. (Although Spyglass suffered at the client side of its business, the server side continued to grow apace. The company licensed commercial Web servers to Oracle, and in 2000 it was acquired by OpenTV for $2.5

billion.) As most of the world adopted the HTML standards backed by the W3C, Netscape made its remaining technology available as an open-source product by giving its code to the community-based, not-for-profit Mozilla Foundation, now creators of Firefox.[35]

Was Netscape Communications Corporation doomed now that browsers were practically free? Clark and Andreessen had sold before the boom went bust, and they were feeling optimistic that the government would intervene against Microsoft's growing dominance. Netscape was one of many plaintiffs in the U.S. antitrust case brought against it in 1998 for monopolistic practices. The antitrust suit significantly curtailed Microsoft tentacles, opening the door to many other smaller startups. Clark moved on to develop other software ventures. Andreessen has sat on the board of directors of Facebook and eBay and has invested in Twitter, Pinterest, Foursquare, and Skype. As a prominent Silicon Valley venture capitalist, he knows who he is looking for. A 2015 article in the *New Yorker* reported that Andreesen declared, "We are not funding Mother Teresa . . . we're funding imperial, will-to-power people who want to crush their competition."[36]

## The Map (Browser) and the Territory (the Web)

What, then, is Mosaic? Is it a tool? Is it a map? Its developers and users have consistently described it in those terms. It is a "navigational tool for the emerging data highway" and "a map to the buried treasures of the Information Age."[37] Mosaic's salesmen understood it in terms of "the ages-old Problem of Navigation," drawing, in particular, inspiration from Zadok Cramer's *The Navigator* (1802), the field guide that had helped open up the American West to European exploration.[38] But Mosaic was much more than a map, a tool, or even a technology (in the usual sense of these words).[39] Mosaic was a world-making software that turned the dream of the internet into a reality.

When we say we just found something "on" the Web, it is as if it were a stable, concrete thing, not unlike a table "on" which we find other things. But what gives the Web this thingness?[40] In part, it is the browser that permits us to see it that way, because we understand it as a mere in-terface to something else. Mosaic was the first successful browser used to access a system of networked computers, one so successful that most users were unconcerned with the essential role it played in producing the internet as a concrete reality. A look behind the scenes reveals otherwise: the success of the Web as we now know it hinged on complex negotiations that extended far beyond the lines of code that constituted Mosaic as a software product. That all of these elements disappeared so readily from view was a testament of how useful it was—so much so that it shows, by its very unobtrusiveness, how our contemporary point-and-click existence came to be.

## Notes

1. Alexander R. Galloway, *The Interface Effect* (Cambridge, UK: Polity, 2012), 31.

2. For a critique of the teleological and "Whig" aspects of most work on the history of the internet see Campbell-Kelly and Garcia-Swartz, "History of the Internet."

3. During the first Queen Elizabeth Prize for Engineering. Andrew L. Russell and Valérie Schafer, "In the Shadow of ARPANET and Internet: Louis Pouzin and the Cyclades Network in the 1970s," *Technology and Culture* 55, no. 4 (2014).

4. David S. Jackson and Suneel Ratan, "Battle for the Soul of the Internet," *Time*, June 25, 1994.

5. John Markoff, "A Free and Simple Computer Link," *New York Times*, December 8, 1993.

6. Winners announced during the International W3 Conference in Geneva (May 26, 1994). "WWW Awards '94," *The Guardian*, June 2, 1994. Some early accounts describe how Eric Bina "joined" Andreessen and Clark. Dale Dougherty and Richard Koman, *The Mosaic Handbook* (Sebastopol, Calif.: O'Reilly, 1994), 13. Other accounts name Bina as co-author.

7. Alan Deutschman, "Imposter Boy," *GQ*, January 1997, 123.

8. Jackson and Ratan, "Battle for the Soul of the Internet."

9. Ibid.

10. "Your Window to the Internet: The Net on the Net," edited by Mosaic Communications Corporation (Mountain View, Calif.: Mosaic, 1994).

11. Because of the stipulations connected to its funding, the NCSA was obliged to make its research available "for academic, research and internal business purposes only." Dougherty and Koman, *Mosaic Handbook*, 13.

12. Eric Nee, "Jim Clark," *Upside* 7, no. 10 (1995).

13. The government retained the power of specifying what systems would be eligible for defense contract funding. For this history see Nathan Newman, "Net Loss: The Political Economy of Community in the Age of the Internet," PhD diss., University of California, Berkeley, 1998; and Newman, *Net Loss*.

14. Dougherty and Koman, *Mosaic Handbook*, 13.

15. Kevin Maney, "10 Years Ago, Who Knew What His Code Would Do?" *USA Today*, March 3, 2003.

16. Paul Andrews, "Profit without Honor," *Seattle Times*, October 5, 1997.

17. Ibid.

18. Ibid.

19. Jim Crawley, "University of Illinois Moves to Enforce Its Mosaic Trademark," *WEBster, the CyberSpace Surfer for the World Wide Web*, October 25, 1994.

20. Clark explained why he did not want to buy a license: "The university wanted us to take a license, but they didn't have a reasonable license to offer us. They wanted us to pay an ongoing per-copy royalty. And I said, 'Look, we're not going to do that, our business model won't allow that.' I didn't tell them, but we had intended to allow people to download it, and they were going to charge me." Nee, "Jim Clark."

21. Crawley, "University of Illinois Moves to Enforce."

22. Ibid.

23. Dougherty and Koman, *Mosaic Handbook*, 13. But the role played by NCSA was not so easily dismissed, as it had hired many other students to develop Windows and Mac versions.

24. For Jim Clark's thoughts about himself see Jim Clark and Owen Edwards, *Netscape Time: The Making of the Billion-Dollar Start-Up That Took On Microsoft* (New York: St. Martin's, 1999). For a book-length account of Andreessen see Ehrenhaft, *Marc Andreessen*.

25. Andreessen's supervisor, Ping Fu (3D graphics expert who had studied at UIUC on a doctoral assistantship from Bell Labs), claimed it was her idea to incorporate graphics into the browser. Dave Thompson, a key programmer, was sidelined, as was Rob McCool. Another student (Chris Wilson) took Mosaic with him to Seattle and eventually partnered with Compuserve and later Microsoft. Compuserve's Spry/Internet Division created and trademarked "Mosaic in a Box" and "Internet in a Box." "The project coordinator, Joseph Hardin, however, said the idea arose 'organically' from discussions among Andreessen, Bina and another NCSA programmer, Dave Thompson, as well as key managers, including Ping Fu, Andreessen's supervisor. Fu herself recalls suggesting the idea of a graphical browser to Andreessen." Andrews, "Profit without Honor."

26. Nee, "Jim Clark."

27. Donald K. Rosenberg, *Open Source: The Unauthorized White Papers* (Foster City, Calif.: M and T, 2000).

28. David Bank, "Netscape Settles Mosaic Dispute," *San Jose Mercury News*, December 22, 1994.

29. Mark Pesce, "A Brief History of Cyberspace," *ZDNet*, October 15, 1995. Mosaic's main benefit was how it provided access to the World Wide Web, but it also incorporated content found via FTP, Gopher, and WAIS.

30. Jackson and Ratan, "Battle for the Soul of the Internet."

31. "Your Window to the Internet."

32. Tim Krauskopf was co-founder, Chief Technical Officer and Vice President of Research and Development for Spyglass. Chris Nerney, "The Up and Coming: Get to Know Five Companies That Could Shake Up the NW200 in Years to Come," *Network World*, April 20, 1998, 60.

33. Bruno Latour, *Science in Action: How to Follow Scientists and Engineers through Society* (Cambridge, Mass.: Harvard University Press, 1987), 254.

34. "Your Window to the Internet."

35. Rosenberg, *Open Source*.

36. Quoted in Friend, "Tomorrow's Advance Man."

37. Markoff, "Free and Simple Computer Link."

38. Dougherty and Koman, *Mosaic Handbook*, 42.

39. Bernhard Siegert, "The Map is the Territory," *Radical Philosophy* 169 (2011): 15.

40. Martin Heidegger, "The Thing," in *The Craft Reader*, edited by Glenn Adamson (London: Bloomsbury, [1950] 2009).

## Sources

Among the most readily available sources for the story of Mosaic, see the following: Martin Campbell-Kelly and Daniel D. Garcia-Swartz, "The History of the Internet: The Missing Narratives," *Journal of Information Technology* 28 (2013): 18–33; Jim Clark and Owen Edwards, *Netscape Time: The Making of the Billion-Dollar Start-Up That Took On Microsoft* (New York: St. Martin's Press, 1999); Daniel Ehrenhaft, *Marc Andreessen: Web Warrior* (Brookfield, Conn.: Twenty-First Century Book, 2001); Tad Friend, "Tomorrow's Advance Man: Marc Andreessen's Plan to Win the Future," *New Yorker*, May 18, 2015; and Nathan Newman, *Net Loss: Internet Prophets, Private Profits and the Costs to Community* (University Park: Pennsylvania State University Press, 2002).

# Superfluidity

*Tim Brown*

Anthony Leggett

In the spring of 1964, Anthony J. Leggett, a freshly minted PhD in physics from Oxford, considered the next steps in his career. He wanted to pursue his theoretical research interests in condensed matter physics and to join a challenging scientific community. And he wanted to get away from the university where he had spent the past nine years of his life. Aware of the work of David Pines, John Bardeen, and other physicists at the University of Illinois, Leggett decided to apply to the Physics Department in Urbana-Champaign for a postdoctoral appointment. It was the only application he made that year, and, happily for all concerned, he was successful. When he arrived on campus that fall, Leggett was unimpressed by the midwestern landscape. The campus, recently decimated by Dutch elm disease, looked particularly barren. But the young Englishman was quickly drawn into the physics community's exciting intellectual culture.

During his first year at Illinois, Leggett began his interest in the superfluid liquid isotope called "$^3$He." What interested him most about this element was how it acted when cooled down to absolute zero (0 K). While experiments demonstrated that at these low temperatures, magnetic forces that had been previously negligible caused the flow of the liquid to acquire zero resistance, the mechanism behind this phenomenon was unknown. Leggett's theoretical insights into how this "superfluidity" occurred and how it challenged previous assumptions about quantum mechanics attracted international attention. The year at Illinois, Leggett later recalled, was "a turning point in my career."

Leggett soon left Illinois and within a few years had established himself as a professor at the University of Sussex, but his colleagues at the University of Illinois did not forget him. In 1982 the John D. and Catherine T. MacArthur Foundation established a new endowed chair at the University of Illinois, and the search began for its first occupant. In the Physics Department, a committee of six faculty members decided to nominate Leggett for the position. He later recalled that he was astonished to receive the offer "out of the blue" and excited at the prospect of returning to the Urbana campus. At Illinois, he expanded his interests in the foundations of quantum mechanics to theoretical investigations of other systems, including unconventional superconductors, degenerate atomic gases, and low-temperature properties of glasses. Most recently, he has been interested in how the quantum mechanics of condensed matter systems could be exploited for quantum computing.

In 2003 he was awarded the Nobel Prize for his seminal contributions to the theory of superconductors and superfluids. A continuing interest has been how the microscopic theory of quantum mechanics could be extrapolated to our macroscopic world of everyday objects.

## Sources

The best published source on Leggett is a profile in a university publication, "MacArthur Professor Tests Basic Physical Ideas" *Illini Week*, April 28, 1984. The University Archives also maintains a small file of material on Leggett's life and career. Finally, the website of the Nobel Prize (nobelprize.org) contains an extended autobiographical statement by Leggett.

# Bottled Sunshine
## Discovering and Harnessing the Power of Photosynthesis

Claire Benjamin and Claudia Lutz

The energy that flows through almost every living thing on Earth comes from the light of our sun. Plants, algae, and bacteria harness light's energy and use it to convert carbon dioxide and water into life-giving oxygen and sugar in a process called photosynthesis.

As our global population continues to grow, so do our demands on the crops that can turn light into food we can eat. The key to increasing our food supply is hidden inside the elaborate molecular processes that make photosynthesis possible. The innovative work of a succession of Illinois researchers—Robert Emerson, William Ogren, Stephen Long, and Donald Ort—over the course of almost a century has given us the knowledge and the tools we need to create crops that can feed future generations.

Yet this research began not with a practical goal but with a passionate desire to discover and understand.

## Emerson: Photosynthetic Efficiency and a Search for Truth

A great-grandnephew of nineteenth century philosopher Ralph Waldo Emerson, Robert Emerson planned to become a physician like his father. With this goal in mind, he matriculated at Harvard University in 1920 and graduated with a master's degree in zoology in 1925.[1] During that time, however, he encountered the renowned botanist and pioneer of biochemistry, Winthrop John Van Leuven Osterhout,[2] whose compelling lectures inspired

Emerson to change the trajectory of his career. He moved to Germany to pursue plant science research, joining the laboratory of Otto Warburg at the University of Berlin; this began a professional relationship that would lead to some of the brightest—and darkest—moments of Emerson's academic career.[3]

Warburg, who received the Nobel Prize in Medicine in 1931 for his research on metabolism in cancer cells,[4] also had a strong interest in photosynthesis and respiration in plants. While earning his doctorate in botany in Warburg's laboratory in Berlin, Emerson learned manometry, a technique for measuring gas pressure used to quantify the consumption of carbon dioxide and release of oxygen that takes place during photosynthesis. He investigated the relationship between the rate of photosynthesis and chemical factors, including the concentration of chlorophyll. Emerson completed his doctoral studies in 1927; after returning to Harvard as a Research Council Fellow, he joined the faculty of the California Institute of Technology's Department of Biology in 1930 and established a research program examining the effects of chemical concentrations, light, and temperature on the rate of photosynthesis.

Emerson demonstrated that for every two thousand chlorophyll molecules stimulated by a brief flash of light, only one molecule of oxygen is generated.[5] This apparent wastefulness is actually caused by the then-unknown structure of the light-capturing molecular complexes found within plant and algal cells. Most photosynthetic pigment molecules act like components of a large antenna, capturing the energy from light and passing it to a central molecule, where it is transformed into chemical energy. Emerson's results were the first to suggest the existence of this molecular teamwork.

At Caltech, Emerson became interested in yet another important aspect of photosynthesis.[6] Just two decades earlier, physicists had recognized that light can be measured in discrete units, now called photons. In the 1920s Otto Warburg posed a question that dominated the field for the next forty years: What is the minimum amount of light energy, or number of photons, required to produce one molecule of oxygen? Researchers thought this value might help clarify the unknown mechanisms underlying photosynthesis, just as knowing the cost of manufacturing a machine might suggest something about how it was made. In 1922 Warburg and his collaborator, Erwin Negelein, found that one molecule of oxygen is produced for every four quanta of light captured in optimal conditions.[7]

In California, Emerson began to question Warburg's findings.[8] He started his own investigation, which continued after his move to a faculty position at the University of Illinois in 1946. In these experiments, algal cultures were briefly exposed to carefully calibrated flashes of light. Manometry was used to quantify changes in the concentration of carbon dioxide and oxygen during photosynthesis (in the light) and during respiration (in the dark). Results were easily affected by the health of the cultures, the reagents used, and the handling of the equipment. Emerson became confident that there were systematic problems with Warburg's methods.[9]

At Illinois, Emerson worked with several collaborators, including physicist M. Shimpe Nishimura, physical chemist Eugene Rabinowitch, and expert technician Ruth V. Chalmers, to address discrepancies between Warburg's findings and those of other laboratories, including his own. Warburg's prior role as Emerson's mentor and his frequent changes to details of his experimental approach without explanation[10] presented significant obstacles for Emerson. In response, Emerson methodically identified differences between his and Warburg's experiments and determined how results might be affected by those differences. Ultimately, he proposed a minimum light requirement of eight photons per oxygen molecule generated, twice the minimum published by Warburg but in close agreement with other laboratories using various experimental approaches. In 1955 Emerson published a paper that delineated potential sources of error in Warburg's methods and offered mechanistic explanations for his results, as well as confirming his own minimum value.[11]

Warburg's unwillingness to cooperate with colleagues to establish the facts of photosynthetic efficiency eventually frustrated many of his contemporaries and prolonged the debate for many years. However, the limitations of the technology available at the time were also a significant impediment to resolving the question. It is impressive that

Robert Emerson and Eugene Rabinowitch

researchers were able to reach a conclusion that, today, has been confirmed by more reliable methods and by a much more complete understanding of photosynthesis.

As the controversy finally waned, Emerson returned to an observation that he had made many years before: the rate of photosynthesis is affected by the wavelength of available light. Exploring this phenomenon further, he found that although the rate of photosynthesis dropped in red light at the far end of the visible spectrum, photosynthesis could be "rescued" by supplementing with certain blue or green wavelengths. Tragically, this work was cut short when Emerson died in a plane crash in 1959, on his way to a scientific conference at Harvard University.[12] However, Emerson's "enhancement effect" helped other researchers, including Rabinowitch, theorize and eventually confirm the existence of two independent complexes of photosynthetic pigments called photosystems, each with its own complement of pigments and light requirements. The partnership of the two photosystems accounts for the eight-photon requirement established by Emerson and others; each photosystem must absorb four photons for each oxygen molecule produced.[13]

Emerson met controversy and bitter conflict with forbearance, patient work, and a determination to establish the truth. His efforts greatly advanced our knowledge of photosynthesis, setting a high standard for future plant science research at the University of Illinois and breaking ground for his successors.

## Ogren: Diagnosing and Confronting the Achilles Heel of Photosynthetic Efficiency

As Emerson, Warburg, and others were struggling to understand photosynthesis, a broad agricultural research initiative was creating huge changes in worldwide food production. Led by biologist Norman Borlaug, the Green Revolution improved global food security by providing farmers with better irrigation, improved access to pesticides, and newly developed high-yield crop plants.[14] Continuing this dramatic improvement of vital food crops was the motivation behind William L. Ogren's research as a United States Department of Agriculture (USDA) scientist based at the Urbana campus.

Like Emerson, the origins of Ogren's lifelong career in photosynthesis research were serendipitous.[15] After graduating from the University of Wisconsin in 1961 with a bachelor's degree in chemistry, Ogren accepted a job at the Parker Rust Proof Company in Detroit. He enrolled in evening graduate studies at nearby Wayne State University. The only chemistry night course offered that year was taught by David Krogmann, then an assistant professor of chemistry who specialized in photosynthesis research. Krogmann was so impressed by Ogren's performance on the first exam that he urged Ogren to accept a full-time graduate position in his laboratory. His argument must have been compelling—Ogren accepted, left his job at Parker, and joined the doctoral program. He graduated in 1965, converted from an industrial researcher to lifelong plant scientist.[16]

The USDA research laboratory in Urbana hired Ogren to investigate photosynthesis in soybeans, a key food crop, to identify ways to improve yield. (For the background to the USDA laboratory at Illinois, see chapter 3.1, "The Morrow Plots.") Ogren began by screening soybean plants for naturally occurring genetic variation in photosynthetic efficiency. Plants with higher efficiency, and thus higher potential yield, could be used to improve existing varieties through crossbreeding.[17]

Ogren's initial results showed large variation in photosynthetic rate, but he found that these differences were simply due to variable leaf thickness. He shifted to a more targeted strategy, concentrating his efforts on identifying inefficient aspects of the molecular mechanisms of photosynthesis. One possible candidate was the recently discovered phenomenon of photorespiration,[18] a process in which some of the carbon dioxide captured during photosynthesis is released back into the air instead of being successfully incorporated into sugar. In most plants, for every four photosynthetic "steps" forward, photorespiration slides carbon fixation one step back. At the time, there was no mechanistic explanation for this process.

Ogren's interest was piqued by the pioneering work of Canadian plant physiologist Gleb Krotkov, who quantified a phenomenon first observed by Warburg in 1920,[19] that higher concentrations of oxygen inhibit photosynthesis. Krotkov had also shown that higher levels of carbon dioxide promote photosynthesis.[20] His mathematical formulation of this relationship, which implied a positive correlation between the rates of photosynthesis and photorespiration, enabled Ogren's daring insight—that both processes were regulated by a common mechanism.[21]

Ogren and his postdoctoral fellow, George Bowes, had begun to examine oxygen's effects on Ribulose bisphosphate (RuBP) carboxylase, an enzyme (protein catalyst) that facilitates carbon fixation in photosynthesis. Researchers thought that oxygen could irreversibly damage the enzyme. In 1969, through a lucky error, Bowes and Ogren discovered that rather than disabling the protein, oxygen shoves carbon dioxide aside and replaces it in the subsequent reaction.[22] This alternative reaction is, in fact, the first step of photorespiration. The enzyme was eventually renamed RuBP carboxylase/oxygenase, or Rubisco, to represent the duality of its activities.

Obtaining and verifying these results and the end products of the newly discovered reaction was incredibly difficult to accomplish in Ogren's (or any) laboratory. This technical challenge and the unexpectedness of the findings, published in 1971, initially provoked skeptical reactions from colleagues. One legend has it that a graduate student in biochemist Ed Tolbert's laboratory at Michigan State University became so frustrated with his failed attempts to reproduce Ogren's results that he drove from Lansing to Urbana to argue about the data in person.[23] In reality, the student, George Lorimer, came at least in part to obtain some of the isolated enzyme Bowes used in his experiments.[24] With Bowes's enzyme in hand, and later using enzyme he isolated himself, Lorimer successfully verified Ogren's findings.[25] This success was not the end of the controversy over Rubisco, though. The ensuing battle—waged via contradictory publications and shouting matches at conferences—continued for the better part of a decade.[26]

Ogren continued to investigate the properties of Rubisco and photorespiration to better understand their findings as well as to reinforce them. Ogren's work with a graduate student in his laboratory, William Laing, led to a series of equations that formalized the relationships between oxygen concentration, carbon dioxide concentration, and the rate at which Rubisco interacts with each. These equations—published in 1974—proved consistent with the experimental results of Ogren, Krotkov, and others.[27] Laing's equations formed the basis for present-day models used to predict how food and energy crops will respond to global climate change.[28]

The next researcher to join Ogren's laboratory, Chris Somerville, also made a lasting contribution to the methodology of modern plant science. Somerville, who began his postdoctoral work with Ogren in 1978, was looking for a project that could serve as a proving ground for a relatively unknown experimental plant, *Arabidopsis thaliana*. Somerville thought that a genetics experiment in Arabidopsis could help settle the debate over photorespiration and in doing so could persuade the research community of the small, fast-growing, easily reared mustard plant's utility as a genetic experimental organism. By working with Ogren, Somerville was picking a side in the Rubisco controversy and also aiding Ogren's continued efforts to discover genetic variation that could affect photosynthetic efficiency.[29]

Somerville created and described several lines of Arabidopsis plants with possible photorespiration-related mutations that were only able to photosynthesize at very low oxygen levels. He and Ogren identified the gene affected in each mutant and what part of photorespiration each contributed to, providing a picture of the process that confirmed Ogren's earlier work.[30] Arabidopsis has since become one of the most important plants in the research world and the first to have its complete genome sequenced.[31] Ogren had hoped his work with Somerville might also produce plants with increased photosynthetic efficiency, but this effort failed.

Ogren's career-long quest to produce a higher-yield crop through improvement of photosynthesis did not succeed. Yet in this quest he overcame widespread opposition to solve the mystery of photorespiration. Under his leadership, the Illinois laboratory demonstrated a key second function of the enzyme RuBisCo, produced a robust mathematical model for the basic mechanisms of photosynthesis and photorespiration, and established Arabidopsis as a key research tool. Like Emerson, Ogren created a legacy for a new generation of researchers, who, equipped with a new set of experimental tools, might complete the quest he had begun.

## Illinois: Ushering in the Next Green Revolution

Today's crops cannot adapt quickly enough to the world's rapidly changing, postindustrial climate. After the Green Revolution, population growth, dwindling natural resources, and limited arable land have caused food prices to rise and agricultural productivity once again to become strained.[32] By 2050, feeding a global population of more than nine billion will require a 70 percent increase in food production.[33]

Previous improvements to food crops such as wheat had redistributed the fruits of photosynthesis, thus doubling the yields of staple food crops. Before 1930, grain accounted for 30 percent of a plant's mass; today it ac-

> "The pioneering work of previous scientific generations has enabled Long, Ort and their colleagues to construct sophisticated *in silico models* to identify multiple bottlenecks and inefficiencies in photosynthesis."

Stephen Long in his laboratory. Photo by Kathryn Faith, courtesy of the Carl R. Woese Institute for Genomic Biology.

counts for 60 percent. However, scientists believe this to be the biological limit, as the remaining mass—in the form of stems, leaves, and roots—is needed to sustain the plant.[34]

Two Illinois professors, Stephen Long and Donald Ort, are building on the legacy of researchers like Emerson and Ogren to engineer the next Green Revolution. Their vision expands on Ogren's: optimize multiple aspects of the photosynthetic pathway in key food crops—rice, cassava, cowpeas, and soybeans—to increase the total growth potential, and therefore food yield, of each type of plant. This large-scale research project, Realizing Increased Photosynthetic Efficiency (RIPE), receives its funding from the Bill and Melinda Gates Foundation. Researchers working on the RIPE project will engineer more efficient pathways through a combination of gene editing and transplantation from more efficient species.[35]

The pioneering work of previous scientific generations has enabled Long, Ort, and their colleagues to construct sophisticated *in silico models* to identify multiple bottlenecks and inefficiencies in photosynthesis. These quirks of nature make plants better evolutionary competitors, but selfish and wasteful neighbors in a field of crops.[36] Long and Ort plan to use their models to determine the optimal levels and functions of each photosynthetic gene.

Researchers in Ogren's generation had limited tools with which to explore and manipulate plant genes; modern day tools make it possible to read plant DNA quickly and to edit it precisely. For example, Long and Ort hope to borrow the molecular mechanisms used by microbes to pump more carbon dioxide to Rubisco, helping it avoid the inefficiency of photorespiration Ogren described. In a practical application of Emerson and Ogren's observations that more light is absorbed by plants than can actually be used, Long and Ort plan to alter the regulation and distribution of photosynthetic pigment in each plant and the orientation of leaves to ensure that light is evenly distributed throughout the canopy and to maximize photosynthesis in each leaf.

RIPE researchers will test their predictions in another unlikely crop, tobacco, which like Arabidopsis is an easy-to-use plant genetic model. The most promising approaches will then be transferred to target crops, which are more difficult and time consuming to bioengineer. Because photosynthesis is similar in most plants, these photosynthetic improvements could eventually be implemented in other staple crops, like wheat and potatoes.[37] Ultimately, Long and Ort hope to improve photosynthetic efficiency by 60 percent and eventually to produce a comparable increase in crop yields.

The ancient Greeks believed that fire was a gift stolen from the sun and given to humanity by a god, and that curiosity was humanity's punishment for receiving that gift. Contemplation of the history of scientific exploration suggests that instead, curiosity is a gift—one that leads to the discovery of ways to understand the natural world, to harvest its fruits, and to conserve its splendor. A quest that began with curiosity has led to a newfound ability to harness the light of the sun and, perhaps, to feed the world.

## Notes

1. "Robert Emerson, 1903–1959." *Plant Physiology* 34 (1959): i4, 179–84.

2. Lawrence Rogers Blinks, *Winthrop John Vanleuven Osterhout: August 2, 1871–April 9, 1964* (National Academy of Sciences, 1974).

3. Kärin Nickelsen and Govindjee, *The Maximum Quantum Yield Controversy: Otto Warburg and the Midwest Gang*, Bern Studies in the History and Philosophy of Science (Books on Demand, 2011).

4. *Otto Warburg: Documentary*, Nobel Media AB, 2014, available at http://www.nobelprize.org/nobel_prizes/medicine/laureates/1931/warburg-docu.html.

5. Robert Emerson and William Arnold, "The Photochemical Reaction in Photosynthesis," *Journal of General Physiology* 16 (1932): 191–205.

6. Nickelsen and Govindjee, *Maximum Quantum*.

7. Otto Warburg, "Über den Energieumsatz bei der Kohlensäureassimilation," *Zeitschrift für Elektrochemie und angewandte physikalische Chemie* 28 (1922): 449–52; Otto Warburg and Erwin Negelein, "Über den Einfluss der Wellenlaenge auf den Energieumsatz bei der Kohlensaeureassimilation," *Zeitschrift für Physikalische Chemie* 106 (1922): 191–218.

8. Robert Emerson and Charlton Lewis, "Factors Influencing the Efficiency of Photosynthesis," *American Journal of Botany* 26 (1939): 808–22; Robert Emerson and Charlton M. Lewis, "The Dependence of the Quantum Yield of Chlorella Photosynthesis on Wave Length of Light," *American Journal of Botany* 30 (1943): 165–78.

9. Nickelsen and Govindjee, *Maximum Quantum*.

10. Dean Burk, Sterling Hendricks, Mitchell Korzenovsky, and Otto Warburg, "The Maximum Efficiency of Photosynthesis: A Rediscovery," *Science* 110 (1949); Otto Warburg and Dean Burk, "The Maximum Efficiency of Photosynthesis," *Archives of Biochemistry* 25 (1950): 410–43; Otto Warburg, Dean Burk, Victor Schocken, and Sterling B. Hendricks, "The Quantum Efficiency of Photosynthesis," *Biochimica et Biophysica Acta* 4 (1950): 335–48.

11. Robert Emerson and Ruth Chalmers, "Transient Changes in Cellular Gas Exchange and the Problem of Maximum Efficiency of Photosynthesis," *Plant Physiology* 30 (1955): 504–29.

12. "Robert Emerson, 1903–1959."

13. Robert Emerson and Eugene Rabinowitch, "Red Drop and the Role of Auxiliary Pigments in Photosynthesis," *Plant Physiology* 35 (1960): 477–85.

14. William S. Gaud, "The Green Revolution: Accomplishments and Apprehensions," address by the Honorable William S. Gaud, Administrator, U.S. Agency for International Development, Department of State, before the Society for International Development, Shoreham Hotel, Washington, D.C., 1968, 8.

15. Henry A. Schuette, "Badger Chemist: A Newsletter from the Department of Chemistry of the University of Wisconsin," Winter 1961.

16. Archie R. Portis Jr., "William L. Ogren Was Honored with a Lifetime Achievement Award by the Rebeiz Foundation for Basic Research," *Photosynthesis Research* 110 (2012): 213–20.

17. W. L. Ogren, "Affixing the O to Rubisco: Discovering the Source of Photorespiratory Glycolate and Its Regulation," *Photosynthesis Research* 76 (2003): 53-63.

18. Brian James Atwell, Paul E. Kriedemann, and Colin G. N. Turnbull, *Plants in Action: Adaptation in Nature, Performance in Cultivation* (South Yarra: Macmillan Education Australia, 1999).

19. Otto Warburg, *Über die Geschwindigkeit der photochemischen Kohlensäurezersetzung in lebenden Zellen* (Berlin: Springer, 1928).

20. Marlene L. Forrester, Gleb Krotkov, and C. D. Nelson, "Effect of Oxygen on Photosynthesis, Photorespiration and Respiration in Detached Leaves. I. Soybean," *Plant Physiology* 41 (1966): 422–27.

21. Chris R. Somerville, "An Early Arabidopsis Demonstration: Resolving a Few Issues Concerning Photorespiration," *Plant physiology* 125 (2001): 20–24.

22. William L. Ogren and George Bowes, "Ribulose Diphosphate Carboxylase Regulates soybean Photorespiration," *Nature* 230 (1971): 159–60; George Bowes, William L. Ogren, and Richard Hageman, "Phosphoglycolate Production Catalyzed by Ribulose Diphosphate Carboxylase," *Biochemical and Biophysical Research Communications* 45 (1971): 716–22.

23. Somerville, "Early Arabidopsis Demonstration."

24. Ogren, "Affixing the O."

25. George H. Lorimer, Nathan E. Tolbert, and T. John Andrews, "Oxidative Activity Associated with Ribulose 1,

5-Diphosphate Darboxylase," *Federation of American Societies for Experimental Biology* (1972).

26. Somerville, "Early Arabidopsis Demonstration."

27. William A. Laing, William L. Ogren, and Richard Hageman, "Regulation of Soybean Net Photosynthetic CO2 Fixation by the Interaction of CO2, O2, and Ribulose 1, 5-Diphosphate Carboxylase," *Plant Physiology* 54 (1974): 678–85.

28. Ogren, "Affixing the O."

29. Somerville, "Early Arabidopsis Demonstration."

30. William L. Ogren, "Photorespiration: Pathways, Regulation, and Modification," *Annual Review of Plant Physiology* 35 (1984): 415–42; Chris Somerville and William L. Ogren, "Inhibition of Photosynthesis in Arabidopsis Mutants Lacking Leaf Glutamate Synthase Activity," *Nature* 286 (1980): 257–59; Chris R. Somerville and William L. Ogren, "A Phosphoglycolate Phosphatase-Deficient Mutant of Arabidopsis," *Nature* 280 (1979): 833–36.

31. The Arabidopsis Genome Initiative, "Analysis of the Genome Sequence of the Flowering Plant Arabidopsis Thaliana," *Nature* 408 (2000): 796.

32. Norman E. Borlaug, "Ending World Hunger: The Promise of Biotechnology and the Threat of Antiscience Zealotry," *Plant Physiology* 124 (2000): 487–90.

33. David Tilman, Christian Balzer, Jason Hill, and Belinda L. Befort, "Global Food Demand and the Sustainable Intensification of Agriculture," *Proceedings of the National Academy of Sciences* 108 (2001): 20, 260–64.

34. Donald R. Ort, Sabeeha S. Merchant, Jean Alric, Alice Barkan, Robert E. Blankenship et al., "Redesigning Photosynthesis to Sustainably Meet Global Food and Bioenergy Demand," *Proceedings of the National Academy of Sciences* 112 (2015): 8529–36.

35. Gilbert, "Gates Foundation Backs High-Risk Science." *Nature Plants* 1, no. 15022 (2015).

36. Ort et al., "Redesigning Photosynthesis."

37. Ibid.

## Sources

For comprehensive history of Emerson's career, and particularly the years of controversy with Warburg see Nickelsen and Govindjee's *The Maximum Yield Controversy: Otto Warburg and the "Midwest Gang"* (2011); his obituary in *Plant Physiology* also includes some noteworthy and touching details. Emerson's correspondence, laboratory notes, and other files are preserved in the University of Illinois Archives. Ogren provides a helpful summary of his own career in his perspective piece, "Affixing the O to Rubisco: Discovering the Source of Photorespiratory Glycolate and Its Regulation" in the April 2003 issue of *Photosynthesis Research*. Natasha Gilbert's 2015 article (no. 15022) in *Nature Plants*, "Gates Foundation Backs High-Risk Science for Big Wins," is a good starting point for understanding the background and goals of the RIPE project led by Long and Ort.

# Interdisciplinary Scholarship at the College of Law

*Michael Hughes*

Since its founding in 1897, the University of Illinois College of Law has emerged as a leading institution in the training of scholars and legal practitioners. The college's first publication, the *Illinois Law Bulletin*, was published in 1917; it is now distributed nationally as the *University of Illinois Law Review*. For more than seventy years the college occupied historic Altgeld Hall (the original university library), but in the 1950s it moved into a modern facility on Pennsylvania Avenue. That building was renovated and transformed into a state-of-the-art facility in the early 1990s (Supreme Court Justice Ruth Bader Ginsburg presided over its rededication in 1994).

The training of lawyers typically follows a predictable path, with basic courses and other aspects of education largely dictated by American Bar Association accreditation. This framework generally emphasizes passing on the doctrinal framework of the law to future practitioners. Remarkably, however, despite the College of Law's traditional strength as a training ground for practicing lawyers, it has also established itself as a center of innovative, interdisciplinary research and pedagogy. Beginning in the late 1980s, faculty and students made concerted efforts to explore interdisciplinary perspectives on the law. The most successful aspect of this effort has occurred among scholars interested in

The University of Illinois College of Law building. Photo courtesy of the College of Law.

linking the fields of law and economics in order to broaden the profession's understanding of the economic implications of legal rules and processes. The College has promoted their efforts in a variety of ways, notably by hosting the initial annual meeting of the American Law and Economics Association in 1991 and by the early 2000s hiring core faculty in law and economics to make Illinois Law one of the best groups of scholars in that discipline in the world. Additionally, the College of Law has hosted interdisciplinary symposia on major issues such as the impact of sovereign loan defaults, the problem of regulating foreign banking in the United States, the creation of international banking rules, and the causes and legal consequences of widespread consumer bankruptcy. The college also explored the relationship between economic change and corporate reorganization when it sponsored a widely noted "Uncorporation" symposium that explored the ways corporations create nontraditional business associations in response to tax laws.

The College of Law has also fostered interdisciplinary course and scholarly work in law and philosophy, law and psychology, law and history, and, most recently, law and the behavioral and social sciences. The college has long sought to build on the university's strengths in scientific research and engineering. Professor Jay Kesan, a specialist in technology and business law, has spearheaded some of these efforts, most notably by founding, with the university's Institute of Government and Public Affairs, the *Journal of Technology, Law, and Policy* in 2001. In its first years, the journal's student editors and their faculty mentors sought to highlight issues associated with the regulation of digital technologies and the effects of those regulations on both security and privacy. As the journal's readership has expanded, it has addressed the ever-shifting terrain of technology, economics, and the law and has been a leading forum for scholarly inquiry into the legal implications of technological innovation. Extending this involvement with issues related to technological innovation and the law, the College of Law has also established an Intellectual Property (IP) and Technology Law program.

The faculty at the College of Law have demonstrated that despite the Law School's basic (and challenging) task of introducing students to the existing legal landscape, that landscape exists in a complex world where technological innovation, government action, and the challenges of a global economy demand vision and innovation.

# PART THREE

# PLACES OF INNOVATION

Where Ideas and People
Meet to Produce Innovation

# The Morrow Plots

Kathleen Mapes

On September 12, 1968, barely six months after the University of Illinois's centennial celebrations had come to an end, an esteemed assortment of dignitaries gathered to mark the designation of the Morrow Plots as a National Historic Landmark. Established in 1876, the Morrow Plots were distinguished as both the oldest agricultural experiment plots created by a college or university in the United States and the oldest continuous experimental corn plots in the world. One of the speakers that day, Dr. Morell B. Russell, director of the University of Illinois Agricultural Experiment Station, likened the 1876 founding of the Morrow Plots to the nation's Declaration of Independence a hundred years earlier, proclaiming, "It is now clear that the lesson of the Morrow Plots represents a new kind of declaration of independence— not of political independence but independence from one of the fears that man has had since the dawn of time, the fear of hunger." Russell continued, "[The Morrow Plots] stand as a symbol of hope that hunger and privation are not the historic fate of man."[1]

The original Morrow Plots consisted of ten half-acre parcels of farmland. In 1895 two of these plots were discontinued to make room for the campus observatory. Eight years later, five of the remaining plots were seeded back to grass, leaving three half-acre plots. A year later, the remaining plots were further reduced to one-fifth of an acre, with each divided in half, leaving a total of six plots, each one-tenth of an acre—the size of the plots to the current day.

The relatively small size of the Morrow Plots belies their historical and continued significance. When they

Dedicating the National Historic Landmark at Morrow Plots, 1968

tablish colleges "for the benefit of agriculture and the mechanical arts," offered a new vision for both higher education and for agricultural research. But how these newly formed colleges would "benefit" agriculture and the mechanical arts remained very much up for debate. Initially, it proved much easier to focus on the teaching of traditional academic subjects than to develop a research agenda that could reach the masses and would have practical application.

In the early years, leaders at what was then known as Illinois Industrial University sought out ways to fully enhance agricultural practices without abandoning classical education. In 1871 Willard C. Flagg, secretary of the university board of trustees, convinced university regent John M. Gregory to call a meeting of representatives of twelve of the newly formed land-grant colleges so that fellow leaders could discuss ways to develop agricultural extension. By the end of the meeting, the representatives passed a resolution calling for the creation of experiment stations at each college where long-term practical and applied agricultural research could be conducted. The participants stipulated, however, that they did not want the limited Morrill funds to be used for that purpose. The following year U.S. Commissioner of Agriculture Frederick Watts called for a meeting of Department of Agriculture officials and land-grant college leaders. Once again, Gregory assumed a leading role and, in conjunction with others, formed a Committee on Experiment Stations. The committee renewed the previous year's call for the creation of campus-based experimental stations, noting that the nation's farmers expected the newly established land-grant colleges to help meet their need for applied and practical research.[2]

Considering the leading role Regent Gregory played in calling for the creation of experiment stations at land-grant colleges, it is not surprising that Illinois would establish experimental farms under his watch. The 1875 hiring of Manly Miles as a professor of agriculture and the appointment of George E. Morrow two years later as dean of the College of Agriculture proved to be pivotal moves for the history of University of Illinois as well as for the future of practical and applied agricultural research. Miles, who graduated with a medical degree from

were established in 1876, practical agricultural science was still in its infancy. For much of the nineteenth century, agricultural experimentation remained the domain of myriad local and state agricultural societies who engaged in experiments and shared results at county fairs and in farm journals and newspapers. While these efforts reflected a keen appreciation for the fact that agriculture would need to become more economically and technically advanced, and that scientific principles and experiments would provide a pathway forward, the lack of institutional continuity or assured public support limited the impact of early experimental efforts.

The passage of the Morrill Land-Grant College Act of 1862, which provided federal land for states to esthe Rush Medical College in 1850, was known as the first "professor of practical agriculture" when he was hired by Michigan Agricultural College in 1865. Miles came to Illinois Industrial University in 1875, and though his time at Illinois would be short, he is credited with the idea to create the Morrow Plots. Morrow, after whom the Morrow Plots were named, took a different path to Illinois Industrial University. After graduating from the University of Michigan Law School in 1866, Morrow spent a decade as editor of a prominent agricultural magazine, *Western Rural* (later the *Western Farmer*). He moved on to Iowa Agricultural College in 1876, where he became a professor of agriculture. Gregory recruited him to Illinois the following year. Morrow would remain at Illinois for nearly two decades. Morrow proved to be the first of many capable stewards and visionaries, ensuring that the Morrow Plots would become a long-term experiment rather than a short-term project. The questions that initially concerned both Miles and Morrow—how the growing of corn year after year would affect yields and soil properties, how crop rotation might help to maintain soil productivity, and whether fertilizers would need to be applied—may appear simple and straightforward today, but they had yet to be studied rigorously. It is important also to appreciate the extreme optimism that pervaded settlers throughout the Illinois prairies and even farther west in the Great Plains during the second half of the nineteenth century. The vast expanse of seemingly endless land and the promise of the opening frontier, long a motif in American culture, lulled many into believing that the nation had boundless resources. Too often, boosters and settlers believed that the rich soil would forever sustain increasing numbers of farmers and burgeoning numbers of homesteads. Testing these assumptions through practical experimentation—and ensuring that the results would be shared with farmers who could then improve their farming practices to be both more productive and sustainable—became the mission of the Morrow Plots.

Over the course of the next century and a half, the Morrow Plots would provide a number of valuable lessons: first, that even the highly fertile and rich soil of the Illinois prairies was not immune to overcropping; second, that soil depletion represented a very serious threat to the maintenance and future growth of Illinois agriculture; and third, that proper crop rotation could help to stave off soil depletion. The Morrow Plots also helped establish the importance of proper fertilization to crop production. After fertilizer was first introduced to the southern half of the Morrow Plots in 1904—in the form of manure, lime, and phosphorous—yields increased dramatically. More than a half-century later, researchers announced that the continuous corn plots produced twenty-five bushels a year, while the fertilized plots that had remained part of a three-year crop rotation averaged more than one hundred bushels per acre. Reflecting advances in fertilizer treatment, in 1955 researchers began to apply limestone, nitrogen, phosphate, and potassium (LNPK) to two plots: one that had received no treatment since 1876, and another that had been treated with manure, limestone and phosphorous since 1904. Both plots responded to the new fertilizer treatments with increasing yields. Most significant, the plot that had formerly never been treated seemed to come back to life. Yields there doubled in just the first year.

The transformation and enduring presence of the Morrow Plots is best understood as part of a much larger history of the institutionalization of applied agricultural research, community outreach, and the rise of industrial agriculture. A crucial development in this history was the founding of the Illinois Agricultural Experiment Station in 1888, made possible by the passage of the Hatch Act of 1887, which provided federal funds for the creation of a nationwide network of experimental stations that would work with agricultural colleges to insure that the valuable research being pursued at agricultural colleges would be available to farmers. What had been a goal of Regent Gregory's since the 1870s seemed finally to be coming to fruition.

During this new stage of federal engagement with agricultural research, Eugene Davenport, who was hired as dean of the College of Agriculture and director of the Illinois Agricultural Experiment Station in 1895, oversaw the transformation of the agricultural college from an institution with just a handful of students and little equipment into a nationally respected leader in research and outreach. The son of Michigan farmers, and a graduate of Michigan Agricultural College who had returned to the family homestead near Woodland following his graduation, Davenport combined interests in scientific research and practical applications. Following a decade as a Michigan farmer, he returned to his alma mater to study for a master's degree, and then traveled first to Brazil and later to England to learn new agricultural techniques and new approaches to farm management. With his combination of university and practical experience, Davenport proved the perfect person to create a bridge between science/research and the economic interest of farmers, agricultural industries, and farm organizations in Illinois. In spite of somewhat lukewarm support from presidents Andrew Sloan Draper (1894–1904) and Edmund Janes James (1904–1920), Davenport managed to garner much needed state funds and support for the experiment station by winning over the state's farmers as well as specialized producers' associations and agricultural industries. One historian later noted that as a result of Davenport's political acumen and close ties to members of the legislature, state support for the university's farming programs increased so much that "by 1910, the university's orphan child [the College of Agriculture] had become at once a leading advocate of and argument for legislative largesse."[3]

Under Davenport's leadership, the College of Agriculture and the Illinois Agricultural Experiment Station blossomed. The number of students graduating from the College of Agriculture increased from none in the year Davenport arrived on campus (1895) to 176 by 1921. The number of experimental plots, of which Morrow was the first, increased dramatically between the end of the nineteenth century and the early twentieth century, highlighted by the creation of the Davenport Plots in 1895 and South Farms in 1903. By 1919 the university could point to nearly a thousand acres of experimental farms on campus and an additional 827 acres of experimental plots at forty different locations throughout the state. The experiment station conducted soil surveys throughout the state and by 1919 station researchers had completed soil surveys in eighty of the state's 102 counties. By 1922 the experiment station had published 237 bulletins and nineteen soil reports, totaling nearly ten thousand pages. Farmers regularly encountered Illinois researchers and

station agents during the various demonstration and outreach activities, including soil, seed, and dairy trains, short courses in agriculture, one-day farmers' institutes, fairs, expositions, and exhibits. Even farmers as far away as Greece benefited from the expansion of agricultural expertise at Illinois. During World War I, Professor Cyril G. Hopkins, chair of the Agronomy Department and a leading force in the scientific survey of Illinois soils, traveled to Greece as part of a Red Cross expedition to share the discoveries of the experimental plots and help Greek farmers institute better soil management.

Morrow's vision of long-term agricultural experiments and Davenport's politically astute efforts to secure powerful allies in support of extension work was complemented by the original research of a number of pioneering scientists on campus. Two of the most important researchers working during this era were Thomas Jonathan Burrill and, later, William Leonidas Burlison. As Morrow oversaw the early years of the Morrow plots, his colleague Burrill engaged in groundbreaking research that would establish him as a "pioneer in plant pathology." The son of an English immigrant weaver, Burrill moved with his family from his childhood home in Massachusetts to far-northern Stephenson County, Illinois, when he was nine years old. After growing up on a struggling farm, he studied botany at Illinois Normal University (he later assisted John Wesley Powell on his first Rocky Mountain expedition). Following graduation in 1865, Burrill took up the position of principal in the Urbana public schools. After the university was founded in his new hometown, Regent Gregory hired the young man as an algebra instructor. Burrill was named professor of botany and horticulture in 1870 and then professor of botany alone from 1903 until his retirement in 1912. During his forty-four-year tenure at Illinois, Burrill taught a wide variety of subjects, including general horticulture, forestry, vegetable physiology, cryptogamic botany (the study of spore-producing organisms), and, perhaps most important of all, bacteriology. All of this in addition to his duties as the horticulturist to the Illinois Agricultural Experiment Station. (Burrill even assumed the position of university president during the three years the trustees searched for a replacement for Selim Hobart Peabody, who had resigned under fire in 1892.)

Cyril Hopkins with Morrow Plot crops

Burrill is best remembered, however, for his commitment to agricultural extension work as well as his original research on the bacterial causes of plant and fruit diseases. Over time he developed measures for preventing diseases in plants, innovations that helped establish the field of plant pathology. Spurred by a deep religious faith, Burrill sought out the causes of diseases, such as fire blight, that affected Illinois farmers and orchardists. He introduced his students to the major bacterial diseases and fungi that affected local crops while also teaching them the habits of insects that could destroy local farms. He was among the first in the nation to teach a course in plant pathology and to use microscopes in a botany classroom.

The same year Burrill retired, the university renewed its commitment to agricultural research and scientific farming by appointing W. L. Burlison to the Agronomy Department. A native of Harrison, Arkansas, and a 1905 graduate of Oklahoma A&M College, Burlison earned his graduate degrees from the University of Illinois in 1908 (MS) and 1915 (PhD). By 1920 Burlison would assume the post of chair of the Agronomy Department, the same year he became a founding member of the American Soybean Association. Like Burrill, Burlison focused first on the crops that were most important to Illinois farmers. When he assumed his first appointment in 1912, for example, soybean production in the state of Illinois was minimal. Although both Cyril G. Hopkins and Eugene Davenport had published bulletins on soybeans in 1896 and 1897 respectively, and the university's South Farms had begun planting soybeans as part of the regular crop rotation in 1903, soybean production in the state stood at a mere two thousand acres in 1914. (The Morrow Plots were first planted with soybeans in 1912, and in 1967 soybeans became a permanent part of the crop rotation there.) Within a decade, Illinois would overtake North Carolina as the leading soybean state in the union, with more than a half-million acres planted.

This dramatic increase in soybean production in the state can be credited to the groundwork laid by J. C. Hackleman, an agronomy professor and crops extension specialist from 1919 until his retirement in 1956. Recognizing that the replacement of horses and mules with trucks, cars, and tractors would mean that farmers would require less oats and hay, Hackleman promoted the growing of soybeans as a replacement crop. Beginning in 1920, Hackleman was the leading force behind soybean demonstrations in seven counties, outreach efforts that reached at least five thousand growers. During these demonstrations, extension workers provided information about the value of planting soybeans and how to choose high-yielding varieties that would be best suited to the soil and climate of Illinois farmers.

Recognizing that soybean crops could hold significant commercial possibilities, Professor Burlison not only supported Hackleman's work but also became a leading researcher of the possible industrial uses of soybeans. Burlison oversaw a number of experiments by the Illinois Agricultural Experiment Station that ultimately led to the industrial use of soy in paint manufacturing. Burlison also helped to ensure that the University of Illinois would become an institutional base for soybean research nationally and globally by helping to found the U. S. Soybean Laboratory on campus in 1936. This laboratory represented the cooperative effort of the experiment stations of twelve states and the USDA and was made possible by the Bankhead-Jones Act of 1935, which provided funding for the creation of regional agricultural laboratories. (For more on the long-term impact of the Soybean Laboratory, see chapter 2.17.) More than two decades later, in the 1960s, the University of Illinois initiated a cooperative soybean development program with India, and in the 1970s the University of Illinois became home to the International Soybean Program (INSTOY), which provides planting, harvesting, processing, marketing, and utilization advice to U.S. farmers as well as international partners to make the most of soybean production in terms of human consumption, animal nutrition, and industrial uses.

Today the Morrow Plots remain a popular site for campus visitors and an internally recognized symbol of the promises and perils of agriculture. In the years since the first planting of the Morrow Plots, corn production has increased dramatically, becoming not only the most important cereal crop in the world but the centerpiece of an industrial food chain that envelops the globe. Corn can be found not just in the foods that we eat but also in the cleaners we use, the trash bags that hold our refuse, the matches and charcoal briquettes we use for grilling, and the ethanol that fuels some engines. Journalist Michael Pollan estimates that of the roughly forty-five thousand items carried in supermarkets, at least one-quarter of these items contain some form of corn. While there is much to celebrate about the increasing production of corn, and other crops as well, there is also a growing appreciation for the challenges facing the globe in the twenty-first century. The questions that led to the creation of the Morrow Plots—questions regarding soil fertility, sustainability, and conservation—remain at the center of the University of Illinois's College of Agricultural, Consumer, and Environmental Sciences as well as the Illinois Agricultural Experiment Station.

## Notes

1. *The Morrow Plots: A Symbol of Hope*, 12–13.

2. Paul E. Waggoner, "Research and Education in American Agriculture," *Agricultural History* 50, no. 1 (1976): 238 and 244–45.

3. Charles E. Rosenberg, "Science, Technology, and Economic Growth: The Case of the Agricultural Experiment Station Scientist, 1875–1914," *Agricultural History* 45, no. 1 (1971): 11.

## Sources

Manly Miles's papers are at Michigan State University Archives and History Collection, 1826–1898. The papers of Thomas J. Burrill, Eugene Davenport, and William L. Burilson are at the University of Illinois Archives. On the Morrow Plots see *The Morrow Plots: A Century of Learning*, Agricultural Experiment Station Bulletin 775, College of Agriculture, University of Illinois at Urbana-Champaign (Urbana, 1982); *The Morrow Plots: A Symbol of Hope*, Special Publication 16, University of Illinois College of Agriculture (Urbana, January 1969); *The Morrow Plots: A National Historic Landmark*, Circular 777, University of Illinois, College of Agriculture (Urbana, June 1957). On the rise of industrial agriculture see Michael Pollan, *The Omnivore's Dilemma: A Natural History of Four Meals* (New York: Penguin, 2006).

# Bringing Innovation to the Farm through the Farmers' Institutes

*Kristen Allen*

In 1894 Charles F. Mills, secretary of the Illinois State Board of Agriculture, headed a committee that proposed the formation of the Illinois Farmers' Institute. The purpose of the institute would be to disseminate scientific information to ordinary farmers in order to improve their methods and increase their yields. Despite the fact that the university featured an active College of Agriculture, its farming programs had thus far attracted few students. Local farmers seemed to have little use for scientific innovation.

Initially, the institutes were county gatherings where faculty and researchers could share their ideas in informal settings. This format became so popular that in 1910 the university began sponsoring annual gatherings on campus that were open to farmers from across the state. These on-campus institutes followed a standard format. On the first day five or six lecturers would offer practical instruction in small settings that encouraged questions and discussion. These sessions were punctuated by elaborate noon meals served by students and faculty in the home economics program. (The home economics program soon sponsored an equivalent program for women that ran concurrently with the Farmers' Institute. Organized by the Illinois Association of Domestic Science, this program introduced farm families to modern ideas regarding hygiene, food safety, and nutrition.) Most institutes included evening programs that mixed education with entertainment and special events for children.

Soon the Illinois Farmers' Institute also began distributing farming education materials for teachers. This educational effort, which began just as 4-H clubs were becoming a visible part of farm life in the Midwest, drew even more participants to the institutes. Individual institute sessions ranged across topics from dairy management and wheat cultivation to cattle feeding and rural road construction. The Thirty-Seventh Annual Illinois Farmers' Institute Meeting program in 1932, for example, featured sessions on farm poultry problems, the supplies of vegetables in winter, legislative stumbling blocks, farm finance, and world trade.

Eugene Davenport in the field

The Farmers' Institute not only spread the lessons of scientific farming across the state, but it also stimulated new government programs. Among these were the state soil survey (launched in 1902) and an extensive program of rural road construction. The greatest achievement of the institutes, however, was that they bridged the distance between innovative research emerging from the university and the needs of rural farmers.

## Sources

Information on the Illinois Farmers' Institute can be found in Roy V. Scott's *The Reluctant Farmer* (1970) and Winton Solberg's two volumes of University of Illinois history. The Illinois Farmers' Institute also published an *Annual Report*. The University Archives holds additional materials, including minutes of the organization's steering committee and minutes of annual meetings.

# The Story of the University of Illinois Library

Winton U. Solberg

Libraries are the bedrock on which civilization is built. They contain the learning that people need to profit from the past and point the way to the future. Since time immemorial, people have viewed libraries as essential to their well-being.

When the University of Illinois opened in 1868, the library was on the second floor of University Hall and a faculty member doubled as university librarian. In the early years a young librarian shelved Neander's *Planting of the Christian Church* among books dealing with agriculture. In 1894 the library held twenty-six thousand volumes and the first full-time librarian arrived. Three years later this collection was moved into Altgeld Hall, the first building on campus designated as a library, and Katharine L. Sharp became the head librarian and the founding director of the university's library school. A graduate of Melville Dewey's New York State Library School, Sharp brought a new level of professional expertise to the facility. Aided by a largely female staff, she ran an efficient operation. By the time of her retirement in 1907 the library had grown to 95,946 volumes and 12,696 pamphlets and was receiving 1,224 periodicals. Despite this growth, Sharp had, during her tenure, emphasized the standardizing of procedures more than collection development.

These priorities changed after Sharp's departure. Edmund J. James, who had been president of the university since 1904, used the occasion of hiring a new librarian to initiate a new era of collection development. He separated the positions of librarian and director of the library school (which Sharp had combined) for the coming year,

Altgeld Hall, the university's first library building

and appointed Francis K. W. Drury, the order librarian since 1905, as acting head of the library. Drury read Latin, Greek, French, and German. He had been assistant librarian in the Theological Seminary of the Reformed Church at New Brunswick, New Jersey, and had studied one summer at Dewey's New York State Library School. In 1905 he received a master's degree from Rutgers and a library science degree from Illinois. He wrote readily, worked with a staff of more than twenty, refined Sharp's practices, kept meticulous records, and submitted annual reports to President James. In 1908 the library owned 108,383 bound volumes and 13,079 pamphlets; a year later it held 127,106 volumes. Drury also collected and purchased newspapers for the library.

President James himself took an active part in building the collection. He had a doctorate from the University of Halle and kept in touch with German booksellers. He also promoted the idea—common among American librarians at the time—of purchasing entire libraries from European scholars and collectors. In 1907 he persuaded the trustees to authorize $2,500 to purchase the library of Karl Friedrich Wilhelm Dittenberger, a former professor of classical philology at the University of Halle. The books would lay the foundation for advanced work in classics. The arrival of fifteen boxes with about seven thousand titles was a high point in the development of the classics library. In 1909 the University purchased the library of Moriz Heyne, a former professor of German philology at the University of Göttingen. Heyne's library of about 5,200 volumes was strong in philology and comparative literature and contained documents of all periods of German literature as well as German dictionaries.

Although Drury was a worthy candidate for librarian, James wanted someone with better scholarly credentials for the post. He turned to Phineas L. Windsor, who was born in Chenoa, Illinois, in nearby McLean County. The son of a Methodist minister, Windsor had earned a bachelor's degree at Northwestern University (1895) and had graduated from the New York State Library School (1899). He had also attended the Albany Law School in 1900 while working at the New York State Library. Windsor had a broad background. From 1900 to 1903 he had worked in Washington, D.C., as an assistant in the Copyright Office in the Library of Congress, and since 1903 he had served as librarian at the University of Texas. He came to Illinois in 1909 and took up Katherine Sharp's old double appointment—university librarian and director of the Library School.

President James and Phineas Windsor differed in temperament and in style. James was aggressive and decisive; Windsor was retiring and deferential. James kept close watch on the library, badgering Windsor about details of his administration and recommending books for library purchase. As a thoroughly modern librarian, Windsor was active in the American Library Association (where Dewey was a leading figure) as well as in other professional associations. His accomplishments notwithstanding, James was often unduly sharp with his librarian. Whatever their differences, during Windsor's tenure the library grew at the rate of nearly thirty thousand volumes a year.

> "The University, James informed the trustees, should establish the goal of building its collection to at least a million volumes within ten years."

Windsor presided over routine collection development, while James devoted himself to special acquisitions. In practice, the lines were intermixed. Windsor bought many ephemeral items that were likely to be valuable for research—telephone directories, newspapers, and municipal documents. By 1915 the library had 6,416 volumes and 10,634 pamphlets of such material. The library made most of its purchases to meet the needs of some particular course offering or research work. In 1909 President James declined to buy the library of a German scholar of Indic philology, which was strong in Sanskrit and related subjects, because the university had no one to teach the subject at that time. A few years later a linguistics scholar introduced courses in Sanskrit.

In 1911 James began to enlist ethnic and religious groups in America to contribute materials to the library that related to their own history and culture. With board approval, he appointed commissions on both Jewish-American history and culture and German-American history and culture. He intended to appoint commissions on seven other ethnic elements in America, but he was unable to fulfill this laudable plan. The main object of these commissions was to secure for the library materials bearing on the history of various ethnic and national groups. These materials would also support research in literature and history, but they would as well prove significant to students of linguistics, immigration, the history of science, and other fields that had yet to become part of the university curriculum.

James continued to be a zealous buyer of foreign libraries. In 1911 he was willing to pay $5,000 for the pedagogical library of twenty-thousand pieces of Rudolf Aron of Berlin, but Aron wanted $8,000 so the case was closed. In 1912, while in Berlin, James acquired the library of Gustav Gröber of the University of Strasbourg, a leading Romance languages scholar. This treasure of 6,367 volumes and pamphlets was particularly valuable for Provençal and Italian linguistics. James purchased the holding, apparently for $2,500.

While in Berlin, James studied the library of the University of Berlin, which he called the greatest library in the world. Within twenty-five miles of the city hall, he noted, scholars had access to five million volumes in various libraries. This experience shaped James's notion of what must be done in Urbana. In June 1912 he laid his views before the trustees in an essay published that year as part of the board's *Annual Report*. No part of a university was more necessary than the library, he said, and a great library "will under favorable conditions become a great university. Books are not dead. They are alive to the man who comes in contact with them and knows how to use them. They are the sources of inspiration and power, and not merely of knowledge." Comparative data showed that Illinois was inferior to a dozen other leading American

can universities. It could not hope to be a great center of learning until it had much larger library facilities. One reason American scholarship trailed European scholarship, he argued, was the lack of great collections of books. The university, James informed the trustees, should establish the goal of building its collection to at least one million volumes within ten years.

In 1913 James was able to buy two libraries that he had failed to obtain earlier. One was the classical philological library of Johannes Vahlen, late of the University of Berlin. It contained two or three times as many important sets as the Dittenberger library. The other was the library of Rudolf Aron of Berlin, a scholarly collection on all the great pedagogical movements in European, especially German, elementary education from Luther and Comenius forward. After haggling over the price with a German book dealer, James bought the two libraries for $16,500.

In 1914, addressing students in Urbana, James demonstrated passion about the future greatness of the university. Observing that the library had held sixty thousand volumes ten years earlier and three hundred thousand as he spoke, he declared that Illinois must have a library of at least one million, "and when we have a library of two million it will be only a fair beginning, and when it is four or five millions, as it must be if it is going to suit our purposes, it will have become one of the great libraries of the world."

In 1916 the friends of Heinrich A. Ratterman bought his library and presented it to the University of Illinois. Ratterman had immigrated from Germany and settled in Cincinnati, where he had become a noted historian of the German people in the United States. For many years he had edited *Der Deutsche Pionier*. His library was therefore rich in materials on the German experience in the United States. In a similar vein, in 1918 James also negotiated the purchase of the library of Julius Doerner, an eccentric Chicago book collector and antiquarian who amassed materials on Chicago.

In 1919, shortly before leaving office, James made an important contribution to the development of the University of Illinois Library—he bought the library of Count Antonio Cavagna Sangiuliani di Gualdana for $17,989.31. This notable treasure contained more than forty thousand books and pamphlets, several thousand manuscript documents and maps, seven incunabula, rare and early printed books, first editions, and many books printed before 1560. Mostly in Italian, the library included French editions of Italian works, Italian editions of French works, Latin works, translations from the Italian, and some German works. Acquisition of the Cavagna Giuliani collection was a landmark in the development of the library.

President James set a high standard in library development, and he made the case for the centrality of the library to the university's academic mission. It remained for others to follow his example. The university enlarged its library rapidly in the 1920s, but it still lagged behind the leaders. In 1911, for example, Harvard had almost 700,000 volumes more than Illinois, but in 1925 it had 1,761,000 more volumes. Illinois was making a worse showing every year. As librarian Phineas Windsor declared, Illinois need not allow its university to be surpassed by any American university in the things that money could buy.

Before World War I the university had established departmental libraries to complement the collection housed in the main library. These specialized libraries became a noted feature of the Illinois campus. In 1923, for example, the university supported twelve departmental libraries, while Michigan, Minnesota, and Wisconsin had from three to seven each. The close collaboration of the staffs of the library and the library school was also distinctive. At Illinois, the library staff had teaching duties, while those at Minnesota and Wisconsin did not.

In the postwar years a turn in public opinion toward conservative politics and cultural standards confronted libraries with the problem of ordering and handling condemned and unpopular literary works. In 1924, although the Senate Library Committee was averse to any formal action, Windsor, the librarian, had declared that when such books came into the library, they were guarded from handling by the library staff and from general circulation after they were cataloged. These materials would be locked up or otherwise hidden and could be borrowed only on special permission. President David Kinley, after consulting legal counsel and learning that there was no lawful way by which the library could secure such books, declared that the library should decline all requests to purchase or

Circulation area in the new university library. Reproduction rights granted courtesy of the University of Illinois at Chicago, University Library.

secure them. And yet, in a discussion of books debarred from the mails, Kinley could understand why the library, as an institution, should have everything published.

To what extent could or should a state university library serve the needs of both students and scholars on the one hand and the public on the other? That question arose when someone wrote and asked the following questions: Who suffered severely because of the collapse of the German mark in 1923? And what country's flag was flown by citizens whose history goes back nine centuries? And what section of the world, from which before the World War, much grain was shipped and to which now is imported? These vague queries were from a female Illinois resident who turned to the university library for information. Did librarians have an obligation to respond? Within the limits of their capacity, they should respond.

The university library was gradually improving both absolutely and relatively. In 1923 Illinois was in eighth place among university libraries in the number of volumes held. Harvard led with 2,256,500 volumes, Yale followed with 1,580,102, Columbia with 863,341, Cornell with 688,686, Chicago with 670,749, Pennsylvania with 554,507, Michigan with 545,675, and Illinois with 541,941. Princeton was in ninth place with 525,939, and California tenth with 511,259 volumes.

With more than half a million volumes in its collection, the library was outgrowing its thirty-year-old home in Altgeld Hall. As a mark of the library's increasing significance on campus, the trustees authorized the construction of a grand new library to be built in the Georgian style of architecture on a new plaza west of the main quad. The new structure, built at a cost of $1.75 million, was dedicated in October 1929. The building was—and remains—an impressive headquarters for research. The main reading room on the second floor measured three hundred feet by fifty feet and had capacity for 516 seats. It was the largest reading room in any American state university library building. The windows in the reading room were decorated with renderings of printers' marks, and the main stairwell contained large-scale reproductions of maps of the world.

The new library became a special point of pride on the campus. The pace of growth of the collections accelerated—the university acquired its one-millionth volume in 1934—and by 1940 the library had become the largest state university library and the fifth largest university library in the nation. It contained approximately 1,175,000 volumes, 330,000 pamphlets, 3,909 maps, and 10,600 pieces of sheet music. And it was still growing to meet the needs of students, faculty, and scholars.

For years the efficiency of the library was handicapped by the fact that the greater part of its professionally trained personnel had to be rated by the Civil Service System in order to be employed. As a result, the library was often unable to hire qualified specialists as needed. As librarian, Robert B. Downs freed librarians from the civil service incubus by awarding librarians faculty rank in varying degree. The new system solved an old problem but introduced an entirely new set of challenges.

The growth of the collection made it necessary to enlarge the holding capacity of the library. So in 1984 a seven-story structure was added to the southwest side of the original building. With high density, mobile book-stack shelving, this facility could house more than two million volumes.

In 1972 a group known as the Library Friends formed with a goal to increase financial support for and the visibility of the library. In 1982 the Library Friends purchased John Flamsteed's *Historiae Coelestis* (1712) for the library. This addition marked the six-millionth volume in the library. Other milestone markers followed. In 1986 the Library Friends purchased and presented to the library its seven-millionth volume. This book, *Peregrinatio in Terram Sanctam* (1486), or *Journey to the Holy Land*, was described as the first travel book ever published. The commemora-

tive eight-millionth volume presented in 1992 was Frank Lloyd Wright's book *The House Beautiful*. The commemorative volume that celebrated the University of Illinois Library at ten million volumes came in 2003, and in 2012 the library acquired its thirteen-millionth volume.

The library's special collections holdings continue to draw researchers to its reading rooms from across the campus and around the world. Among the special collections, for example, the library holds the third-largest collection of Slavic and East European titles in a North American library, a complete first edition of John James Audubon's *The Birds of America*, and extensive holdings by and about William Shakespeare, John Milton, and Marcel Proust. Over time, the library has also acquired the papers of historical and literary figures such as H. G. Wells and Carl Sandburg and organizations such as the American Library Association. For years the rank order of the American libraries with the largest collections has been as follows: the Library of Congress first, Harvard second, Yale third, and the University of Illinois fourth. Among university libraries, Illinois is regularly listed in third place.

A library can exist without a university, but a university cannot exist without a library. Libraries are gauges of intellectual development and provide essential resources for scholars in all fields. Libraries enable people to flourish in both body and spirit. They are essential in creating and preserving a campus community as well as a just and prosperous society. The University of Illinois Library, from its simple beginnings in University Hall to the present imposing buildings and collections, has enabled not only university students and faculty but also the people of Illinois and those far beyond to flourish in countless individual ways.

## Sources

The early years of the library are covered in Solberg's two volumes on the university's history to 1904. One can learn of later developments from Winton U. Solberg, "Edmund Janes James Builds a Library: The University of Illinois Library, 1904–1920," *Libraries and Culture* 39, no. 1 (Winter 2004): 36–75.

# Improvising an Innovation

## Stadium Terrace Housing and the Arrival of "Nontraditional Students"

*Lauren Tokarewich*

At the end of World War II, the Servicemen's Readjustment Act (popularly known as the "GI Bill") enabled nearly eight million male and female veterans (roughly half of all who served in the war) to attend college. In 1946, 5,730 veterans were attending the University of Illinois. Their presence expanded the school's enrollment by almost 50 percent, from thirteen thousand to nearly nineteen thousand. This huge influx of new students not only created an unprecedented demand for campus housing, but it also added a new element to the university community. Complicating the situation was the fact that 30 percent of the returning veterans were married (and 85 percent of those seeking housing had children).

University officials quickly realized that existing dormitories—and the model of a campus composed solely of eighteen- to twenty-two-year-olds—was no longer suitable. In September 1945 the board of trustees came up with a solution for the crisis: the university would set aside eleven acres of land between First and Oak Streets as a temporary housing site and erect temporary structures there to house the new arrivals. Campus officials quickly began moving decommissioned portable housing units from army bases in Indiana onto the property. By September 1947, 233 buildings had been erected, providing 493 units of housing. For the next sixteen years this "temporary" location housed married undergraduates and graduate students (and some faculty). The innovation transformed both the campus and the university's expectations regarding its student population.

Despite complaints of discomfort and shoddy construction, "Stadium Housing" became the center of an unprecedented new community. The university now included older students, spouses, and children. It provided them with playgrounds and other services (administered by a Stadium Terrace town council) and even welcomed their newspaper, *The Prefabricator*, as a feature of student life. A temporary "fix" nurtured a new dimension of campus life and demonstrated the university's ability to incorporate a unique element into the campus. For the first time, "nontraditional" students (and their children) became a part of the university community. (When the university replaced Stadium Terrace with permanent married-student housing units, the site was rededicated as Stadium Terrace Play Field.)

### Sources

There are no published histories of Stadium Terrace, but the University Archives contains significant material on this unique community in its files on Student Housing and Veterans' Education.

Stadium Terrace housing

# Across the Pacific
## The University of Illinois and China

Poshek Fu

In a recent issue, *Inside Higher Education* reported that the University of Illinois at Urbana-Champaign should be labeled the "University of China at Illinois." This eye-catching sobriquet was no doubt triggered by the enormous increase of Chinese students in recent years at the flagship campus of the state university. Just as a rapidly growing number of students from China have come to study in the United States since the turn of the twenty-first century, making them the largest group of international students in the nation, so the Urbana-Champaign campus has witnessed a massive expansion of its Chinese student population. They grew from thirty-seven undergraduates in 2000 to 2,898 in 2014, a 7,000 percent increase. Adding to this number the 1,973 graduate students on campus,

the university ranks first in public institutions nationwide for the number of international students from China.[1]

The "University of China at Illinois" can conjure up another dimension of meaning that *Inside Higher Education* might not have understood. It actually brings to mind of those who are familiar with the university's long history of connection and engagement with China (or to be more precise, Greater China—a term that includes mainland China, Hong Kong, and Taiwan). This history started in 1908–09, when U.S.-China relations existed as an insignificant aspect of an age of global politics dominated by the imperialist rivalry of European powers and their struggle with Japan over dominance in the Pacific. Since China's loss in the Opium War to the British in 1842–43, a combination of imperialist assaults and internal turmoil had pushed imperial China from one crisis to another. In a matter of less than half a century, particularly after its humiliating defeat by Japan in 1895 and the subsequent "scramble for concessions" by various European forces, the "Middle Kingdom" fell from the apex of world politics to become the victim of contesting imperialist powers. Struggling to preserve China's sovereignty in the new world order, defined by the Western system of "wealth and power" rather than by the Confucian civilization of "All under Heaven," Chinese political and intellectual elites debated incessantly about how to navigate the conflicts between the values and principles that made China unique and the imperative to acquire modern technology and industry and thereby insure China's security. From these debates, which were often intertwined with violent political struggles, emerged the dominant discourse of China's early efforts to modernize, as memorialized in 1898 by Qing Governor Zhang Zhidong's phrases: "Chinese learning for essence (*ti*), Western learning for practical use (*yong*)." This *ti-yong* vision of modernity conceded the superiority of Western science and technology without questioning the supremacy of China's cultural tradition. While the question of what constituted Chinese "essence" has been an enduring and bitterly contested theme in modern Chinese cultural and intellectual history, the instrumental emphasis on acquiring knowledge of modern machinery, technology, and commerce played a powerful role in shaping China's cultural relations with the United States.

By 1899, after its victory over Spain and subsequent acquisition of the Philippines, the United States joined the ranks of the world's imperialist powers. With its economic and military focus on Latin America, however, the U.S. presence and influences in Asia were limited. In response

> "Edmund James's deep interest in building a strong relationship between America and China, together with his tireless promotion of the Chinese students' well-being and intellectual development, drew many Chinese youths to the university."

to the European powers' "Scramble for Concessions" after Japan's defeat of China in 1895 (which had the effect of reducing China into a semi-colony), American Secretary of State John Hay proposed an "Open Door" policy so that all powers, whether or not they had acquired spheres of influence (like Japan in the northeast or England in central China), enjoyed equal access to the China market. With this policy, the United States sought to extend its economic interests in China, even though it did not control any sphere. The acquiescence of imperialist powers to Hay's policy (especially on the part of Japan—widely perceived as the dominant force in the western Pacific) amplified demands within the United States for stronger relations with China. It was in this national and global context that the University of Illinois began to build connections across the Pacific.

## The Pioneer: Edmund James's Innovative Engagement with China

In the first years of the twentieth century the University of Illinois was beginning to transform itself into a national research institution. Leading this transformation was President Edmund James, who served from 1904 to 1920. By the time he came to Urbana-Champaign, he had already served as director of the Wharton School of Finance at the University of Pennsylvania and founded the American Academy of Political and Social Science. He was determined to raise the University of Illinois to the level of elite schools in the East and to use education as an instrument of expanding American cultural influences in the world.[2] James acted on these ambitions just two years into his office when he joined a group of eminent missionaries and opinion leaders in urging President Theodore Roosevelt to return to China the excess money of the Boxer Protocol indemnity funds (the Protocol settled the hostilities set off by the Boxer Uprising between Qing China and various imperialist powers) paid to the United States to provide American education for young Chinese.

Why would America act in 1906? China had been on the margins of Roosevelt's international strategy, and the president had favored the dominant interests of Japan in his Asian foreign policy. An Anti-American Boycott launched in Chinese cities in 1905, however, forced Roosevelt to reconsider his policy. The nationwide boycott of American goods movement was organized by educated elites and merchants in various cities to express their deep anger against the racist policy of discrimination and harassment of the Chinese diaspora in the United States. After decades of sinophobic agitation, the U.S. government had passed the Chinese Exclusion Act in 1882, banning further entry of Chinese laborers for ten years and outlawing the naturalization of the Chinese already in the United States. In 1904 Congress extended the exclusion law indefinitely. Although scholars, merchants, and officials were exempted from these racist restrictions, they were constantly humiliated and harassed as they tried to enter the country. Roosevelt appeared to understand that this outrage against American racism marked a new phase in the development of Chinese nationalism and decided to devise ways of improving relations with China.[3]

In 1906 Edmund James wrote a letter to Roosevelt. Just prior to his letter, American missionary Arthur Smith (whose many books on Chinese culture and society had helped shape early-twentieth-century American views of China) had met with the president at the White House to propose that the Boxer indemnity funds be used for education. It was evident in his letter that James's formulation of ideas resembled Smith's missionary conviction to civilize the Chinese. He declared to Roosevelt that in the "Open Door" era, a modern American education should play a significant role in U.S.-China relations because it could enable Americans to capture the hearts and minds of the next generation of Chinese elites:

> The nation which succeeds in educating the young Chinese of the present generation will be the nation which for a given expenditure of efforts will reap the largest possible returns in moral, intellectual, and commercial influences. . . . Trade follows moral and spiritual domination far more inevitably than it follows the flag. . . . If the U.S. had succeeded thirty-five years ago as it looked at one time as if it might, in turning the current of Chinese students to this country, and had succeeded in keep[ing] that current large, we should to-day be controlling the development of China in that most satisfactory and suitable of all ways,—through the intellectual and spiritual domination of its leaders.[4]

When Edmund James referred to the "current of Chinese students" "thirty-five years ago" he was describing the first wave of Chinese students who came to the United States. In 1847 Yung Wing became the first Chinese to study in the United States. His education was sponsored by an American missionary, and he returned home after seven years with a degree from Yale University and a dream of bringing more Chinese youths to the United States. With the support of a senior Chinese official who wanted to have more engineers and merchants to help with China's reform efforts, Yung Wing brought a total of 120 boys to New England to study between 1872 and 1876. However, in 1881, as anti-Chinese sentiment rose in the United States, the Qing court changed its mind and recalled all the students. Its decision ended the first wave of Chinese students to the United States.[5]

Two years after Edmund James's letter to Roosevelt, Congress authorized the remission to China of the excess funds from the Boxer indemnity. The returned funds were then used in 1909 to establish the Boxer Indemnity Scholarship Program to bring Chinese students to the United States and to found Tsinghua Preparatory School in Beijing. Tsinghua would become Tsinghua University in 1928. With Congress's action, the second wave of students from China to the United States began.

It was therefore far from inconsequential that in 1909 President James invited Chinese diplomat Wu Tingfang to Urbana-Champaign to give a commencement speech at the University of Illinois. A preeminent London-trained barrister and an ardent nationalist who had been involved in the Anti-American Boycott four years earlier, Wu served as the Qing Minister to the United States from 1907 to 1910. Wu came to the university in June, seemingly enjoying the hospitality of the James family and the simplicity of midwestern campus life. Perhaps to show his enthusiasm for the university as a place for Chinese students, he posed for portraits with all the current and future scholars he met there (including Weitsen Tu, James Yiko Hu, and Wu Hei-Lui). The photograph remains in the University Archives. Shortly after his visit, Wu wrote to Edmund James, recommending two students to the College of Law and asking for details about the university's admission policy and tuition. Edmund James replied

Ambassador Wu Tinfang at the 1909 Illinois commencement

came to Illinois.[6] To pursue his dream of building a research university that could contribute to U.S. foreign relations by shaping the hearts and minds of young Chinese elites, then, Edmund James turned early on to the task of creating a host of recruitment and retention strategies that were innovative and effective. First, he recruited students through the various kinds of networks he had built with the American missionary communities in China and the lesser-known provincial-level preparatory schools there. For example, two senior leaders of the Henan Preparatory School, Chang Hung-lieh (BA in political science, 1918) and Chung Pun-sien (BS in animal husbandry, 1918), were so impressed by the president's fervent support of the Chinese students in the United States when they studied at the University of Illinois that they sent Henan graduates to Urbana-Champaign there throughout the 1920s.[7]

Second, probably with the help of Wu Tingfang, the low tuition and living cost of studying in Champaign-Urbana that Edmund James had emphasized as a major advantage of Illinois for foreign students were widely circulated in China. (This effort was launched by an article published in the influential Shanghai-based magazine *Dongfang zazhi* (Eastern Miscellany) that compared the cost of studying at different American universities.) This publicity was especially effective in attracting self-supporting students, who had made up more than half of the second-wave Chinese students studying in the United States.

quickly and enthusiastically, emphasizing the relatively low fees and living expenses in central Illinois. Asking Wu for new information about the Boxer Indemnity Scholarship, he added: "I desire to extend through you . . . a cordial welcome for any Chinese student who may desire to pursue their studies in the University of Illinois. . . . I'd be glad if you would send me the names and addresses of the men who have been entrusted by the Chinese government with the actual execution of the plan."

As it turned out, however, (surprisingly, after all of James's campaigning) the University of Illinois benefited relatively little from the Boxer Indemnity program, which was deemed the most prestigious government scholarship available at the time. According to the official record, in the three years from 1909 to 1911, the overwhelming majority of the 180 recipients of this government support went to the Ivy League schools, and only eighteen

Third, Edmund James's deep interest in building a strong relationship between America and China, together with his tireless promotion of the Chinese students' well-being and intellectual development, drew many Chinese youths to the university. For example, after Illinois students "covered themselves with glory" at the Third Conference of the Chinese Students Alliance (the national organization of Chinese students in the United States) at Michigan in 1913, Edmund James wrote to the alliance offering to host the next conference at Urbana-Champaign. With the president's supervision, the 1914 gathering was a huge success, bringing national attention to the university among the Chinese students then studying in the country. To express their respect for the president, members of the alliance selected James as one of its honorary members (others granted this status included luminaries such as John Dewey). The students also pleaded with James to support the development of the recently declared Chinese Republic.

Despite this apparent enthusiasm, however, Chinese students faced a variety of problems at Illinois, as they did on other campuses across the United States. Among these were acts of overt racism and a consequent sense of personal isolation. While the University of Illinois promised the Chinese students a "cordial welcome," they often found themselves subject to suspicion and Orientalist caricature, if not outright hostility. For example, a 1910 report on the "Chinese Students at Illinois" in *The Alumni Quarterly* described:

> In the early days no one here ever dreamed of enrolling a Chinese student. In that period of history, China was held in truly horror, her citizens were "heathen Chinese," her prospects as a nation, dark as a dungeon. Imagine one of our institution's pioneers . . . [upon meeting] the Chinese . . . he will be heartily, scarcely warmly, greeted in truly American fashion. Although the handshake may not be Rooseveltian or Taft-like—the hand of the Chinese students is remarkably small, slight, cold, long-fingered, even frail.[8]

In fact, as late as 1945, more than 92 percent of landowners in Urbana-Champaign refused to rent to foreign students.[9] And everyday microaggression prevailed. As alumnus Chen Loh-kwan (MS in civil engineering, 1924) recalled, when he was a student at the university, whenever he sat down to eat at the student union, white students would turn their backs on him. Chen later won fame during World War II when his work as the chief engineer directing the construction of a massive airfield near Chongqing with an unskilled labor force of thousands for the planned use of the American Air Fortress attracted the attention of writer Ernest Hemingway, who was visiting China. Hemingway reported admirably on the human feat, presenting Chen as a symbol of China's wartime heroism.[10]

Despite these barriers, the university became increasingly cosmopolitan during Edmund James's tenure as president. The Chinese remained by far the largest foreign student group on campus, but there were also other nationalities represented in the student body: those from Japan, Brazil, the Philippines, and India were now attending classes in Urbana-Champaign. In an effort to help Chinese and other foreign students better adjust to the American academic culture, James established the Office of the Advisor of Foreign Students in 1913 (upgraded to Assistant Dean of Foreign Students in 1919). This position became one of the most important legacies of Edmund James at Illinois. What distinguished him from later practice in this area was his insistence on appointing a faculty member to this post (rather than an administrator) who had intimate experiences with foreign cultures. James's first appointment as foreign student advisor was James Seymour, a professor of Romance languages known for his expertise in foreign-language pedagogy. In an attempt to emphasize the importance of the position, President James gave Seymour an attractive extra stipend of $300 (and later increased to $700).

Knowledgeable and dedicated, Seymour soon launched (with Edmund James's blessings) a series of innovative programs such as language enrichment classes, private language tutors, and a citywide host family system, which, along with the countless hours he had spent talking to students about the problems they had in adjusting to American life, made the Office of the Advisor of Foreign Students (like the Chinese Student Club) a home away from home for the Chinese students and others from overseas as well. Its success inspired other universities to set up similar offices in the ensuing years to provide advice and support for their foreign students. (Seymour became deeply engaged in this work. In 1921, he took a two years' leave of absence

The university Chinese Club, 1914

from Illinois to take up an invitation from the university's Chinese alumni to travel around China and help establish an English program at the Henan Preparatory School similar to the one he had started in Illinois.)

## The Turning Point

Thanks to Edmund James's commitment to promoting U.S.-China relations through education and innovative approaches to recruitment and student services aimed at foreign students, the University of Illinois became a Mecca of learning for Chinese students eager to discover the ingenuity of the West in the 1910s and 1920s. His innovative policies were largely sustained by his successor, David Kinley (1920–1930), who had served previously as dean of the Graduate College and vice president of the university and was therefore familiar with the emphasis on building connection across the Pacific. Although he had never launched any innovative programs on his own, Kinley closely followed the careers of Chinese alumni and became the first top university official to visit China. In 1930, shortly after stepping down from the presidency,

David Kinley took a long trip to Asia, including visits to several Chinese cities.

After he returned to Illinois, Kinley wrote a long report to his successor, President Harry Chase. The report was full of detailed observations of the several top Chinese universities he had visited and candid observations of China's educational developments. (It remains the only official report on China written by a senior university official on that nation's educational system—a striking fact in light of Illinois's long history of connection with China.) Unlike the missionary idealism of Edmund James, who imagined a big role for the United States in China's quest for modernity, David Kinley's report was marked by a guarded optimism and clearer-eyed reflection about U.S.-China cultural relations. Kinley noted the magnitude of anti-imperialist nationalism among Chinese intellectuals at the time and described the extent to which the country remained in the grip of Western powers while struggling to counter Japan's mounting military incursion into the northeast (primarily in Manchuria).

While the archival record is unclear, David Kinley's trip to China was likely arranged by prominent Chinese alumni. In fact, from the 1910s until the defeat of the Chinese Republic by the communists in 1949, there was an active "Illini Alumni Club" in China with branches in major cities such as Shanghai, Beijing, Tianjin, Canton, and (during World War II) Chongqing. The club included some University of Illinois graduates who had played important trailblazing roles in modernizing China and promoting U.S.-China relations. C. C. Wang (Wang Jingchun), for example, came to Illinois in 1909 with Wu Tingfang's support and received a master's in railway engineering and then a doctorate in economics under David Kinley in 1911. At a time when graduate fellowships and practical training were legally out of reach for international students, Edmund James and David Kinley personally intervened in arranging for Wang to teach a course on "Oriental culture" and work as an intern with railway interests in Chicago.

When Dr. Wang returned home, China's railway system was small and fragmented into various uncoordinated sections operating under the control of European powers and Japan. The Illinois graduate set out with the dream of reclaiming, reunifying, and overhauling the communication system for the service of national integration and economic modernity. His integrity and deep knowledge of railway management had earned him the reputation as "one of the three leaders in Chinese Railway Administration." Like his teacher David Kinley, with whom he had maintained friendship for many years, he was also passionate about promoting U.S.-China cultural exchanges. He was the perennial leader of the Chinese Educational Mission, which worked with officials in Washington, D.C., to promote the welfare of all Chinese students in the United States.[11]

Another influential Chinese graduate from this era was H. Y. Moh (Mu Ouchu), known as the "Cotton King" of China. He came to study in the United States in 1909 at age thirty-three. After receiving a bachelor's degree in agriculture from Illinois in 1914 and a master's from the University of Texas, where he focused on cotton production, Moh returned to China with the dream of building a modern textile industry that could support China's struggle to become a modern, industrialized nation. With his amazing energy and discipline, Moh quickly set up three

cotton mills, where he experimented with the cottonseed and scientific management techniques he had learned in the United States. Adapting both cotton production and manufacturing to local conditions in China required enormous effort, and Moh was generous in sharing the results of his experiments widely with other cotton producers and manufacturers. He also helped establish the Chinese Cotton Goods Exchange in Shanghai and the Chinese Industrial Bank in an effort to provide standards and stability for the cotton textile market. Even Mao Zedong applauded Moh's public-minded entrepreneurial spirit. The communist leader declared the Illinois graduate a "new kind of capitalist." (Nevertheless, Moh's cotton dream suffered repeated setbacks as the Japanese intensified their encroachment into the Chinese mainland during the 1930s.) Throughout his tumultuous career, Moh remained a dedicated Illinois alumnus. Corresponding regularly with David Kinley, he had been a member of the University Alumni Association since he graduated, and he had contributed to the Alumni Fund as well. He was also a principal sponsor of the Illinois Alumni Club in China and a stalwart leader (and longtime president) of the nation's American Returned Students Club.[12]

Leading members of the "Illini Alumni Club" extended a warm welcome to David Kinley once he arrived in China, most notably C. C. Wang and M. T. Moh, who hosted lavish parties for Kinley and accompanied him throughout his trip across the country. Probably through conversations with these two remarkable graduates, Kinley came to the surprising realization that Western scientific and technical knowledge the returned students had acquired could not be applied directly to "the requirements of life" in China. Kinley learned that Western ideas and technology required extensive and sometimes fundamental adaptation to be effective in a new setting. He also came to appreciate that modernizing intellectuals in China were fiercely patriotic and nationalistic in their outlook. He presented these lessons with a remarkable amount of both sympathy and alarm. He explained:

> The country which gives its wealth and its citizens to the development of another country, while met at first with applause and gratitude, in times finds itself looked on as imperialistic and is seeking to exact tributes from the

people it has tried to benefit. . . . [This antagonism] has not been lessened by the attitudes and remarks of some foreign, particularly American visitors to the country who have gone out as "advisors." . . . There has been too often an assumption of superiority, of teaching the Chinese how to do things [in American ways].[13]

The appearance of David Kinley's sober report coincided with the onset of a financial crisis at the University of Illinois—triggered by the Great Depression as well as the advent of isolationism in American foreign policy and a shift in public opinion. Preoccupied by other pressing issues, and without the bold leadership of Edmund James and David Kinley, the university allowed its ties with China to fade. Over the course of the 1930s no new initiatives or student programs arose to build on the institution's connections across the Pacific. The number of Chinese students dwindled, rising again only in 1946, when the Republic of China (America's ally in World War II) sent a huge number of students to study in the United States. But the postwar surge did not last long. The second wave of Chinese students to America had come to an abrupt end in 1949 when the Chinese Communists took power.

Following the onset of the Korean War in June 1950, China entered a long period of Cold War hostility and isolation from the United States. During this period, Taiwan (where the exiled Nationalist regime ruled) and to some extent British Hong Kong became the major sources of students to the United States. Some of them came to the University of Illinois. Like the Chinese students who had arrived before the war, most pursued graduate degrees in engineering and science, but a few swam against the tide to study arts and social sciences. The latter group included Oscar-winning film director Ang Lee (BFA in theater, 1980) and Annette Lu Hsiu-lien (Master of Laws, 1971), the first woman vice president of the Republic

> "The creation of a campus-wide exchange program at Illinois, however, occurred slowly, but the university's long history of trans-Pacific relationships had created a strong reputation in China of innovative research."

of China. A champion of women's rights, Lu went on to a successful career in both academics and journalism.

## Looking Back, Looking Ahead

In 1978, with the launch of the "Reform and Opening Up" by Deng Xiaoping and his associates aiming at revitalizing China's economic fortunes, the third wave of Chinese students who traveled across the Pacific to study at American universities began. Decades of isolation ended with the arrival of a small group of visiting scholars, but by the mid-1980s significant numbers of students began appearing on U.S. campuses to pursue graduate studies, both government-sponsored or privately financed degree programs. The university was not among the first group of American colleges where leaders in Beijing chose to send their students. Competition among U.S. universities for these renewed opportunities to establish cultural ties with Chinese academics became quite intense. The creation of a campus-wide exchange program at Illinois, however, occurred slowly, but the university's long history of transpacific relations had created a strong reputation in China of innovative research. Yan Dongsheng, a prominent material scientist who earned a doctorate at Illinois in 1949 and returned to China to become vice president of the Chinese Academy of Science, explained the significance of that history in a 1983 letter to university president Stanley Ikenberry:

> University of Illinois has been well-known [in China] for her outstanding contribution in many disciplines of science and engineering and has been successful for promoting interaction and friendship between academic communities and scientists . . . I myself is [sic] an Illini and earned my Ph.D. in 1949 and worked there till 1950. Being able to host a delegation from my Alma Mater will be, personally, a great [honor].[14]

Yan Dongsheng invited Ikenberry to lead a University of Illinois delegation to visit China. We do not know what the president saw there and what he proposed to do afterward, as he, unlike David Kinley, did not record the details of his trip. Nevertheless, once Beijing began allowing Chinese students to study abroad with private funding, the flow of applicants to Illinois (particularly in the sciences and engineering) increased dramatically. Like the first and second wave generations, almost all of the new arrivals were graduate students living on a tight budget and trying to save money to send home to support their families.

The composition of the Chinese students on campus began to change after 2000, however, when a rapidly increasing number of young Chinese came to pursue undergraduate degrees, and largely self-funded. As China's new middle class grew and began planning their children's future, the number of Chinese undergraduates in the United States skyrocketed. For example, in 2013–14, almost 280,000 Chinese students (accounting for one of every three foreign students enrolled in U.S. colleges) came to America to pursue their education. Particularly noteworthy was the dramatic rise of undergraduate students, who now made up almost half of the Chinese student population.

In recent years, critics have pointed out that Chinese students have become a major marketing target for the U.S. higher education. At a time of financial exigency following the economic crisis of 2008 that hit higher education hard, Chinese undergraduates who pay full (and often premium) tuition fees have helped many universities balance their books while fulfilling their missions of fostering equality and continuing academic competitiveness. These same critics often deplore that campus services for this unprecedented wave of undergraduates have been woefully inadequate.[15] Boasting a total of nearly five thousand young Chinese at the Urbana-Champaign campus, Illinois became emblematic of these trends.

In fact, as high as the number of its Chinese students is, University of Illinois, ironically, has continued to be slow and halting in developing sustainable academic exchange programs and strong institutional relations with China. For example, when I was the director of the Center for East Asian and Pacific Studies, a private foundation considered canceling a successful humanities-centered exchange program with Chinese universities (organized on the model of the Harvard-Yenching fellowship program) in part because of its growing skepticism about the commitment of university leadership to stronger ties with Chinese educators. (This skepticism was only strength-

ened following the last-minute cancellation of a long-planned network-building reunion conference at Nanjing University in 2011.) Moreover, the Chinese students have been largely unprepared for navigating the increasingly fragmented and financially beleaguered college culture: how to make sense of the racial politics, for example, or how to make sense of the problems of racialization and minoritization they faced on campus and beyond.

When he accepted the invitation in 1912 to become honorary vice president of the prestigious China Society of America (a position already held by both President William Howard Taft and President Yuan Shikai of China), President Edmund James wrote: "We have a large number of Chinese students at the University of Illinois, between forty and fifty I think, and they have shown themselves well able to profit by the facilities placed at their disposal and some of our Chinese graduates have already done notable service at home in their public and private relations."[16]

The foresight and innovative approaches Edmund James, and his successor David Kinley, brought to educating young Chinese, which included setting up English classes and the Office of Advisor to Foreign Students to help them adjust to a new cultural environment, as well as the attention they showered on the new arrivals, gave the University of Illinois a formidable reputation across the Pacific. Now, with a Chinese student population thousands of times larger than in the early twentieth-century, and as China has come a long way to become the world's second-largest economy and the "strategic partner" of the United States, the soaring aspirations and gallant efforts of Edmund James and David Kinley to make the University of Illinois a significant player in forging strong cultural relationships between China and the United States remain a powerful reminder of how important and rewarding this effort can be and yet how long the road ahead of us remains.

## Notes

1. See https://www.insidehighered.com/news/2015/01/07/u-illinois-growth-number-chinese-students-has-been-dramatic.

2. For an in-depth study of Edmund James's contributions to the university, see Winston Solberg, "President Edmund J.

James and the University of Illinois. 1904–1920: Redeeming the Promise of the Morrill Land-Grant Act," unpublished manuscript. My gratitude to Professor Solberg for sharing with me this valuable manuscript.

3. See Peter Kwong and Dušanka Miščević, *Chinese America: The Untold Story of America's Oldest New Community* (New York: New Press, 2005), chapters 7 and 11; Warren Cohen, *America's Response to China: A History of Sino-American Relations* (New York: Columbia University Press, 2010), chapters 1–3.

4. Quoted from Qian Ning, *Chinese Students Encounter America*, translated by T. K. Chu (Seattle: University of Washington Press, 2002), xvi–xvii. Edmund James's letter was originally collected in Arthur Smith, *China and America Today*, first published in 1923 (Ithaca, N.Y.: Cornell University Press, 2009), 213–16.

5. See Qian Ning, *Chinese Students Encounter America*, ix–xv; Liel Leibovitz and Matthew Miller, *Fortunate Sons* (New York: Norton, 2011).

6. "Diyici Gengzi Peikuan liuxuesheng liebiao" (A List of the First Boxer Indemnity Scholarship Program Returned Students), Zh.m.wikipedia.org.

7. See Carol Huang, "The Soft Power of U.S. Students and the Foundation of a Chinese American Intellectual Community in Urbana-Champaign," PhD diss., University of Illinois at Urbana-Champaign, 2001, 49.

8. "Chinese Students at Illinois" in *Alumni Quarterly* 1 no. 4 (October 1910): 363.

9. Carol Huang, "Soft Power," 190–91 and 303–5.

10. Ibid.

11. See Carol Huang, "Wang Jingchun: Zhongguo diyiwei tielu guanli boshi" ("C. C. Wang: The First Chinese Railway Administration," PhD diss.); *China Times*, December 15, 2001; Stacey Bieter, "Wang Jingchun," in *Biographical Dictionary of Chinese Christianity*, http://www.bdcconline.net/en/stories/w/wang-jingchun.php.

12. Moh Hsing Yueh, Alumni Biographical File, 1913–1936, RS 26/4/1, University of Illinois Archives; Mu Jiaxiu et al. eds., *Mu Ouchu xiansheng nianpu* (The Chronicle of Mr. Mu Ouchu) (Shanghai: Shanghai guji chubanshe, 2006).

13. "Some Cursory Observations of Educational Policy and Sundry Educational Institutions in the Philippines, China and Japan," David Knight to President H. W. Chase, June 8, 1932, President Harry W. Chase subject file, 1930–1933, RS 2/7/5-1.

14. Yan Dongsheng to President Stanley Ikenberry, August 13, 1983, Administrative subject file, 1932–2005, RS 7/1/7-30.

15. See, for example, Bethany Allen-Ebrahimian, "Chinese Students in America: 300,000 and Counting," *Foreign Affairs*, http://foreignpolicy.com/2015/11/16/china-us-colleges-education-chinese-students-university; Matt Schiaverza, "The Tenuous Relationship between American Universities and Chinese Students," *Atlantic Monthly*, available at http://www.theatlantic.com/education/archive/2015/05/american-universities-are-addicted-to-chinese-students/394517; Sarah Svobada, "Why Do So Many Chinese Students Choose U.S. Universities?" *BBC News*, http://www.bbc.com/news/business-32969291.

16. Edmund James to Louis Livingston Seaman, November 4, 1912, President Edmund James general correspondence, 1904–1919, RS 2/5/3-31, University of Illinois Archive.

## Sources

The University Archives holds a wealth of material on the institution's connections with China. Most of these sources are included in the presidential papers of the campus leaders involved in China relations. My study in the archives was supported by an outstanding group of students. In fact, I could not have finished this essay so quickly and with so much enjoyment without the research support of these students—Huiyi Chen, Jiayi Li, Junyi Tang, and Mindi Zhang—all history majors from China. We had so much fun digging up materials in the University Archive and spent so many cheerful hours discussing our findings. I am also thankful to Zeyu Hu for his enthusiasm.

# The ILLIAC Computers

## Product and Source of Innovation (and Controversy)

*Rafal Ciolcosz*

ILLIAC (Illinois Automated Computer) is a term coined to describe a series of complex supercomputers built at the University of Illinois in the aftermath of World War II. ILLIAC I (1952) was largely a copy of the ORDVAC, a supercomputer the university built in 1952 to perform ballistic trajectory calculations for the U.S. Army. Louis Ridenour, dean of the Graduate College (and a technology advisor to President Eisenhower), had been instrumental in the development of ORDVAC. Following the success of that machine, Ridenour proposed the creation ILLIAC in Urbana-Champaign.

ILLIAC was the first automatic digital supercomputer built and owned by a university. The computer not only had revolutionary arithmetic capabilities (for example, it could analyze extensive seismic data to help predict earthquakes), but it could also be used for evaluations of antenna patterns, construction plans, and weapon damage assessments.

The new Illinois computer was most notable because it was made available to students and faculty across campus. (For example, ILLIAC attracted the attention of chemist Lejaren Hiller, who used it for the composition of

ILLIAC I

experimental music. See chapter 2.9.) Researchers across campus quickly embraced the new technology. In 1962 ILLIAC I was replaced by ILLIAC II, designed by computer science professor James E. Robertson and powered by recently developed transistors and semiconductors (the ILLIAC I had been powered by 2,800 vacuum tubes). ILLIAC II was one hundred times faster than the previous model. ILLIAC III debuted in 1967; it allowed researchers and students to analyze visual data, such as high-energy particle events. The pace of change continued to accelerate. Daniel Slotnick, a mathematical physicist, began designing ILLIAC IV even before III became operational. Version IV was vastly more powerful than its predecessors. Its use in space exploration and missile research attracted wide attention among American scientists. Unfortunately for the campus engineering community, however, this interest came at a politically awkward moment.

In January,1970, the *Daily Illini* revealed that two-thirds of ILLIAC IV's operational time had secretly been committed to the Department of Defense, the source of most of the project's funding. This news sparked protests by students opposed to the American war in Vietnam; they condemned the machine as an instrument of destruction. These protests reached their peak in March of that year when, fearing damage to campus property, the university administration summoned more than one thousand National Guard troops and state police officers to campus. They arrested two hundred protestors. Eventually, the university moved ILLIAC IV to NASA's Ames Research Center in California, where it was used for classified research until 1981.

## Sources

The University Archives holds substantial material on the ILLIAC computers. The *Daily Illini* covered the protests over ILLIAC IV on January 6, 1970.

# The Krannert Center for the Performing Arts

Harry Liebersohn

When I first visited the University of Illinois campus for my job interview in the spring of 1989, the distinguished diplomatic historian Paul Schroeder, one of my future colleagues, urged me to visit the Krannert Center for the Performing Arts before I left. It wasn't on my schedule, and in the normal order of things I wouldn't have been able to follow his advice. But luckily—as I now view it in retrospect—I missed my return flight and had to stay an extra day. And that gave me my first chance to visit a magical performance space that exerts a deep attraction on artists and audiences alike. The Krannert Center is not just a house; it is home to a creative community nurtured by the arts. Thanks to a remarkable consensus of donors, administrators, architect and faculty, the foundations of that community were laid at the moment of its founding in the early 1960s.

The story of the Krannert begins with the chief donors, Herman C. and Ellnora Krannert. Herman came from Chicago and attended the University of Illinois, where he graduated with a degree in mechanical engineering in 1919. In 1925, after years of working for a manufacturer of "ventilated corrugated boxes for the shipment of baby chicks," he started his own company. Known publicly after 1930 as the Inland Box Company, this Indianapolis-based enterprise thrived during the Depression. It added branches across the country, sold large quantities of its boxes to the federal government during World War II, and continued its geographic expansion and develop-

Aerial view of Krannert Center for the Performing Arts. Photo courtesy of Krannert Center for the Performing Arts.

ment of new products into the 1960s.[1] By then, Herman and his wife Ellnora had become generous philanthropists who supported major educational and arts projects in both Indiana and Illinois.

One of the Krannerts' gifts was the founding donation for the creation of the university art museum—named after them—which opened in 1961.[2] On a campus dominated by handsome but conventional Georgian brick buildings, the Krannert Art Museum was a spanking-white example of postwar modernism, winking at classical tradition but fresh and bold. The year after the art museum opened, the Krannerts disclosed that they wished to make a second major gift to the university.[3] Campus administrators conferred among themselves but could not settle on a clear sense of direction. James C.

Colvin, director of the University of Illinois Foundation (the fundraising unit associated with the university), nervously noted to President David D. Henry that the Krannerts generally preferred to fund buildings. The administration appeared willing to follow their donors' wishes, but they remained uncertain how a new building would fit into the university's long-range plans.[4] Interestingly, from today's perspective when different parts of campus often compete for new resources, President Henry and his colleagues do not appear to have favored one part of the institution over another. They struggled to identify a project that would advance the interest of the whole campus community.

In October 1962, Henry, Colvin, and H. O. Farber, the university comptroller, met with the Krannerts at the offices of the Inland Container Corporation in Indianapolis. They presented a long list of possible projects. These included a conference center, a foreign students' center, an acquisitions program for the art museum, a student center for the university's Chicago medical school—and a combination concert hall and space for music and theater activities. The Krannerts' response surprised and stunned the campus leaders. They made an offer that completely surpassed what Henry and his colleagues had expected. In a letter dated December 17, Herman Krannert approved the plan for an ambitious array of performing arts facilities.[5]

At this point a new group entered the discussions and made an important intervention: a faculty committee, appointed by President Henry and chaired by Allen S. Weller, dean of the College of Fine and Applied Arts, developed an ambitious and detailed plan for a comprehensive performing arts center. They were able to move quickly in part because a previous faculty committee had delivered a report in 1958 making the case for such a unified space for teaching and performance. The arts faculty of the early 1960s included a number of remarkably talented arts professionals. In the early planning stage, for example, Ludwig Zirner, a Viennese émigré and the head of the Theater Department, quickly produced a detailed building plan for the new theater facilities. Zirner's design was shaped by one of the fundamental principles guiding the overall creation of the center: "the strongest possible interaction between the various performing arts—opera, theatre, and dance." Zirner underlined this commitment to interaction and collaboration by proposing shared service areas, overseen by a staff of experts who would direct and teach their crafts—a plan enacted a half-century ago and still in place on the Krannert Center's second floor.[6]

The Krannerts' proposal and the Illinois faculty's deliberations were occurring at a pivotal moment in the history of university arts programming in the United States. Their discussions were part of a national movement to give the arts new prominence on the nation's campuses and to integrate the various genres of performance as never before. Marginal before World War II, university arts programs had grown dramatically during the period of postwar expansion, and by the early 1960s they were

Herbert and Ellnora Krannert. Photo courtesy of Krannert Center for the Performing Arts.

asserting their centrality alongside liberal arts and technical fields in the American definition of higher education.[7] The situation at the University of Illinois demonstrated precisely why there was a need for such a center. In the 1950s, music, dance, and theater were scattered in inadequate facilities across the campus; the older performance halls like Lincoln Theater and Smith Hall were beautiful but completely inadequate to student needs and the faculty's critical standards.[8] Moreover, a center bringing together the performing arts corresponded to the aspirations of cultural modernists who had argued since the late nineteenth century that the arts languished when kept in isolation. Arts advocates believed that when nurtured in close proximity, the arts awoke and inspired one another. Unity—unity of the different performing arts, unity of

Theater department head Ludwig Zirner and students

teaching and performance, unity of the campus community and the general public—became the shared credo of the makers of the Krannert Center. Donors, faculty, and administrators believed in it and with remarkable speed worked toward realizing it.

By June 11, 1963, Dean Weller, together with the heads of the Illinois Foundation and the campus's physical plant, could meet with the Krannerts in Indianapolis and present them with the university's plan for a comprehensive performing arts complex. Herman Krannert was impressed, and at the end of the month he and his wife met again with university officials. He was ready to underwrite the entire undertaking of a performing arts center. But he brought his business experience to bear on the plan with a few fundamental demands. He wanted to be sure that the center was the university's highest priority among donor-funded projects. And he insisted that none of his money or the university's be used for interest on loans, a requirement that may have been intended to pressure

the state to fund its share of the building.[9] Herman Krannert's voice comes through in his correspondence with the university officials as jovial and sometimes ironic; at one point he apologized to the foundation director for bringing up center business when there were more important things to think about, like the performance of the Illinois football team in the upcoming Rose Bowl game.[10] But he was also the project's commanding personality from beginning to end, cool and decisive. Early on, the estimate for total costs rose from $10 million to $16 million, and for a moment the university officials were paralyzed; Krannert simply threw in another $3 million, provided it would be matched by the state.[11] Henry and the other university administrators made a point of deferring to his planning and organizing skills.

The planning of the center became a partnership when the firm of Harrison and Abramovitz was hired, with Max Abramovitz appointed as its architect in September 1963, less than three months after the Krannerts' approval of the project.[12] Abramovitz was the second inspired creator of the new center. Like Herman Krannert, he came from Chicago; in fact, they had attended Crane Technological High School together and were both graduates of the University of Illinois.[13] On the faculty side, Joseph W. Scott, the director of the University Theater, admired the architect's concern for "the philosophical and educational implications" of the performing arts center.[14] As for the university administrators, they were already used to working with Abramovitz, for he had designed the university's Assembly Hall, a futuristic-looking building on the edge of campus that still turns heads today. (The football stadium, across the street and not far away, is an architecturally ordinary-looking brick-and-mortar coliseum; Abramovitz's building for graduation ceremonies and mega-concerts is often compared to a flying saucer, one in the shape of a silvery half-sphere that has landed on a prairie field.) Decisive for the administrators was that Abramovitz had also been the architect for Avery Fisher Hall in New York's Lincoln Center (now David Geffen Hall) and therefore had the experience to take on another performing arts assignment. The New York concert hall was savagely criticized for its poor acoustics, but the university administrators were confident that they could collaborate with Abramovitz to produce a better building.[15] Their confidence was well placed: Foellinger Great Hall, the large concert space of the Krannert Center, has a warm sound that carries an orchestra's blend of parts and the pianissimo of a pianist all the way to the back rows of the balcony.

Less promising—though the university administrators and Krannerts may not have thought so at the time—was Abramovitz's architectural oeuvre. He had absorbed a wide range of American and European influences after studying at Illinois and Columbia University and spending two years in Europe; but he tended to work as a quiet technician who was teased in a *New York Times* article for being a colorless man in a grey flannel suit.[16] Neither the marble glitziness of Avery Fischer nor the bureaucratic anonymity of another of his prominent commissions, the CIA headquarters in Langley, Virginia, boded well for a building that was supposed to bring together the different parts of an artistic and academic community. But the prairie setting and collaboration with the Krannerts led the architect to turn away from cold glass and metal. Instead he created a building that was, and remains, a provocation from the outside and a welcoming interior space stimulating conversation, collaboration, and shared enjoyment.

The building rises from broad staircases to a plateau where the doors lead to the lobby, its brick façade and sloping towers having the combined effect of a teasing enigma. Only a semi-circular outdoor amphitheater gives away its function. The overall effect is that of a temple, which it is—a temple of the arts, in keeping with the aspirations of high modernism. Go through the glass doors, though, and the kingdom of art turns out to have an unassuming elegance, with a teak floor, brick walls, and sparing use of marble and glass. Donal Henahan, the music critic for the *New York Times*, especially admired the Krannert Center interior, contrasting it with the meretricious public spaces in other performing arts halls with their chandeliers and dramatic staircases.[17] The Krannert Center was designed with four performance spaces of different sizes, from Foellinger Hall that seats twenty-one hundred to the experimental Studio Theatre, accommodating fewer than two hundred. The variety of the spaces stimulates thinking about performance genres and their expressive demands. Despite his Chicago origins, Abramovitz had never been a follower of Prairie School architecture, but now his insistence on natural materials complemented his European functionalist style to produce a place that was a pleasure for the eye and the ear, for the hieratic aspirations of high modernism, and for relaxed entertainment.

On critical points the Krannerts pushed Abramovitz in the right direction. Herman Krannert cared about parking, and two floors of underground parking space were built. This was not a humble detail: as a result, concert-goers feel an ease of access and entry that encourages them to show up on the coldest winter nights. He also wanted plenty of outdoor lighting, which again is a practical issue that integrates audience and center; on the darkness of evening in a prairie town of a hundred thousand, the lighting serves as a transition from the prosaic outdoors to the imaginative realm of Krannert Center performances. Ellnora Krannert was at least an equal partner to her husband in making suggestions that humanized the design. One in particular was transforming: tired of intermissions on Broadway where one had to go out onto the street, she asked Abramovitz to provide a large interior space that could hold the crowds pouring out of the theaters at intermission.[18] What Abramovitz created leaves behind the word "lobby" and comes closer to the piazza or public square. The founders of the Krannert anticipated that different parts of the campus community would mingle there; and so it is, especially on nights when different performances may appeal to family, student, specialized, and town audiences, who may know one another from business, school, or academic settings and come together in the Krannert setting before, during, or after concerts. The addition of a bar, a café, and Stage 5—a lobby area for free performances—later multiplied these relaxed exchanges, changes that are very much in the spirit of the founders.

Abramovitz was confident that he could realize the Krannerts' and university planners' hopes for a unified

> "The overall effect is that of a temple, which it is—a temple of the arts, in keeping with the aspirations of high modernism."

The Krannert Center lobby area. Photo courtesy of Krannert Center for the Performing Arts.

center for the arts—so long as the entire project could be realized in one fell swoop according to his plan. Herman Krannert was his ally: he saw the project through its rapid completion in the space of five years, from the moment the Krannerts approved his architectural plans on May 22, 1964, to the center's dedication festival of April 19 to May 18, 1969. By then the planners had also hired John Burrell as the center's first director. Burrell came from the theater—he had revived Old Vic in London in the mid-1940s and then enjoyed a successful stretch of years on Broadway—but expressed the ambitious intentions of the place from the beginning when he wrote: "The Center is intended as a unified concept where music, opera, theatre, and the dance can operate both in training and performance as interrelated and complementary to one another, bringing these arts close together both for performers and for audiences."[19] Burrell packed a great deal into that one sentence, but it reinforced the concept that

had guided the Krannert Center founders: the vision of the arts as a unified totality that has antecedents going back a century to creative artists like Richard Wagner and Claude Debussy, and to the Arts and Crafts movement and Bauhaus School. Thanks above all to the arts faculty's sophistication, the Krannerts' articulation of audience needs, and Abramovitz's architectural conception, the Krannert Center was and is the realization of a complex concept, bringing different arts and different human roles together as a unified whole. Moreover, that whole immediately had the vibrant artistic drive that its planners wished to encourage. The dedication concert on April 19 was a nervy event. On the program was music by Aaron Copeland (Fanfare from Symphony no. 3), Beethoven (Overture: The Consecration of the House, opus 124), the Mexican composer Manuel Enriquez (Transición I), Bartók (Concert no. 2 for Violin and Orchestra) and, for the entire second half following intermission, Britten

(Spring Symphony, op. 44).[20] It was an offering of living artists and twentieth century artists, with a nod back to Beethoven, the original revolutionary of modern music.

The message was one of daring, celebration, and new beginnings. It lives on in innovations like the free concerts at Stage 5; Opening Night, annually packed with visitors, music, food, and drink; and the Ellnora guitar festival, a biennial fireworks of music that crosses worldwide places and genres. All of these events remain true to the founders' vision of a community of free expression. From their time to ours, the bold new beginnings have never stopped.

## Notes

I wish to thank Mike Ross, Maureen Reagan, and Bruno Nettl for sharing with me their knowledge of the Krannert Center's history and current aims. Of course, I am solely responsible for any errors of fact or interpretation.

1. Emily Castle, "Historical Sketch," in *Guide to Inland Container Corporation Papers, 1921–2001*, Indiana Historical Society, Manuscript and Visual Collections Department, http://www.indianahistory.org/our-collections/collection-guides/inland-container-corporation-papers-1921-2001.pdf, accessed September 26, 2015.

2. "About Krannert Art Museum: History," http://kam.illinois.edu/about/history.html, accessed October 10, 2015.

3. Krannert Center for the Performing Arts, Office Materials; Anon., *The Story and Facts about the Krannert Center for the Performing Arts*, University of Illinois at Urbana-Champaign (no place, publisher or date), 1. Hereinafter Krannert Office Materials. Hereinafter *Story and Facts*.

4. University of Illinois Archives, President David D. Henry, general correspondence, 1955–1964: Faculty Letters—Gifts (#1-307), 1963–1964, series no. 1/12/1, box 115, University of Illinois, folder: Fine and Applied Arts, College of. Center for the Performing Arts. Colvin to Henry, cc: Weller, May 10, 1962. Hereinafter Henry Correspondence 1955–1964.

5. Henry Correspondence 1955–1964. Herman Krannert to David Henry, December 17, 1962. See also Krannert Center Office Materials, Anon. (probably James C. Colvin), *Krannert Center for the Performing Arts: The Concept and the Design* (Urbana: University of Illinois Press, n.d.), Krannert Office Materials. Hereinafter cited as Colvin, *Krannert Center*.

6. University Archives, Fine and Applied Arts, Dean's Office: Allen S. Weller Papers, Krannert Center for Performing Arts,

1956–64, series no.: 12/1/20, box 32, folder Krannert Center, 1956–1963. Ludwig Zirner to Allen Weller, April 19, 1963. Zirner and Joseph W. Scott, the executive director of the University Theatre, based their space estimates on the so-called Cohn Report of February 19, 1958. The report by Rubin G. Cohn, "Report of University Committee to Plan Auditorium Facilities for Drama and Music," is appended to a letter in the same file from Scott to Weller, April 19, 1963. Hereinafter cited as Weller Papers 1956–64. On Zirner's Austrian background, see Lisa Silverman, *Becoming Austrians: Jews and Culture between the World Wars* (Oxford: Oxford University Press, 2012), 221n1–2.

7. Jack Morrison, *The Maturing of the Arts on the American Campus: A Commentary*, foreword by Clark Kerr (Lanham, Md.: University Press of America, 1985). See also Sue M. Lawson, *An Atlas of Performing Arts in the United States* (April 1985: no place, no publisher); Margaret Mahoney, ed., *The Arts on Campus: The Necessity for Change* (Greenwich, Conn.: New York Graphic Society, 1970). There is a dour prognosis of the Krannert Center's prospects for success in Martin Mayer, ed. *Bricks, Mortar and the Performing Arts: Report* (New York: Twentieth Century Fund, 1970), 73–74.

8. See the Cohn Report in Scott to Weller, April 19, 1963. See also a second report, no author, "Proposal for a Music Hall-Theater and Concert Hall as the Central Unit of a Performing Arts Center," December 7, 1962; Joseph W. Scott, executive director of the University Theatre, to Fred H. Turner, dean of students, February 8, 1956; Joseph Scott to Duane A. Branigan, director of the School of Music, no date; and "A Center for the Performing Arts: Drama Theatre Unit"; in Weller Papers, 1956–64.

9. Colvin, *Krannert Center*, 10–13.

10. Weller Papers, 1956–64. Herman C. Krannert to James C. Colvin, December 10, 1963.

11. Colvin, *Krannert Center*, 42.

12. Ibid., 13.

13. For biographical perspectives, see the essays in John Harwood and Janet Parks, eds., *The Troubled Search: The Work of Max Abramovitz*, foreword by Gerald Beasly (New York: Wallach Art Gallery, Columbia University, 2004).

14. Weller Papers, 1956–64. Scott to Weller, September 10, 1963.

15. Weller Papers, 1956–64. Physical Plant Department, "Memorandum Concerning Selection of Architect on the Center for the Performing Arts, Urbana-Champaign," September 11, 1963.

16. "Concern for Detail: Max Abramovitz," *New York Times*, September 24, 1962; Randy Kennedy, "Max Abramovitz, 96,

Architect of Avery Fisher Hall, Dies," *New York Times*, September 15, 2004.

17. Krannert Office Materials. Donal Henahan, "A Middle Western Arts Dream Thrills Its Architect," April 21, 1969. The photocopy in this file differs from the online version of the article, which does not include the lines comparing the Krannert Center's interior to other, less tasteful spaces.

18. *Story and Facts about The Krannert Center*, 9–11; Colvin, *Krannert Center*, 19; Henry Correspondence 1955–1964, Charles Havens, Physical Plant, to Max Abramovitz, August 20, 1964; Weller Papers, 1956–64, Physical Plant, Memorandum of meeting with Mr. and Mrs. Krannert on May 22, 1964.

19. This statement comes from the cover verso of Anon., *Dedication Festival: The Krannert Center for the Performing Arts*, University of Illinois at Urbana-Champaign, April 19 to May 18, 1969. On Burrell, see also Colvin, *Krannert Center*, 67.

20. The program is in *Dedication Festival*.

## Sources

There is almost no extended treatment in print of the Krannert Center. The exceptions are privately published occasional works (for the opening in 1969 and other publicity moments), several of which are stored in the center's files. The best of these is Anon. (probably James C. Colvin), *Krannert Center for the Performing Arts: The Concept and the Design* (Urbana: University of Illinois Press, n.d.). The University of Illinois Archives are well-organized and well-preserved, but the researcher must comb through scattered files to reconstruct the center's history. Both the archival sources and the occasional publications must be used with critical caution, for they are written from the University of Illinois administration's point of view. They tend to downplay the role of faculty as an essential actor in the creation and implementation of the Krannert Center's design, a part of the story that one glimpses indirectly among the letters and memos.

For more on the role of performing arts centers in the modern history of public higher education, see Jack Morrison, *The Maturing of the Arts on the American Campus: A Commentary* (Lanham, Md.: University Press of America, 1985). The Krannert Center embodies longstanding conceptions of architecture and design as shapers of community in modern democracies. The essay on urban modernism in Carl E. Schorske, *Fin-de-siècle Vienna: Politics and Culture* (New York: Knopf, 1980) remains the most penetrating historical treatment of this movement.

# Ebertfest

## Where Hollywood Comes to the Prairie

*Tim Brown*

Roger Ebert while a student at the University of Illinois

"Ebertfest," a five-day film festival held at Champaign's historic Virginia Theater, originated in 1997, when Roger Ebert (1942–2013) hosted a screening of *2001: A Space Odyssey* in 70mm film at the Virginia. The occasion was sponsored by the university as part of a "Cyberfest," organized to celebrate the school's innovations in computer science. Roger Ebert, a 1964 Illinois graduate, was the most famous and influential film critic of his day. Born and raised in Urbana, Ebert had cut a wide swath through the university, serving as editor of the *Daily Illini* and organizer/editor of *Illini Century*, a centennial history of the institution.

Despite his distinguished career at Illinois, Ebert was an unlikely celebrity. He had moved to Chicago after graduation to pursue a graduate degree in English. Unexpectedly, however, a part-time job at the *Chicago Sun Times* suddenly evolved into a full-time assignment as the paper's film critic. Eight years later, in 1975, Ebert and crosstown rival Gene Siskel (film critic of the *Chicago Tribune*) launched a half-hour television show, *Sneak Previews*, in which the two debated the virtues and failings of recent films. Their program became a hit, catapulting both men to careers as the voices of American film criticism. Ebert himself took a turn at screenwriting when he wrote scripts for *Beyond the Valley of the Dolls* (1970) and other films. Ebert won the Pulitzer Prize for his critical writing in 1975.

The first official Ebertfest took place in the spring of 1999, when Ebert, with the help of the College of Media, organized "Roger Ebert's Overlooked Film Festival" at the Virginia Theater. The program for the festival was set by Ebert himself and ranged from well-known classics such as *Patton* to obscure cult films and forgotten silent features.

The initial festival established the pattern for later events: great, often forgotten works such as *Days of Heaven* would be paired with underappreciated American or neglected foreign films, animated features, and recent films Ebert simply believed deserved more attention. Every film was introduced by Ebert or a fellow critic, and discussions followed every showing. Many of these included directors, cinematographers, and even movie stars. Recent examples of celebrity appearances include Richard Linklater, Patton Oswalt, and Spike Lee.

From almost the very start the festival was a success, drawing visitors who were attracted by the unpredictable and unpretentious program and the festive atmosphere surrounding the Virginia Theater (the theater's organ was often dusted off to warm up the crowds). Over time, the festival was also supplemented by workshops, seminars led by visiting artists, and programs for Illinois undergraduates. Sadly, Ebert's declining health drew him away from the festival, but he continued to set its program until 2013, the year of his death. In the years since his passing, Roger's wife, Chaz Ebert, and a global network of Ebert colleagues have continued to produce this unique and stimulating festival with the support of local donors and the university.

### Sources

Information about Ebertfest can be found at the University of Illinois Archives and on the event's website. Roger Ebert's memoir, *Life Itself* (2011), tells the story of his life and recounts the early years of Ebertfest.

# Innovation across Disciplines

## The Institute for Genomic Biology

*Nicholas Hopkins*

One of the paradoxes of modern research institutions is that most innovations arise from the collaboration of colleagues who approach a problem from different disciplines, while universities are organized around discipline-based departments. The Institute for Genomic Biology (IGB) has ameliorated this conflict by bringing scientists from many disciplines together to explore the history and function of the fundamental building blocks of life. The university also intended to use the institute as a means of positioning itself at the forefront of biotechnology research so that Illinois could participate in an area of scientific work that had significant intellectual and commercial potential. The architects of the IGB sought to bring together the plethora of biotechnology researchers at the university in the hope that their interaction would lead to syntheses of ideas and additional innovations that would benefit everyone involved. The whole, they hoped, would be larger than the sum of its parts.

This ambitious project did not always include constructing a new building. Vice Chancellor Richard C. Alkire first proposed bringing all campus biotechnology projects together in the 1990s. This plan garnered such support from the State of Illinois, however, that the university soon began to receive public funds for the project. While levels of state backing initially varied considerably, public interest in the project continued. University support for the project was spurred on by calls of faculty, such as National Medal of Science recipient Carl R. Woese, who implored the administration not to miss the opportunity for IGB to become a "world-class institute" for genomic biology. By 2003 campus leaders decided to propose the construction of a physical space to showcase its work in biotech research. With timely support from then-Governor George Ryan's Venture-TECH initiative, the project was soon underway.

In November 2006 the new $75 million, 186,000-square-foot facility opened on a site only a few yards from the campus's Morrow Plots. Its first director, mammalian geneticist

Professor May Berenbaum with participants in an IGB summer program. Photo by Kathryn Faith, courtesy of the Carl R. Woese Institute of Genomic Biology.

Harris Lewin, got the facility up and running, accommodating researchers and announcing IGB's research areas: systems biology, cellular, metabolic engineering, and genome technology. Entomologist Gene Robinson, an expert in the genetic dimension of regulatory mechanisms, succeeded Lewin in 2012. In 2014 the university renamed the IGB to honor Professor Woese: the Woese Institute for Genomic Biology.

Since opening its doors IGB has pursued its mission to "advance life science research and simulate bio-economic development." It has done so by providing space to groundbreaking interdisciplinary projects like antibiotic creation through mining microbial genomes. IGB has also hosted scholarly competitions and summer camps for young researchers and has sponsored seminars on topics as varied as the use of DNA evidence in legal proceedings, nutrition learning and memory, and biomedical engineering. These efforts have produced hundreds of scholarly publications as well as new products: an antibiotic to combat food-borne diseases, a yeast strain that improves biofuels production, a technique for isolating tumor-seeding cancer cells, and a genome map of the energy crop *Miscanthus sinensis*.

The institute has focused especially on research on legal and social issues related to genomic science, as well as international food security. It hosts regular symposia to showcase and disseminate achievements of its fellows working on different aspects of food production and processing. Recent conference topics have included sequencing microspore pathogens on North American bumblebees, quantifying the effects of phthalates (commonly found in dust and dairy products) on human fertility and cancer rates, and measuring ozone-sensitivity of new soybean strains.

As with other places of innovation, the Woese Institute for Genomic Biology represents a major investment in creativity and exploration, one that rests on the assumption that exchanges, debate, and collaboration will spark new ideas and inventions.

## Sources

The University Archives holds primary materials on the planning and construction of the IGB. Coverage of the institute's construction and renaming can be found in the *Daily Illini*, September 16, 2004, and September 25, 2014.

# The Business Instructional Facility

## Designed for Innovation

*Jonathan Binkley and Kelsey Reinker*

In the spring of 2006, the College of Business announced its plan to meet the pressing need for new classroom space by constructing a 160,000-square-foot Business Instructional Facility (BIF) that would contain not only teaching facilities but also spaces for conferences, career services, and hands-on learning. The college also declared that the new building would be the first environmentally sustainable building on the campus and would not require public support. University of Illinois alumnus Cesar Pelli was chosen to design BIF. One of the most distinguished architects in the world, Pelli was best known for building the Petronas twin towers in Kuala Lumpur, Malaysia, the Wells Fargo Center in Minneapolis, and the World Financial Center complex in lower Manhattan. His design goal was to create a space that would encourage interaction and teamwork among students and also to accommodate alumni events

The Business Instructional Facility. Photo courtesy of the College of Business.

and corporate receptions. With support from alumni and corporate sponsors, the BIF project quickly took shape and was ready for students by the fall of 2008. A platinum-certified LEED building (the Leadership in Energy and Environmental Design certification is awarded by the U.S. Green Building Council), the new building was designed to reduce energy costs by 75 percent over conventional buildings. It featured triple-layered windows, solar panels in its roof, a green roof area planted in grass to absorb heat and water, maximum use of natural light, and air circulation systems that use convection and gravity rather than electric power.

In addition to classrooms, the new structure also contained an auditorium, interview rooms, faculty offices, meeting rooms, a 3D printing lab, and a market-information laboratory featuring trading simulators that enable students to test the results of short-term trading strategies. The new interview facilities allow students access to present themselves in a professional atmosphere and to practice and prepare for upcoming interview sessions. Responses to the new building were enthusiastic. Dean Larry DeBrock of the College of Business summarized these reactions when he declared, "The BIF represents the collective aspirations of many generations of College alumni, students, and friends."

The emphasis throughout the building is on collaboration and teamwork. Architect Pelli and the College's faculty argued that in the modern business environment, it is essential that individuals be able to maximize their creativity and problem solving by gathering the strongest ideas possible from a team of committed practitioners. From the building's soaring atrium where students gather to study and socialize, to the conference rooms and trading simulator, the BIF encourages interaction and group effort.

## Sources

The most accessible information about the BIF is in the *Daily Illini*, particularly articles published during the weeks surrounding the building's 2008 opening. See especially "New Business Facility May Be Most Sustainable on Campus," August 28, 2008, and "Business Instructional Facility Makes Its Debut," October 17, 2008.

# The Beckman Institute
## Imagining Interdisciplinarity

Stephanie A. Dick

The Beckman Institute for Advanced Science and Technology is an interdisciplinary research center at the University of Illinois, Urbana-Champaign. It houses hundreds of researchers from across the sciences under one (very large) roof. Since its doors officially opened in 1989, the institute has been the site of countless innovations, ranging from the development of new medical devices to the exploration and engineering of materials at the molecular level. But the Beckman Institute is not just the *site* of scientific and technological innovations. The institute *itself* was an innovation. Its creation involved years of planning. It was designed to offer a new kind of academic research environment—one that fostered forms of research, inquiry, and development that weren't believed possible within the confines of traditional university in-frastructure, one that transcended so-often-entrenched disciplinary and departmental boundaries.

Today, interdisciplinarity is a hallmark of American academia. Universities boast of their interdisciplinary research initiatives, the National Science Foundation (NSF) and other funding bodies privilege and prioritize interdisciplinary proposals, and countless industrial, governmental, and academic research institutions have been founded on the grounds of large-scale interdisciplinary promise. Much twenty-first-century research is premised in part on the belief, as the National Science Foundation states on its program website, that "important research ideas often transcend the scope of a single discipline or program." In all disciplines there are questions scientists want to answer and subjects they want to explore, paths of inquiry we now believe to be beyond the reach of any one discipline and its tools.

However, it was not always so. Although some forms of academic collaboration have existed for centuries, interdisciplinary research did not become an explicit or dominant dimension of modern American scholarship until after World War II. Moreover, interdisciplinarity is *hard*. Scholars spend decades learning the modes of reasoning and practice particular to their field of study. They are trained to see, think, and work in specialized and very different ways. There are many obstacles to overcome in order for scholars of one field to collaborate meaningfully with people who are equally embedded in their own research paradigms. Interdisciplinarity takes work and, as we shall see, it takes many different kinds of work.

The Beckman Institute was among the earliest interdisciplinary research centers to be created at a university with the support of a private philanthropist. Earlier interdisciplinary centers in the postwar era were generally funded and founded with governmental, military, and industrial sponsorship, and they tended to be oriented toward explicit and specific programs, like the development of nuclear weapons, radar defense, or modern digital computers. (The University of Illinois's successful ILLIAC computer projects described in chapter 3.6 were examples of this trend.) The Beckman Institute and others like it represented something new. They reflected a basic investment in large-scale (and long-range) interdisciplinary research on university campuses.

Planning for what later would become the Beckman Institute began in 1983 with a meeting between Chancellor John Cribbet and faculty members Ned Goldwasser, Mort Weir, and Theodore L. Brown (who would become the institute's first director in 1987) to discuss the possibility of acquiring private funds for interdisciplinary research at the university. By 1984, faculty and administrators were hard at work drafting and redrafting proposals to send to potential donors. A year later the institute transitioned from a paper concept into bricks and mortar after Arnold and Mabel Beckman agreed to donate $40 million to launch the project. Beckman, the son of a blacksmith from Cullom, Illinois, had earned his undergraduate and master's degrees in Urbana-Champaign before going on to

Theodore Brown at the Beckman Institute topping-off ceremony

a remarkable career as a research scientist and inventor. The Beckmans' sponsorship of the new institute represented the largest philanthropic gift ever given to a public university at that time. (It was later supplemented by a $10 million grant from the state of Illinois.) Chancellor Cribbet extolled the significance of this gift at a university senate meeting in October 1985: "The first weekend of October 1985 will surely go down in history as one of the most remarkable weekends in the history of the University of Illinois, particularly at this campus. [ . . . ] I think it is an Institute that is being announced at the right time and in the right fields."[1]

Designing programs for the new institute fell to Professors Brown (chemistry) and Goldwasser (physics), as well as Bill Greenough and Morton Weir (psychology), Karl Hess and Greg Stillman (electrical and computer engineering), and an array of university administrators, including officials of the University Foundation, President Stanley Ikenberry, Chancellor Thomas Everhart, and Vice Chancellor Sarah Wasserman. This group discussed ideas for the institute in extensive conversations with the Beckmans. The planning for the new Beckman Institute was so exciting that faculty and staff began moving into the new building as soon as spaces became ready for occupancy. Researchers began taking up residence in 1987, even though the formal opening of the institute would not occur until 1989.

Planning for the new institute focused on the question of how to make interdisciplinarity *possible*, in spite of its many obstacles. The faculty and administration involved thought long and hard about what would be required—architecturally, intellectually, and administratively—to enable new and difficult forms of research that crossed disciplinary boundaries. Many of the questions they would have to address were raised in April 1982 at a "Graduate Faculty Seminar on Interdisciplinary Research." The symposium focused on several compelling questions: "What do we mean by interdisciplinary research?" "To what extent do the tensions between different disciplines contribute to or inhibit interdisciplinary research?" "What are the essential conditions for interdisciplinary research? Do they exist at the UIUC?" "Does the strong departmental emphasis on this campus inhibit interdisciplinary research?" "Is there a need for new mechanisms to stimulate cross-disciplinary cooperation?"[2]

> "At its heart, the Institute was to be 'a single site' that could enable sustained and meaningful collaboration between scientists previously kept apart by discipline and geography."

Because interdisciplinary research has become so dominant in the American academy, these questions are seldom asked explicitly anymore. But in the 1980s they were difficult questions, and their solutions were far from obvious. The Beckman Institute was the University of Illinois's answer. It embodied a vision of the kind of space and place that would enable interdisciplinary work. It represented a philosophy of scientific research and development in the twentieth century. And it was made possible by an administrative infrastructure that differed significantly from those that governed traditional university departments.

## Building the Beckman

In proposing the Beckman Institute, faculty and administrators emphasized that the University of Illinois would be an ideal place for an interdisciplinary institute in part because a number of interdisciplinary initiatives were already underway there. In the early 1980s the university had, among other things, a Center for Supercomputing, a Microelectronics Center, a campus-wide Biophysics program, and a Neural and Behavioral Biology graduate training program, all of which transcended traditional disciplinary boundaries. Money was coming in from the Department of Energy (DOE), the National Science Foundation (NSF), the National Institutes of Health (NIH) to fund these new collaborative forms of research at the university. However, these initiatives did not have viable homes—existing facilities in academic departments and buildings could not accommodate the growing range of research projects, and there was a campus-wide need for significant "modernization and renovation."

Research in modern technical fields often requires dedicated facilities and specialized equipment. Many scientists depend on the spaces they inhabit and the access they have to human, technological, and experimental resources. The founders of the Beckman Institute argued that scientific interdisciplinarity could never work when the researchers involved "are dispersed around the campus in several different departments, often in buildings that are far apart."[3] The Beckman Institute was put forward both as a solution to the existing facilities problem and as a condition of possibility for future development in interdisciplinary research at the university. At its heart, the institute was to be a "single site" that could enable sustained and meaningful collaboration between scientists previously kept apart by discipline and geography.

What kind of space would this institute be? Well, for one thing, it would be large—so large that part of the planning involved the acquisition of privately owned land in the vicinity of the northern campus. When it was completed, the building, at 405 North Mathews Avenue, contained 313,000 square feet of space for researchers.

Every square foot was designed to embody a philosophy of interdisciplinary research. "The facility must be more than merely a collection of offices, laboratories, and support facilities," Theodore Brown wrote in 1984. "We have planned the Institute to foster lifelong, continuing learning and engender the kinds of day-to-day interactions that lead to fruitful collaborative research, through the inclusion of common areas, food service facilities, and seminar and conference rooms." He and his colleagues planned for all of this in addition to auditoriums, libraries, and reading rooms.[4] The founders recognized that meaningful interdisciplinary engagement would be as likely to emerge over sandwiches as in an office or classroom. They imagined it would grow out of formal but also informal encounters, and they sought to maximize the possibilities for both in the new space.

The building was also designed to be *dynamic*. The institute was not supposed to enshrine any particular interdisciplinary configuration or set of research questions. Brown and his colleagues imagined that the building would change as its inhabitants, their research agendas, and their needs changed. In consultation with Smith, Hinchman, and Grylls (SH&G)—the architectural firm chosen in 1985 to actualize their vision—the planning group imagined everything from movable walls to modular furniture that could be rearranged to accommodate new forms of scientific work being pursued within. They also placed laboratory space in one wing and office space in another so that even those researchers who occupied different labs could have offices close to one another. All of these choices were meant to differentiate the institute from traditional department and laboratory infrastructure that tended to compartmentalize and isolate faculty within their disciplinary paradigms.

The aesthetic of the building—instantly perceptible to anyone entering its soaring atrium—is one of openness and connectivity. The massive skylights and windows enveloping this welcoming space open onto numerous common areas and reveal several bridges connecting the different wings of the building. The bridges symbolically reinforce the institute's commitment to traversing existing disciplinary, intellectual, and institutional boundaries.

Beckman Institute under construction

## Intellectual Framework

The planning group's proposals went far beyond issues related to the physical design of the new institute. Brown and company also had to develop a *conceptual* framework and a research philosophy that would make future interdisciplinary work possible. As academics are still learning today, you can't just put researchers from different back-

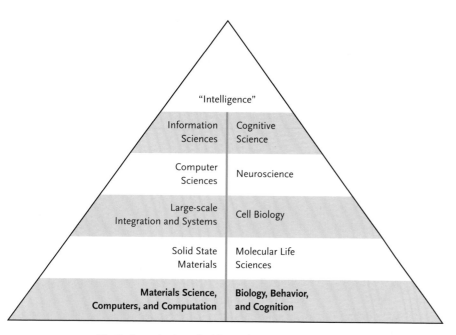

"Intelligence"

| Information Sciences | Cognitive Science |
| Computer Sciences | Neuroscience |
| Large-scale Integration and Systems | Cell Biology |
| Solid State Materials | Molecular Life Sciences |
| **Materials Science, Computers, and Computation** | **Biology, Behavior, and Cognition** |

The Beckman Institute for Advanced Science and Technology

The intellectual blueprint for collaboration at the Beckman Institute. Reprinted with permission from the University of Illinois Press

grounds into a shared space and expect that collaboration and understanding will emerge. Although they sought to traverse boundaries and create new research possibilities, the planning faculty also recognized that there would have to be constraints and guiding infrastructure. Not all disciplines could be included. Not all questions could be asked. As Brown put it, "We must be careful that it [the mandate of the institute] not be defined so broadly as to lack of proper focus."[5]

In 1983 and 1984 the planning group considered numerous proposals for research areas that would guide the institute's intellectual focus, ranging from global warming and public health to management and manufacturing. But ultimately they decided that, based on the perceived existing strengths of the university and maximal possibilities for the future, the institute would be composed of two centers: a Center for Biology, Behavior, and Cognition, and a Center for Materials Science, Computers, and Computation. In one sense, these centers could not be more different—the former constituted by the life sciences and the study of natural and organic phenomena, the latter

by the physical sciences, engineering, and inorganic material. But the faculty convened to adjudicate the issue thought they had two important things in common. They believed the two research areas shared a profound and parallel hierarchy, at the bottom of which was the study of microscopic things—atoms and molecules—and at the top of which was the study of high-level phenomena like information processing and cognition.

Moreover, the planning committee also believed that in spite of their very different objects of interest, research in these two centers could be directed toward a single subject: "*Intelligence*" (see figure 1). What is intelligence? How is it made manifest in living things? How might it be made manifest artificially in computers or other materials? No discipline, equipped with its methods and practitioners alone, could adjudicate these questions.

Here was the intellectual framework through which the Beckman Institute was first imagined: "There is a remarkable parallelism in the organizations of the two centers, a parallelism that suggests the possibilities for interdisciplinary interactions between the two centers as well as within each center. Indeed, many researchers would be involved in the work of both centers, particularly in the areas of artificial intelligence and cognitive sciences; and many would work actively in the boundaries between areas within a center, for example, between quantitative biology and neuroscience."[6] The program was open and interdisciplinary enough to admit scientists from very diverse fields engaged in various kinds of research, from the microscopic scale to the macroscopic. It was simultaneously constrained by a set of questions focused around "intelligence." Crucially, no definition of intelligence was offered—that was part of what was at stake in the research program. Instead, that concept was used to mobilize a heterogeneous community in a shared intellectual project that would engage what were seen as important and basic research questions.

On the ground, research at the Beckman Institute is and always has been far more complicated than the diagram in Figure 1 would suggest. In the 2014–15 academic year, for example, the institute undertook projects as diverse and seemingly unrelated as researching sexual harassment during scientific field studies to the development of an electronic heart membrane that could replace pacemakers. But the development of an overarching conceptual framework was nonetheless a crucial element in the realization of an interdisciplinary institute. It offered a mechanism for selecting between research proposals submitted to the Beckman Institute and a founding charter to guide future planning. It offered a vocabulary for explaining to faculty, the Beckmans, the public, and the government what the institute was, what it was *for*, and how it would work. Thanks to the planning group's efforts, the institute came with ready-made and built-in possibilities for interdisciplinary collaboration. This framework, however much it was realized on the ground, was itself an intellectual innovation and a model for other interdisciplinary institutions of this kind.

Today the institute is organized around four "research themes" that reflect both the original vision for the institute and the many developments that have taken place since its founding: biological intelligence, human-computer intelligent interaction, integrative imaging, and molecular and electronic nanostructures. These themes still aim to cut across the physical sciences, life sciences, and engineering and to investigate phenomena at vastly different sites and scales. Although the intellectual framework has changed, and there remains significant space for interpretation within and between major "research themes," the institute remains faithful to its founding intellectual innovation. It is still structured around a set of unifying questions. In the absence of more traditional academic infrastructure, like departments and schools, intellectual organization offers coherence and direction to the institute. After all, there can be no innovation without constraints. The Beckman Institute's example teaches that in order to make interdisciplinarity work, it is essential to define a vision of research that can accommodate a specific community of vastly different researchers and provide motivation and mechanisms for meaningful communication and collaboration between them.

> "Thanks to the planning group's efforts, the institute came with ready-made and built-in possibilities for interdisciplinary collaboration."

The Beckman Institute has been enabling groundbreaking work across the sciences since its doors opened in 1989. But it was neither obvious nor certain when the idea for the institute was first proposed that a center for interdisciplinary scientific research could be made operational. The degree to which the center succeeded in fostering interdisciplinary research that would have been a struggle in other more traditional settings was a function of the imagination and foresight of the faculty and administrators who asked and answered difficult questions before they secured funding for the new enterprise or broke ground for the building. The planners struggled to define what interdisciplinary research would *be* at Illinois and what exactly would be needed—in terms of policies, architecture, ideas, and institutional support—to realize that vision. The center was, of course, made possible by Arnold and Mabel Beckman's generous gift, but its success as a globally celebrated center for innovation was equally dependent on the fact that the Beckmans imposed no agenda or constraints on what kind of research would be undertaken there. They engaged in discussions with the campus planning team, but in the end they trusted the vision that emerged from conversations among the experts on campus. Because the Beckman Institute was among the earliest efforts in the country to bring interdisciplinary scientific institutes to university campuses and to move beyond government, military, and industry-sponsored research centers, the story of its planning and construction constitutes a model for others to study and follow.

The questions faculty and administration asked in planning the Beckman Institute cut to the heart of twentieth-century science and its increasingly technological, large-scale, and interdisciplinary character. Their answers—in the form of architectural design, intellectual framing, policy development, and organizational structure—created a unique interdisciplinary space that challenged—and changed—many traditional features of the university.

## Notes

1. "Minutes, Urbana-Champaign Senate Meeting, October 14, 1985: Chancellor's Remarks," Stanley Ikenberry Papers, record series 2/14/1, box 74, University of Illinois Archives.

2. "Questions for Discussion, Graduate Faculty Seminar on Interdisciplinary Research, April 22, 1982," Dean's Office Papers, record series 7/1/7, box 11, University of Illinois Archives.

3. "Proposal Draft 8/27/84," Theodore L. Brown Papers, record series 15/5/33, box 5, University of Illinois Archives, p. 2.

4. "A Summary Supplement to a Proposal from the University of Illinois at Urbana-Champaign," ca. 1984, Theodore L. Brown Papers, record series 15/5/33, box 5, University of Illinois Archives, p. 22.

5. "Historical Development and Current Status of the Arnold O. and Mabel M. Beckman Institute for Advanced Science and Technology," 1984, Theodore L. Brown Papers, record series 15/5/33, box 5, University of Illinois Archives, p. 2.

6. "Summary Supplement," ca. 1984, Theodore L. Brown Papers, p. 7.

## Sources

For a history of American science in the postwar era see Peter Galison and Bruce Hevly, eds., *Big Science: The Growth of Large-scale Research* (Stanford, Calif.: Stanford University Press, 1992). For a comprehensive, firsthand history of the Beckman Institute see Theodore L. Brown, *Bridging Divides: The Origins of the Beckman Institute at Illinois* (Urbana: University of Illinois Press, 2009), with forewords by Stanley Ikenberry and Richard Herman. Several works explore the life, career, and philanthropy of Arnold O. Beckman, including Arnold Thackray and Minor Myers Jr. *Arnold O. Beckman: One Hundred Years of Excellence*, Chemical Heritage Foundation Series in Innovation and Entrepreneurship (Philadelphia: Chemical Heritage Foundation, 2000), and National Research Council, ed., *Instrumentation for a Better Tomorrow: Proceedings of a Symposium in Honor of Arnold Beckman* (Washington, D.C.: National Academies Press, 2006). Archival materials concerning the founding of the Beckman Institute in the University of Illinois Archives include Beckman Institute Publications, 1984–, record series 7/22/801; Building and Statue Dedication Programs, record series 2/0/808; President Stanley O. Ikenberry, General Correspondence, 1979–2000, record series 2/1/4/1; Graduate College Dean's Office Administrative Subject File, 1932–2005, record series 7/1/7; Facilities and Services Project Drawings and Plans, 1980, record series 37/2/11; Theodore L. Brown Papers, 1951–96, record series 15/5/44. Photographs of the Beckman Institute are located in Publications Office Records, Stock Publicity Photographs, 1985–2002, record series 39/4/10, and subject files for several departments contain materials related to the Beckman Institute, including original proposals for major centers: Physics, record series 11/10/1; Bioengineering, record series 11/16/1; Chemistry, record series 15/5/1; National Center for Supercomputing Applications Subject File, 1978–2000, record series 7/5/1.

# Nevada Street

## A Center for the Study of Race and Ethnicity

*Frederick E. Hoxie and Michael Hughes*

There is one block on Nevada Street—between Goodwin Street and Mathews Street—that is the center of activity for four academic units devoted to the history, experience, and future of the United States' four major racial minorities: the African American Studies Department, the Department of Asian American Studies, the Latina/Latino Studies Department (actually located just behind the Department of Asian American Studies on Oregon Street), and the American Indian Studies Program. Nevada Street is also home to La Casa Cultura Latina, the Asian American Cultural Center, and Native American House, administered by the Office of Inclusion and Intercultural Relations. Situated on a majority-white campus, the academic programs clustered along Nevada Street foster research that explores the racial, class, and gendered structures of power in the United States by focusing primarily on the histories, experiences, and world views of nonwhite peoples. While the programs each retain a distinctive identity, scholars associated with them work to understand a series of related questions. Among these are what it means to belong or to possess citizenship in a nation that was structured in an age of white supremacy. They also explore the meaning of diaspora in the experiences of all four groups, as well as issues of belonging, transnational identity, group autonomy, educational opportunity, poverty, and social conditions.

Each of these programs arose out a unique set of circumstances, but they all followed a common trajectory, marked by phases of organization, founding, and consolidation. They began when nonwhite students in each group who had experienced institutional marginalization and instances of racial hostility began to call for academic and cultural centers that would give them both visibility on campus and opportunities to learn more about their heritage. In each instance as well, university administrators responded by gradually facilitating the institutionalization of cultural centers and studies programs. After years of campaigning by students and faculty, these units gained enough legitimacy in the eyes of the institution to become academic programs, to hire faculty, and to chart a course as integral members of the campus community.

La Casa. Photo courtesy of the University of Illinois Archives/UIHistories and Kalev Leetaru.

Asian American Studies and Cultural Center. Photo courtesy of the University of Illinois Archives/ UIHistories and Kalev Leetaru.

Before 1968 the University of Illinois was almost entirely a white campus. Black students accounted for approximately 1 percent of the student population, and the other minority groups were barely represented at all. In 1967 the Black Student Association (BSA) emerged as an autonomous organization, arguing that blackness lay at the center of their political consciousness. Influenced by the race riots and segregation occurring in Chicago and nationally, the BSA sought equality through a program of black self-determination and empowerment rather than through the pursuit of a conventional civil rights agenda. The BSA was deeply engaged in the university's 1968 Special Equal Opportunities Program, commonly called "Project 500," and energized by its outcome. (For more on Project 500 see chapter 1.16.)

In the wake of Project 500's tumultuous launch, the BSA demanded that the university hire more black professors, establish a black cultural center, and organize an African American studies program. In early 1969 Chancellor Jack Peltason formed the Faculty-Student Commission on Afro-American Life and Culture to oversee the development of a cultural center, an academic program, and related student service programs. The Afro-American Cultural Program was established that same year to oversee black cultural activities on campus. The cultural center hosted writers' workshops for prose and poetry, a dance program, and workshops in which students discussed gender roles in black communities.

In 1974 the African American Studies and Research Program was organized within the College of Liberal Arts and Sciences. This program quickly developed courses focused on the experiences of people of African descent in the United States and the Western Hemisphere. These academic offerings also proliferated to embrace faculty members from across the social sciences and humanities as well as experts in fine arts, education, journalism, and law. The university approved an interdisciplinary minor in African American Studies in 1988.

In recent years the African American Studies and Research Program has experienced tremendous growth. Renamed the Department of African American Studies in 2008, the unit now boasts a core faculty of twelve and an affiliated group of more than thirty others who link the department to a number of other campus units, including History, Anthropology, Linguistics, and Gender and Women's Studies. Indicative of these cross-departmental ties, the department now grants the Ida B. Wells-Barnett Certificate in Black Women and Gender Studies to students who complete coursework that integrates gender into their study of the lives of black women. Meanwhile, the African American Culture Center was renamed the Bruce D. Nesbitt African American Cultural Center (BNAACC) in 2004 in recognition of the contributions of the former director. Perhaps not the hotbed of student political activity it was in the early 1970s, the BNAACC continues to hold cultural events throughout the year, a graduation ceremony, programs and workshops that reach across the campus and into the local community.

Almost immediately following the creation of the African American Studies and Research and Cultural Centers, La Colectiva, a new Latino student organization, began a campaign to establish a place of its own. The formation of La Colectiva in the early 1970s occurred when Illinois students and their allies overcame many of the same problems the BSA had encountered only a few years earlier. La Casa sought to expand the definition of "minority" to include bilingual students who descended from Latino families who were either citizens in the United States or immigrants from Latin America. Like the BSA, Colectiva brought attention to the severe underrepresentation of Latino students and faculty on campus and demanded that the university develop a recruitment initiative to remedy the situation.

La Casa Cultura Latina opened its doors in 1974 and set out to provide a home for Latino students and to spread awareness of Latino cultures across the campus. Despite this victory, however, student morale remained low. Hampered by limited budgets, La Casa was forced to rely on one overworked doctoral student as its sole administrator—and he soon resigned in despair. At the same time, the part-time recruiter working in the admissions area found it impossible to reverse a decades-long pattern of underrepresentation. Renewed student activism seemed to be the only tactic that would produce results. Additional student protests produced a full-time director for La Casa (as well as additional support staff) and eventually a recognition among campus leaders that the house provided an important space to promote and encourage Latino cultural expressions. Students published a newsletter, *La Carta Informativa*, which addressed the local, national, and global concerns of Latino students, and a magazine, *Profile*, which featured poetry and prose of these students.

By the end of the 1980s, with the Program in African American Studies established, Latino students began to imagine a similar program. In April 1992, after several rounds of protest and negotiations, a group of these students staged a sit-in at the Office of Minority Affairs, in which they demanded an enhancement of the programming at La Casa, the formation of a representative student group to address Latino concerns, and the establishment of a Latino Studies Program. The board of trustees soon approved the establishment of a Latino Studies Program, with Rafael Nunez-Cedeno, a professor of Spanish originally from the Dominican Republic, serving as the acting director. Over the next two decades, the program expanded its course offerings, developed an undergraduate minor (1997), lobbied intensively for the hiring of Latino faculty, and ultimately proposed reconstituting itself as the Department of Latina/Latino Studies (LLS), which the university officially approved in 2010. The department is now home to

Native American House and American Indian Studies building. Photo courtesy of the University of Illinois Archives/ UIHistories and Kalev Leetaru.

eleven core faculty and twelve additional professors who are affiliated with both LLS and a variety of campus programs, including Communication, Curriculum and Instruction, Art and Design, Media and Cinema Studies, Spanish and Portuguese, and History.

Both LLS and La Casa mount an array of academic and general interest programs. LLS hosts a postdoctoral fellows program and organizes symposia that draw together faculty and students at Illinois and other institutions to discuss recent developments in the field. La Casa maintains a steady stream of cultural programming and sponsors recruitment events, student orientation programs, and support activities such as house dinners, lectures, and service projects that provide support for Spanish-speaking immigrant families in the Urbana-Champaign community.

In the years prior to 1980, Asian and Asian American students had organized a number of student associations based on national origin. In 1985, however, a new organization came on the scene. The appearance of the Asian American Association signaled the development of a distinctly Asian American political identity and consciousness on campus. In the following year the Asian Pacific Coalition to Combat Oppression, Racism, and Discrimination was formed; it promoted the establishment of an Asian American cultural house. Like African American and Latino students, Asian students argued for a place on campus where their concerns could be central and where they would have the ability to shape programming. As had been the case with the other groups, Asian student activists in the 1990s cited instances of individual and institutional bias and racism on campus and called for the creation of an Asian American Cultural Center. That center opened its doors in 2005 and today provides support to Asian American students by offering walk-in services, a student orientation program (Asiantation), art exhibits, brownbag lectures that feature work by students and visitors, book clubs, and programming every April for Asian American and Pacific Islander Heritage Month.

While seeking the establishment of a cultural center, Asian American student activists also called for the establishment of an academic program. Courses in Asian American studies appeared in the early 1990s, but it was not until 1997 that the Asian American Studies Committee was organized and charged with creating an academic program. In 2002 the board of trustees approved the Asian American Studies Program to offer an interdisciplinary undergraduate minor in which students learn about the histories, contributions, and experiences of Asian immigrants in the United States. The program began to award graduate minors in 2009; in 2012 the Asian American Studies Program was reconstituted as the Department of Asian American Studies. Operating on a model similar to the African American program and LLS, Asian American Studies is now home to ten core and six affiliated faculty members, the latter maintaining ties to Social Work, History, Gender and Women's Studies, Media and Cinema Studies, Political Science, and Anthropology.

The fourth program focusing on an American racial minority emerged in the immediate aftermath of the creation of Asian American Studies. Native American Studies programs had emerged on many campuses in the United States during the "Red Power" era of the 1970s, but there was little movement to create such a program at Illinois until late in the 1980s, when Native American students on campus lodged many of the demands made by earlier

groups: the creation of a cultural center, an academic program, and a campus effort to recruit and retain Native American students. The concerns of indigenous students assumed additional meaning on the Illinois campus because of the institution's public commitment to its mascot, Chief Illiniwek. Native American students sought to move the university away from the atmosphere that had created this caricature by exposing students to cultural activities and to academic experiences that would teach them about native people and their distinctive experience in North America. This pressure finally bore fruit in 2002 when the university established an indigenous-oriented cultural center, Native American House. In its new home next door to the Asian American Studies Program and Cultural Center, and across the street from La Casa and the African American Studies Department, Native American House quickly began to support programs for Native American students (orientation, scholarship advice, mentoring programs, graduation ceremonies) as well as symposia, "Chat and Chew" lunchtime discussions, and Native American Heritage Month programs.

An academic program in American Indian Studies (AIS) quickly followed. In 2003 the Committee on Native American Programs began work to develop a curriculum in the field, and the following year the university appointed its first tenure-track faculty member in AIS. The board of trustees approved of the American Indian Studies program in 2005, and the program began offering an undergraduate minor in 2008 and a graduate minor in 2009. The program is currently planning for the transition to departmental status.

In its relatively short life, the American Indian Studies Program has hosted a number of events that have showcased innovative thinking in the emerging field of indigenous studies. In 2006 leading indigenous thinkers came to campus for the "Native Feminists: Without Apology" conference, in which indigenous feminist theorists spoke on how structures of race and gender interlock to confine native women's lives. Between the 2009 and 2011 academic years, the program, in conjunction with the Center of Advanced Study, hosted the Sovereignty and Autonomy in the Western Hemisphere initiative. This project brought speakers to Illinois and engaged students and faculty from across campus units together to consider what the concepts of sovereignty and autonomy meant for both indigenous peoples and for nation-states across the Western Hemisphere. Unfortunately, the controversy triggered in 2014 by the board of trustees decision not to confirm the hiring of a tenured faculty member, Steven Salaita, in AIS disrupted the program's activities and plans. Five of six core faculty members left the unit, and an international boycott temporarily ended most academic activities involving off-campus scholars, thus putting the future of the program in doubt. The elements that produced all of the Nevada Street programs, however—student activism, faculty support, and educational and social need—remain in place, and an eventual restoration of AIS as an academic unit on campus remains an achievable goal.

The Nevada Street units reveal that innovation at Illinois is not inevitable but that it often occurs through the efforts of dedicated students and faculty. The related histories of these programs also suggest that *where* something occurs is also important. The accident of geography—that these programs have pursued broadly similar goals in a setting where their students and staffs see and speak to one another on almost a daily basis—has clearly accelerated their rise and progress. Student activists have recognized that despite different perspectives, they have shared a common commitment to making the university a better, more inclusive place for themselves and others. Faculty members have also welcomed the idea that the units' academic programs not only further understanding of a single group, but they also teach campus community members—regardless of their background—about the experiences of peoples whose individuality and complexity is often denied by stereotypes and conventional ways of thinking.

The synergy and mutually reinforcing success of the Nevada Street units demonstrate that, despite their separate histories of protest and struggle, significant innovation in a difficult and controversial arena of learning can arise from a combination of outspoken students who are unafraid to bring racial bias and injustice to the attention of the public, a dynamic and collaborative relationship between students and faculty committed to developing academic and cultural programming, and campus leaders who recognize the power and persuasiveness of these efforts and then encourage and reward them. The lively community of programs now filling this quiet block in Urbana is vivid testimony to the efforts of all partners in that effort.

## Sources

The University Archives holds a number of sources for the history of the four programs/departments and cultural centers discussed in this essay. These include record series (RS) 15/42/805 for newsletters published by the Afro-American Studies and Research Program, RS 15/42/5 for the program and department in African American studies, RS 41/64/40 for La Casa Cultura Latina, RS 41/12/18 for the Bruce Nesbitt Center, and RS 41/64/852 for the Asian American Cultural Center. Joy Williamson's *Black Power on Campus*, cited in this volume's bibliography, discusses founding of the Afro-American Studies and Research Program and the African American Cultural Center. For information about the founding of these academic programs, the University of Illinois Senate has digitized their agendas and minutes, available at http://www.senate.illinois.edu. Readers are encouraged to visit the websites of these departments, programs, and cultural centers for more information on recent department functions.

# SNAPSHOTS OF UNIVERSITY HISTORY

## 1867–1890

### PRESIDENTS

John Milton Gregory (1867–1880)

Selim Hobart Peabody (1880–1891)

John Milton Gregory

Selim Hobart Peabody

## EVENTS

### Morrill Act Passes (1862)

Responding to a national call for educational reform (in which Jacksonville's Jonathan Turner was a leading voice), Congress approved a law that would subsidize the creation of public universities with grants of federal land in the West. Urbana mayor Clark Griggs led the campaign to locate Illinois's new school in his town rather than in Jacksonville, Normal, or Bloomington. Governor Richard Oglesby signed the law creating Illinois Industrial University in Urbana on February 28, 1867.

Women studying (1878)

### Morrow Plots Established (1876)

Professor George Morrow established these experimental farm plots to test the sustainability of prairie soils. Experiments today are conducted in three of the original ten plots, one of which has been planted continuously with corn since 1876.

Jonathan Turner

### Women Admitted (1870)

While women attended lectures from the founding of the university, they were not admitted as students until 1870. That fall, twenty-four women matriculated at Illinois, composing approximately 10 percent of the student body.

These plots are older than most of us! (1913)

### First Degrees Granted (1878)

Because the university's founding trustees wanted to separate themselves from older institutions in the East, they prohibited the granting of formal degrees, preferring to issue certificates to students who completed coursework. Students and alumni petitioned for a change in this practice, and after consulting leaders of other land-grant institutions, the university trustees approved their request. Campus leaders specified the coursework required to earn undergraduate and graduate degrees.

### Name Changed to University of Illinois (1885)

In another move away from its founding intention to build an institution unlike others, the board of trustees bowed to the desires of faculty and students and accepted their demand for a broad, comprehensive curriculum. As a consequence of this shift, the trustees changed the school's name to the University of Illinois.

### Hatch Act Passes (1887)

The provisions of the Hatch Act granted federal funds to support the creation of experimental farms at universities that sponsored research in the crop sciences. By 1910, the College of Agriculture used this law to establish extension programs that brought recent advances in agricultural technology to thousands of farmers.

Illinois farmers inspecting Illinois Experiment Field in 1903

---

## 1890—1920

### PRESIDENTS

Thomas Jonathan Burrill (1891–1894)

Andrew Sloan Draper (1894–1904)

Edmund Janes James (1904–1920)

Thomas Jonathan Burrill

Edmund Janes James

# EVENTS

### UIUC Exhibits at Columbian Exposition (1893)

The University of Illinois organized an exhibit at the 1893 Columbian Exposition in Chicago to advertise the innovations being introduced to farmers by its Agricultural Experiment Stations.

Graduate Library Students in Study Hall circa 1898

### Graduate School Created (1893)

The creation of a university graduate school enabled departments to offer fellowships to advanced students in exchange for their service as teachers. Limited to one class per day, these graduate students were also expected "to make research a part of his daily life" and to contribute "to the world's knowledge."

### Library School Transferred to UIUC (1897)

Pioneer librarian Katharine Sharp first established a library school at the Armour Institute in Chicago. In 1897, at the invitation of President Andrew Draper, Sharp transferred her program to the University of Illinois, where she became University Librarian and head of the Illinois State Library School.

### First Chinese Students Arrive (1909)

Seeking to transform Illinois into a more worldly institution, President Edmund James proposed Illinois as a school to host Chinese students who would be educated in the United States as part of the Chinese government's indemnification of the West for damages sustained during the Boxer Rebellion. The first students from China arrived to Illinois in 1909. They have been a continuous presence since then; today they make up approximately 12 percent of the student population.

Chinese Students' Club

### President Taft Visits Campus (1911)

President William Taft made the first appearance by a sitting United States president to the University of Illinois campus in 1911. Taft reviewed the student cadets and delivered a short address in Champaign. President James promoted the cadets' performance as part of his effort to secure federal funds for a facility for military education.

Cadets in field south of the Armory—1916

Taft inspects cadets

### Armory Completed (1914)

Construction on the distinctive structure, characterized by ninety-eight-foot-high ceilings standing without center supports, began in 1912. Dedicated in 1914 before a crowd of more than fifteen thousand, the structure soon added office spaces and classrooms. Today the Armory also houses ROTC programs, the program in Arms Control, Disarmament, and International Security, and the Center for Innovation in Teaching and Learning.

### University Press Established (1918)

The University of Illinois Press's first publications were a history of the first fifty years of the University of Illinois and a study of Abraham Lincoln. It is now one of the largest university presses in the United States and is recognized as a leading publisher in the fields of communications, musicology, labor history, African American studies, and gender and women's studies.

University Print Shop (1919)

## PRESIDENTS

David Kinley (1920–1930)

Harry Woodburn Chase (1930–1933)

Arthur Hill Daniels (1933–1934)

Arthur Cutts Willard (1934–1946)

George Stoddard (1946–1953)

David Kinley          Arthur Cutts Willard

## EVENTS

### Hillel Foundation Established (1923)

Rabbi Benjamin Frankel spearheaded the founding of Hillel to promote opportunities for students to reconcile the demands of religion, academic study, and social life in modern America. The organization quickly expanded to other campuses and is now the largest Jewish student organization in the United States.

### Memorial Stadium Dedicated (1924)

At the stadium's dedication, Trustee William Noble announced that the new facility would "memorialize those who sacrificed their lives in World War I for the 'Illinois spirit,' a spirit that exemplifies fair play, honest work, a respect for the rights of others, and an undying devotion to justice and truth."

President Kinley speaks at Memorial Stadium dedication service

## Main Library Dedicated (1929)

When Edmund James announced his aim to expand the library, Library Dean Phinneas Windsor co-designed a building that could facilitate a rapidly growing collection of books that would enrich students for generations to come.

Main Library construction

## Alma Mater Dedicated (1929)

Sculpted by Lorado Taft, the Alma Mater was dedicated on June 11, 1929. At the dedication, university president David Kinley praised the statue for the collaboration, good feelings, and posterity it memorialized.

Alma Mater dedication with Lorado Taft and David Kinley

## Illini Union Building Dedicated (1941)

At its dedication in 1941, Illinois governor Dwight Green celebrated the Illini Union as a place that "can be of real service to the citizens of the state of Illinois," where social, intellectual, and professional contacts can be made between students and faculty.

Illini Union Building 1941

## University Airport Opened (1945)

More than twenty thousand spectators watched dozens of World War II veterans fly aircraft at the opening of the University Airport in 1945. Willard Airport has hosted student aviation clubs, commercial flights (beginning in 1954), and, until 2014, the University of Illinois Institute of Aviation.

## University Acquires Allerton (1946)

Robert Allerton, son of a Chicago banking and stockyard tycoon, styled his Monticello house on English Georgian manors. Allerton donated the house and its grounds to the University of Illinois in 1946. Today, it is open to the public for recreation and special events.

Flying Club inspecting homemade plane

Art students on Allerton's front lawn

## PRESIDENTS

Lloyd Morey (1954–1955)

David Dodds Henry (1956–1971)

John E. Corbally (1971–1979)

## CHANCELLORS

Jack Peltason (1967–1977)

Morton Weir (1977)

William Gerberding (1978–1979)

John Cribbet (1979–1984)

David Dodds Henry

Jack Peltason. Photo courtesy of the University of Illinois Archives and the *News-Gazette*.

## EVENTS

### Howard Bowen Resigns as Dean of College of Commerce (1950)

Dean of the College of Commerce Howard Bowen resigned in 1950 after incurring the wrath of the faculty's conservative members. Bowen had attempted to eliminate old departmental customs by recruiting young staff members. His opponents sought to discredit Bowen by claiming his espousal of Keynesian economists indicated that he was too liberal for the university. Bowen went on to serve as president of the University of Iowa and to receive an honorary degree from Illinois in 1975.

### ILLIAC I Completed (1952)

Completed in 1952, faculty at the university used the ILLIAC I, a five-ton computer, to develop the first electronic musical composition, the binary division used in microprocessors today, and PLATO, the first computer program that assisted in academic instruction.

Ralph Meagher and the ILLIAC

### George Stoddard Fired (1953)

The resignation of Howard Bowen in 1950 presaged the erosion of trustee confidence in President Stoddard. Originally appointed to revive the university, Stoddard sustained criticism for his attempts to engage the university with national movements, his religious and political liberalism, and his aggressive leadership style.

No-Vote against Stoddard. Photo courtesy of the University of Illinois Archives and the *News-Gazette*.

### Bardeen Wins His First Nobel Prize (1956)

In 1956, Bardeen and colleagues Walter Brattain and William Shockley were awarded the prize (in physics) for building the first point-contact transistor. Their design has since found broad application in myriad electronic devices, including televisions, radios, computers, calculators, and many more.

John Bardeen

## JFK Visits Campus (1960)

John F. Kennedy became the first presidential candidate from a major party to speak at the University of Illinois. Ten thousand students filled the quad to listen to Kennedy, who criticized Republicans for ignoring upheavals in Latin America and decolonization in Africa.

JFK's motorcade passes through Champaign.
Photo courtesy of C. F. Marley.

## Assembly Hall Completed (1963)

The University of Illinois constructed Assembly Hall to accommodate a rapidly expanding student body. Spacious enough to contain a single class of students, Assembly Hall was the largest edge-supported structure in the world when it was dedicated in 1963.

Carl Sandburg at Assembly Hall dedication

### AAUP Censures UIUC (1963)

The American Association of University Professors censured the University of Illinois for firing Leo Koch without a hearing, after the psychology professor indicated in the *Daily Illini* that he endorsed consensual sex outside of marriage. The AAUP lifted the censure in 1966 after the University clarified its tenure policy.

Leo Koch

### Krannert Center Hosts Opening Festival (1969)

Allen S. Weller, dean of the College of Fine and Applied Arts, led initiatives that developed the Krannert Art Museum, the Krannert Center for the Performing Arts, and the Festival of Contemporary Arts.

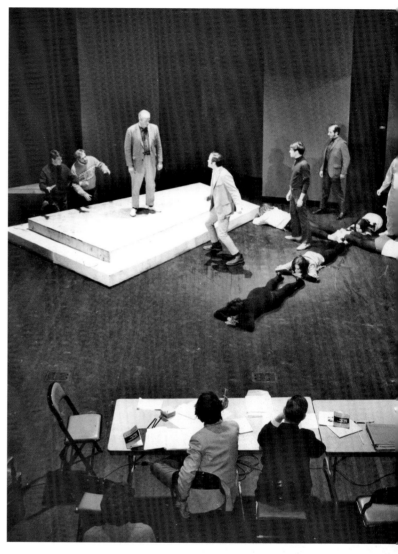

John Burrell observing a production of *Murder in the Cathedral*

### Project 500 Created (1968)

After the assassination of Martin Luther King Jr., the University of Illinois created the Special Educational Opportunities Program (SEOP), or Project 500, to increase accessibility for disadvantaged high-school graduates, primarily African Americans. Disputes over housing and financial aid (together with what many felt was indifference from administrators) prompted the students to announce a sit-in at the Illini Union; police arrested 248 of them.

### ILLIAC IV Protests (1970)

Proposals for the construction on campus of a new super-computer, ILLIAC IV, became the focus of protests after students learned that the project would be managed by a new unit of the Computer Science Department, to be funded by the Department of Defense. Fearing the machine could not be installed safely on campus, DoD officials moved ILLIAC IV to NASA in 1970.

### Bardeen Wins His Second Nobel Prize (1972)

John Bardeen won the prize again with Leon Cooper and Bob Schrieffer, who together developed the theory of superconductivity, which explained why cold metals conduct electricity more efficiently.

### Office of Women's Studies Founded (1978)

The University of Illinois offered its first courses in women's studies in 1970 as a result of feminist activism on campus. The Office of Women's Studies was founded in 1978, and in 2003 the department renamed itself Gender and Women's Studies to reflect scholarly trends.

March 1970 disturbance on campus. Photo courtesy of the University of Illinois Archives and Terry Zimmerman Wyffels.

Women's Week 1974. *Illio* (1975), p. 149. Photo courtesy of the University of Illinois Archives and the *Daily Illini*.

## PRESIDENTS

Stanley O. Ikenberry (1979–1995)

James Stukel (1995–2005)

B. Joseph White (2005–2009)

Michael Hogan (2010–2012)

Robert Easter (2012–2015)

Timothy Killeen (2015– )

## CHANCELLORS

Thomas Everhart (1984–1987)

Morton Weir (1987–1993)

Michael Aiken (1993–2001)

Nancy Cantor (2001–2004)

Richard Herman (2004–2009)

Robert Easter (2009–2012)

Phyllis Wise (2012–2015)

Robert J. Jones, (2016– ).

Stanley O. Ikenberry

James Stukel

## EVENTS

Beckman Institute Founded (1989)

The Beckman Institute was founded to be a center for interdisciplinary research, bridging the physical, life, and behavioral sciences with engineering. Its faculty and students conduct research in the material sciences, neuroscience, physics, bioengineering, robotics, and cognitive sciences.

2012–2013 *Annual Report*, simulation apparatus. Photo courtesy of the Beckman Institute for Advanced Science and Technology.

## Mosaic Browser Released (1993)

Released by the National Center for Supercomputer Applications, Mosaic was the first web browser to become popular among the general public. The project developers, Marc Andreesen and Eric Bina, introduced the technology to the private sector in 1994 by founding Netscape, the dominant web browser in the 1990s.

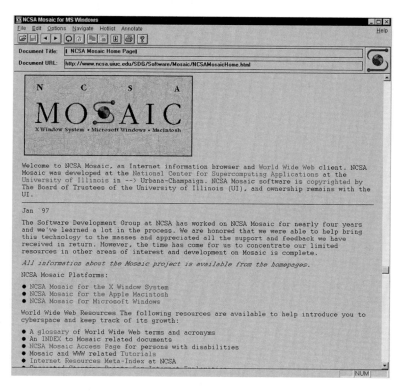

Mosaic Browser 3.0. Photo courtesy of the National Center for Supercomputing Applications (NCSA) and the Board of Trustees of the University of Illinois.

## Bill Clinton Visits Campus (1998)

At his speech to an overflow audience at Assembly Hall, Clinton declared that continuing "scientific research, [securing] universal access to university education, reforming Social Security for the twenty-first century, [and] dealing with the challenge of climate change" were the four major problems facing students.

Bill Clinton at Assembly Hall

## Ebertfest Launched (1999)

School of Journalism graduate Roger Ebert launched the film festival in 1999 to provide a venue for films that he felt had merit but had received little attention. The festival screens several movies each day for five days at the Virginia Theater, and the College of Media hosts panels in which the public can engage with the writers, actors, and directors whose work is shown.

### Nancy Cantor Appointed Chancellor (2001)

Nancy Cantor, the first woman appointed chancellor, endorsed cross-campus initiatives, employee benefits, and the graduate student union. She left to become president of Syracuse University following attacks on her from supporters of the school's controversial mascot, Chief Illiniwek.

### Institute for Genomic Biology Dedicated (2007)

A plan emerged in the 1990s to centralize campus biotechnology projects. Dedicated in 2007, the Institute of Genomic Biology has launched interdisciplinary programs related to nutrition, food security, and the use of "big data" in medical research.

Photo courtesy of the University of Illinois Archives and the University of Illinois News Bureau.

Image from the institute's Overview Booklet. Photo courtesy of the Carl R. Woese Institute for Genomic Biology and Don Hamerman.

### Two Nobel Prizes Awarded (2003)

In 2003, the University of Illinois enjoyed the distinction of having two of its faculty members win Nobel prizes: Anthony Leggett (physics) for groundbreaking contributions to the theory of superconductors and superfluids, and Paul Lauterbur (medicine) for discoveries that led to development of the MRI machine. Twenty-three Illinois faculty members and other scholars associated with the university have won the Nobel Prize in physics, economics, medicine and physiology, and chemistry.

### Chief Illiniwek Retired (2007)

The University of Illinois retired the school's mascot, Chief Illiniwek, following the announcement of sanctions against the institution by the National Collegiate Athletic Association.

### AAUP Censures UIUC (2015)

The American Association of University Professors censured the institution following the board of trustee's decision not to ratify Steven Salaita's appointment as an associate professor of American Indian Studies. The board's action was taken following Salaita's posting of anti-Israel messages during the 2014 Gaza War. Salaita's dismissal triggered several departmental votes of no confidence in the campus leadership, an academic boycott of the campus, and a critical report from the Committee on Academic Freedom and Tenure of the Faculty Senate.

# ACKNOWLEDGMENTS

*The University of Illinois: Engine of Innovation* began with a proposal from History Department chair Diane Koenker. She and her colleagues on the departmental executive committee suggested to the university administration that a volume of essays on campus achievements would be an appropriate way to celebrate the 150th anniversary of the institution's founding. Pradeep Khanna, associate chancellor for corporate and international relations, shepherded the proposal through the campus leadership and found the support necessary for the project. This book would not have been possible without their leadership and advocacy.

After agreeing to edit the volume, I benefited from the wise counsel of two people who know the university's history far better than I: Winton U. Solberg, emeritus professor of history, and William Maher, university archivist. They patiently coached me through the process of organizing the structure of the volume. Scott Schwartz, director of the Sousa Archives and the Center for American Music was a wonderful guide to the history of music making at the university. Archivist Maher also provided continuous advice on sources and images for the book, and he and his staff were steady guides for the undergraduate researchers who took up the task of writing the sketches between the longer essays. I am particularly grateful to Archivist for Reference and User Engagement Jameatris Rimkus

for this help with students, as well as to archives staff members Cara Bertram, Linda Stahnke Stepp, and Katie Nichols, who assisted immeasurably in the production of the book. Thanks also to Mr. C. F. Marley for granting permission to use, in the centerpiece of this book, his wonderful photograph of Senator John F. Kennedy campaigning in Champaign.

Two excellent research assistants, both doctoral students in history, supported my work on this project, particularly when I was preoccupied with teaching and other responsibilities. David Greenstein located materials in the university archives for several essay authors, particularly those far from campus. He also helped assemble the volume bibliography and other reference materials and provided feedback on early drafts of the book's organizational plan and preface. Michael Hughes took over David's role during the final stages of the book's development, carrying out photo research, running down errant sources, and tackling the difficult task of locating the rights holders of the images in this book that are not drawn from the university archives. He also drafted the sketch about Nevada Street, which I later revised with input from several colleagues.

Several others supported the project. These include the History Department's business manager, the indefatigable Thomas Bedwell, who managed the project budget and guided me through the maze of vendor contracts, student time sheets, and photographic reproduction fees. Willis Regier and Laurie Matheson at the University of Illinois Press have been excellent partners in this endeavor, guiding me to new ideas and helping me think about how best to tell this story for a general audience. We have also benefited from superb copyediting by Julie Gay and editorial guidance from Julie Laut. History Department chair Clare Crowston has been a steady source of support, as have several colleagues who were willing to comment on drafts of the project overview, the preface, and the introduction. These include Antoinette Burton, Harry Liebersohn, Leslie Reagan, and Carol Spindel. Finally, the undergraduate authors of the sketches were both tireless and thick skinned, responding gamely to my edits and tossing back revised drafts with speed and good humor. I hope they learned as much in the process as I did.

Any history that aspires to tell a vast story with a series of single-topic essays is asking for trouble. In my selection of essay subjects, I have no doubt passed over important people and events and failed to recognize the achievements of many campus innovators. To this I plead guilty in advance, noting only in my defense that the topic is huge and this book is already longer than I had anticipated. My hope is that what is here is accurate and fair; if it is not, that is my fault, too.

# BIBLIOGRAPHY

## General Bibliography: The University of Illinois

Allen, Walter C., and Robert F. Delzell, eds. *Ideals and Standards: The History of the University of Illinois Graduate School of Library and Information Science, 1893–1993*. Urbana-Champaign, Ill.: The School, 1992.

Baker, Willis C. *History in Postcards: Champaign, Urbana, and the University of Illinois*. Champaign: Illinois Heritage Association, 1993.

Bateman, H. Paul, William A. Foster, Benjamin A. Jones Jr., and Walter D. Lembke, eds. *Agricultural Engineering on the Prairie: Illinois Style; A History of the University of Illinois Department of Agricultural Engineering, 1921–1997*. Urbana, Ill.: Scherer, 1998.

Burford, Cary C. "We're Loyal to You, Illinois." Danville, Ill.: Interstate, 1952.

Clark, Thomas A. *The Sunday Eight O'clock: Brief Sermons for the Undergraduate*. Urbana: Illini, 1916.

Demartini, Joseph Raphael. "Student Protest during Two Periods in the History of the University of Illinois, 1867–1894 and 1929–1942." PhD diss., University of Illinois, 1974.

Derber, Milton, and Philip Menzel. *A Brief History of the Institute of Labor and Industrial Relations, University of Illinois at Urbana-Champaign*. Champaign, Ill.: The Institute, 1987.

Ebert, Roger, *An Illini Century: One Hundred Years of Campus Life*. Urbana: University of Illinois Press, 1967.

Eubanks, Lon. *The Fighting Illini: A Story of Illinois Football*. Huntsville, Ala.: Strode, 1976.

Falkenburg, Barth. *The University of Illinois*. Louisville: Harmony House, 1988.

Farlow, Helen. *History [of] the University of Illinois Division of University Extension, 1933–1968: A Progress Report*. Division of Illinois, n.d.

Finnegan, Terence. "Promoting 'Responsible Freedom': Administrators and Social Fraternities at the University of Illinois, 1900–31." *History of Higher Education Annual* (1989).

Gates, Wendy S. "Dr. Laura J. Huelster and Physical Education: The Administrative Years, 1949–1966." M.S. thesis, Illinois State University, Bloomington, 1985.

Griffin, Peter James. "A History of the Illinois Industrial University/University of Illinois Band, 1867–1908." EdD thesis, University of Illinois, Urbana-Champaign, 2004.

Hannah, Harold W. *One Hundred Years of Action. The University of Illinois YMCA, 1873–1973*. Urbana: YMCA, 1973.

Hatch, Richard A. *Some Founding Papers of the University of Illinois*. Urbana: University of Illinois Press, 1967.

Herron, Miriam. *The University of Illinois Library, 1868–1926*. B.S. thesis, University of Illinois, Urbana-Champaign, 1926.

Hoddeson, Lillian. *No Boundaries: University of Illinois Vignettes*. Urbana: University of Illinois Press, 2004.

James, Edmund J. *Sixteen Years at the University of Illinois: A Statistical Study of the Administration of President Edmund J. James*. Urbana: University of Illinois Press, 1920.

Johnson, Henry C., Jr., and Erwin V. Johanningmeir. *Teachers for the Prairie: The University of Illinois and the Schools, 1868–1945*. Urbana: University of Illinois Press, 1972.

Kersey, Harry A., Jr. *John Milton Gregory and the University of Illinois*. Urbana: University of Illinois Press, 1968.

Kiler, Charles A. *On the Banks of the Boneyard*. Urbana: Illini Union Bookstore, 1942.

Kinley, David. *The Autobiography of David Kinley*. Urbana: University of Illinois Press, 1949.

Middleton, Holly. "'I Pay for All': The Cultural Contradictions of Learning and Labor at Illinois Industrial University." *College English* 69, no. 6 (2007): 596–614.

Moores, Richard G. *Fields of Rich Toil: The Development of the University of Illinois College of Agriculture*. Urbana: University of Illinois Press, 1970.

Nevins, Allan. *Illinois*. New York: Oxford University Press, 1917.

Odell, R. T., W. M. Walker, L. V. Boone, and M. G. Oldham, eds. *The Morrow Plots: A Century of Learning*. Bulletin 775. Urbana, Ill.: Agricultural Experiment Station, College of Agriculture, University of Illinois at Urbana-Champaign, August 1982. Revised August 1984.

Peoples, Brock. "A Great Library on the Prairie: The History, Design, and Growth of the University of Illinois Library." *Library Trends* 60, no. 1 (Summer 2011): 134–51.

Piersel, W. G. *The Wesley Foundation at the University of Illinois*. Urbana: Wesley Foundation, University of Illinois, 1945.

Powell, Burt E. *The Movement for Industrial Education and the Establishment of the University of Illinois, 1840–1870*. Vol. 1, Semi-Centennial History of the University of Illinois. Urbana: University of Illinois, 1918.

Smith, Brett H. *Labor's Millennium: Christianity, Industrial Education, and the Founding of the University of Illinois*. Eugene, Or.: Pickwick, 2010.

———. "Reversing the Curse: Agricultural Millennialism at the Illinois Industrial University." *Church History* 73, no. 4 (December 2004): 759–91.

Solberg, Winton U. "The Catholic Presence at the University of Illinois." *Catholic Historical Review* 76, no. 4 (October 1990): 765–812.

———. "The Early Years of the Jewish Presence at the University of Illinois." *Religion and American Culture* 2, no. 2 (Summer 1992): 215–45.

———. *Reforming Medical Education: The University of Illinois College of Medicine, 1880–1920*. Urbana: University of Illinois Press, 2009.

———. *The University of Illinois, 1867–1894: An Intellectual and Cultural History*. Urbana: University of Illinois Press, 1968.

———. *The University of Illinois, 1894–1904: The Shaping of the University*. Urbana: University of Illinois Press, 2000.

Stephens, Carl. *Illini Years: A Picture History of the University of Illinois, 1868–1950*. Urbana: University of Illinois Press, 1950.

Stoddard, George D. *The Pursuit of Education: An Autobiography*. New York: Vantage, 1981.

Tilton, Leon D., and Thomas E. O'Donnell. *History of the Growth and Development of the Campus Plan of the University of Illinois*. Urbana: University of Illinois Press, 1930.

Turner, Fred Harold. *The Illinois Industrial University*. Urbana: University of Illinois, 1931.

Weller, Allen S. *100 Years of Campus Architecture at the University of Illinois*. Urbana: University of Illinois Press, 1968.

Williamson, Joy Ann. *Black Power on Campus: The University of Illinois, 1965–1975: An Intellectual and Cultural History*. Urbana: University of Illinois Press, 2003.

## Fictional Works about Life in Urbana-Champaign and at the University of Illinois

Henderson, Robert. *Whether There Be Knowledge*. Philadelphia: Lippincott, 1935.

Hormel, Olive Deane. *Co-Ed*. New York: Scribner's, 1926.

Maxwell, William. *The Folded Leaf*. New York: Harper, 1945.

Montross, Lynn, and Lois Seyster Montross. *Fraternity Row*. New York: Doran, 1926.

———. *Town and Gown*. New York: Doran, 1923.

Wallace, David Foster. *A Supposedly Fun Thing I'll Never Do Again*. Boston: Little, Brown, 1997.

# ABOUT THE AUTHORS

James R. Barrett is scholar in residence at the Newberry Library, Chicago, and professor emeritus of history and African American studies at the University of Illinois, Urbana-Champaign, where he has taught courses in labor history, immigration and ethnic history, and urban history for more than thirty years. His most recent books are *The Irish Way: Becoming American in the Multiethnic City* (2012) and a volume of his essays, *History from the Bottom Up and Inside Out* (2017).

George O. Batzli is professor emeritus of ecology. He has taught introductory and advanced courses in ecology at the University of Illinois for thirty-three years. He was chair of the Program in Ecology, head of the Department of Ecology, Ethology, and Evolution, and an editor of the journal *Ecology*. His research has focused on nutritional, population, and community ecology of mammals. He has served on several advisory panels for the National Science Foundation, is a fellow of the American Association for the Advancement of Science, and received the C. Hart Merriam Award of the American Society of Mammalogists.

Claire Benjamin is communications coordinator at the University of Illinois for four interdisciplinary, multi-institutional grants related to plant biology. Previously, she was a science writer at the Carl R. Woese Institute for Genomic Biology (IGB), where her news stories were picked up by the *New York Times*, *Yahoo News*, *Wired*, *Smithsonian Magazine*, and *Motherboard*. She earned a bachelor's degree in agricultural communications at the University of Illinois, where she majored in journalism and crop sciences. She will graduate with a master's degree in advertising from the University of Illinois in 2017.

Jeffrey D. Brawn is head of the Department of Natural Resources and Environmental Sciences and professor of wildlife ecology at the University of Illinois. His research interests are in ecology and conservation biology with an emphasis on tropical birds, the ecology of infectious disease, and the interplay of agricultural practices with biodiversity. He came to the University of Illinois in 1991 from the Smithsonian Tropical Research Institute and initially held an appointment with the Illinois Natural History Survey.

Jimena Canales is the author of *The Physicist and the Philosopher: Einstein, Bergson, and the Debate That Changed Our Understanding of Time* (2015) and *A Tenth of a Second: A History* (2009). She currently holds the Thomas M. Siebel Chair in the History of Science at the University of Illinois, Urbana-Champaign, and was previously an assistant professor and associate professor in history of science at Harvard University. She has published widely in specialized journals (*Isis, Science in Context, History of Science,* the *British Journal for the History of Science,* and the *MLN,* among others) and also writes for wider audiences (*The New Yorker, Wired* magazine, BBC, *Aperture,* and *Artforum*).

Stephanie A. Dick is a historian of mathematics and computing in the postwar United States, with a particular interest in how the computer has been used as a scientific instrument. Her first book project, *After Math: Reasoning, Proving, and Computing in the Postwar United States,* documents transformations in the production and understanding of mathematical proof precipitated by the introduction of computing. She is currently a junior fellow in the Harvard Society of Fellows and she will join the faculty of the Department of History and Sociology of Science at the University of Pennsylvania in fall 2017.

Poshek Fu came to the United States from a small fishing town in Hong Kong. He was a first-generation college graduate and the first from his village to earn a PhD. A historian of modern China and the Cold War, he is professor of history at the University of Illinois at Urbana-Champaign. He is also the Zijiang Professor of Humanities at the East China Normal University (Shanghai). He has been a Fulbright Scholar and a fellow at Princeton's Institute for Advanced Study. His publications include *Passivity, Resistance, and Collaboration: Intellectual Choices in Occupied Shanghai, 1937–1945* (1993) and *Between Shanghai and Hong Kong: The Politics of Chinese Cinemas* (2003), which have been translated into Chinese.

Marcelo H. Garcia is M. T. Geoffrey Yeh Endowed Chair and professor of civil and environmental engineering and geology at the University of Illinois, Urbana-Champaign. His main interests are rivers, environmental fluid mechanics, and water resources engineering. He is editor of the Manual of Practice No. 110: "Sedimentation Engineering: Processes, Measurements, Modeling, and Practice," (2008). He joined the University of Illinois in 1990 and has served as director of the Ven Te Chow Hydrosystems Laboratory since 1997. In 2001 he was recognized as University Scholar and became a Distinguished Member of the American Society of Civil Engineers in 2013.

Lillian Hoddeson, professor emeritus at the University of Illinois, Urbana-Champaign, taught in the Department of History from 1989 to 2010. Her solid-state histories include books about the transistor, John Bardeen (with Vicki Daitch), and Stan Ovshinsky (with Peter Garrett, to appear 2017). Her "big science" studies include histories of particle physics, the atomic bomb, Fermilab, and (with Michael Riordan and Adrienne Kolb, 2015), *Tunnel Visions: The Rise and Fall of the Superconducting Super Collider.* Her honors include a Guggenheim fellowship and the Abraham Pais Prize for History of Physics.

Frederick E. Hoxie is Swanlund Endowed Chair and professor of history, American Indian studies, and law at the University of Illinois, Urbana-Champaign. He writes and teaches primarily in the field of Native American history and is author of *This Indian Country* (2012) and editor of the *Oxford Handbook of American Indian History* (2016). He came to Illinois in 1998 from the Newberry Library in Chicago, where he was vice president for research and education.

Michael Hughes earned his PhD in history from the University of Illinois in 2016. His dissertation explored the process of empire making in the North American interior during the late eighteenth and early nineteenth centuries. Fellowships from the Department of History and the Newberry Consortium of American Indian Studies supported the research on that project. A portion of his work was published in the July 2016 issue of *Ethnohistory.*

Harry Liebersohn is professor of history at the University of Illinois, Urbana-Champaign. His most recent books, which examine cultural contact between Europeans and non-Europeans, are *The Return of the Gift: European History of a Global Idea* (2011) and *The Travelers' World: Europe to the Pacific* (2006). Together with colleagues from the arts, he has regularly co-taught "Exploring Arts and Creativity," which links seminar discussions to Krannert Center performances. He is currently writing a history of music and globalization since the nineteenth century.

Claudia Lutz is a science communications specialist and research assistant professor at the Carl R. Woese Institute for Genomic Biology at the University of Illinois,

Urbana-Champaign. She writes about genomics for public audiences and contributes to technical writing projects. Her scholarly work has appeared in scientific and education journals. During her graduate training in the Neuroscience Program at the University of Illinois, she investigated the genomic basis of structural neuroplasticity and learning in the honey bee.

Kathleen Mapes is associate professor of history at the State University of New York at Geneseo. She teaches a variety of courses in nineteenth- and twentieth-century U.S. labor, rural, and immigration history. Her book, *Sweet Tyranny: Migrant Labor, Industrial Agriculture, and Imperial Politics* was awarded the 2010 Richard L. Wentworth/Illinois Award in American History, and her current book project explores the politics of immigration reform and rural America. She earned her doctorate in history at the University of Illinois, Urbana-Champaign, in 2000.

Vicki McKinney is an independent scholar and co-author of *True Genius: The Life and Science of John Bardeen*. She earned a doctorate in history at the University of Illinois. While under contract with the John F. Kennedy Presidential Library, she interviewed President Gerald Ford, Congressman John Lewis, journalist Walter Cronkite, and many others for the library's oral history collection. She currently lives in Rhode Island with her husband, three dogs, and a cat, and volunteers as a long-term-care ombudsman.

Elisa Miller is associate professor of history and gender studies at Rhode Island College. She teaches a variety of courses in nineteenth- and twentieth-century U.S. history, with a research emphasis in the Gilded Age and Progressive Era, and gender and women's history. Her current project is a book manuscript on the history of home economics and women in higher education at the turn of the century, including a chapter on Isabel Bevier and the University of Illinois. She earned her doctorate in history at the University of Illinois, Urbana-Champaign, in 2004.

Robert Michael Morrissey is associate professor of history at the University of Illinois, Urbana-Champaign. His teaching and research interests center on early America, environmental history, and Native American history.

He has written extensively about the colonial-era Great Lakes and Mississippi Valley, including, *Empire by Collaboration: Indians, Colonists, and Governments in Colonial Illinois Country* (2015). He began teaching at the University of Illinois in 2011.

Bryan E. Norwood is a PhD candidate in the history and theory of architecture at Harvard University. His dissertation, "The Architect's Knowledge: Images of History in American Architectural Education, 1797–1930," investigates conceptual and historiographical developments that accompanied the formation of university-based architectural education. The architectural program at University of Illinois plays a key part in his study. His most recent publications are "Working on a Diagonal: Towards a New Image of Architectural History" in *Intensities and Lines of Flight: Deleuze/Guattari and the Arts* (2014) and "Metaphors for Nothing" in *Log* 33 (2015).

Elizabeth H. Pleck is professor emerita at the University of Illinois, Urbana-Champaign, where she has taught courses in U.S. women's and family history. Her most recent book is *Not Just Roommates: Cohabitation after the Sexual Revolution* (2012). As a Fulbright Specialist, she taught world family history at the University of Johannesburg in 2014.

Leslie J. Reagan is professor of history, medicine, law, and gender and women's studies at the University of Illinois, Urbana-Champaign. She teaches and writes primarily on the histories of reproductive health and law; medicine; disabilities; and women, gender, and sexuality. She is author of *Dangerous Pregnancies: Mothers, Disabilities, and Abortion in Modern America* (2010) about the German measles (rubella) epidemic; "Monstrous Births, Birth Defects, Unusual Anatomy, and Disability," in *The Oxford Handbook on Disability History* (2016); and is currently writing on Agent Orange in the United States and Vietnam. She has received numerous teaching and scholarship awards.

Susan M. Rigdon is research associate in anthropology at the University of Illinois, Urbana-Champaign. She has taught comparative and international politics at four American universities, including the University of Illinois, and American politics at two universities in China. Her primary research interests are in the areas of culture and politics, and poverty and development. For twenty years she co-authored an American government textbook and, with Oscar Lewis and Ruth M. Lewis, co-authored the three volume series *Living the Revolution: An Oral History of Contemporary Cuba*.

David Rosenboom is Richard Seaver Distinguished Chair in music, and dean of the Herb Alpert School of Music at California Institute of the Arts. He is a composer-performer, interdisciplinary artist, author, and educator whose work has highlighted new musical forms, interactive media, art-science research, and extended musical interface with the human nervous system. He was founding faculty in the Department of Music, York University (Toronto) in the 1970s and was a Darius Milhaud Professor of Music, head of the Music Department, and director of the Center for Contemporary Music at Mills College (Oakland) in the 1980s. He attended the University of Illinois in the mid-1960s.

Katherine Skwarczek is completing her doctoral work at the University of Illinois, Urbana-Champaign, in the Department of English. Her current project examines the representation of aging and old age in twentieth-century British literature. She is currently an instructor at the University of the Incarnate Word in San Antonio, Texas, where she teaches courses in composition and literature.

Winton U. Solberg is professor emeritus of history at the University of Illinois, Urbana-Champaign. During his twenty years in the History Department, he taught courses and published articles and books in the field of American intellectual and cultural history. He was a Fulbright Professor at the Johns Hopkins University Center in Bologna, Italy, and at Moscow State University, USSR. He was also a visiting professor at the University of Calcutta, India, and lectured in Indian universities under USIA sponsorship. Now retired, he is the author of two volumes on the history of the University of Illinois, covering the years 1867 to 1904 (1968, 2000) and a history of the university medical school from 1888 to 1920 (2009).

He has recently completed one manuscript on Big Ten athletics and another on an Arctic expedition in which the University of Illinois participated.

Carol Spindel is lecturer in the Department of English at the University of Illinois, Urbana-Champaign, and an alumna. She has taught nonfiction writing to undergraduates for twenty-five years in the Unit One Living Learning Community and Campus Honors Program. She is the author of essays, award-winning public-radio commentaries, and the books *In the Shadow of the Sacred Grove* (a *New York Times* Notable Book) and *Dancing at Halftime: Sports and the Controversy over American Indian Mascots*. A native of Memphis, she now considers Urbana home.

William F. Tracy is professor and chair of the department of agronomy, University of Wisconsin-Madison. He earned his bachelor and master of science in plant science at the University of Massachusetts-Amherst and his doctorate in plant breeding from Cornell University. His research involves sweet-corn breeding and maize genetics. At UW-Madison, Bill leads the largest public-sector sweet-corn breeding program in the world. He has developed supersweet corn varieties that are grown commercially on every continent (except Antarctica). Bill publishes research on the genetics and biochemistry of starch and sugar biosynthesis in the maize endosperm.

Joy Ann Williamson-Lott is professor of history of education at the University of Washington, Seattle. Her research and publications focus on the relationship between social movements of the middle twentieth century and institutions of higher education. Her major publications include *Black Power on Campus: The University of Illinois, 1965–1975* (2003), *Radicalizing the Ebony Tower: Black Colleges and the Black Freedom Struggle in Mississippi* (2008), and *Jim Crow Campus: Higher Education and the Southern Social Order in the Mid-Twentieth Century* (forthcoming). She received all of her degrees (bachelor's, master's, and doctorate) from the University of Illinois, Urbana-Champaign.

## Sketch Authors

Most of the sketches in this volume were written by the following men and women while they attended the University of Illinois as undergraduates. These short essays required extensive research in the University Archives. The authors, listed with their hometowns, majors, and graduation years, are:

Kristen Allen, Huntley, Illinois, bachelor's in history and anthropology, 2016 (minor: communications)

Jonathan Binkley, Waukegan, Illinois, bachelor's in political science, 2015 (minors: business and history)

Tim Brown, Chicago, Illinois, bachelor's in history and political science, 2016

Rafal Ciolcosz, Chicago, Illinois, bachelor's in political science, 2016

Alexis Clinebell, Waterloo, Illinois, bachelor's in history and political science, 2015

Nicholas Hopkins, Lawrenceville, Illinois, bachelor's in history and sociology, 2015

Steven Lenz, New Lenox, Illinois, bachelor's in history, political science and economics, 2015

Kelsey Reinker, Crystal Lake, Illinois, bachelor's in anthropology, 2015

Lauren Tokarewich, Bartlett, Illinois, bachelor's in history, 2016

# INDEX

The University of Illinois Press
is a founding member of the
Association of American University Presses.

Text designed and composed by Jim Proefrock
at the University of Illinois Press
in 11/14 Chaparral with Adrianna
and Antique Central display
Cover designed by Jim Proefrock
Cover photos: *Top:* Photo courtesy of the
Carl R. Woese Institute for Genomic Biology
and Don Hamerman. *Bottom:* L. Brian Stauffer/
UI News Bureau
Manufactured by Bang Printing

University of Illinois Press
1325 South Oak Street
Champaign, IL 61820-6903
www.press.uillinois.edu